AF505469

See Red Women's Workshop

See Red Women's Workshop

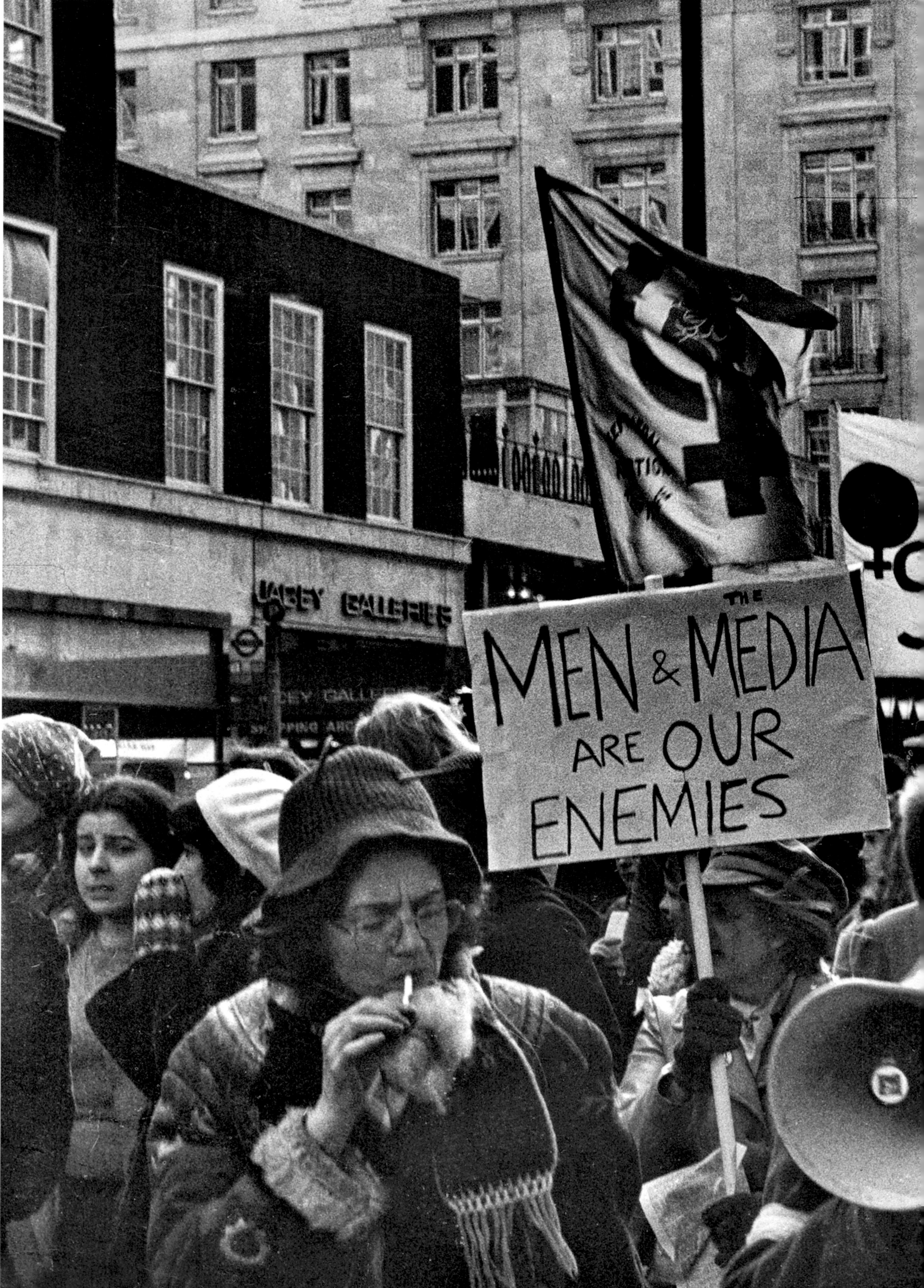

LACEY GALLERIES
THE
MEN & MEDIA
ARE OUR
ENEMIES

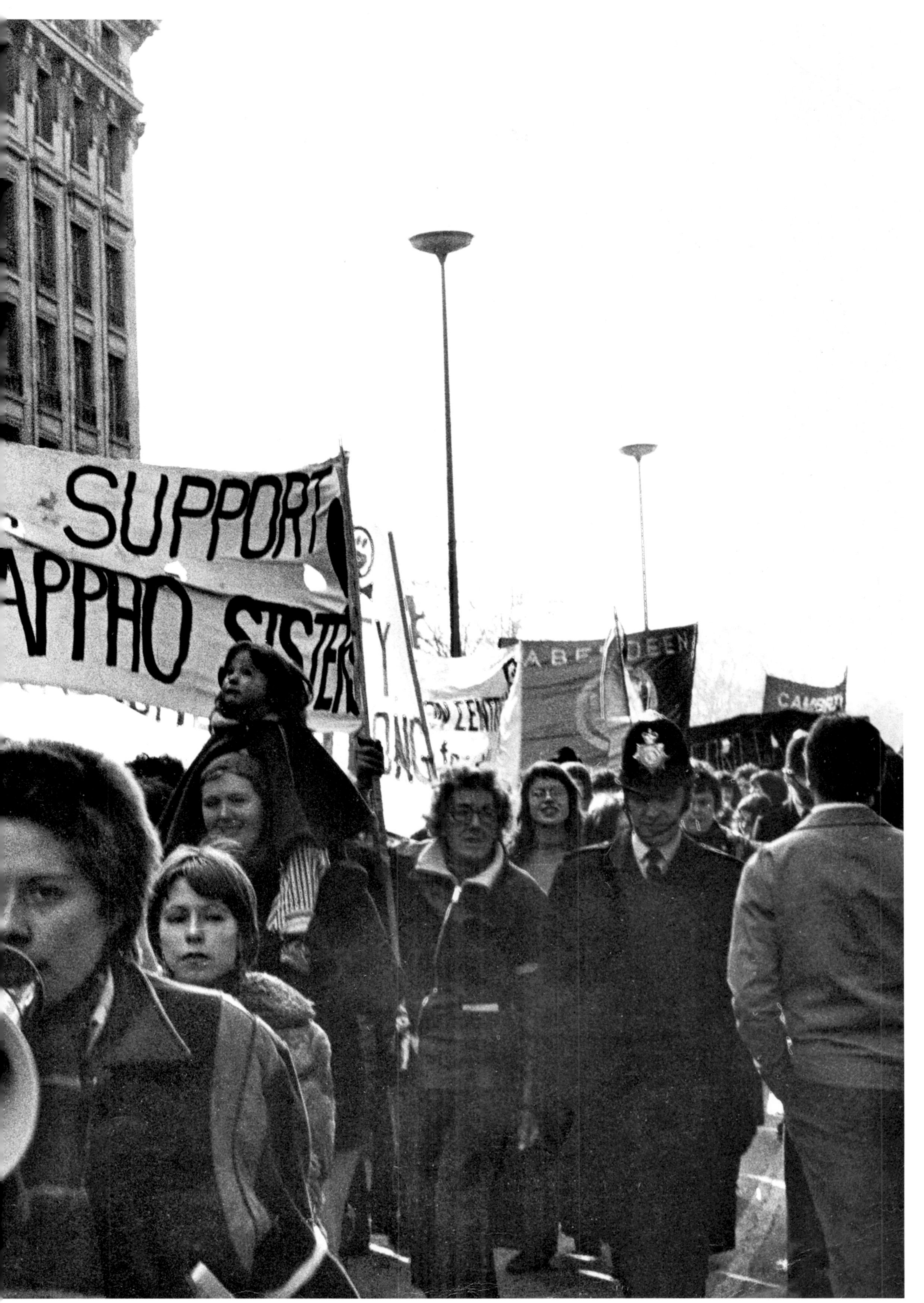
SUPPORT
APPHO SISTER

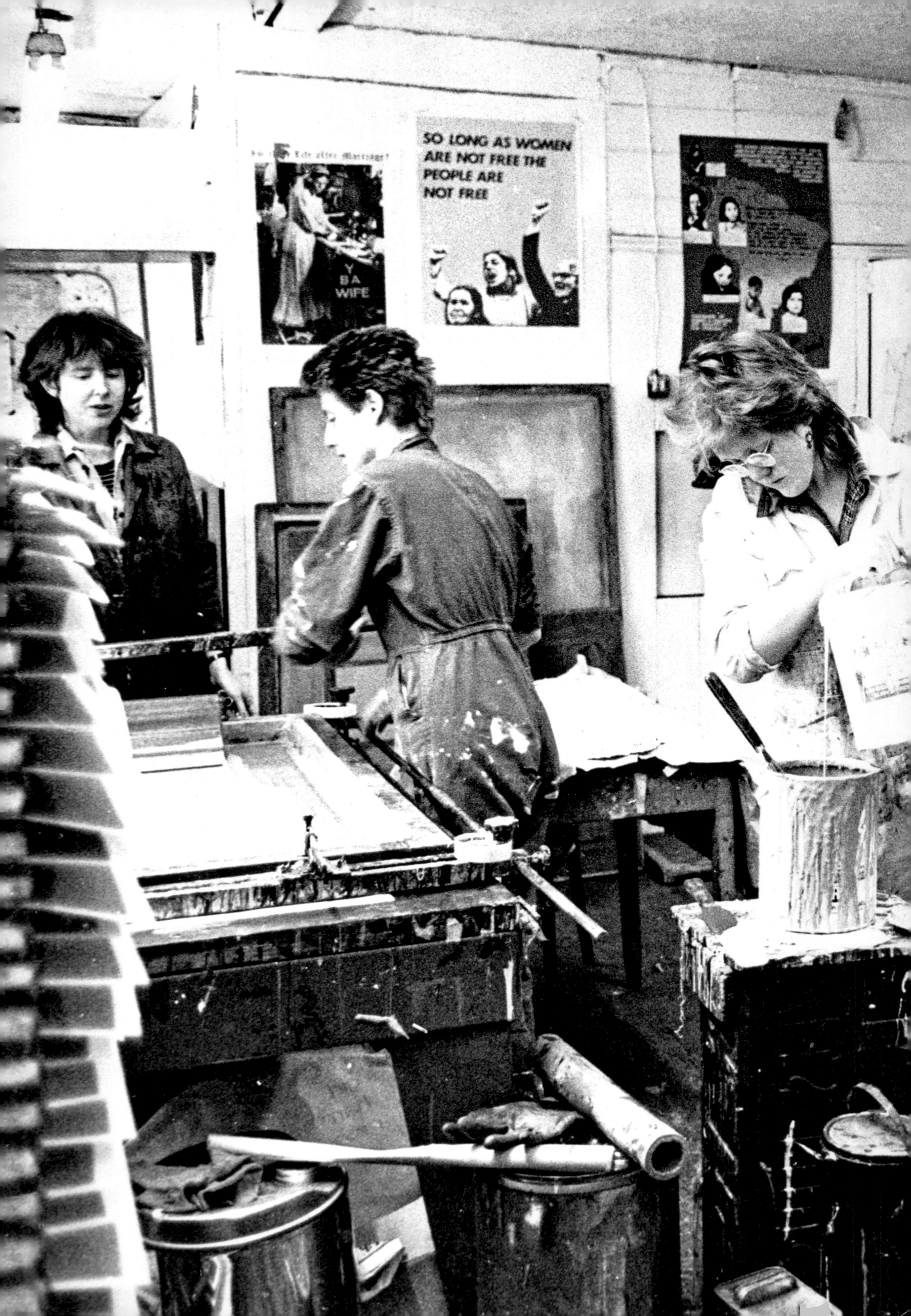
SO LONG AS WOMEN
ARE NOT FREE THE
PEOPLE ARE
NOT FREE
Y
BA
WIFE

See Red

WOMEN'S WORKSHOP

Four Corners Books

First published in 2016 by
Four Corners Books
56 Artillery Lane
London E1 7LS

fourcornersbooks.co.uk

Images © See Red Women's Workshop
seeredwomensworkshop.wordpress.com

This volume © Four Corners Books 2016

Distributed in Europe by Art Data
artdata.co.uk

Distributed in North America by Distributed Art Publishers
artbook.com

Designed by Claire Mason
flushleft.co.uk

Print production by Martin Lee

Image reproduction by DawkinsColour, London

Printed in Italy by Conti Tipocolor
Second printing, 2017

Jess Baines acknowledges support from UAL Research,
University of the Arts, London. *Celebration for Change,* pages
136–137 © Victoria and Albert Museum, London. *See Red 1984 Calendar,*
pages 152–153, courtesy The Women's Library at LSE. Every effort
has been made by the publishers to identify and contact copyright holders,
however, in the event of any oversights of omissions, please contact
hello@fourcornersbooks.co.uk and any corrections will be included
in future editions of the book.

ISBN 978-1-909829-07-7

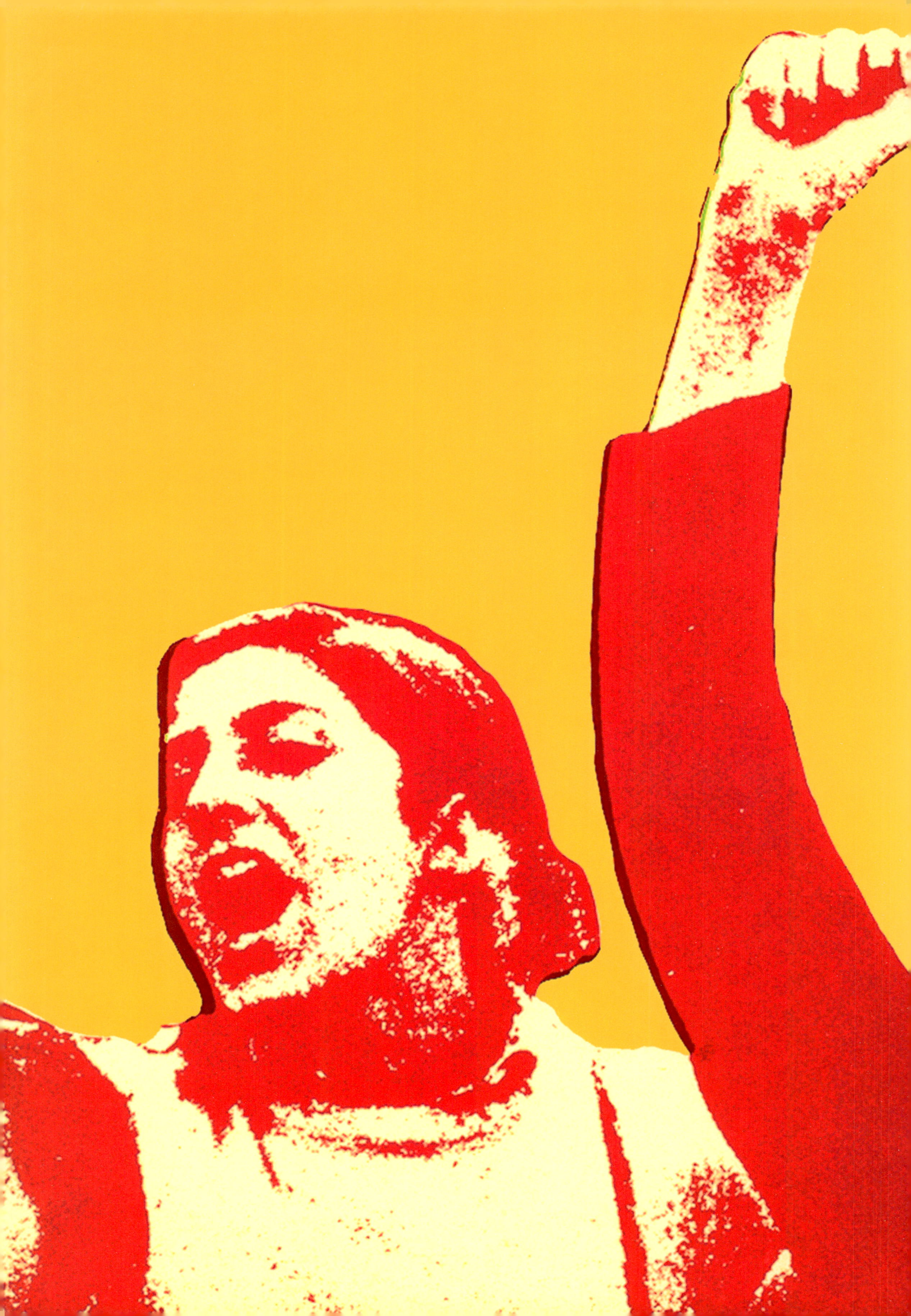

Foreword by
Sheila Rowbotham

It is wonderful, once again, to be able to look at the ingenious posters produced by See Red Women's Workshop during the 1970s and early 1980s … Some relate to historically specific events ranging from Greenham Common to the Grunwick Asian Women's strike; others express broader political concepts in images and words. Founder members recall how the wording for these often caused 'heated debates'. This is not at all surprising, for the small cluster of voluntary designers were trying to subvert the known world from the bottom up, challenging existing political and cultural assumptions.

Ambitiously, See Red were not about selling a product or even getting over a party political message, they were up to something far more complex and far more difficult. They aimed to convey ideas about a transformed society in which relations of gender, race and class would no longer be marked by inequality and subordination. Those messages, on the posters, 'So long as women are not free, the people are not free' and 'Lesbians are everywhere' contested the prevailing 'common sense'. See Red aimed to be clear and wanted to reorient perspectives. Making those posters appear so simple and self-evident must have been agonisingly hard to accomplish. It is not actually that difficult to perplex with layer upon layer of words; to clarify abstraction with just a few constitutes a rare skill.

Their posters contest various forms of male power and also apply a broader lens to the sources of women's oppression by demonstrating links to the political and social context of the era. The 1970s and early 1980s saw violent conflicts in Ireland, racial assaults and a desperate trade union defense of workers' wages and rights, which extended to the poorest. It was a period in which a new trade unionism began to emerge among low-paid, unorganised women and when community activism involved many working class and middle class women around housing, hospitals, nurseries, adventure playgrounds, contraception and abortion rights. Amidst these protests new kinds of everyday living were being envisaged.

The upsurge in militancy and enthusiasm for radical change was accompanied by countless small creative groups — designers, photographers, filmmakers, architects, actors, comedians, writers and musicians who documented and elaborated upon the kind of critical and utopian vision described by See Red. Inspiration for connecting art and daily life came from diverse sources; Angry Arts in America, the Situationists in France, the democratic impulse of the idea of 'workshops' in art schools, John Berger's challenge to 'ways of seeing'. This utopianism imagined new egalitarian and mutual ways of living, relating, and being, but was deeply rooted in the actualities of resistance.

The ferment of intense activism made it hard for groups such as See Red to step back and think through potential problems. Yet these presented nagging dilemmas and erupted in painful clashes, not only for See Red but for many other groups of radical women and men. How to develop resistance on the basis of personal experience when that experience could eclipse the subjectivities of others? How to jolt consciousness while maintaining communication with people who were not necessarily sympathetic towards experimentation with form? How to release everyone's creativity, while respecting craft skill and artistic inspiration?

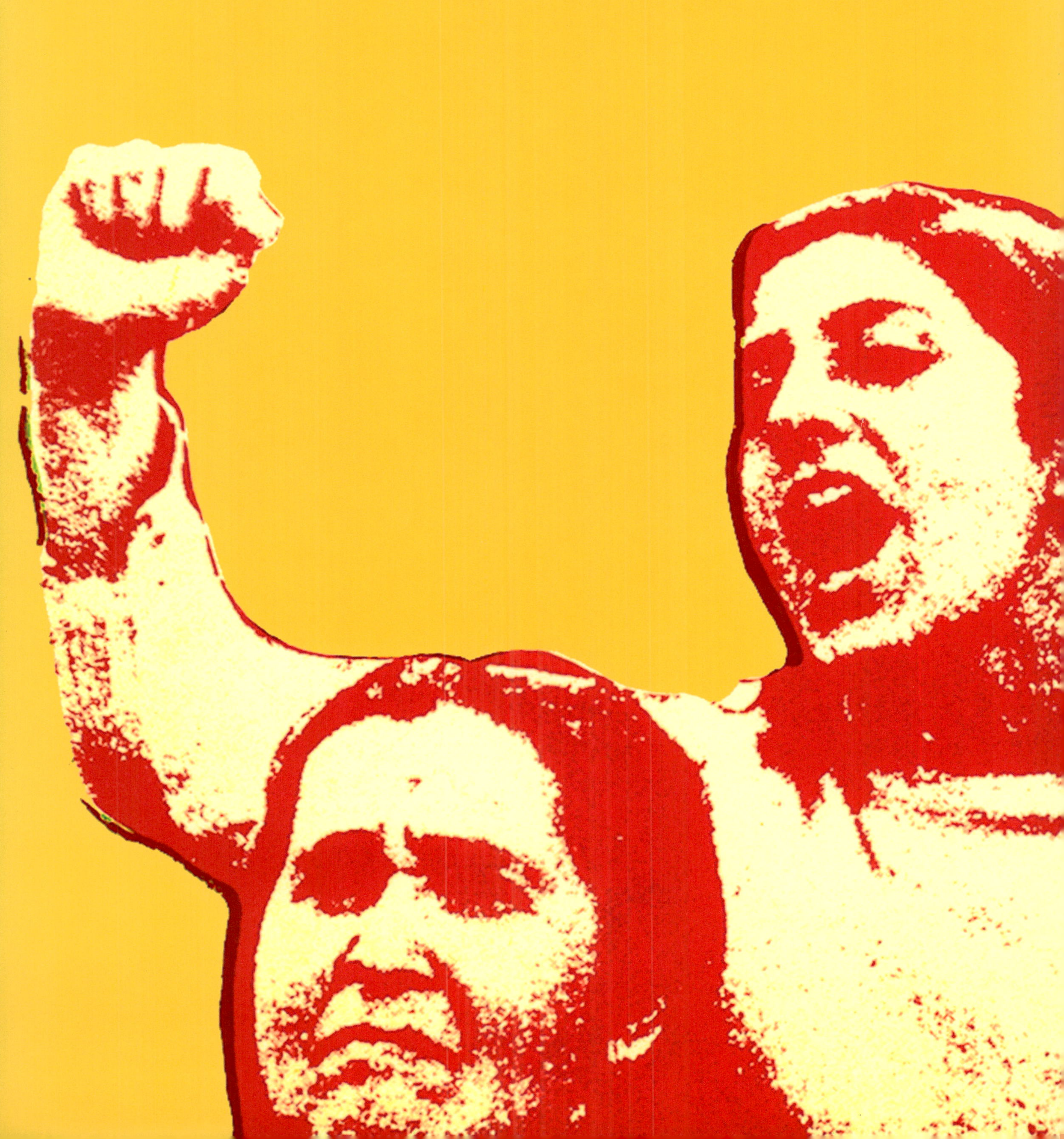

Such problems were not unique to these times, however, because the histories of social and cultural movements can be easily buried, they tended to be faced head-on, without any mediating reference-points.

By the early 1980s, internal conflicts and doubts were tearing and wearing away within the women's movement, community projects, and radical cultural groups. Moreover, the pressure of surviving within capitalism was becoming more acute. Without really realising it those of us who were socialist feminists were confronting a new kind of capitalism. Cut-throat, competitive and ruthless, this was paring down the social and cultural cushioning which, since World War Two, we had grown up taking for granted. Those rights at work and the provision of welfare, wrested from capital, were now surplus to requirements. Cuts, repressive legislation, new forms of management control and intimidation of cultural institutions flourished under Margaret Thatcher, all caught neatly in See Red's poster *Tough!*

Much has been written on the economics of globalisation and the rise of neo-liberal theories. But less attention has been devoted to the manner in which the values and aspirations of both left trade unionism and of myriad groupings like See Red were assailed. Social inequality became blatant in the 1980s. What is more, being individually part of a wealthy elite, was overtly celebrated. Buttons worn by Lord Snooties proudly declared, 'I am rich'. This was the revenge of the powerful and privileged, with a clever twist. Those who could scramble up above their uncompetitive fellows experienced the delights of contempt. Scorn, and an all-pervasive sneer, penetrated English culture by the late 1980s. 1970s radical utopianism was derided as jejune, dull and, most heinous of all, earnest. Efforts to preserve any record were branded as 'nostalgia'. Mainstream historical accounts have tended not to probe this superficial categorisation of 1970s radicalism. If the 60s are delineated as fun but politically irrelevant, the 70s are summed up by the dismissive term 'PC'. Now, however, a new crop of younger researchers are revisiting a maligned era and rediscovering its creative vitality. Much strength to their elbows. Yet, as the years pass, what was self-evident to participants in social movements often eludes the record. This is because perceptions and understandings which are obvious at the time are not explicitly stated. They are implicit and assumed. It is these crucial tacit values that tend to become the blanks. Hence, the testimonies and work of those who remember have much to offer.

The story of See Red Women's Workshop and the posters they made for us contribute a series of mosaics which indicate a larger pattern. They hint at the great hopes that were aroused and sustained through sisterhood and through solidarities of race and class. These were forceful enough to encourage many young women and men to bite the hand that fed them. Our subversive refusal was a profound recoil from a system based on inequality and a culture that confined self-expression and development to an elite.

Much was to be crushed amidst a multitude of defeats. However, as a radical historian I have spent a lifetime chasing memories that appear to vanish below the surface, only to resurface in the most surprising ways.

I sincerely hope that new hands will pick up these posters, bear them aloft and act upon them. For there is indeed a great deal that needs to be done.

Sheila Rowbotham is a historian and writer. Her books include 'Woman's Consciousness, Man's World' ; 'Hidden from History: 300 years of Women's Oppression and the Fight against it'; and 'Dreamers of a New Day: Women Who Invented the Twentieth Century'. Her most recent book is 'Rebel Crossings: New Women, Free Lovers and Radicals in Britain and the United States', Verso, 2016.

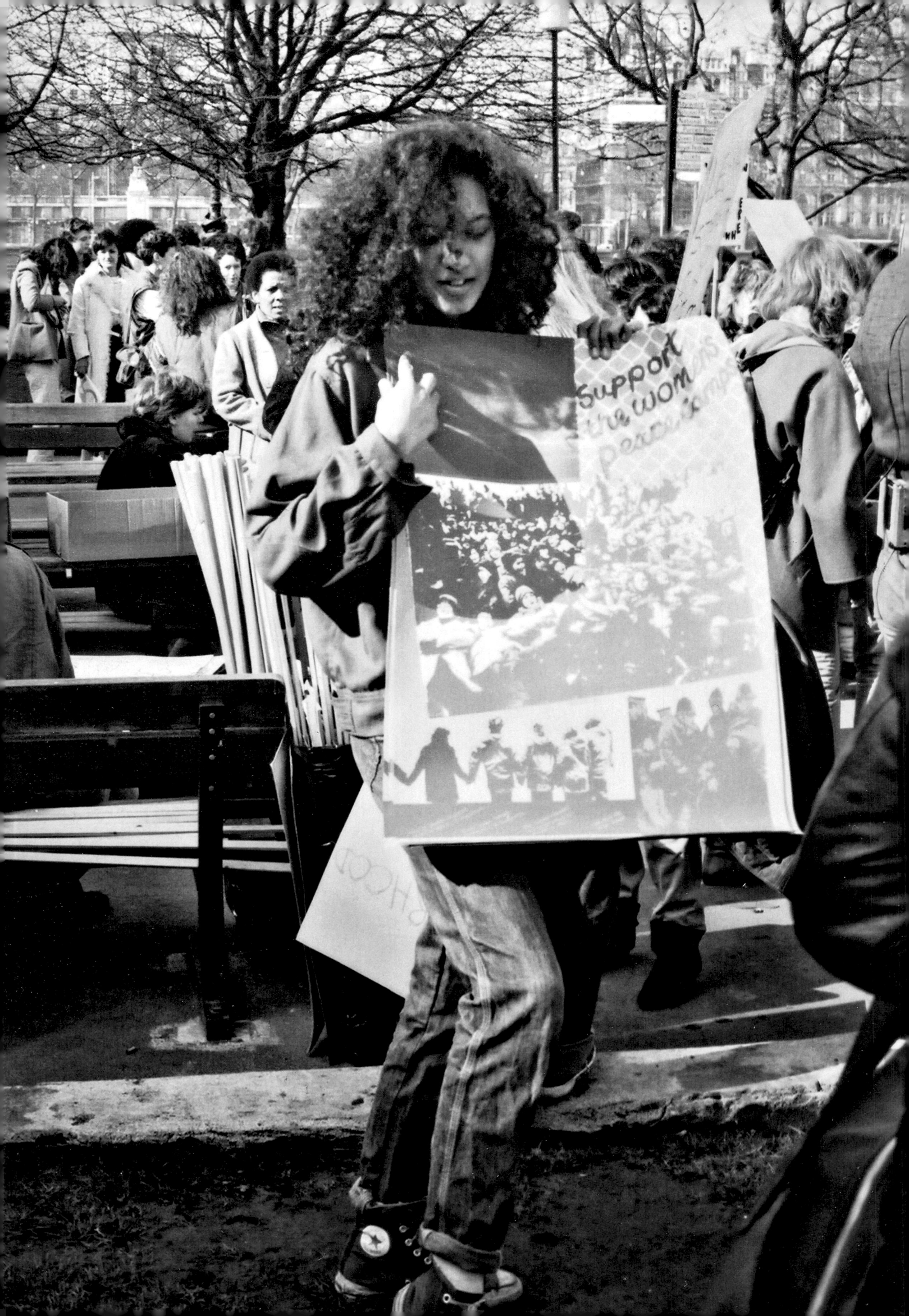

Support
the womens
Peace camp

See Red
WOMEN'S WORKSHOP

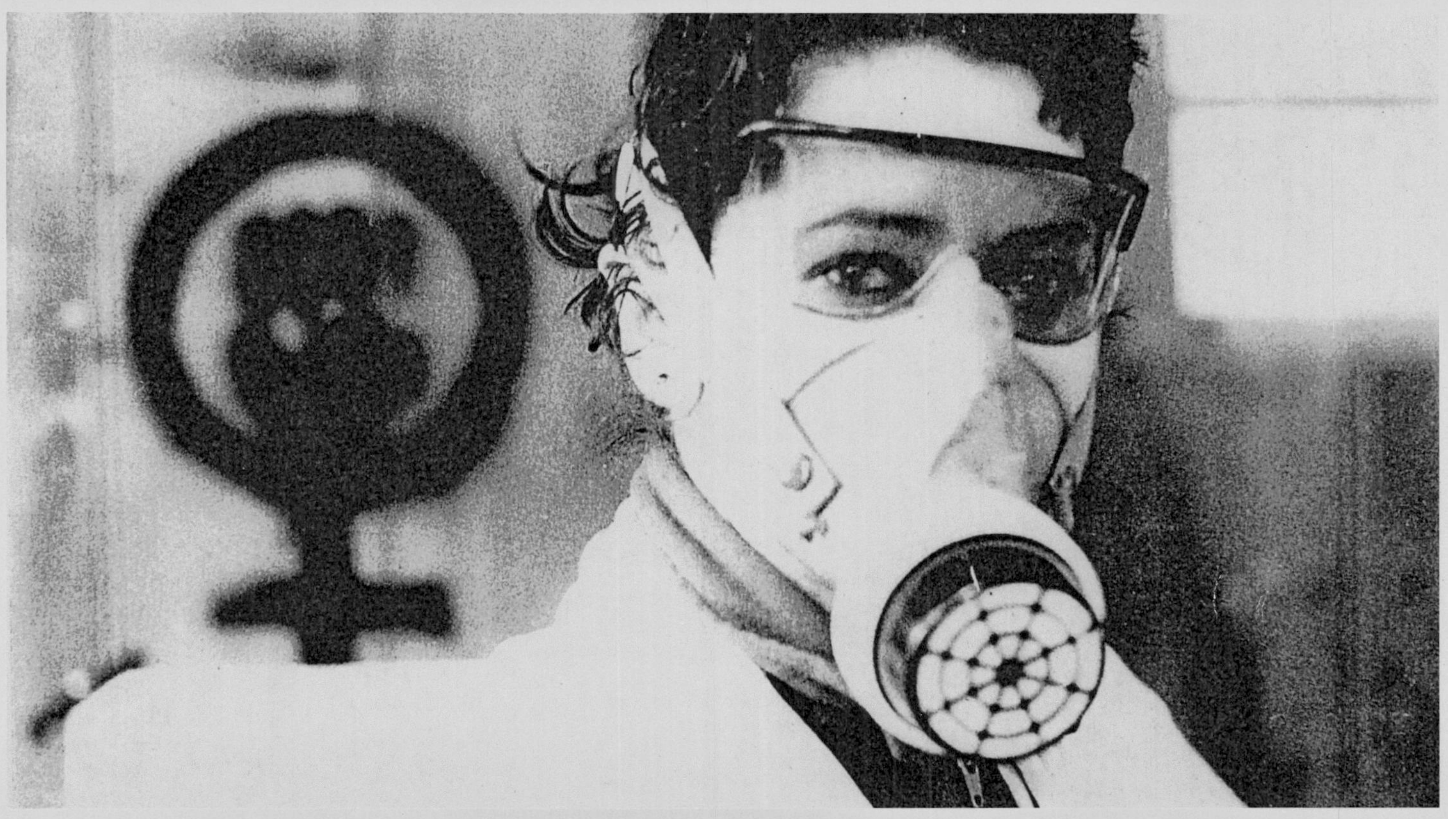

In 1974, an advert placed in a Women's Liberation publication invited women in the visual arts to meet with a view to starting a group to combat the pervasive and negative images of women in advertising and the media. This was a time of great community and political activity, when radicals wanted to use and share their skills to further the aims of grassroots politics. Artists and those involved with visual images were no exception, and silkscreen printing was especially suitable for producing images in large quantities with the minimum of equipment and comparatively little outlay. Many small groups set up workshops in any available spaces — squats, living rooms, playgrounds — to print posters which would help advertise and promote the causes of the new left. See Red Women's Workshop was one of these, formed specifically to make posters to promote Women's Liberation.

At the first meeting were a photographer, an illustrator, a cartoonist, graphic designers, artists and a filmmaker. We initially called ourselves Women's Image Collective, before agreeing on the name See Red Women's Workshop, with an ambitious set of aims, as can be seen from the group's first statement of purpose:

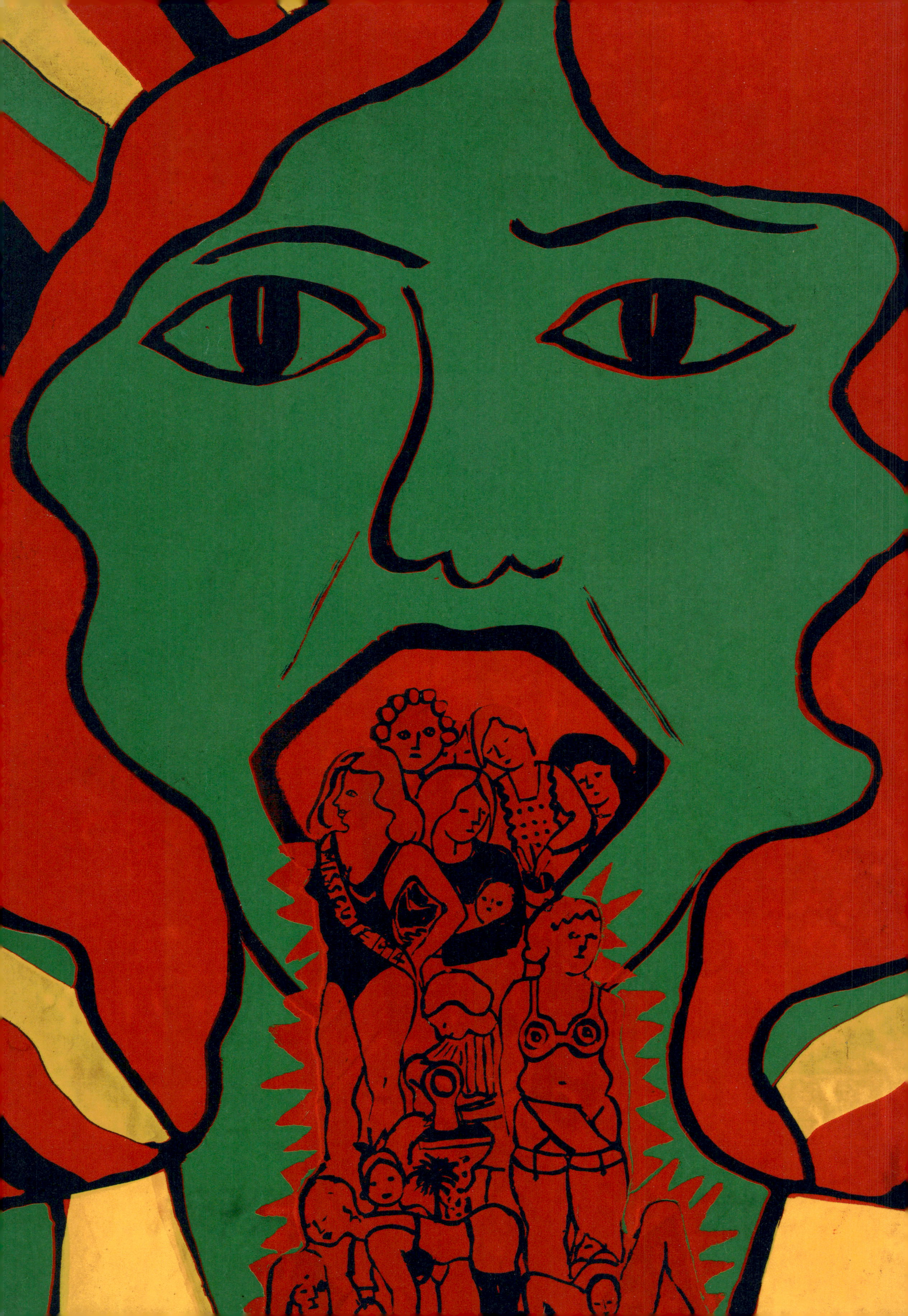

SEE RED WOMENS WORKSHOP

18 Camden Road
N.W.1.

We are a recently formed gr oup of women interested in
visual aspects of the Womens Struggle. We want to combat
images of the 'model womam' which are used by capitalist
ideology to keep women from disputing their secondary
status or questioning their role in a male dominated society.
We hope to do this by putting forward a positive image of
women by:

  a) producing posters, illustrations, cartoons and
     photographs ourselves;

  b) providing visual material for womens publications
     and groups;

  c) providing poster making facilities for other women
     who are fighting for their rights;

  d) collecting images past, present and future which
     indicate the position of women in our society
     today eg. the everyday assaults of advertising, etc.
     We want to build up a collection of examples of the
     positive and negative aspects of the image of women
     for the use of any group, periodical or individual
     presenting a constructive statement on matters
     concerning Womens Liberation. We would like to receive
     any relevant images in order to operate an expanding
     and ongoing collection concerned with Womens Struggle.

Any women interested are welcome to come round to meet us and to use
our facilities and learn printing methods.

It was a very busy time on the left. However, while women were involved and active within various organisations and campaigns, and were attending meetings and rallies to do with housing, work, education and low pay, these meetings were still very or totally male dominated. The left wing at that time, both the radical and the mainstream branches, didn't take the Women's Liberation Movement seriously nor recognise that it would become a major part of people's struggles across the world. Women's issues were seen as a waste of time, frivolous, and diversionary, and were often purposefully misrepresented by the left as well as the right wing. We found ourselves marginalised within these campaigns and were expected to stay in the background, keep quiet and make the tea. Most women who lived with men were still expected to take on full responsibility for all domestic work and childcare, as well as work outside the home. Women who complained were seen as getting in the way of the struggle: 'house work is not important, what I do is — so you should do it.' *

We were not prepared to accept that. How you behaved in your personal life was as important as how you conducted your life in public. We believed that 'the personal is political' encapsulated our emerging understanding of women's place in the world. We lived in shared households where everyone took responsibility for childcare and all domestic chores.

Some households also shared their incomes. We had cooking rotas — sometimes with other homes, there were always lots of people around, and meals were lively with animated discussions around current issues and the politics of the day.

Hundreds of women-only consciousness-raising groups met regularly in the UK during the 1970s and early 1980s. We all met in our local groups to talk about our circumstances and our experiences as women, share the frustrations of motherhood, isolation in the home, loss of independence, sexual harassment on the streets, our relationships, unequal pay, being defined as inferior to men, assumptions made about our sexuality, our status and our availability. We realised through this process that working together made us more confident and therefore more powerful and determined to make changes. Many campaigns grew out of these small groups — including a woman's right to choose abortion, a stop to violence against women, Reclaim the

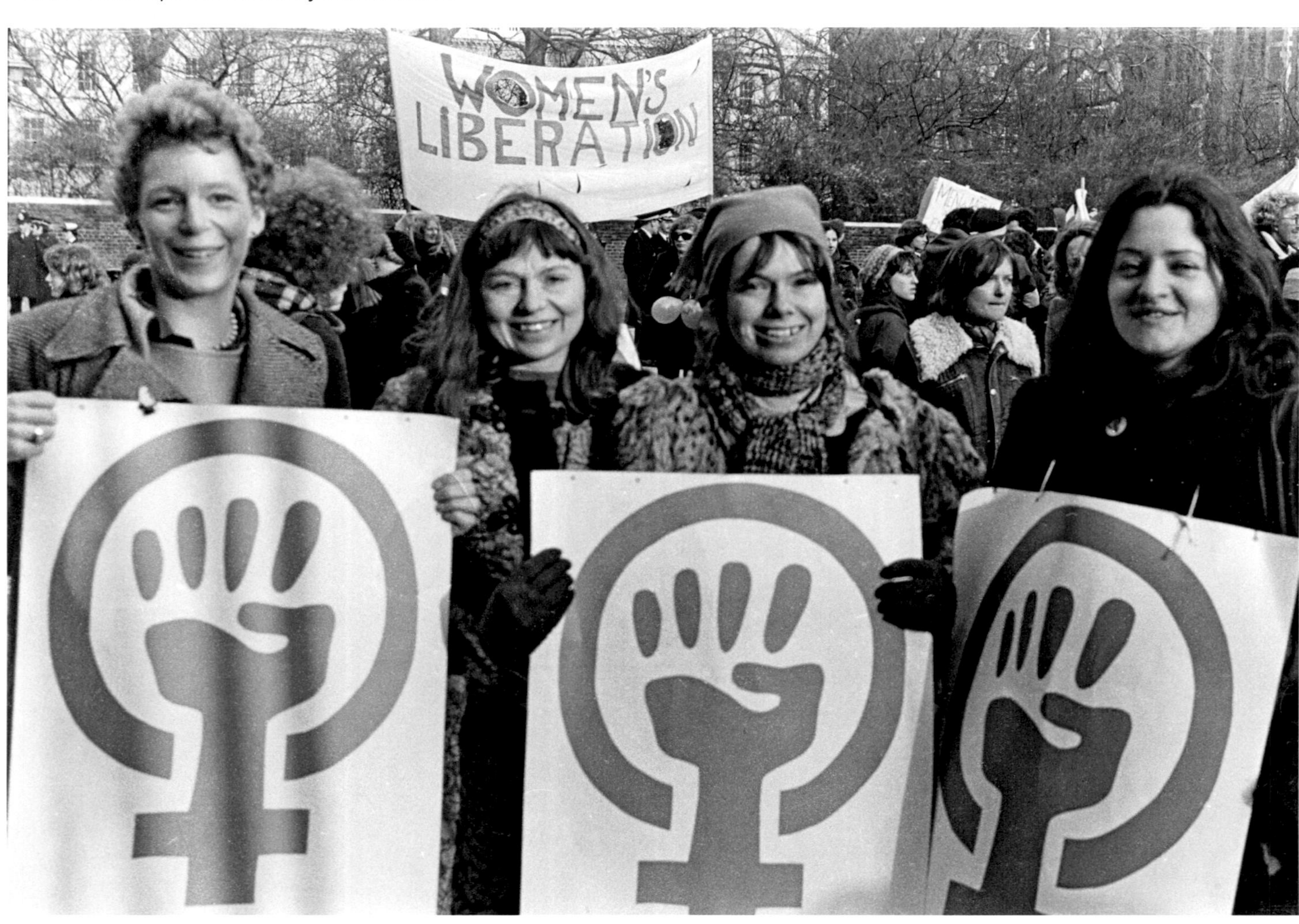

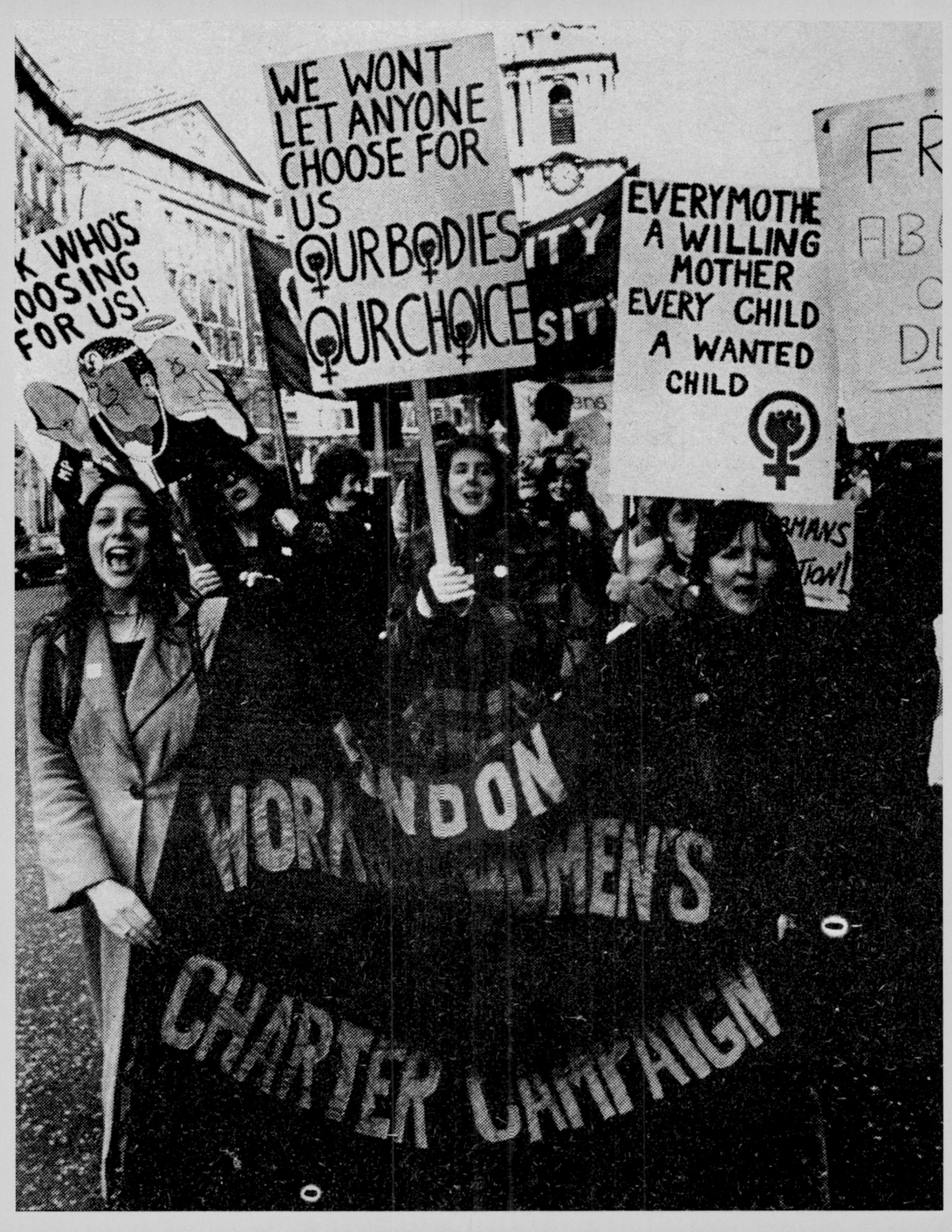

Above: Hand-painted placards made and carried by See Red on the 1975 demonstration against MP James White's Private Members Bill to restrict the 1967 Abortion Act
Facing: See Red silkscreened placards on protest, *c.* 1977

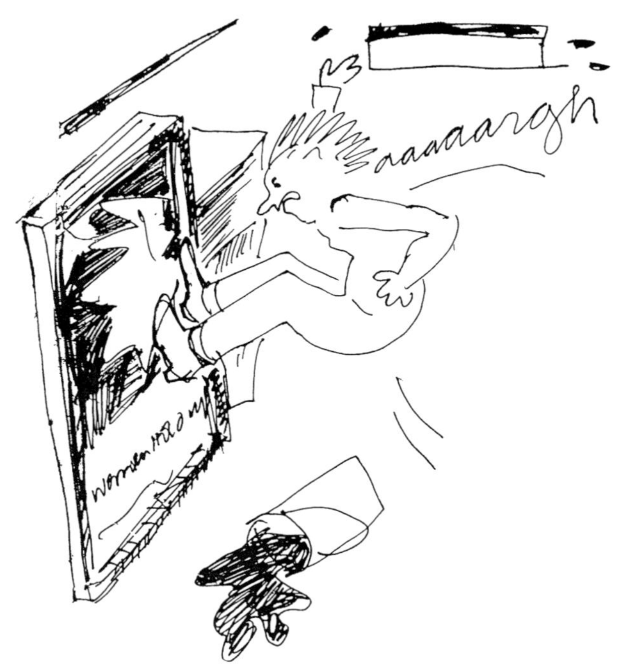

Night, and an end to sexual discrimination. We were politically active in other groups, such as local housing campaigns, Camden Women's Aid and the Grunwick strike. Women's centres were set up and used as places to hold meetings, socialise, run workshops, produce community publications, leaflets, newsletters and posters and spread the word about events, demos and conferences. Vast amounts of information was shared and disseminated from these centres and networks established. It was in this dynamic, creative and politically inspiring environment that we started to produce the posters.

Our own experiences at art school had not been particularly happy. They were staffed by exclusively male tutors and only a third or less of the students were female. The male students demanded and got all the attention and took up all the studio space and there was little respect for our ideas: the assumption often was that we were probably only doing art as a hobby. Pop Art, which was dominant at that time, challenged the tradition of fine art with its choice of subject matter and promised 'sexual liberation', but was largely practiced by men, often using macho and sexist imagery. It was not a creative situation for

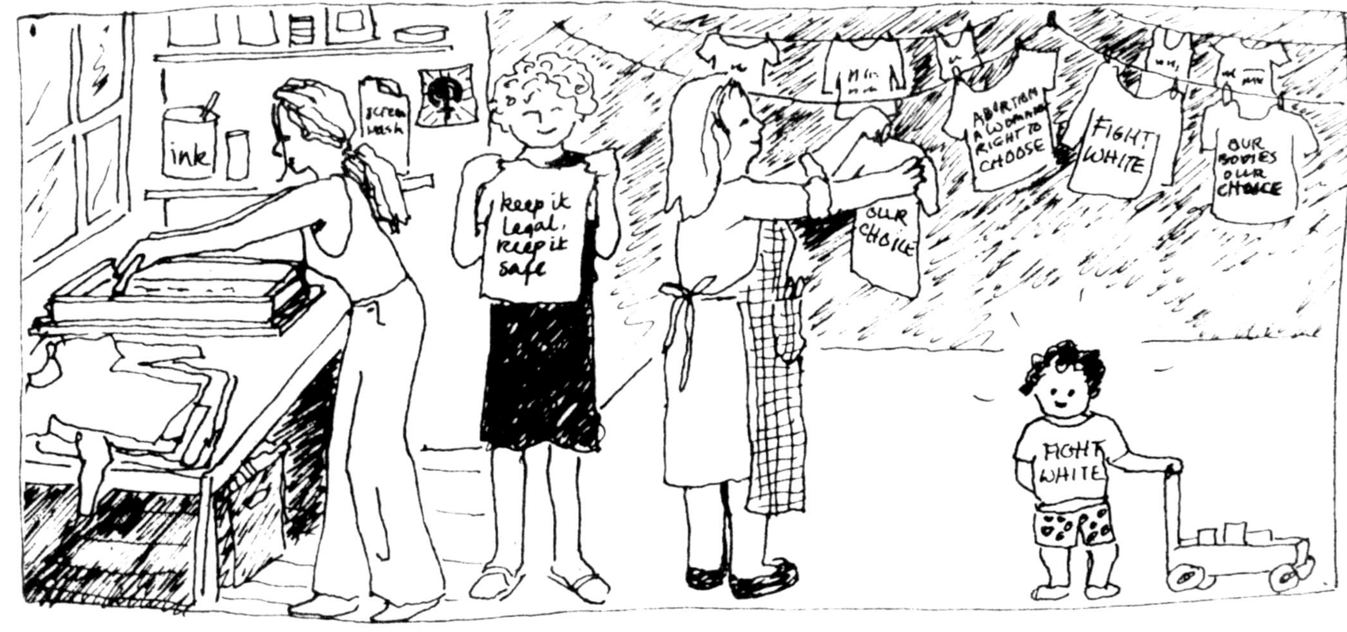

Top: Workshop Sketch, 1977   Bottom: Workshop Sketch, 1974   **6**

any of us: as students we had been encouraged to be secretive and proprietorial about our work and to foster the cult of the artist — a uniquely creative individual. We wanted to challenge this way of working, and we decided from the beginning to work as a collective — to work in a non-patriarchal structure, with no hierarchy and all decisions taken as a group.

All of the ideas for our posters were discussed at length, someone would work up a design, bring sketches back for comment, someone else could then take it, make changes and so on until we were happy with the finished design. This was a way of working that some male artist friends found incomprehensible both as a concept and in practice: 'How do you do it? How do you all design something? Surely someone must hold the pencil.' In many ways it was not easy — it was hard not to say 'it's mine, don't touch it', or to say about someone else's work that it was not good enough, or to take the criticism and change it — but we quickly became committed to this process. Even when this was a challenge, the collective followed through on the ideal of equal shared ownership of the workplace and production, refusing to replicate the silently abusive aspects of top down chains of management even on a small scale. This was quite definitely not just a job and definitely not a way forward for any kind of individual aggrandisement as an artist.

The See Red posters cannot be separated from the wider political context of radical poster making. The posters of the Atelier Populaire (produced during the May 1968 Paris student uprising) and the vibrant posters of the Chinese cultural revolution — together with posters from the US women's movement including Black and Chicano women's groups, and women's freedom and justice campaigns across the world — were particularly influential. Those posters, like ours, were designed to demand attention, to mobilise, inform and inspire. We believed that whilst there is a long tradition of art as social commentary, and whilst posters are part of that tradition, they go further in that a poster doesn't just comment on social injustice — it can actively attempt to generate a response and demand action. Over the following years, we were also influenced by and greatly admired other British radical print collectives including Lenthall Road Workshop, Poster Film Collective, and the Some Girls poster project.

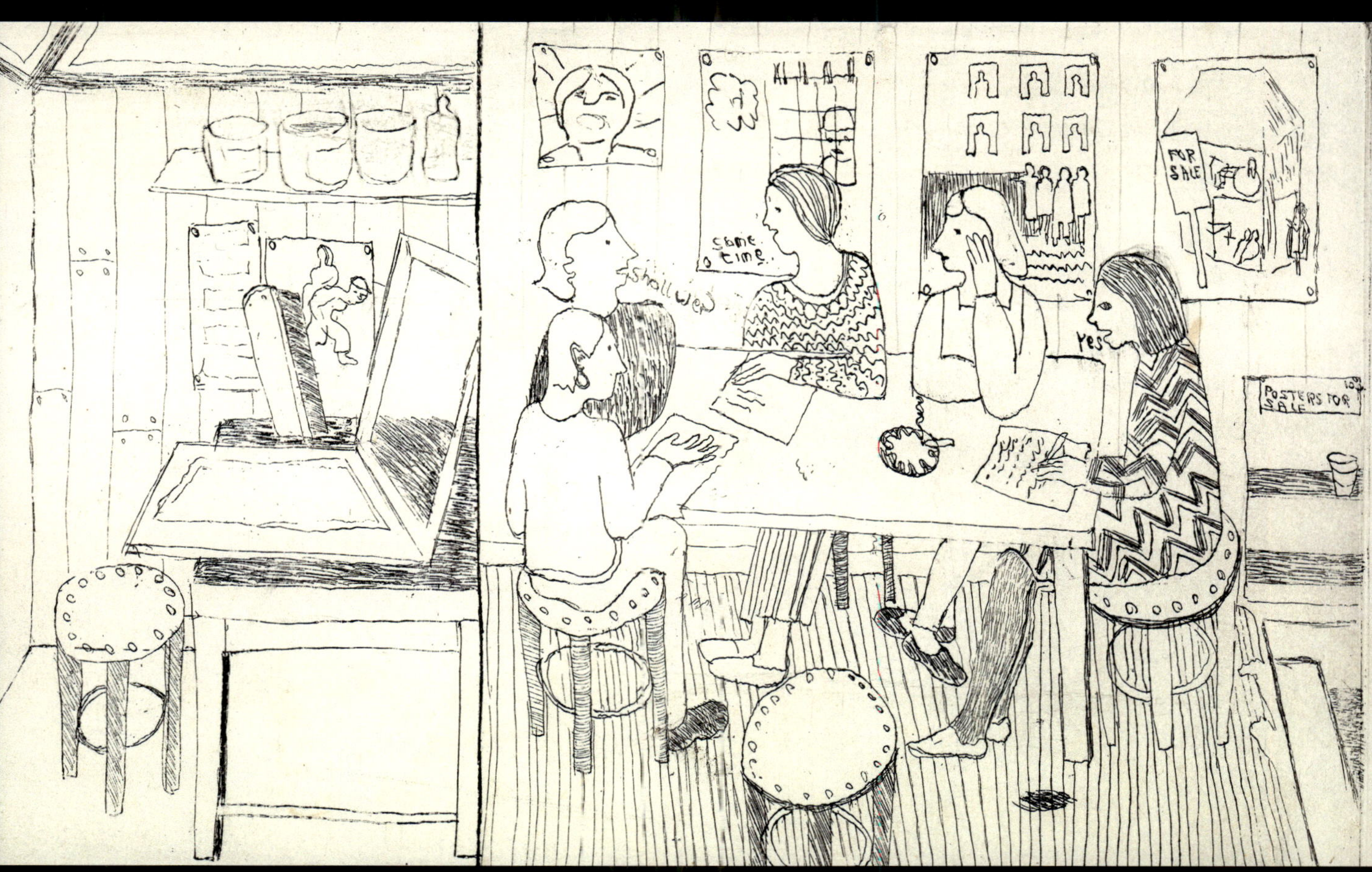

Etching of Camden Road workshop, 1974/5

THESE are a few notes we put together when we were asked todo

this Workshop.

One of the functions of a poster making group is to destroy the
the current images of women that are presented to us , by producing
'new ' images. We try ro do this by making images that question
the ones produced by capitalist society to keep us in our place.

Q. Can you change the image of woman by putting forward only
'positive' images?(from the W.L. point of view),without being
   too utopian and idealistic?

A. You have to use both positive and negative images:

            I. examine the old,negative images(e.g. women isolated
at home in the kitchen) and expose them as sexist conditioning
visually,in a clear way that can be understood by as many women
as possible.
            and 2. produce new positive images(e.g. women together
women as strong)which convey the political spirit of Womens
Liberation.

So an image that doesnt visually suggest an alternative, but only
presents the image we see every day can have a positive effect if
we read   it as as deconstructing (questioning and exposing)
the negative image, and revealing the way the visual oppression
of women works.

Also, we are trying to demystify the'Artistic' process by explaining
the way we produce our images by screenprinting,and showing other
women how to print. By exposing the screenprinting processwe find
that its not that difficult,and we all can do it-- just as by
deconstructing and questioning our roles as women in the male-
defined world,we can understand the nature of our oppression, and
how best to fight it.

By working as a collective we are trying to reject our training
from art school. Many women have said to us:"Oh, I can't draw",
and have   accepted that they can't; we want to destroy
the mystification built around the concept of "The Artist":- it
has a magical quality - someone special - a creator. Accompanying
the term "Artist" is the "given" idea of a strong, individualistic,
self-engrosse d person, which is why we as women find it so
diffic ult to succeed in that role. The ideological assumption
be hind the te rm "artist" is in direct conflict with the accepted
meaning of the term "woman" (a woman creates life not art). Women
are conditioned to be involved with creation by giving birth
and/or caring for man and kids. The"natural" role of a woman is
as a mother and an appendage - we are only supposed to take up
Art as a subsidiary hobby.

The idea of working collectively or even with one other person is
abhorrent to many artists. The idea that their identity - their
mark on the finished creation migh t not be seen, or the idea
of having to share the glory with someone else, stems from fear
of not being recognised. ART today is a way that society allows

the _individual_ to express him/her self and that so-called freedom
of expression is jealously guarded.

Othe r subj ects which would be interesting to discuss:

Ddstrib ution - Who do we sell the posters to?
and
Publicity   - Does our propaganda only reach those who already
                agree with Women's Liberation?
              - How can we reach more women?
Mone y - What grants, etc., are available for poster making group?

SEE RED WOMENS WORKSHOP
 I4 Radnor Terrace
 London
    S.W.4

ACTION GUIDE

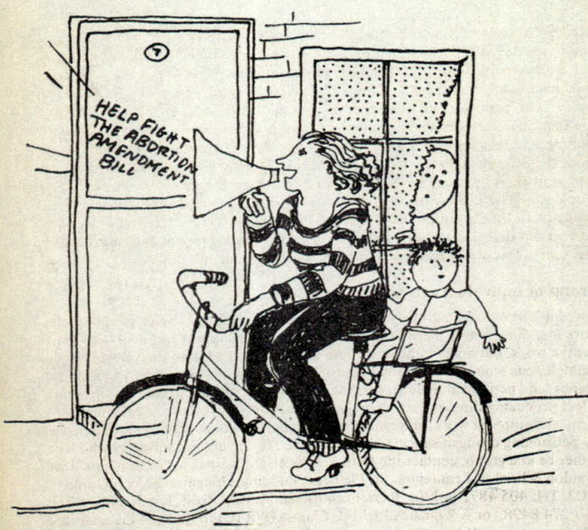

ABORTION LAW REFORM ASSOCIATION
186 KINGS CROSS ROAD   LONDON WC1X 9DE

15p.

This section of the Bill amounts to blanket censorship of information essential to women, and would also restrict the freedom of women journalists to write about their own experiences. If it came into effect, this section would shroud abortion in the secrecy which used to clothe it before 1967. The ability of abortion case witnesses to make outrageous allegations without having their identities revealed seems almost reminiscent of Star Chamber justice.

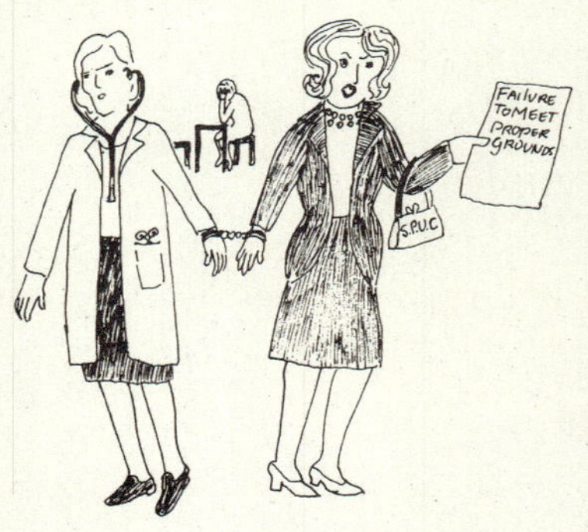

Controls on abortion advice and referral

Mr. White's Bill would permit only registered doctors or people approved by the Secretary of State for Health and Social Services to give advice and information on abortion, unless they were not paid for giving advice. This section would not only catch out the taxi touts and agencies channelling women to extortionate private clinics, but would also catch anyone paid to give general advice. It would apply to Release workers, paid workers for women's groups, Citizen's Advice Bureaux, etc. If a CAB worker who had not been approved by the Secretary of State to give such advice was approached by a pregnant woman the worker could be prosecuted for saying: 'Go to your family doctor and ask for an abortion'. In these circumstances, it is likely that workers in small groups and advice agencies would simply refuse to talk to people about abortion. They would face the same penalties as doctors and nurses carrying out illegal operations, and a heavy fine could destroy a small advice agency.

6

BATTERED WOMEN NEED REFUGES

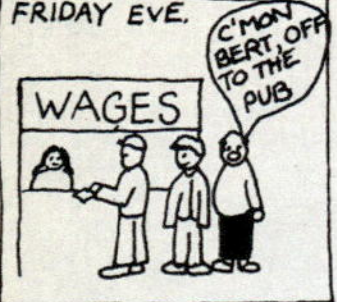

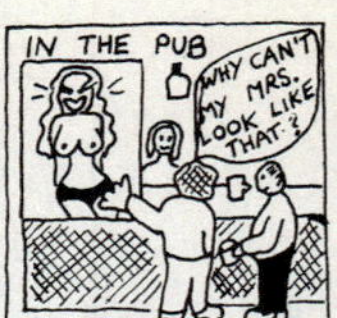

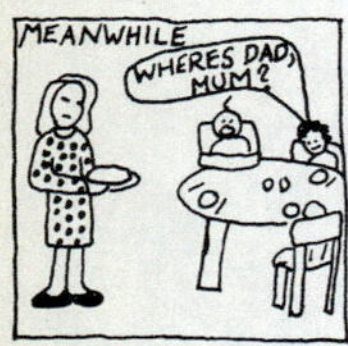

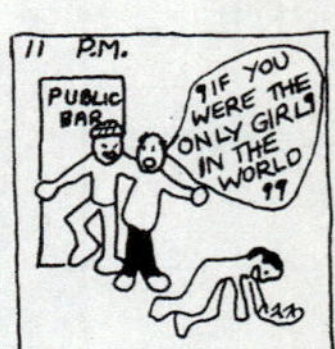

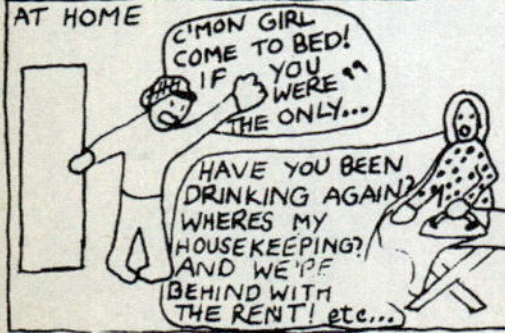

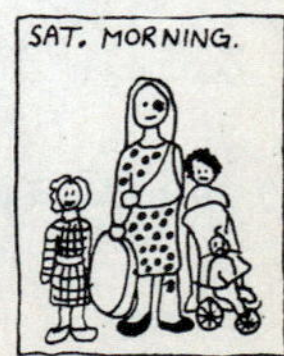

Since 1973, a founder member, Pru Stevenson, had been producing posters in shop premises occupied by the Camden Tenants Association in North London for local community groups and organisations, including for the Women's Liberation Movement. See Red was able to move in and reprint some of these posters to sell and start work immediately.

Initially we envisaged that the collective would work on several different fronts; producing posters, illustrations, cartoons and photographs; providing visual materials for other women's publications and groups to use; and collecting images which illustrated the position of women in our society today — for example, the everyday assaults of advertising. We took on a lot and we worked on a range of jobs, including illustrations for women's campaigns and information booklets for the Abortion Law Reform Association and for Women's Aid and refuges, placards for marches and workshops in schools on Women's Liberation, among many others.

After several months work, the group then split, with three of the founders, Julia Franco, Suzy Mackie and Pru, becoming a women's silkscreen poster making collective (keeping the See Red Women's Workshop name).

Not only was silkscreen printing something we felt would have an impact and would contribute to the Women's Liberation Movement, it was something we wanted to do, enjoyed doing, and could do well. At last we found that we had a chance to use our skills to further a cause that we were personally affected by and that we felt passionately about. We wanted to make posters that were consciousness-raising, humorous and eye-catching: if they were not accessible to all they were not serving their purpose.

For some people they were too provocative: over Christmas, 1974, a passer-by took exception to a display of our posters and hurled a brick through the Camden Town shop window. We were soon looking for new premises.

We moved to South London Women's Centre in 1975, which at the time was in a squat on Radnor Terrace off South Lambeth Road, Vauxhall. With more and more work coming in, we advertised for more members, and Sarah Jones, who became a core member of the group until 1983, joined at this time. The space upstairs was extremely small, with no heating and poor ventilation, but we made it as habitable as we could and carried on printing, hanging the finished posters on a washing line to dry.

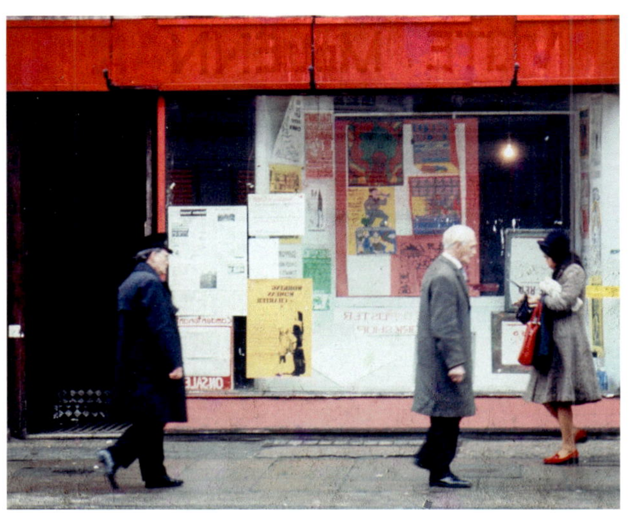

Above: Camden Road Premises, 1974
Facing: Pamphlets illustrated by See Red Women's Workshop, 1974

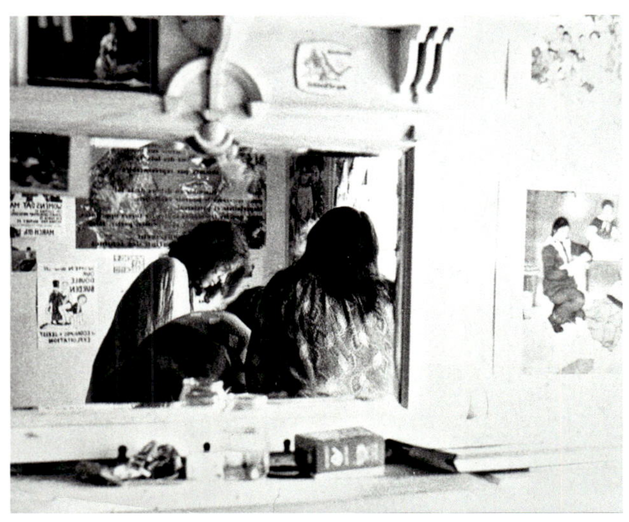

Radnor Terrace Premises, 1975.
The picture had to be taken in the mirror as the room was so small.

We finally found permanent premises in 1977 in
Iliffe Yard, a derelict mews off the Walworth Road
in South London. We worked alongside Women In
Print, a women's offset litho printing co-operative.
They, because of the size of their printing presses,
took the vacant ground floor premises and we took
the first floor workshop across the yard. We were
able to share some equipment and contacts, we
supported eachother and socialised together: they
became a very important part of our working lives.

The workshop was entered via a rickety wooden
staircase. There was no electricity, or plumbing.
On a point of principle and with the aid of the
groups Lambeth Women's Workshop and Women
In Manual Trades, we learnt to do the plumbing,
carpentry and construction work needed to turn
it into a reasonable working environment.

Before we moved to Iliffe Yard our equipment
had been extremely basic: a wooden table with
a couple of screens and washing lines and pegs
for hanging up the posters to dry. For our newly
converted workshop, with the aid of donations,
we were able to buy at auction a silkscreen
printing table, new screens and drying racks large
enough to hold 50 posters at a time. We had
sufficient room to store several reams of the large
paper sizes needed and to store the flammable

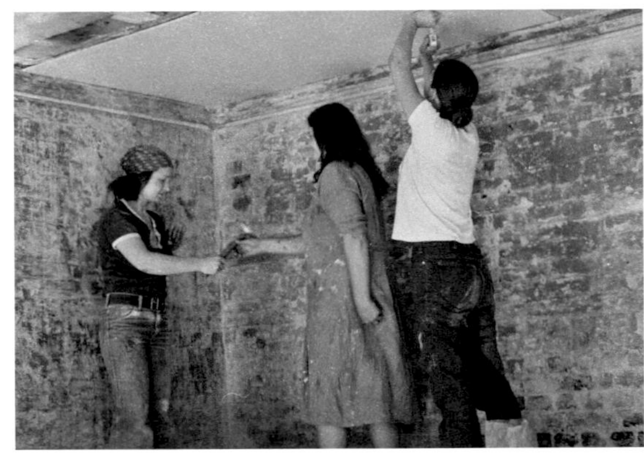

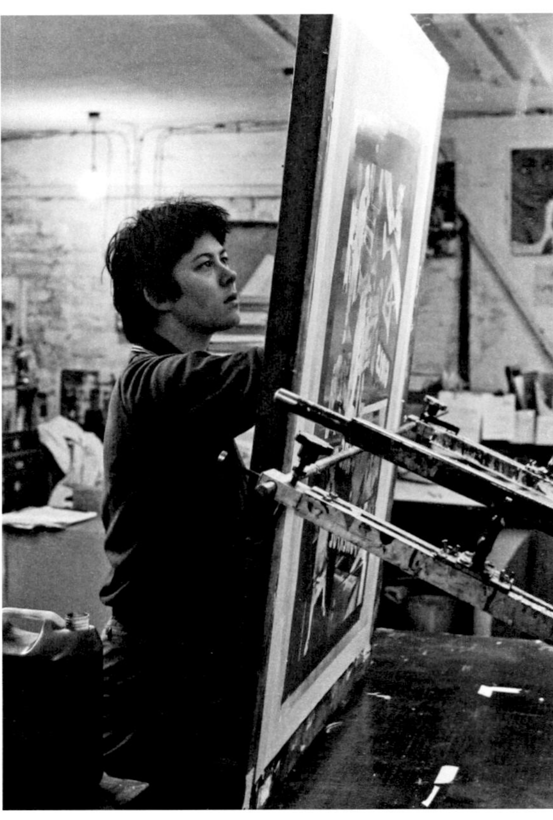

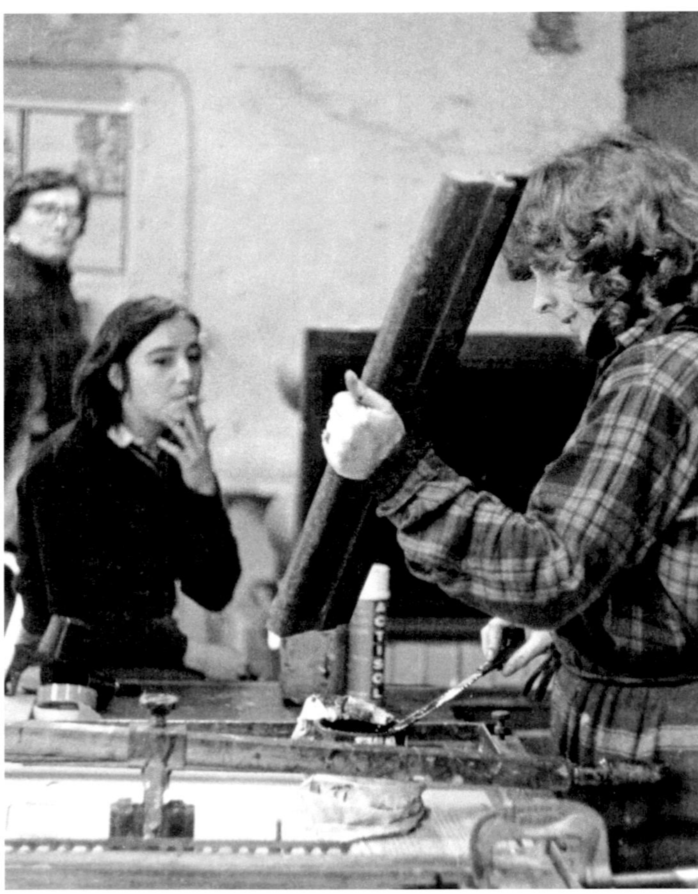

Fixing up premises and printing at Iliffe Yard, 1976–83

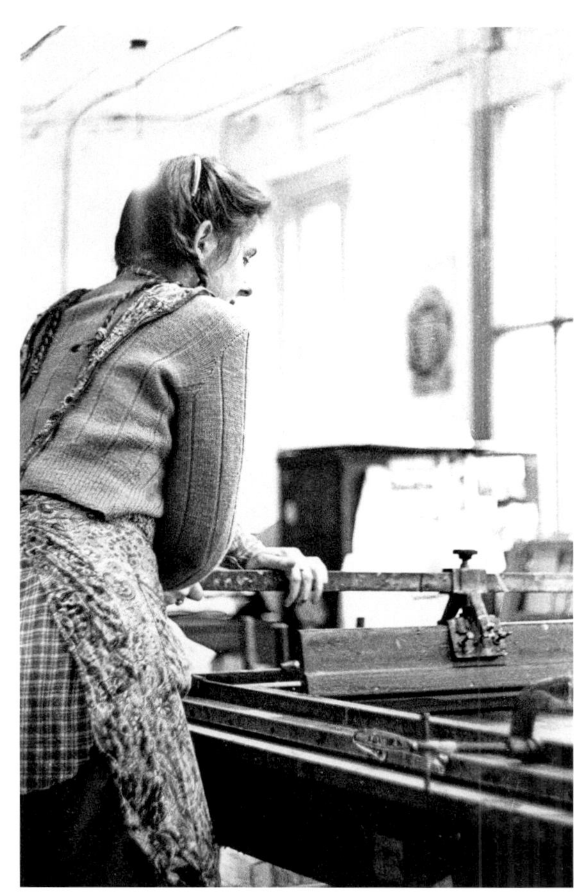

inks in metal cupboards in case of fire — health and safety was not on the agenda in those days. After a couple of years we started trying to protect ourselves and occasionally wore gas masks, and heavy duty rubber gloves and kept the windows open for as long as it was bearable. It was to be some time before we were able to install an extractor fan to suck out all the fumes from the oil based inks used at that time.

The early posters were printed using paper stencils or by blocking out: a blue water based filler was painted onto the screen and this blocked out all the areas not to be printed. Oil-based inks were then drawn across the screen with a squeegee, leaving the water-based filler intact. *Disc Jockey*, *A Woman's Work*, *Capitalism Depends on Domestic Labour*, *My Wife Doesn't Work* and (using a different screen for each colour) *Right on Jane*, *Protest* and *Women Unite* were all printed using this method. These two methods needed the minimum of equipment — paper, stencil knife, filler and paint brush, screen, squeegee, inks and solvent. This meant that we could set up shop almost anywhere — at women's centres, in playgrounds, at Women's Liberation conferences — enabling women to voice their message quickly in a visual form.

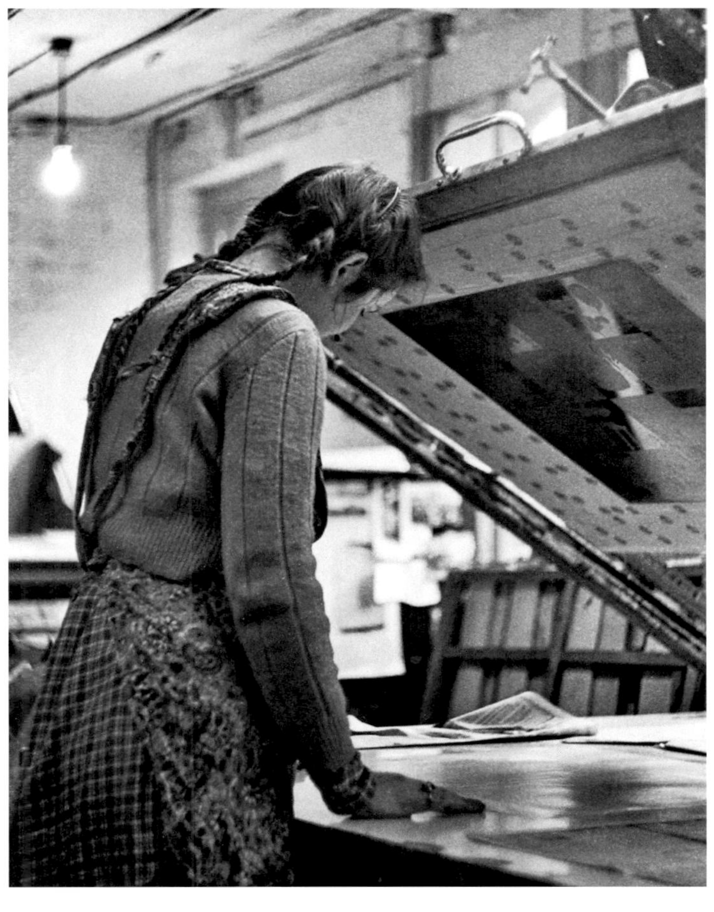

Printing at Iliffe Yard, 1977

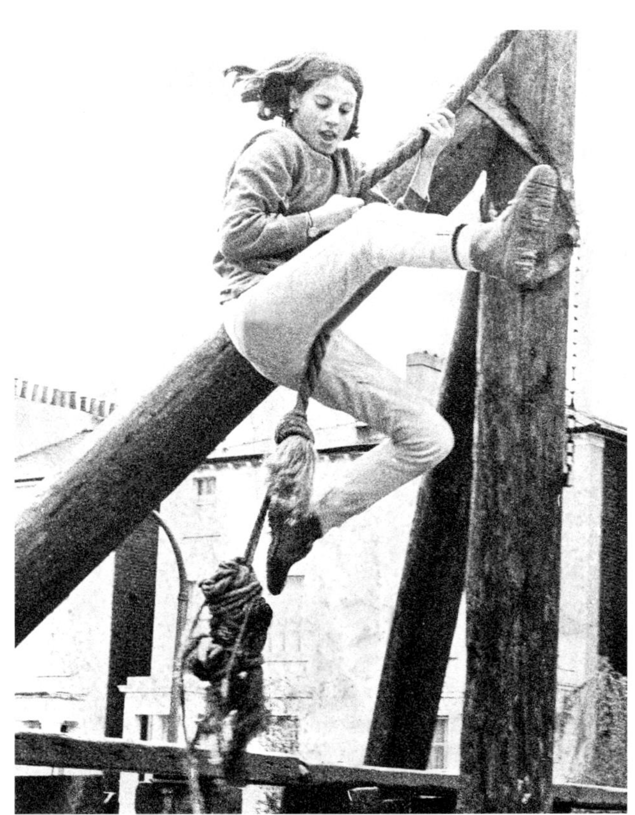

By 1978, we had sufficient funds to install a darkroom; as well as paper stencils and filler we were now able to use photographs which widened the range of images and designs we could produce: *Girls Are Powerful*, and the second version of *Don't Let Racism Divide Us* were among the first posters to use this method. By 1977 we had produced 15 new posters and two calendars. We went on to produce three more calendars (for 1978, 1979 and 1980), each with new designs, many of which went on to become posters.

We wanted all women to be able to buy our posters so we kept them as cheap as possible. From 1976, we produced catalogues, five altogether, printed for us by Women in Print or other radical print co-ops. We sent them to women's centres and bookshops, community and radical bookshops, schools, colleges, and all over the UK and abroad, and we also gave them out at women's events and conferences. The growing number of radical bookshops, such as Compendium, News from Nowhere, First of May, Sisterwrite and Silver Moon, would place regular orders from these catalogues.

Above: Original photograph for *Girls Are Powerful* poster, 1979

Facing: Orders for posters, 1981–82

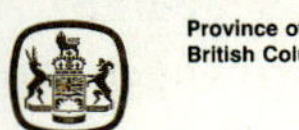

Province of
British Columbia

Ministry of
Labour

Employment Opportunity
Programs
Parliament Buildings
Victoria
British Columbia
V8V 1X4
Telephone (604) 387-1131

120 - 4946 Canada Way
Burnaby, B.C.
V5G 4J6
291-2901

September 21, 1981

Ms. Susan Mackie
c/o See Red Women's Workshop
16A Iliffe Yard
Off Crampton Street
London, S.E. 17
United Kingdom

Dear Ms. Mackie

Thank you for sending your catalogue and price list. Your posters are most interesting!

In answer to your question regarding what promotional purposes the "My Wife Doesn't Work" poster will be used for...

I feel it is important that Women recognize the valuable contribution they make to society as homemakers. I intend to hang the poster in our Women's Office Resource Centre so it gets extensive exposure.

I'd also like men to see it - they may recognize themselves! I'll be showing it to various groups I deal with in hopes that they will order copies.

Please keep me advised of any new posters available. (Our order is attached.)

Yours very truly,

Jule Morrow,
Manager

JM:aas

Sent

FULL MARKS socialist & feminist BOOKSHOP

Telephone (0272) 40491.   110 Cheltenham Rd, Bristol 6.

21.12.81

To

Womens Poster Collective

Greetings.

Could you send us x6 Nº 6

Black Women.

Sent

Thanks,

Marx.

F.M

FULL MARKS LTD, REGISTERED CO-OPERATIVE No. 22227R

WOMENS INFORMATION CENTRE

Tel: Coventry 51756 Ext. 69

Priory Annexe, (Sidney Stringer) Wheatley Street, Coventry, CV1 5NL.

WE HAVE MOVED TO
Vine St. Annexe
(Sidney Stringer)
Vine Street
Hillfields
Coventry
Tel: 51756 Ex. 69

20-4-82.

Dear Sisters,

Please could you send us the following posters :-

Sent   to follow

No1 - Girls - £1
No2 - ABC - 90p
No5 - Racism - 90p
No14 - Lesbians - 90p
No27 - 7 Demands - 90p

PAID.

Sent

We Enclose a cheque for £5.20.

Yours in Sisterhood
Chelly p.p. Womens Centre.

See Red

news from nowhere

· Radical· Books· &· Pamphlets·

100 Whitechapel, Liverpool L1 6EN. Tel: 051-708 7270

29.10.82

Dear Sisters,

We still haven't received your new catalogue of posters (I think it was mentioned in Outwrite or Spare Rib). We now want to do an order to you so would you please send us a catalogue? We're looking forward to getting some exciting new posters from you.

Yours,

Erika Hannerveld

Sent

"People fight and lose the battle, and the thing they fought for comes about in spite of their defeat, and when it turns out to be not what they meant, other people have to fight for what they meant under another name". – William Morris

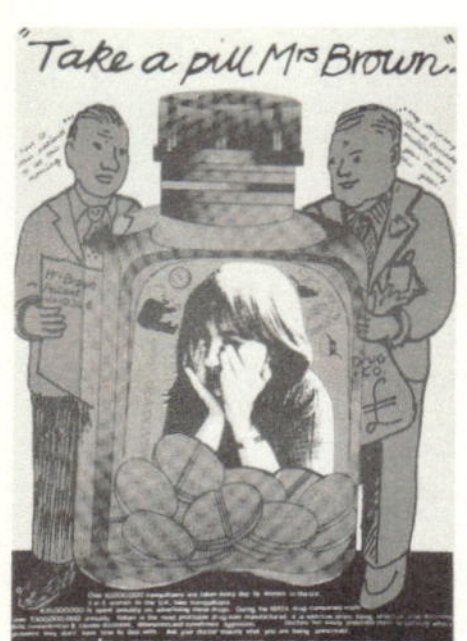

1. PILLS 21"x 31" 80p
green,beige,black.

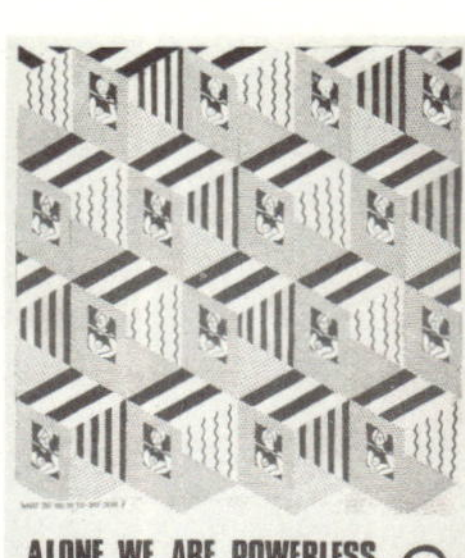

2. ALONE 21"x 28" 70p
red,maroon.

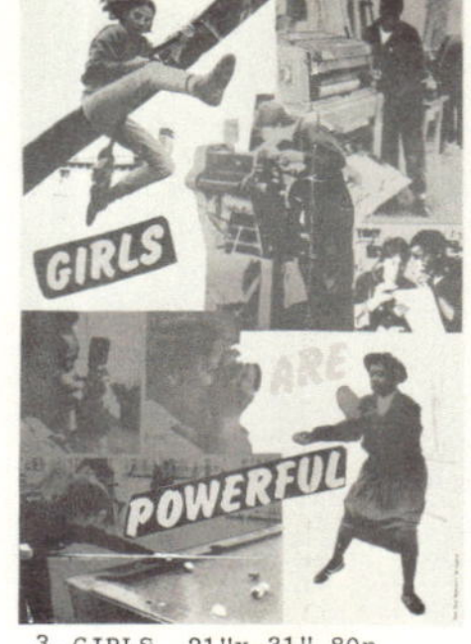

3. GIRLS 21"x 31" 80p
multicoloured.

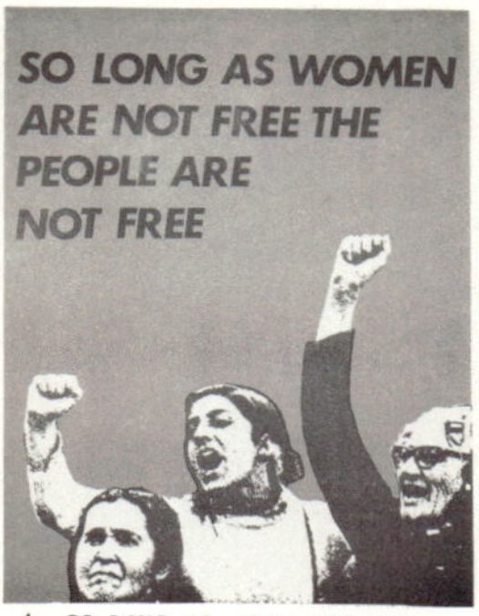

4. SO LONG AS 20"x 26" 70p
yellow, purple/red.

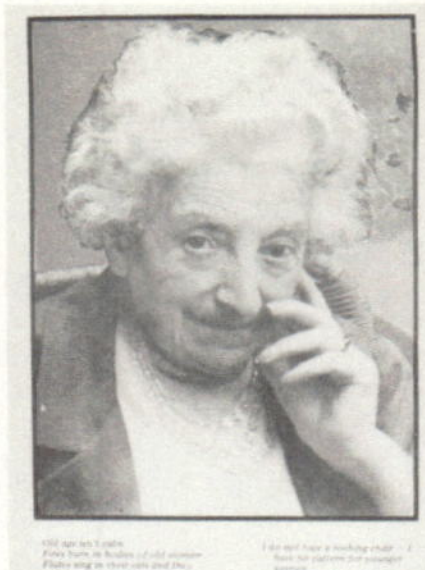

5. OLD AGE 21"x 31" 80p
red, green.

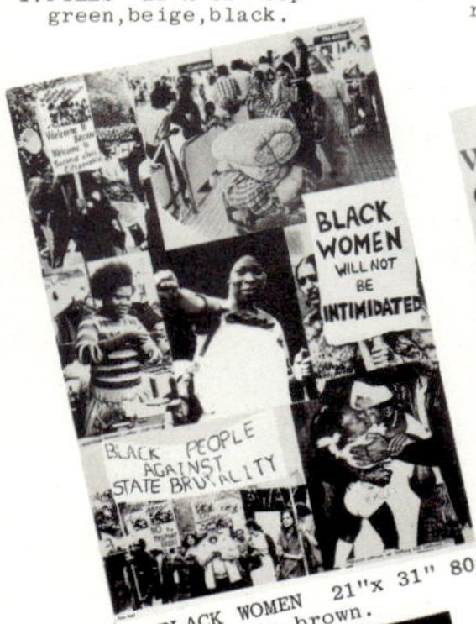

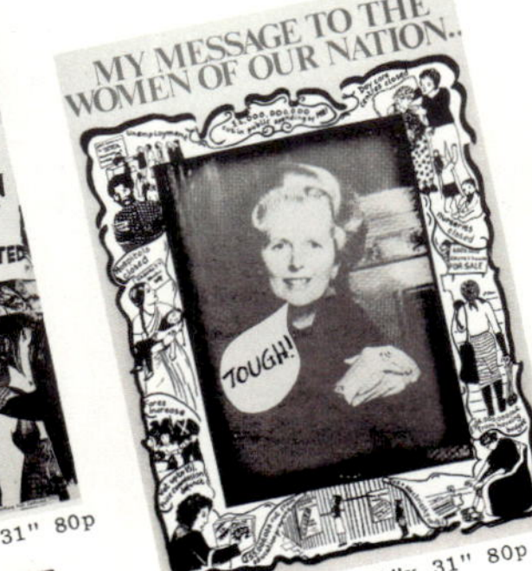

6. BLACK WOMEN 21"x 31" 80p
red,beige,brown.

7. THATCHER 21"x 31" 80p
blue,yellow,red.

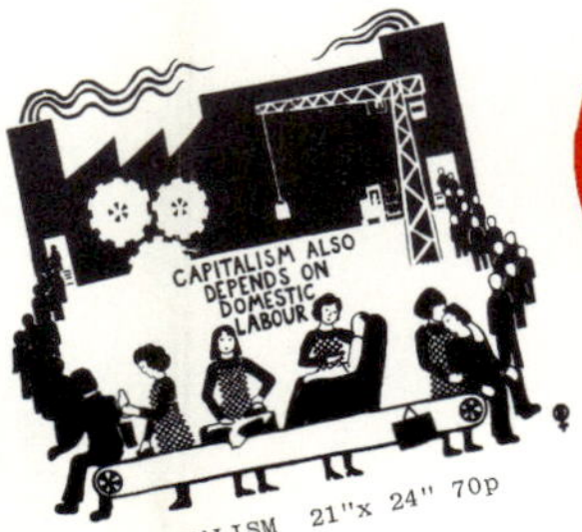

8. CAPITALISM 21"x 24" 70p
brown.

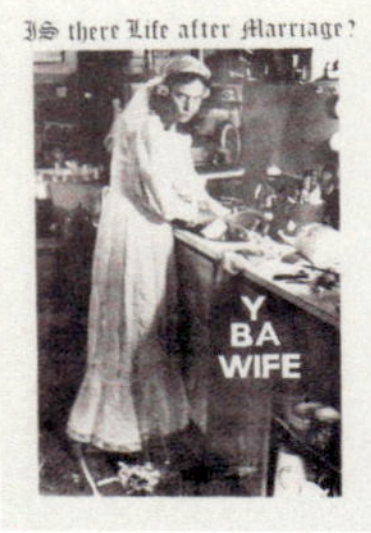

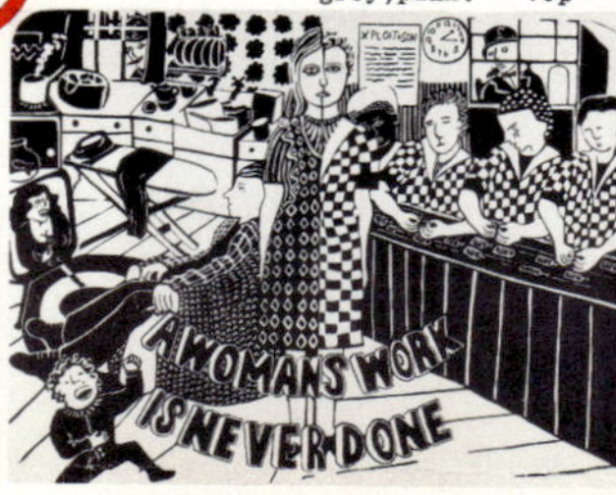

9. YBA WIFE 17"x 24" 70p
grey,pink.

See red womens workshop.

16 a Iliffe Yard,
off Crampton St.,
London, S.E.17.
tel: 01-701-8314

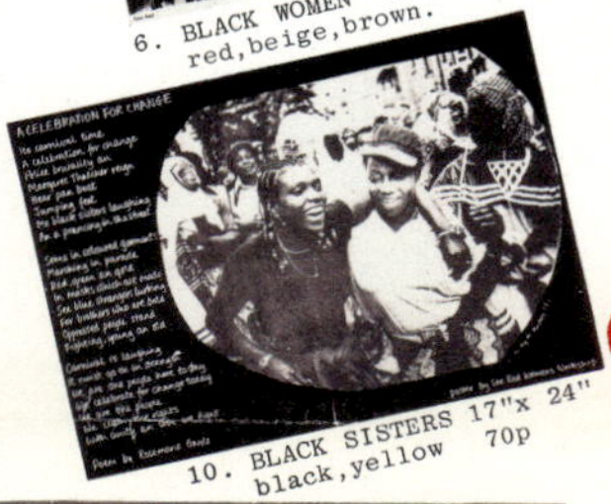

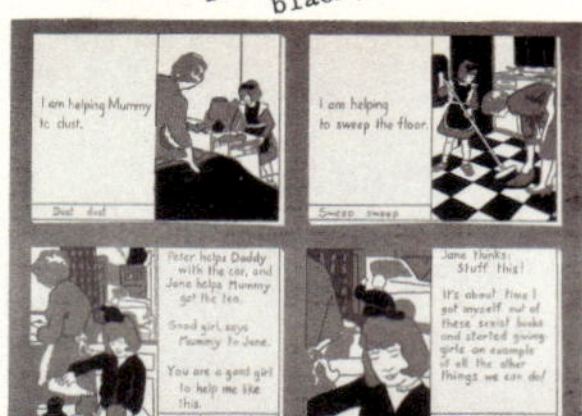

10. BLACK SISTERS 17"x 24" 70p
black,yellow

11. A WOMAN'S WORK 20"x 26" 70p
red.

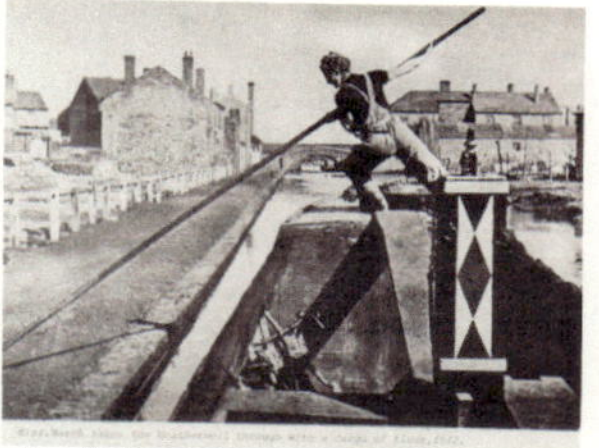

Postage and packing is;
30p for 1 poster
65p for 5
85p for 10
£1.40 for 20

25% discount for bookshops

WE ALSO PRINT T-SHIRTS AND
POSTERS FOR MEETINGS, EVENTS
ETC. AT REASONABLE PRICES.

12. JANE 20"x 26" 80p
red,blue,yellow.

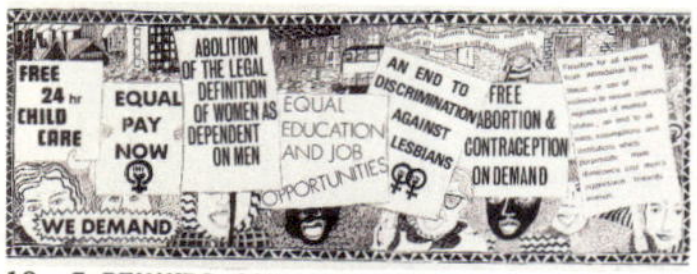

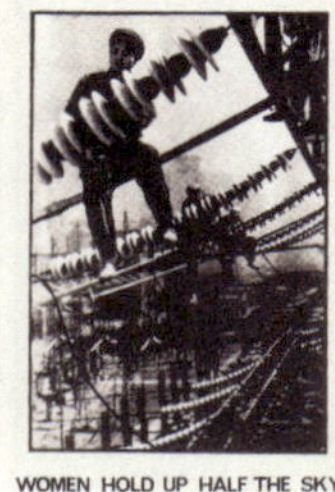

13. 7 DEMANDS 28"x 13" 70p
black.

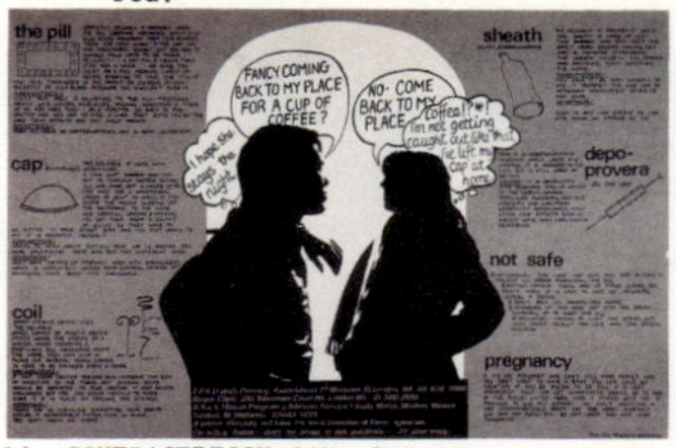

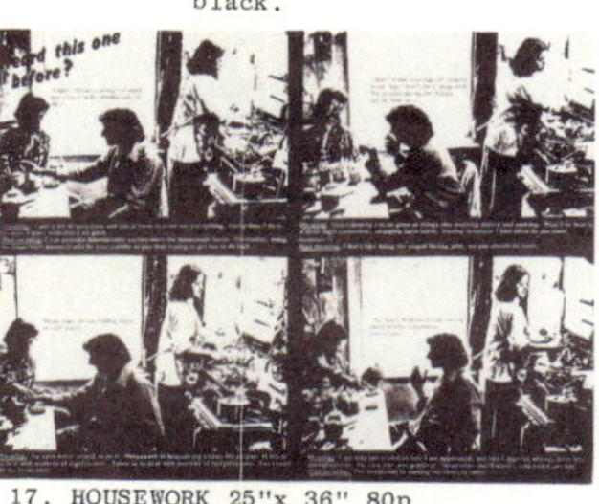

14. CONTRACEPTION 21"x 31" 80p
black,pink/yellow/green.

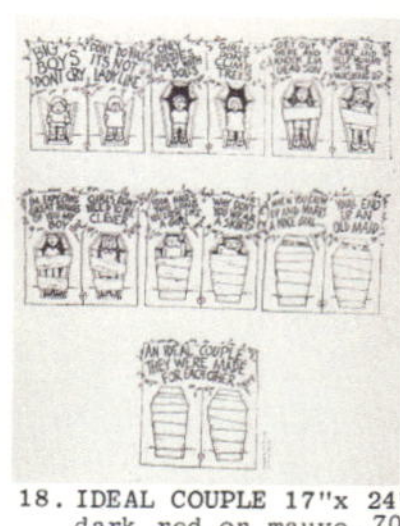

15. MISS MARCH 20"x 25" 70p
green,red.

16. HALF THE SKY 17"x 24" 70p
orange,blue.

17. HOUSEWORK 25"x 36" 80p
multicoloured.

18. IDEAL COUPLE 17"x 24"
dark red on mauve. 70p

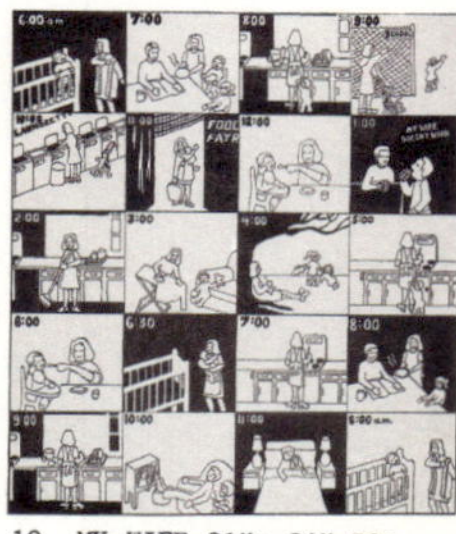

19. MY WIFE 21"x 24" 70p
blue,red.

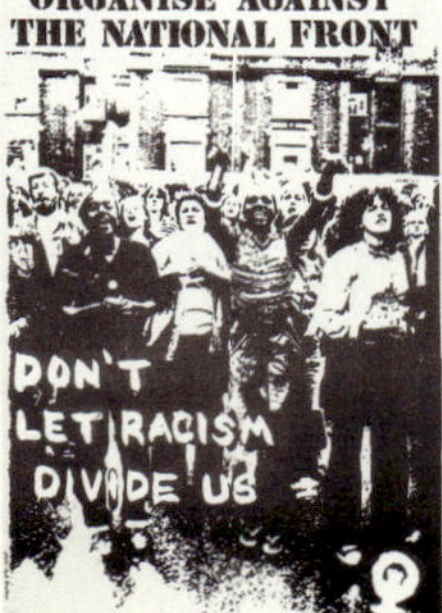

20. RACISM 21"x 31" 70p
black,red.

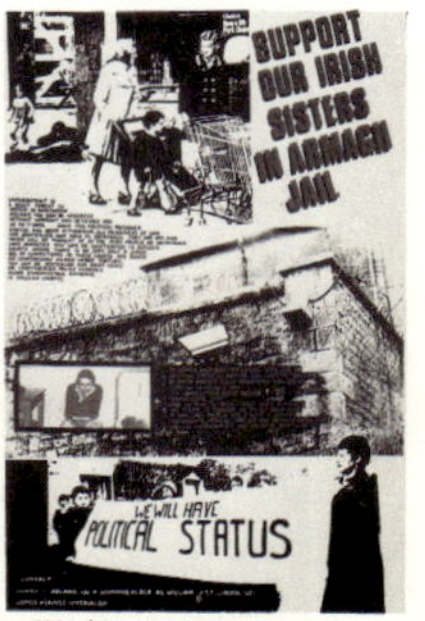

21. WOMEN IN ARMAGH 21"x 31"
80p; green,red,black.

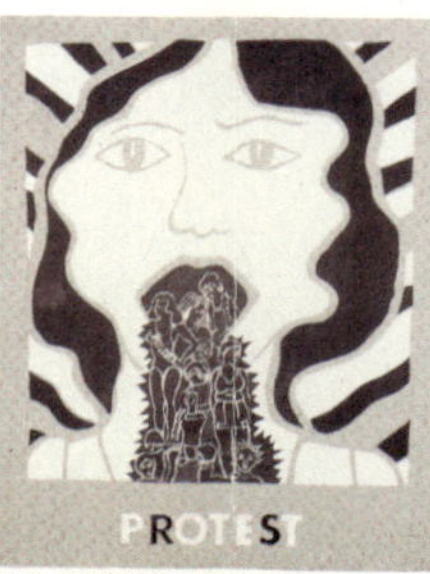

22. PROTEST 21"x 28" 80p
green,red,yellow,blue.

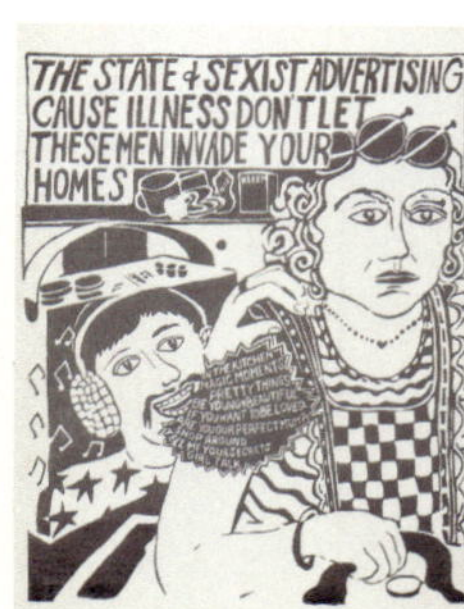

23. DISC JOCKEY 20"x 26" 70p
green.

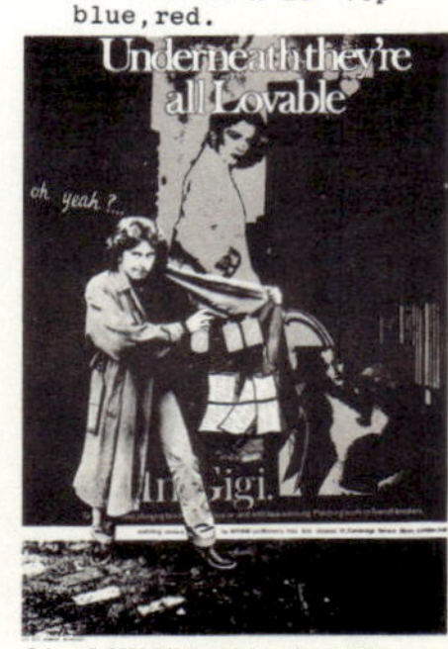

24. LOVABLE 21"x 31" 80p
black,pink,green.

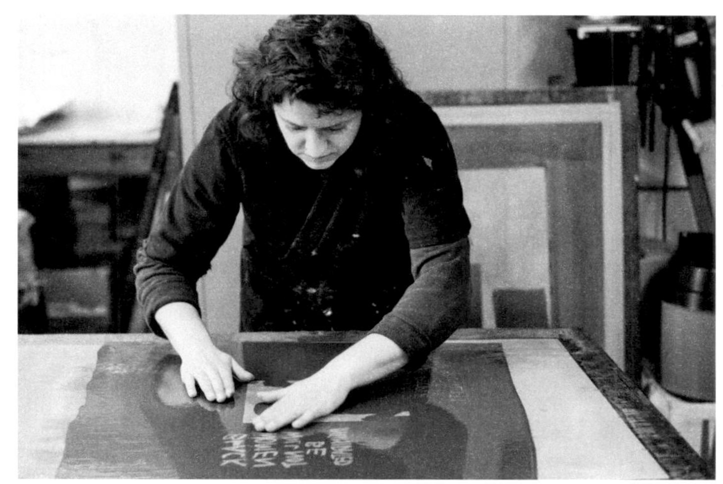

Attending different Women's Liberation Movement conferences and events were annual highlights. With arms full of posters and maybe a screen and inks to do a workshop, we would set up shop and sell hundreds of posters. With debates and workshops on many different topics and new demands for the women's movement made and voted on, the conferences were a source for new ideas and inspiration.

All money from the sale of the posters was ploughed back into the workshop. We received donations and were occasionally given materials for free. We attended sales of printing businesses closing down, scoured nearby East Street shops for their used cardboard tubes which we used to protect posters in the post, and we tried not to waste anything.

Selling didn't pay all the bills though and the collective often found itself in the position of appealing for funds from the women's movement and individual supporters of alternative culture. There are numerous references to this throughout the collective diaries including one entry from 11th February 1982: following one appeal, a mysterious donor pedalled up to the yard with a cheque for a thousand pounds before disappearing.

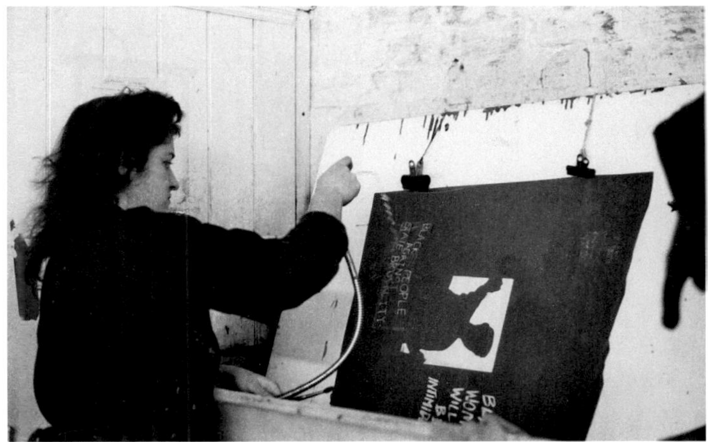

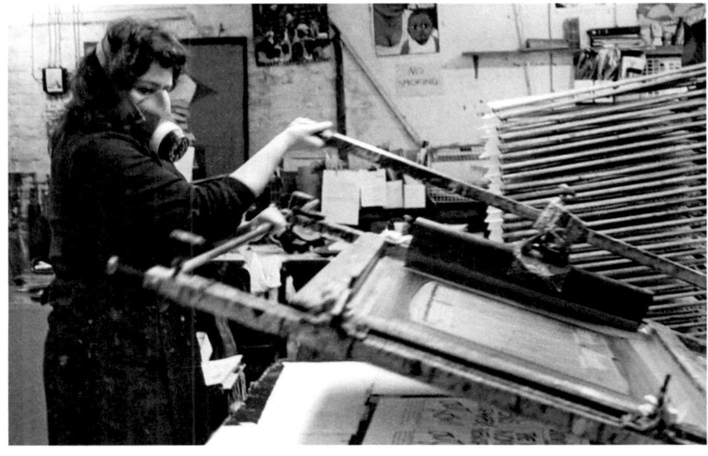

Above: Positioning stencil, washing out stencil and printing
Facing: See Red poster catalogue, 1981

In addition to our See Red designs, we took on printing jobs (posters, cards and t-shirts) for local groups and organisations whose aims we supported. Our first commission was to design a poster for International Women's Day March 1975, and it was followed by posters for the Socialist Feminist Conference London 1977; the Black Information Unit, the Women's Safe Transport service and the London and National conferences of Women Against Violence Against Women, 1982, among many others. This work generated a small income but only enough to keep us solvent, certainly not enough to pay ourselves wages — we received no funding nor were we to receive any until 1982.

We all had part time jobs to enable us to fund our work in See Red — teaching art and crafts in youth clubs, printing in playgrounds, cleaning, teaching silkscreen printing in an adult education college. We wanted to involve other women in the workshop from the start, and had an open invitation for women to join us. We worked for the collective for two and a half days a week each on average, but often took work home to do in the evenings or weekends — the themes we worked on were our lives, and the commitment kept us going.

Sharing our skills, especially with women who ordinarily would not have the opportunity to learn about design and printing, was always important. At any one time there were about five core members of See Red and over its lifespan, 30–40 women joined the workshop for varying lengths of time and for different reasons. Several women became collective members in response to job advertisements placed in *Spare Rib* and other publications and made a commitment to working a few days every week, printing, doing admin and being part of the decision making process. We started a more formal apprenticeship scheme in 1980. Notices were put in local papers and newsletters asking for 'any women interested to come round and meet us and to use the facilities and learn printing methods'. Women would come, and work with us for one day a week for three months, with the option to remain with the collective after that. Two women, political refugees from Colombia and Chile, were referred by a local community worker and joined us in 1980 on that basis. They designed and produced with us the South American poster *Participe de Nostra Luche! Join Our Struggle*.

Though individual black women, lesbians and working class women had worked with us from

Women's Day March
Our first commission was to design a poster for International Women's Day March 1975. We worked on the design as a group, it was printed offset litho by Spiders Web as 5,000 were needed for flyposting, and we went on the march.

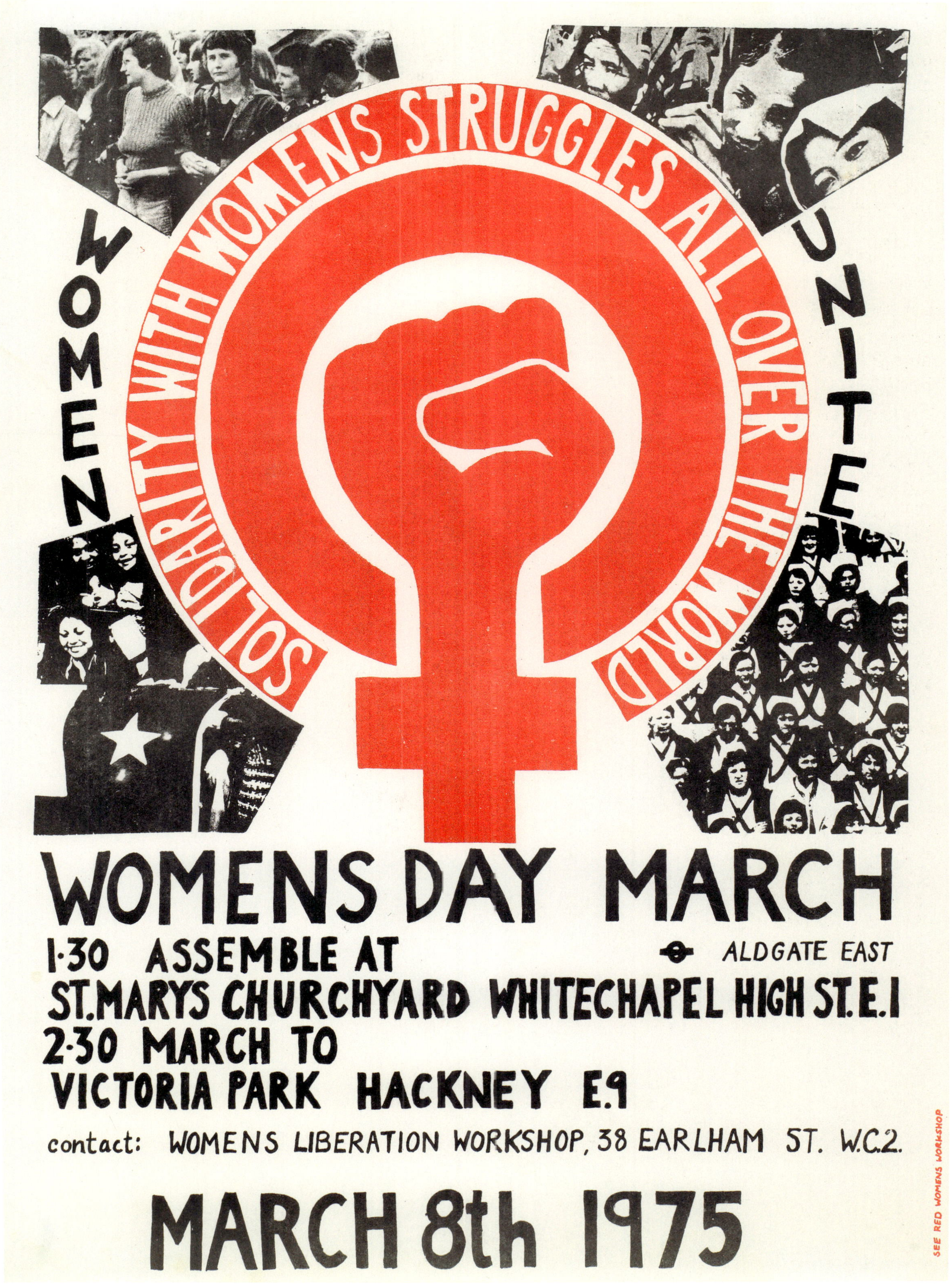

 WOMEN'S DAY MARCH, 1975 *42 × 30.5 cm*

FIGHT
The Corrie
Anti-Abortion
Bill!

LGSM
LESBIANS AND GAY MEN
1984 1985
SUPPORT THE MINERS

NO!
TO MALE
VIOLENCE

MORE
daycare
abortion clinics
now!
nac

WE DON'T JUST WANT
MORE CAKE
STRIKE
WE WANT THE BLOODY
BAKERY

YBA
wife

WOMEN DECIDE
CONTRACEPTION ABORTION STERILIZATION

Don't
do it,
Di!

FIGHT THE CUTS!
STUFF THE JUBILEE

Rock against Sexism

RICH LORDS OUT
ever seen a judge on a bus?
cheap fares in

"IF I CAN'T DANCE...
I DON'T WANT TO
BE PART OF YOUR
REVOLUTION"
EMMA GOLDMAN

NO CUTS
MORE NURSERIES NOW

SANTA SUPPORTS THE YORK's MINERS
NUM

See red
WOMENS WORKSHOP

The GLC
Works for Women
SAVE IT

ADULT
AE
Help us
KEEP it!

March for
abortion
rights
APRIL 3

NATIONAL LESBIAN
CONFERENCE 1981

CHILE FIGHTS

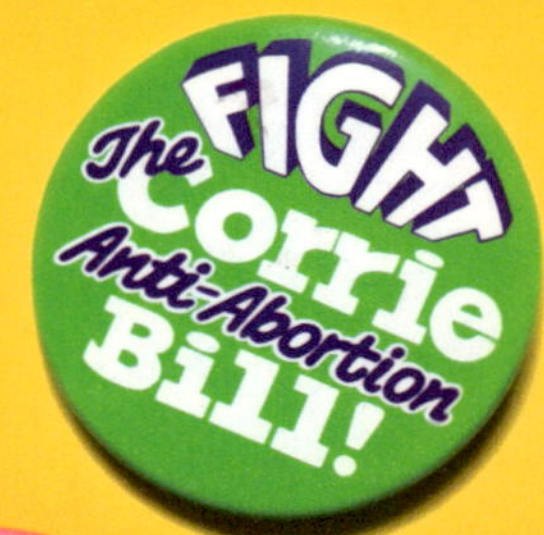

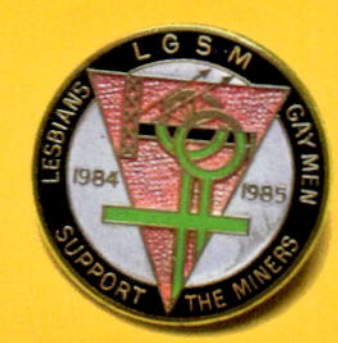

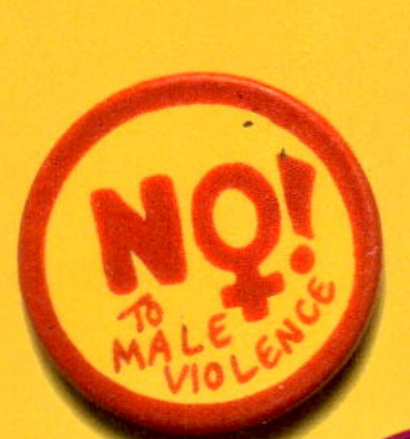

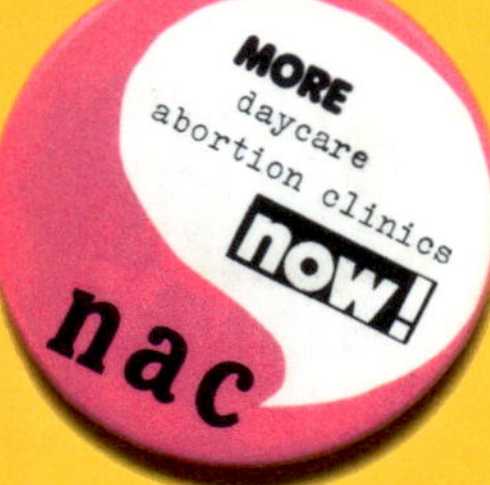

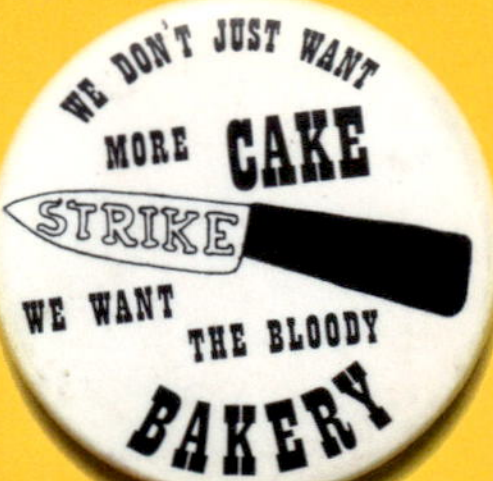

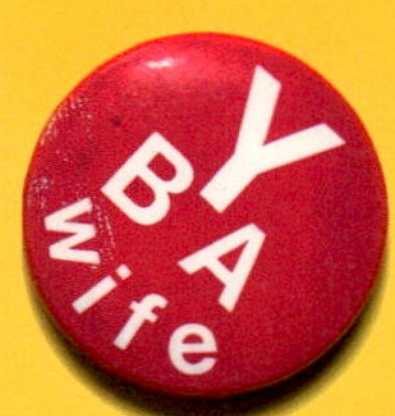

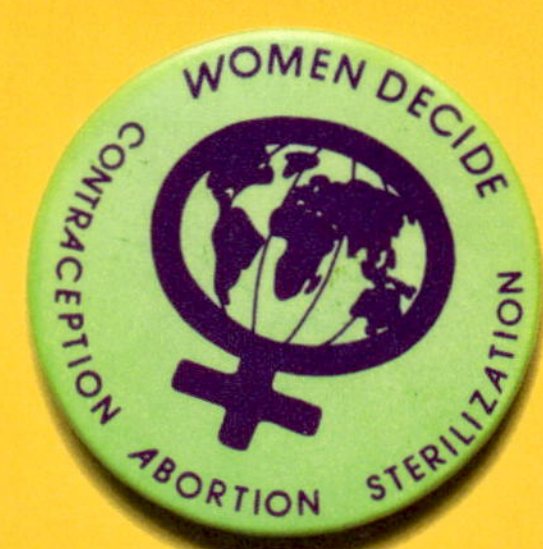

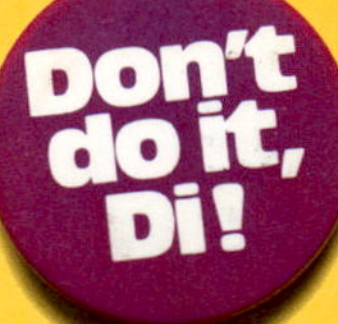

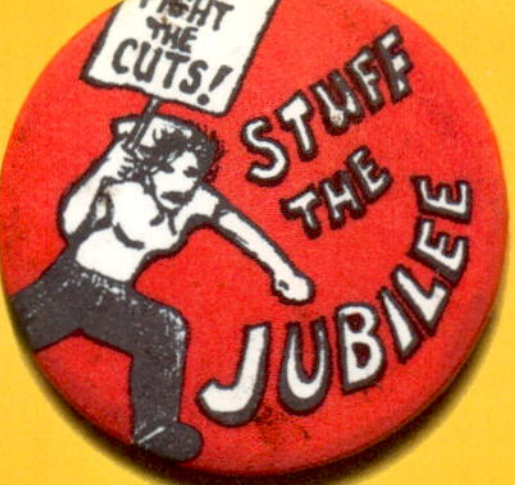

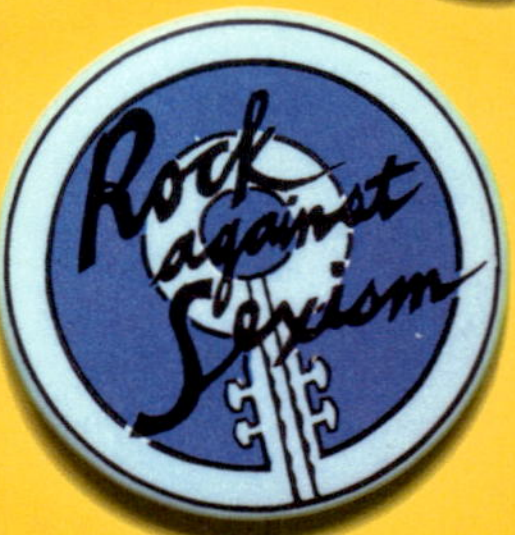

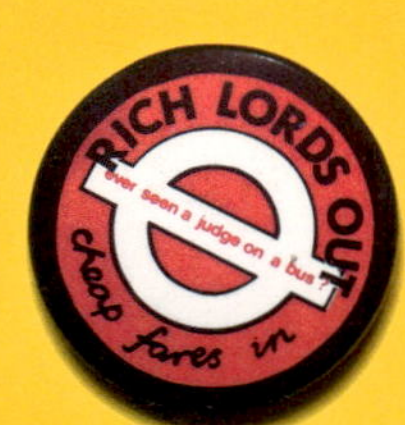

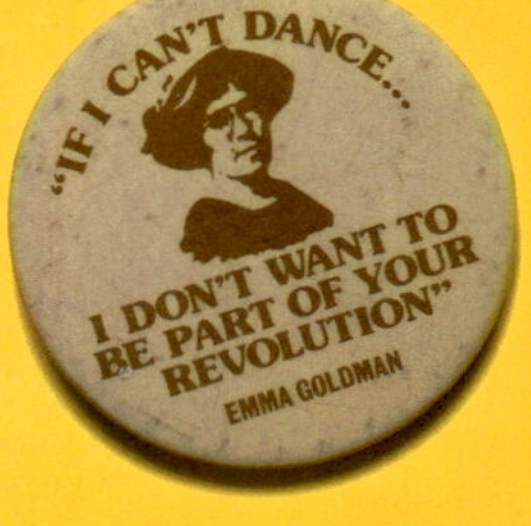

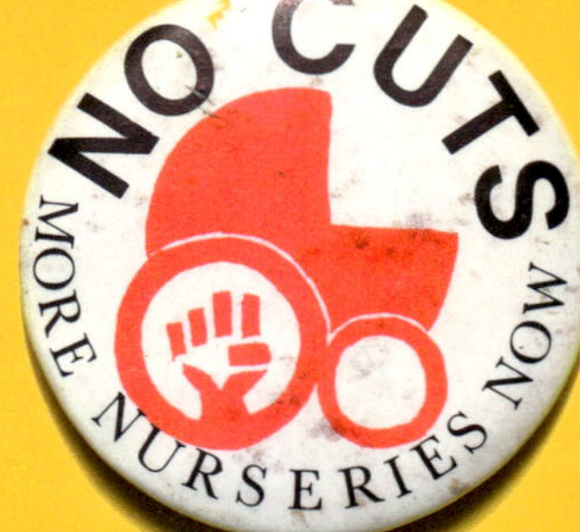

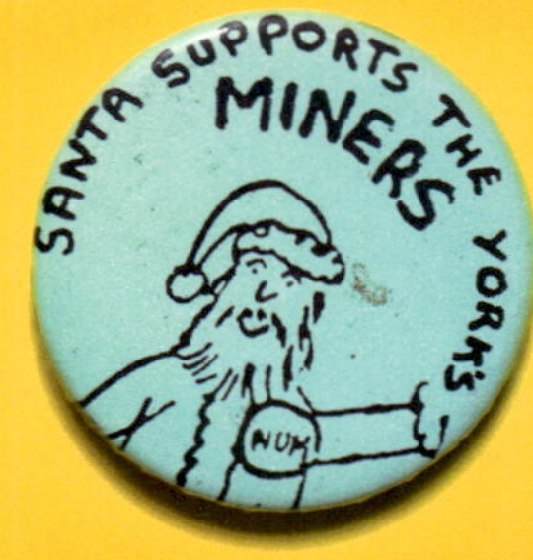

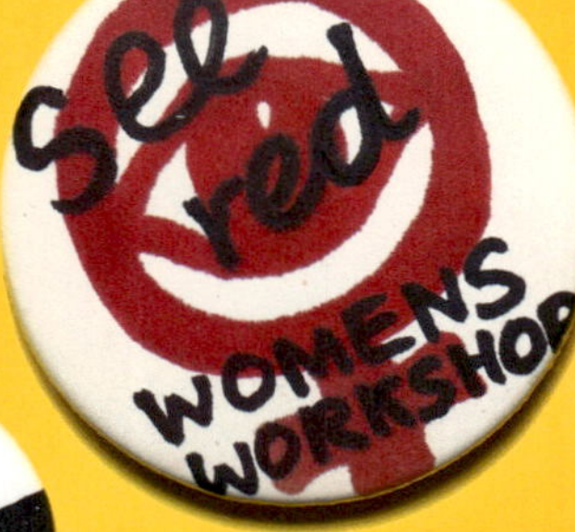

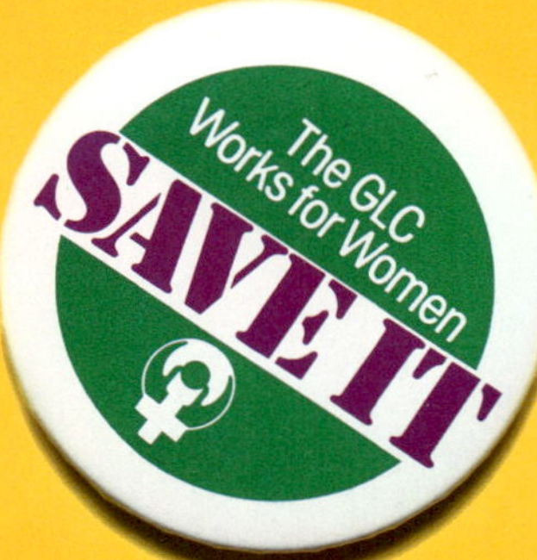

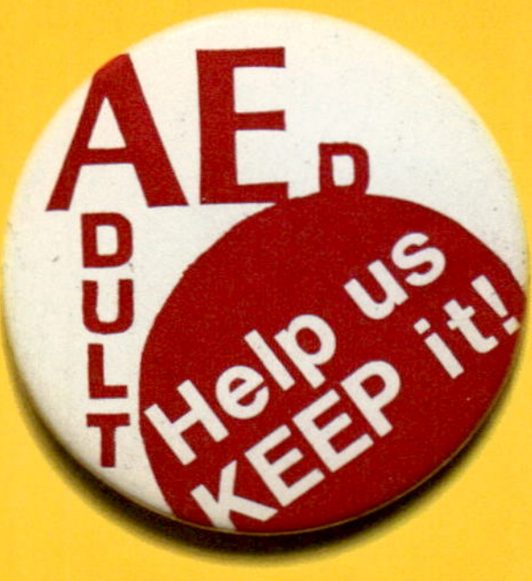

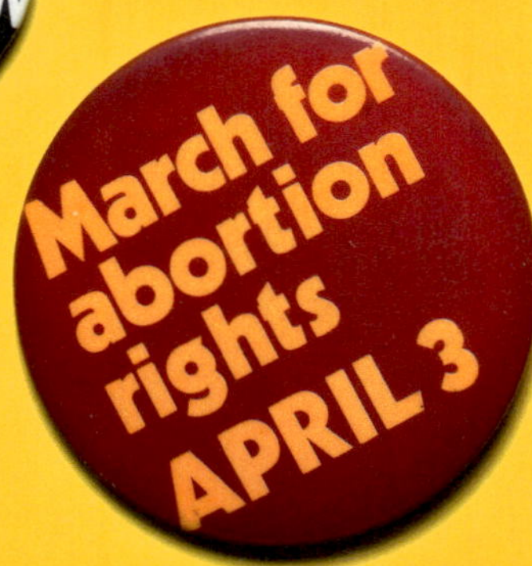

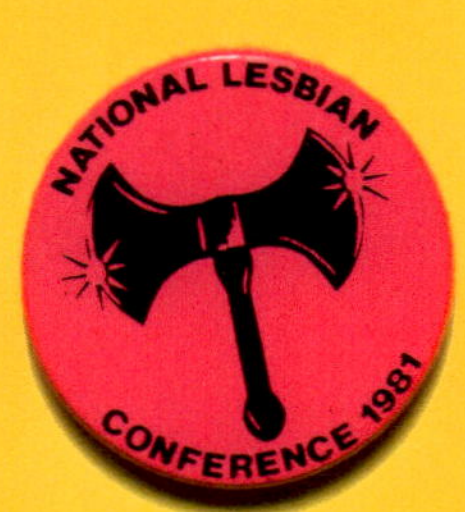

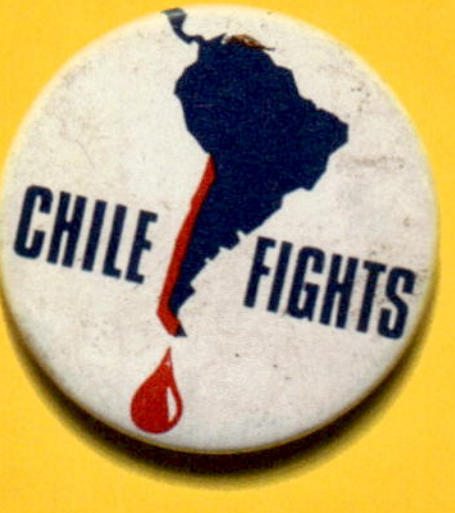

AMAZON

the start, as the Women's Liberation Movement grew and the issues and concerns of different groups of women came to the fore, we were particularly concerned to address issues around race, class and sexuality that sometimes went beyond our immediate experience. So we met with and held discussions with other women and groups, and invited women to join us to express their ideas. These led to the posters *Black Women Will Not Be Intimidated*, *A Celebration For Change*, *Support Our Irish Sisters In Armagh Jail*.

We saw ourselves as accountable to the Women's Liberation Movement and apart from the need to earn an income, we felt that it was important that we were not only poster makers but actively involved in campaigns and outside work, talking with as many women as possible. Feedback was essential, as we would worry that we were not saying things that needed to be said or not saying them in the right way.

Some posters focused on specific, and often little-understood, situations and used more words to help explain and communicate the issues and questions at stake, such as the women's peace camp at Greenham Common and the case of the disappeared women in South America. All these were produced in collaboration with women closely involved with the individual campaigns and had a story to tell.

From early on, we had been involved in flyposting campaigns, including: *Fight For Safe Legal Abortion* (1975), *EGA Call To Action* (1976, protesting against the closure of a much-loved local hospital), *Women Throw Off Our Double Burden* (1976) and a poster challenging the Queen's *Silver Jubilee,* urging women to rebel against the state and the monarchy. Inspired by feminist graffiti and, later, the actions of 'angry women' across the country, we strongly felt that flyposting was an important way of getting feminist messages out and onto the street. Stickers designating women-only tube carriages, using a spoof London Transport logo, were stuck onto tube carriages from December 1981 as part of a campaign about making safe spaces for women to be out at night. In 1982, a poster with the text 'In Loving Memory' printed in sombre black ink on a dark red ground connected violence towards women with a 'male preoccupation' with war (it was also the year of the Falklands war), and was flyposted near war memorials in London on the eve of Remembrance Day.

Some of our early posters were criticized for being depressing: *My Wife Doesn't Work* and *Disc*

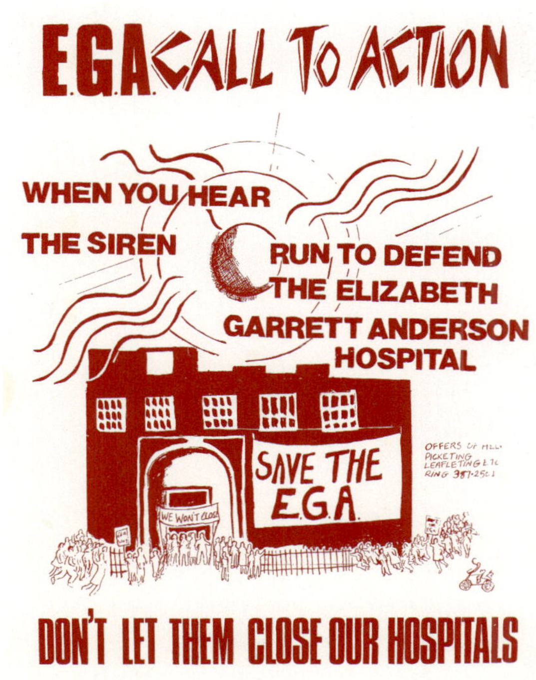

EGA Call To Action
Printed on lightweight paper and flyposted around north London. The much loved Elizabeth Garrett Anderson Hospital for Women was under the threat of closure during the 1960s and early 1970s. Closure was announced in 1976 by Camden Area Health Authority in response, staff occupied the hospital with support from London-wide women's groups. The hospital eventually closed in 1978.

Jockey showed images of women taken from our own experiences. We had always believed that it was possible to use a negative image in a positive way, that women could identify with them and realise that they were not alone. However, we took this criticism seriously and went on to produce a series of posters emphasising positive images of women, such as *Miss March* and *Girls Are Powerful*.

For a poster to be effective the message had to be immediately understood — a simple image, an eye catching heading and as few words as possible. Deciding on the words could be agonising and caused heated debates. We could design something and then spend weeks talking about the caption or the few words needed.

From the start, our posters were designed to look good — we wanted people to want to put them up: no one wants to live with a relentlessly depressing image. Humour had already been an important part of our work (such as in *YBA Wife* and *Tough!*) and it was a way of presenting ideas in an accessible way, encouraging women to challenge the status quo. The use of humour also deconstructed the received ideas about political posters being aggressive, functional and serious — as well as confounding the frequent accusations that feminists were humourless.

Then, as now, women at that time were judged more harshly than men for the quality of their work. Printing was a male-dominated profession. It was essential that the posters and all work that left the workshop was of the highest quality. The accounts in the daily diary reflect endlessly trying to get something right, doing and redoing, terrible frustrations of torn screens, the wrong colour, mis-registration and smudges. Tempers could get very short and frustrations boil over.

A great deal of time was taken up with administration, as orders started coming in from all over the world as well as the UK. All these had to be acknowledged and dealt with, accounts had to be kept, materials kept an eye on. Orders were placed by phone and confirmed in writing and then posted. This involved endless trips to the post office with the cost of postage being a drain on our budget. We did not have the use of computers — everything had to be logged by hand using card index systems and notebooks.

Different women coming in on different days meant that we had to be well organised, A daily diary listing who was due to come in, what had been done the previous day or morning and what needed to be done was essential. It was potentially too easy for everything to descend into chaos. We survived for so long despite the sometimes heated political and other disagreements because of the overriding commitment to the collective, its work and to each other, plus the demand for the posters kept us going and as the work progressed we kept on to see the next stage and the next.

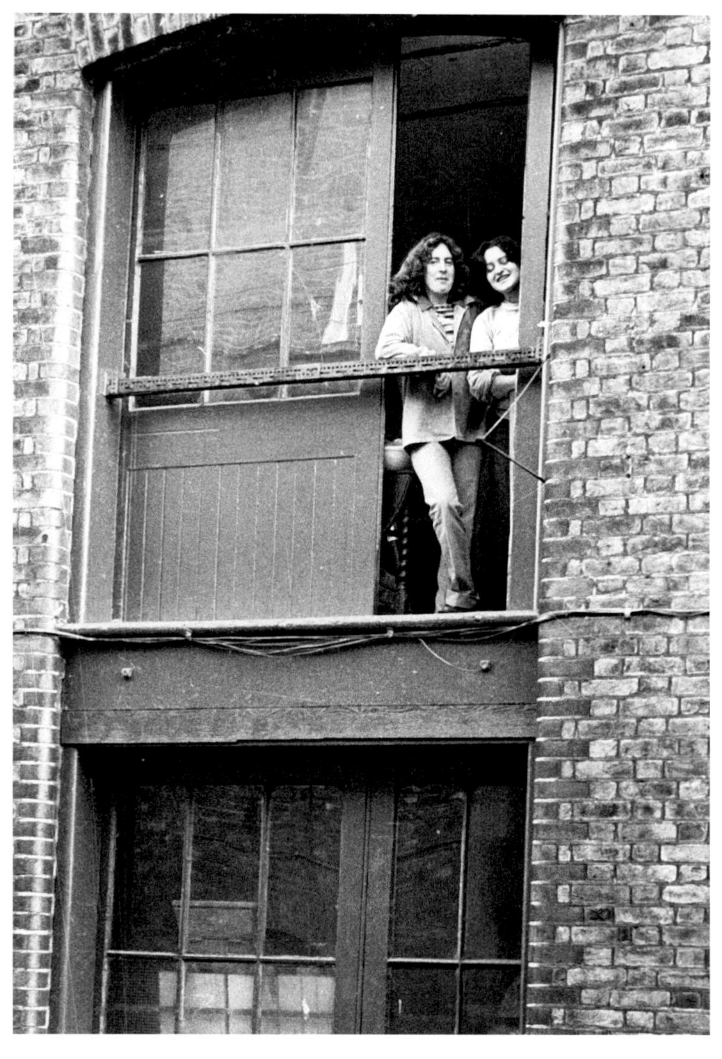

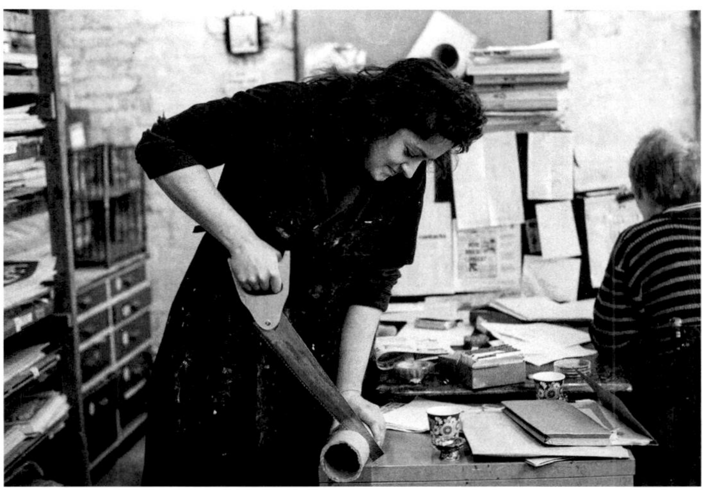

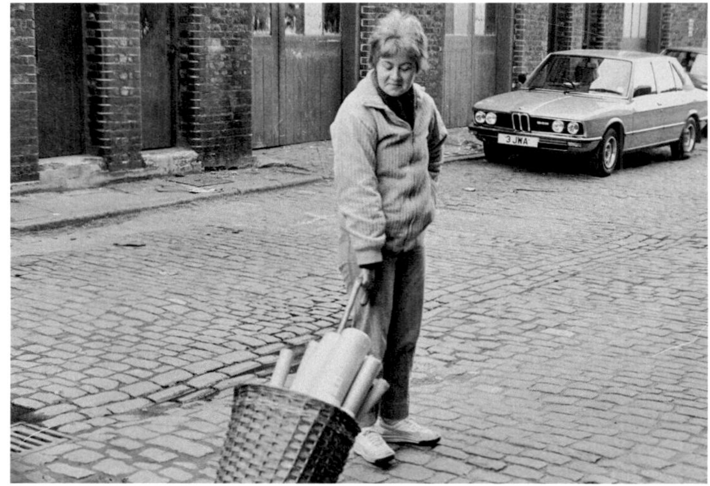

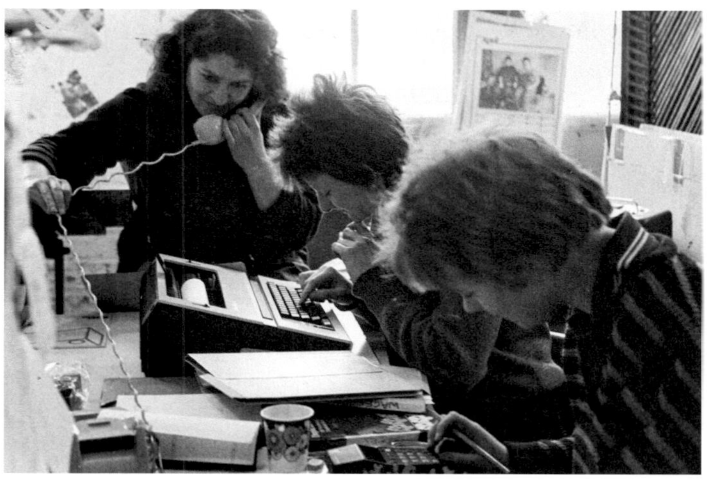

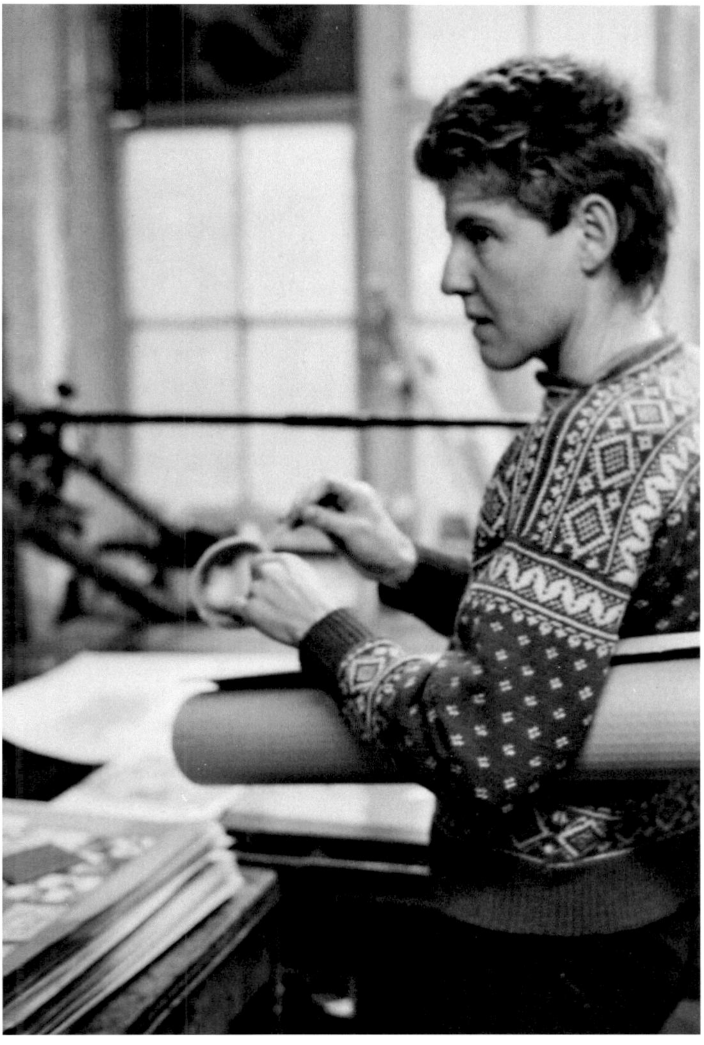

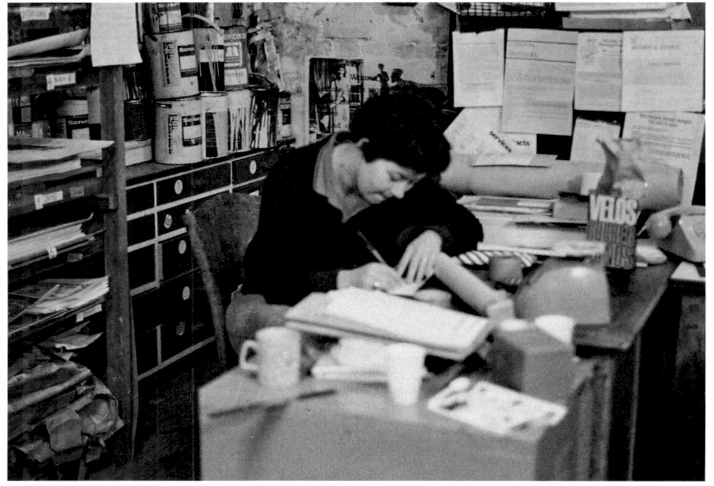

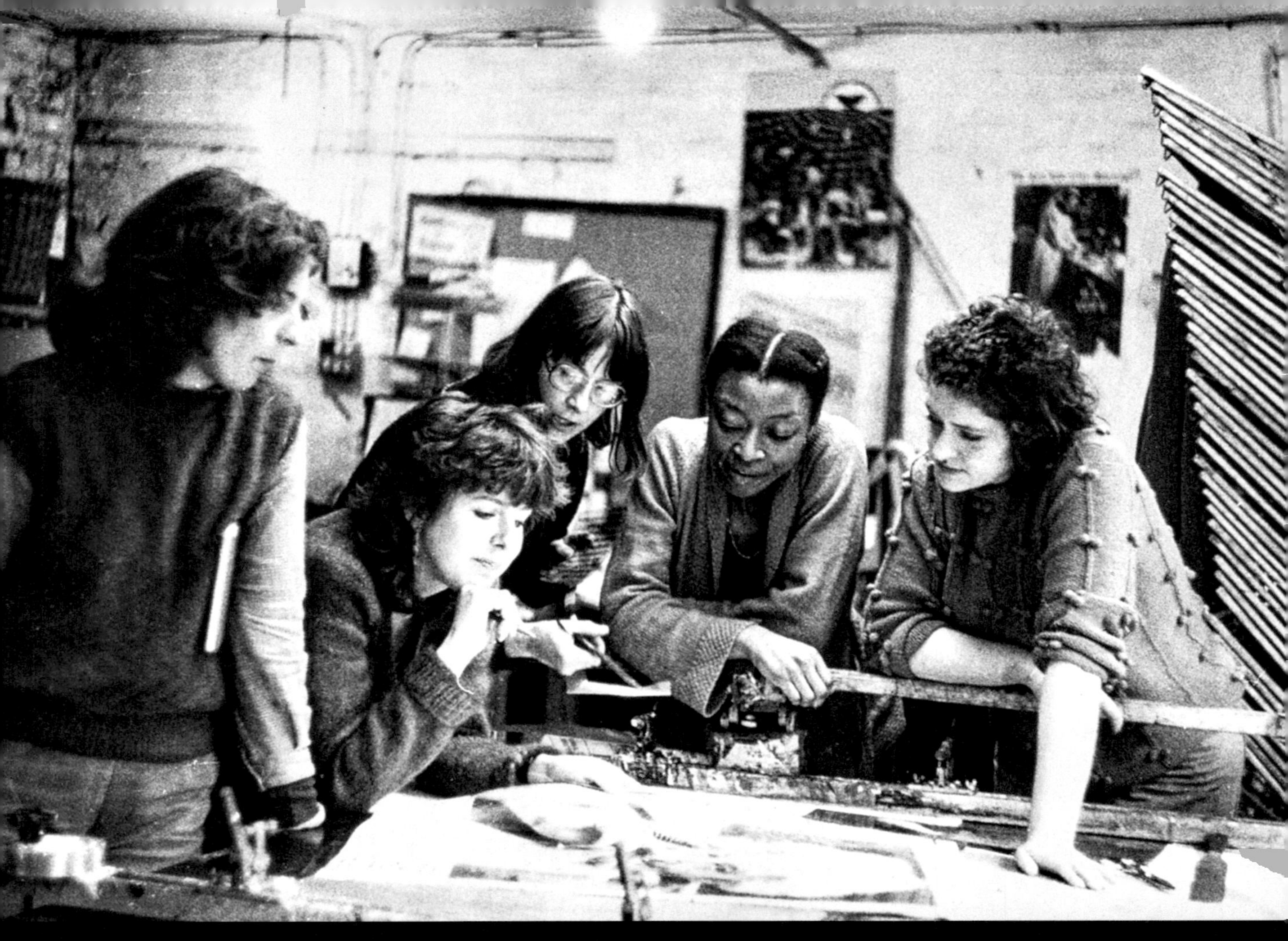

Above: See Red at Iliffé Yard. Photograph by Angela Phillips for *Spare Rib*
Facing: Preliminary sketch for *Don't Let Racism Divide Us*, 1980. Over the page: Workshop at Iliffe Yard, 1982

Our workshop in Iliffe Yard was in an area notorious for far right groups, especially around the nearby East Street market. Neo-Nazi stickers had been posted on the ground floor windows at Women in Print and on See Red's door. One Monday in June 1982, we arrived at work to find that something more serious had occurred. The workshop had been broken into, ink poured around and over machines, paperwork in the desk area ripped and urinated on and structural damage done to the stairwell and the door. The letters NF in the all too familiar joined up logo was scrawled into the wall near the door. Later in the day a young policeman arrived to take down details and when his attention was drawn to the 'logo', he suggested it was probably someone's initials. He then enquired whether we printed any kind of controversial leaflets that people might object to. As feminists, we had little faith in the established forces of law and order at the time. The attack was obviously very upsetting and meant that women in the collective would avoid working at the yard on their own for fear of further attacks. It was happening to other groups, including printshops such as Union Place and Community Press and we didn't know if it would escalate. The July 1982 issue of *Spare Rib* carried a report of the incident: 'Fascists Attack See Red' combined with an appeal for funds to make repairs, 'Being faced at this stage with big repair bills puts our future in jeopardy and we feel that the loss of our workshop would be a loss for the women's movement'. Notes from the daybook indicate women's fears for their personal safety, and the kind of security precautions that were taken during the weeks that followed. This highlighted even more the need for us to find new premises.

'Violence has been much in our lives recently. it started with being stickered by the National Front, then we got threatening phone calls andon Easter Monday and the last bank holiday we got broken into and vandalised by the NF. They smashed the door in, poured ink over machinery, stole equipment and phone numbers, cut the phone wires and pissed over the mail. We see these attacks on us as part of a growing trend from the extreme right who now see women's organisations as a sufficient threat to want to intimidate and attack us. These attacks drain our finances and our energies, but we aren't going to see six years of women's work destroyed.'

Outwrite

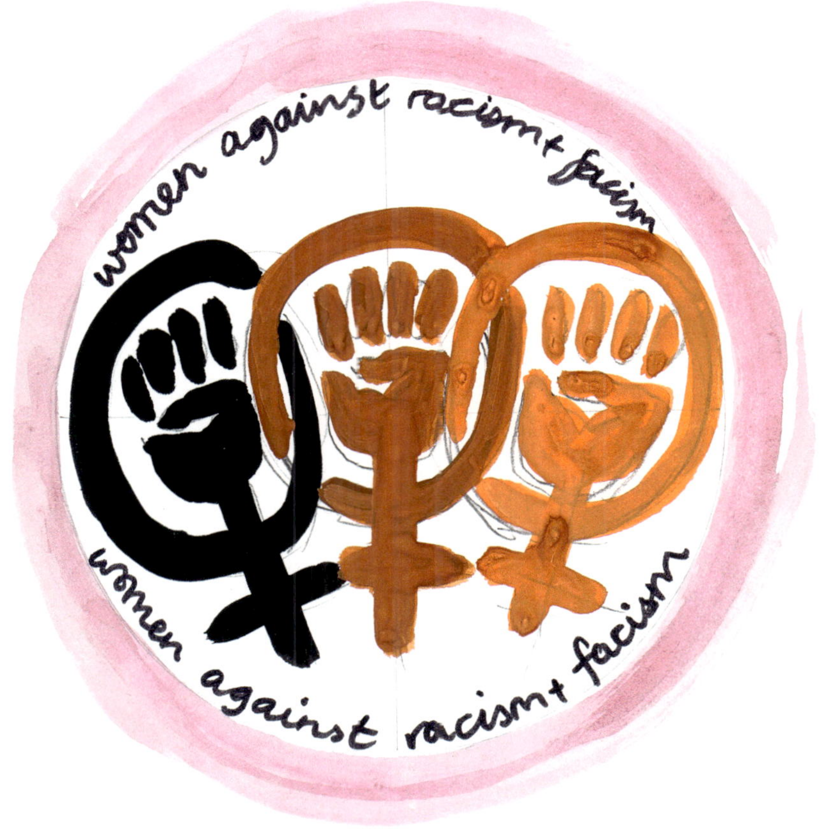

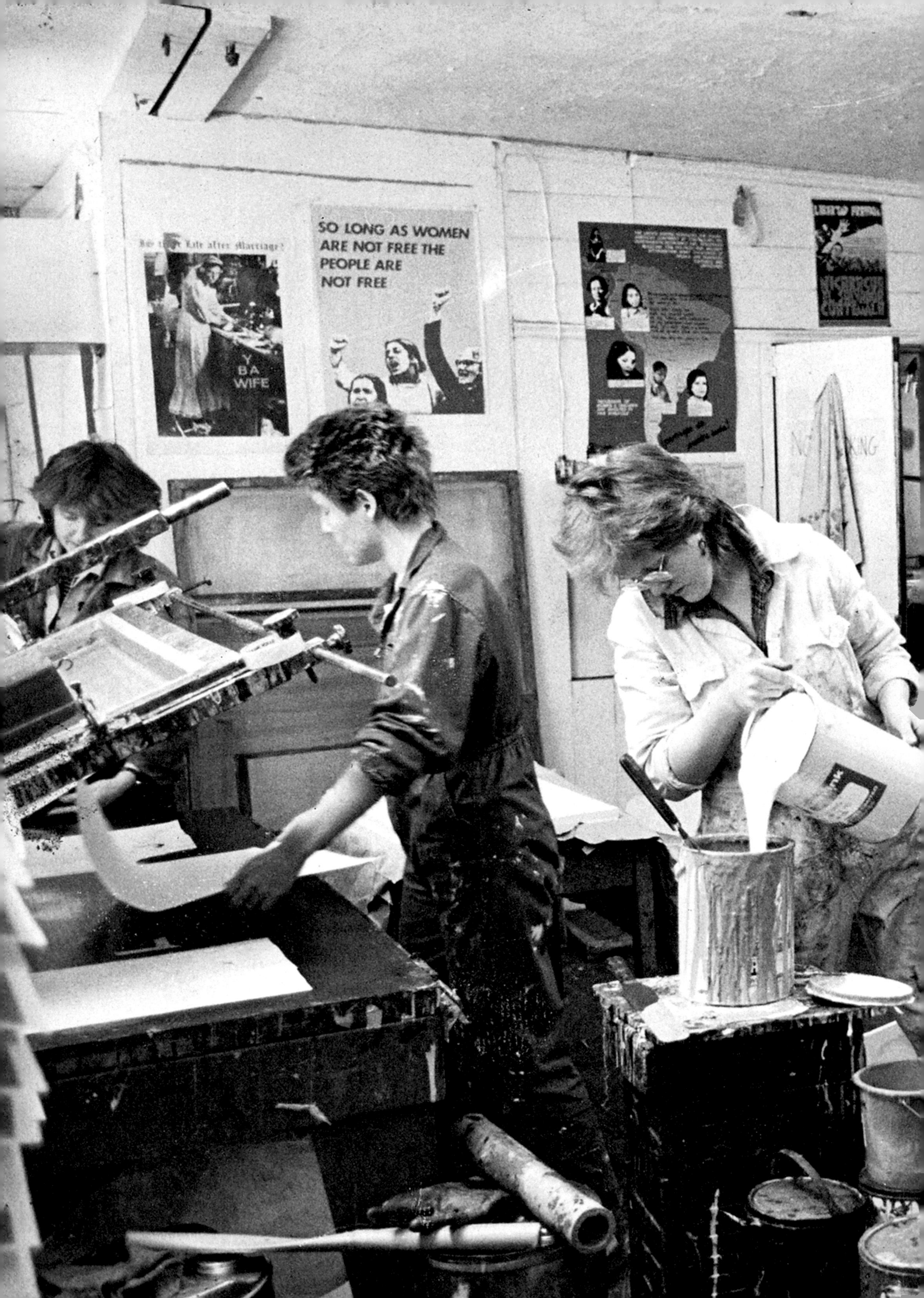

SO LONG AS WOMEN
ARE NOT FREE THE
PEOPLE ARE
NOT FREE

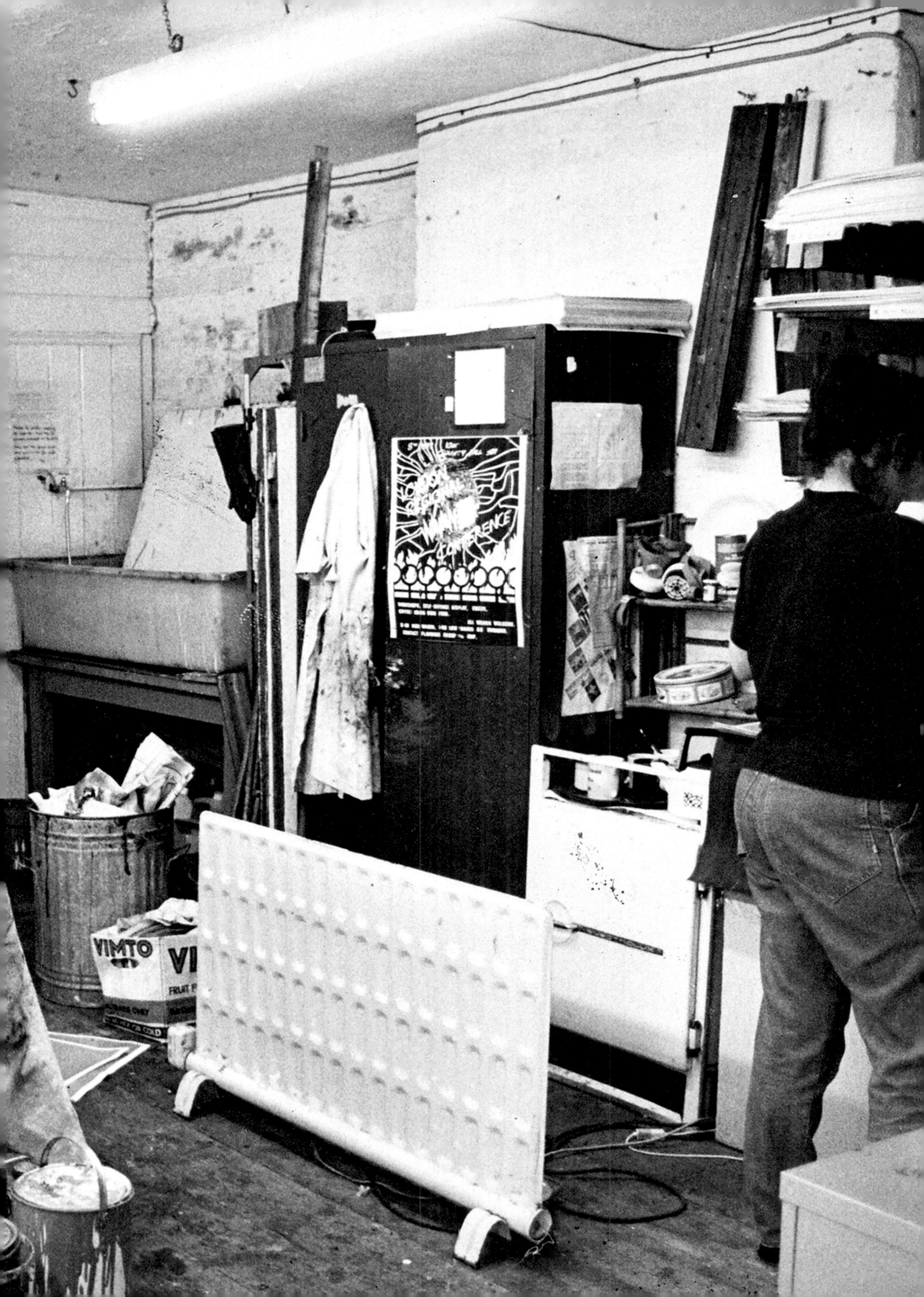
VIMTO

Dealing with security in such a ramshackle space as Iliffe Yard had become a serious issue. The yard was freezing in winter, too hot in summer and riddled with fire hazards, and we were all beginning to worry about the chemical content of silkscreen printing inks. The intention was to move with Women in Print litho printers and share new premises. This was partly to move into a more comfortable working environment where it would also be possible to adhere to better health and safety conditions.

By the spring of 1982, the idea of seeking funding was beginning to be discussed by the collective in order to create a more secure basis for the workshop to move forward. Our first grant was from Southwark Council in the autumn of 1982; £1,000 to support us setting up as a co-operative and to look for new premises.

Meanwhile, a radical Labour group had taken over the Greater London Council (GLC) and soon afterwards formed a GLC Women's Committee with grant giving powers. It was openly sympathetic to left opposition and feminist groups, and See Red successfully applied for funding to buy new up to date equipment and to pay wages for the first time.

The funding from Southwark Council had already prompted newspaper articles in the South London Press about 'Tory fury over political grant'. A more severe media panic about 'Red' Ken Livingstone at the GLC coincided with the opening night of a See Red exhibition at Cockpit, a radical London gallery space. Having recently been awarded a GLC grant and with a self-explanatory name, 'See Red Women's Workshop' seemed like an ideal target, and the event was marred by a crew of ITV Reporting London journalists hungry for a scoop. We duly wrote a piece for *Outwrite*, entitled 'Its Enough to Make You See Red!' warning other feminists to beware of 'the massive amount of power the straight media has to abuse us'. *Outwrite* (No. 14, 1983)

The GLC funding also contributed to a major split between See Red members. By this time the collective was made up of two founder members and four recent members. Within the Women's Liberation Movement there had been a growing debate about how race, sexuality, class, education and economic stability not only shaped the agendas of feminist projects but also participation in them. Women with disabilities raised further issues of access and inclusivity. Job adverts in

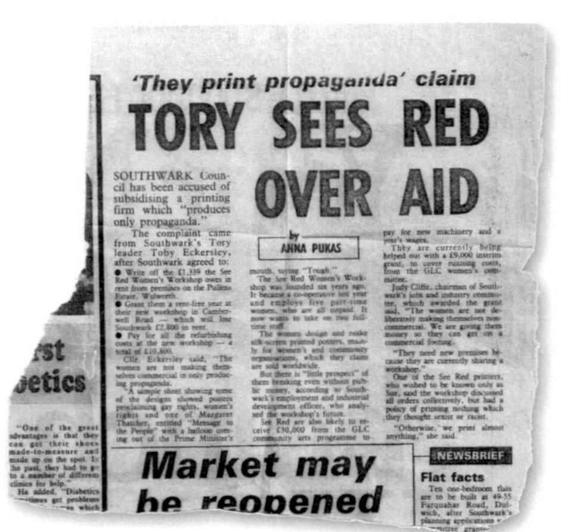

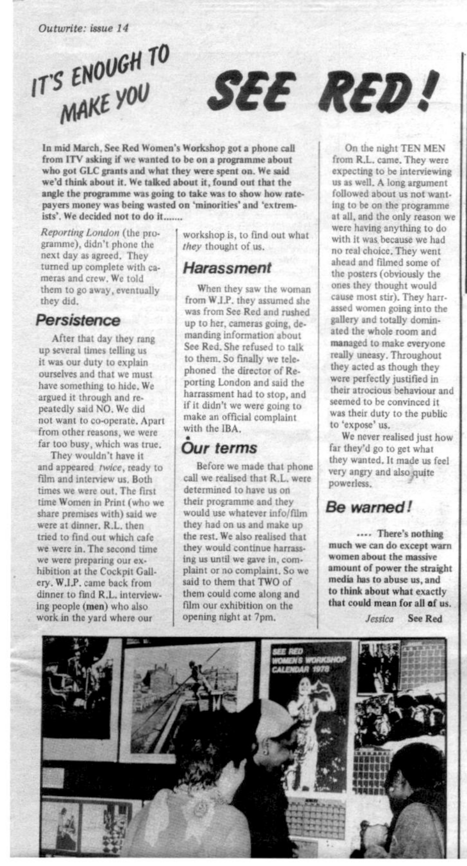

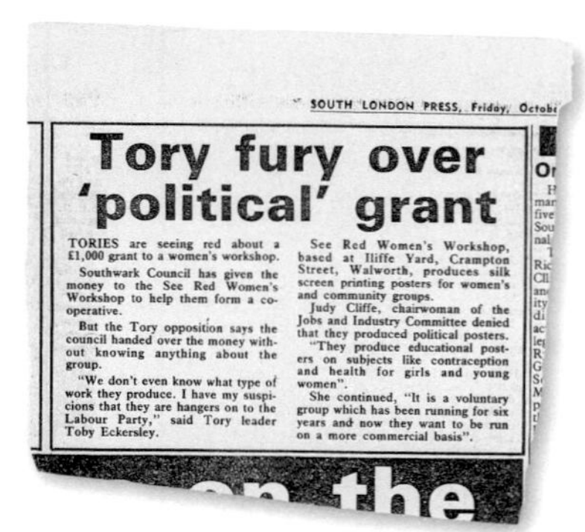

Press furore and Tory anger about council grants, 1982–83

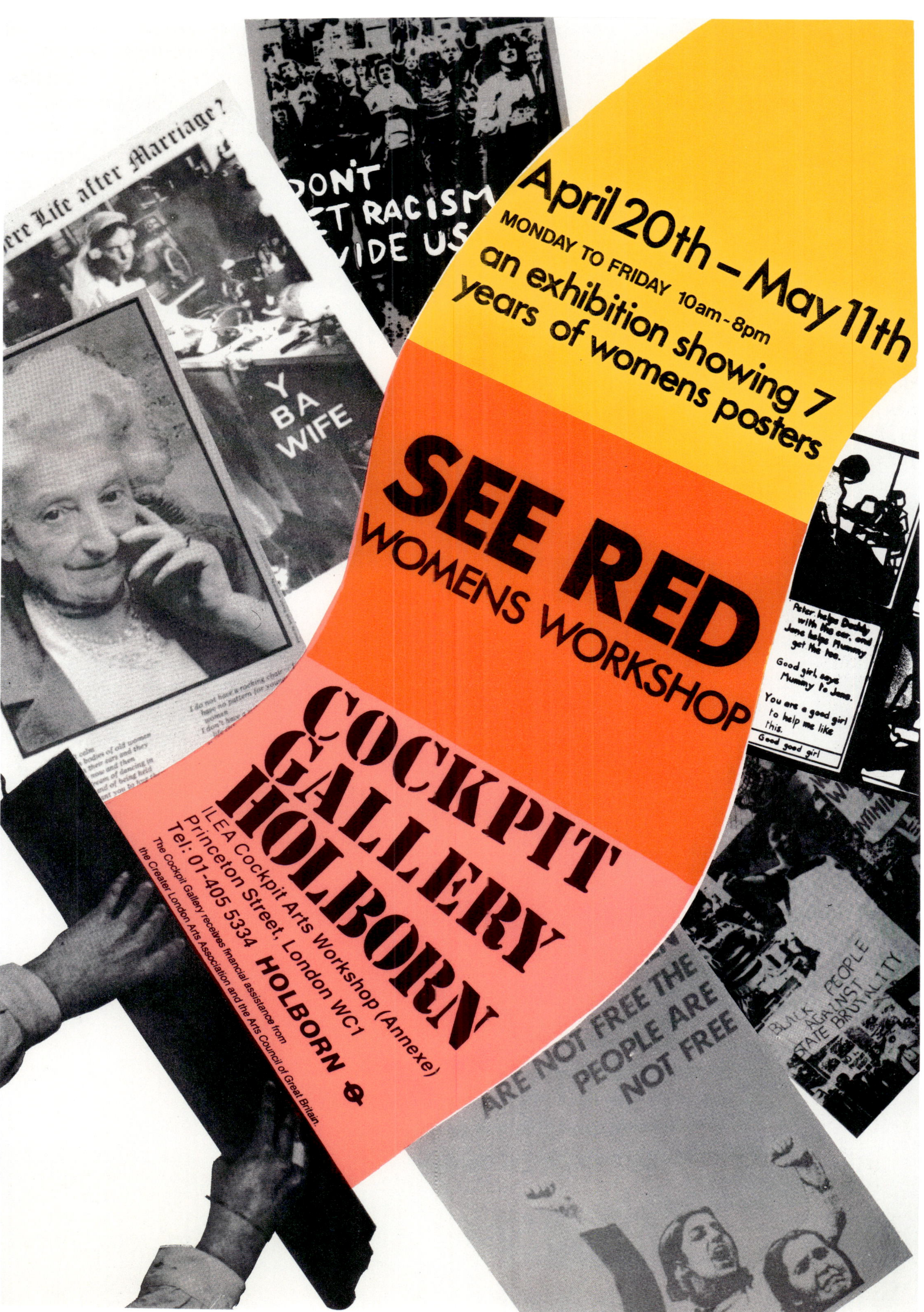

Poster for See Red exhibition at Cockpit Gallery, 1983

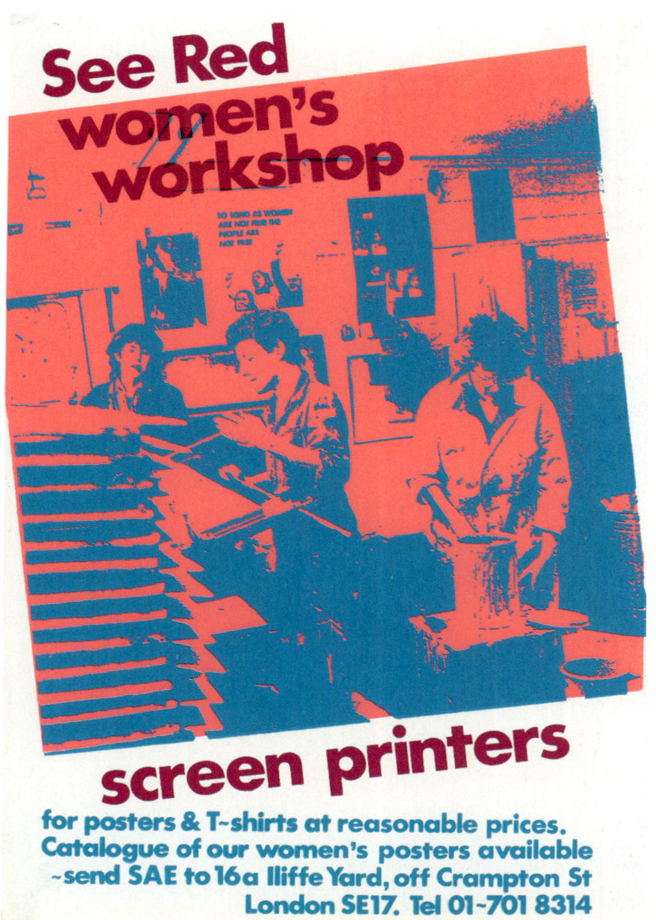
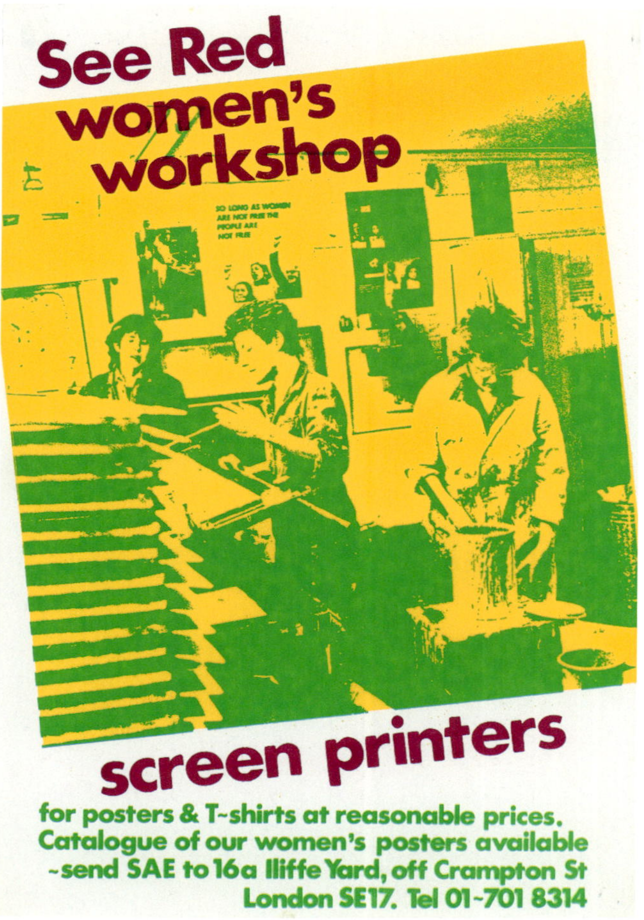

Publicity flyers for service printing work 1983

the feminist press began to show new 'positive action' recruitment policies in terms of race, class and previous educational or training experience. Influenced by aspects of these debates, the newer members of See Red decided that the new paid positions should only be for black or working class women or lesbians, on the premise that it was harder for them to get paid employment and the kind of training opportunity the workshop offered. The two long-term collective members did not fit these criteria and were asked to leave, which they did soon after. See Red then entered a different phase of its history.

In the summer of 1984, the 'new' See Red moved with Women in Print into more spacious and accessible premises in Camberwell Road. Southwark Council's Job & Industries Committee gave a grant to help with the first year of rent and rates. From this time onwards See Red began moving away from its previous core identity of creating its own feminist posters, although continuing to reprint and distribute the existing posters.

With the help of the grants, the aim of bringing more women into printing started to happen in a more structured way: workshops for young women to learn about printing were set up with several local schools and See Red also took part in the Women in Printing Trades video project *No Set Type* (1985), aimed at encouraging women into the trade. We also ran young women's poster competitions, in conjunction with the National Association of Youth Clubs.

There was an increasing focus on service work, not least because other newly funded groups had more money for publicity. Strong relations were built up with many groups in this way, keeping the collective abreast of Women's Liberation Movement developments as well as the emerging gay activism that began to flourish a little later in

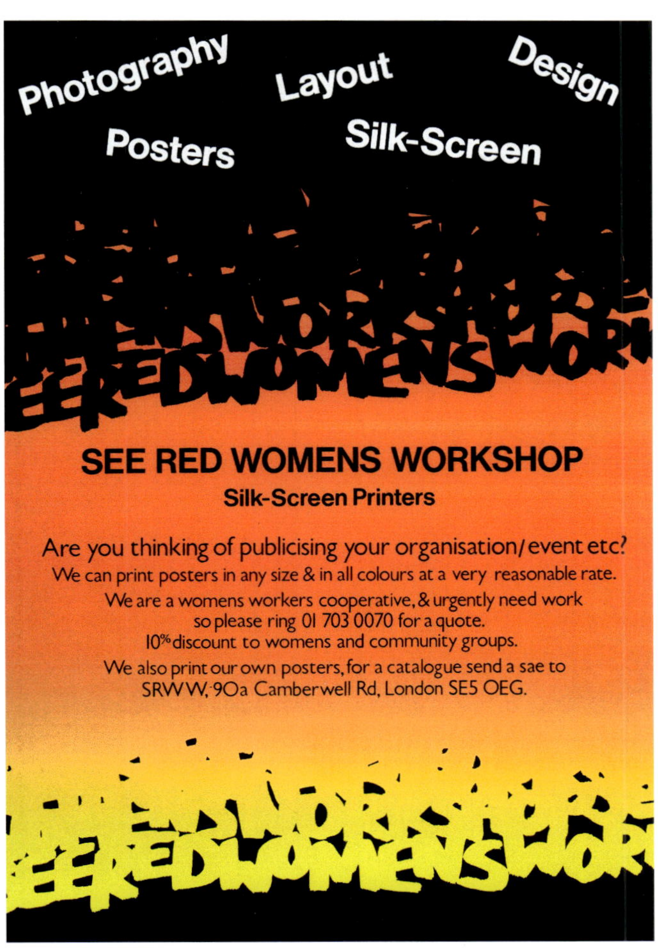

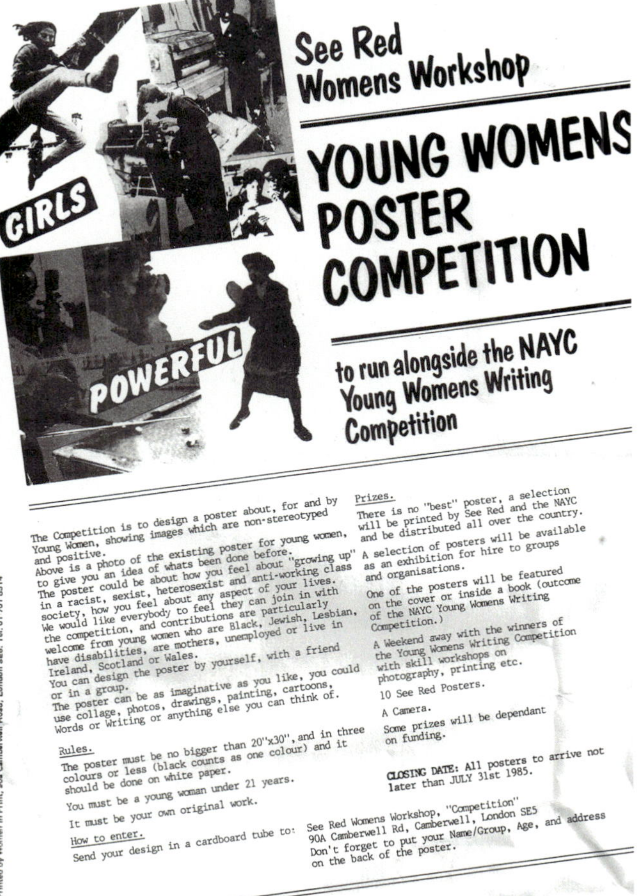

Top: Publicity flyer 1986
Bottom: Red's Young Women's poster competition flyer 1985

response to HIV/AIDS and Clause 28. A particular highlight was designing the logo for the 20th anniversary of Gay Pride. The growth of committee-type feminism in local councils and the professionalisation of what had once been autonomous feminist activity, such as Women's Aid and Rape Crisis, along with the changing tastes of a different generation, brought a greater demands for slicker looking publicity and a more 'sophisticated' look. The finer mesh screens and modern stencil making equipment bought with GLC funds, along with the collective's growing skill base, enabled the collective to meet these demands. The emphasis on service printing was also partly financially motivated, as the workshop lurched between GLC grant cheques, which were always late, even up to a year in one case.

The practicalities of being grant aided were more demanding than we had envisioned. Quarterly reports had to be written in language to meet shifting criteria. Accounts had to be up to date and the bank and suppliers had to be staved off while waiting for overdue payments. We took on a permanent book keeper as part of the collective. This was a break from the older, collective pattern of work and the focus on service work led to greater job division in other areas. Whereas previously

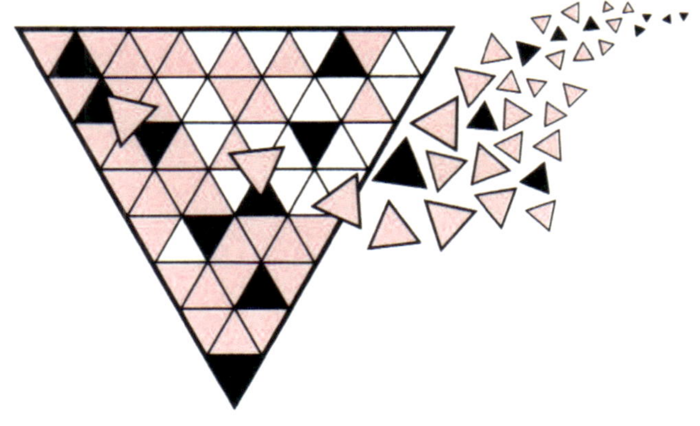

Logo for the 20th anniversary of Gay Pride

several women in the collective had formal art training, now only one did and it tended to be her that took responsibility for design, although still with input from the rest of the collective.

All of this, combined with internal politicking in the women's movement with respect to image-making, hindered the development of new See Red posters. It often felt like walking on eggshells to negotiate the internal divisions of the women's movement and it was not apparent what the new issues for posters should be. See Red weren't alone in trying to work this out; a 1986 double spread in *Outwrite*, also asked, 'Masses of women, but where is the movement?' To some extent, it felt like See Red had 'lost its voice'. This general feeling of a dissipating women's movement, especially in London, compounded the collective's increasing sense that the feminist political poster itself was being seen as a relic from another era. No new posters were added to the catalogue after 1983 and aspirations to do so didn't develop into anything tangible although some of the posters made by the previous collective (such as *Tough!* and *Capitalism*) were modified and updated

In March 1986, with the closure of the GLC, See Red's three-year funded period was over.

Women in Print, with whom they had continued to share premises, finally shut down that year. By the mid 1980s, screen-printing itself was increasingly seen as being an expensive way to produce publicity. Photocopying had become much more widely accessible and creatively used and desktop publishing was in its ascendance. After four years of trying to be self-sufficient the workshop closed in 1990. The early 1990s were a watershed period for many feminist cultural projects born of the energy and excitement of the 1970s Women's Liberation Movement — for example *Spare Rib* magazine and Sisterwrite bookshop also folded at around this time. Feminist inspired activity continued but the dynamic cultural, political — and technological — context that had sustained See Red throughout its lifetime had changed.

The publication of this book is reflective of the resurgence of interest in See Red's posters, from galleries and museums to zine and design festivals and — especially closest to our hearts — from contemporary feminists. The posters seem able to speak to different generations, although it indicates, as if we were in any doubt, that the struggle for women's freedom and equality is far from won.

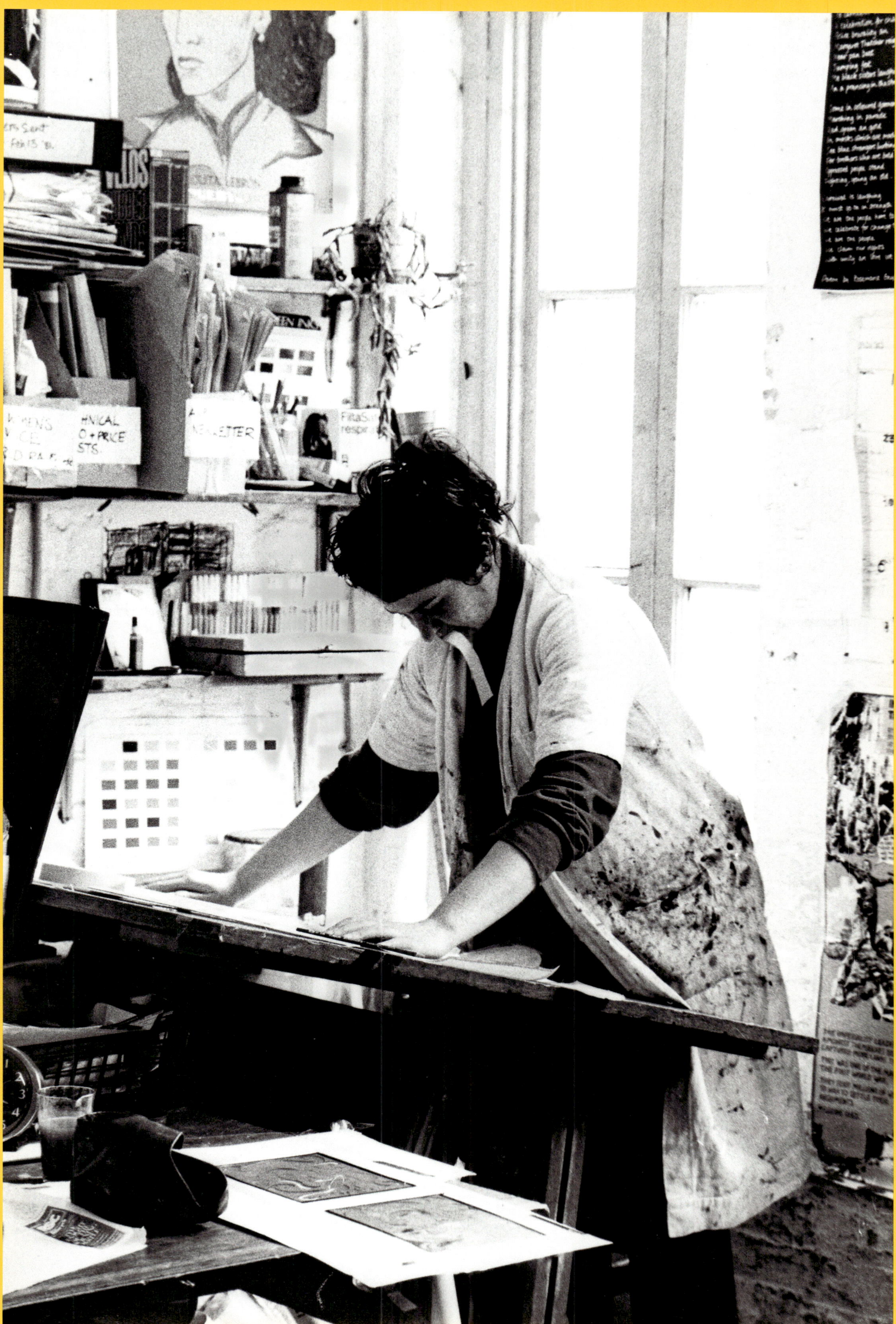

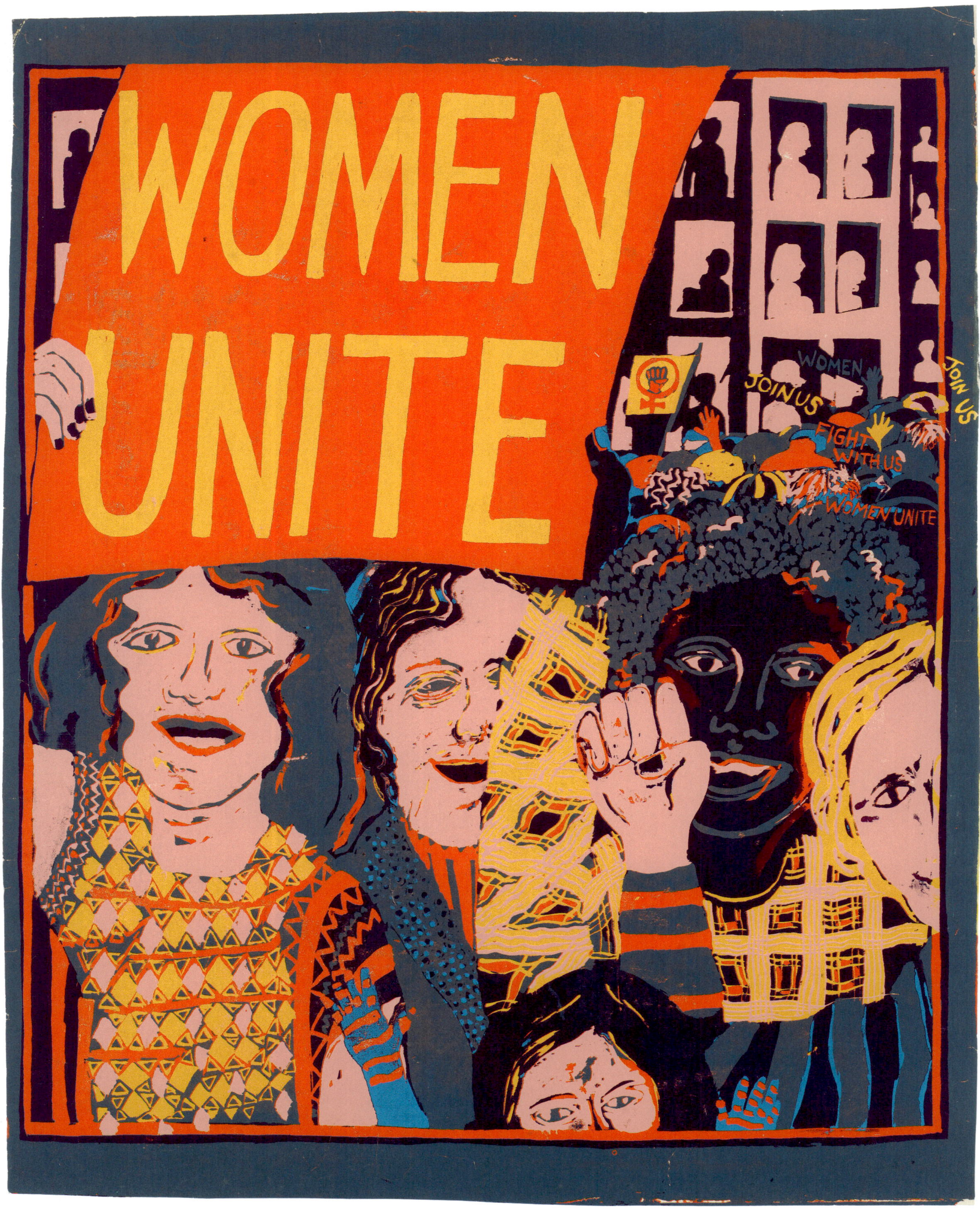

WOMEN UNITE, 1973 56 x 45 cm

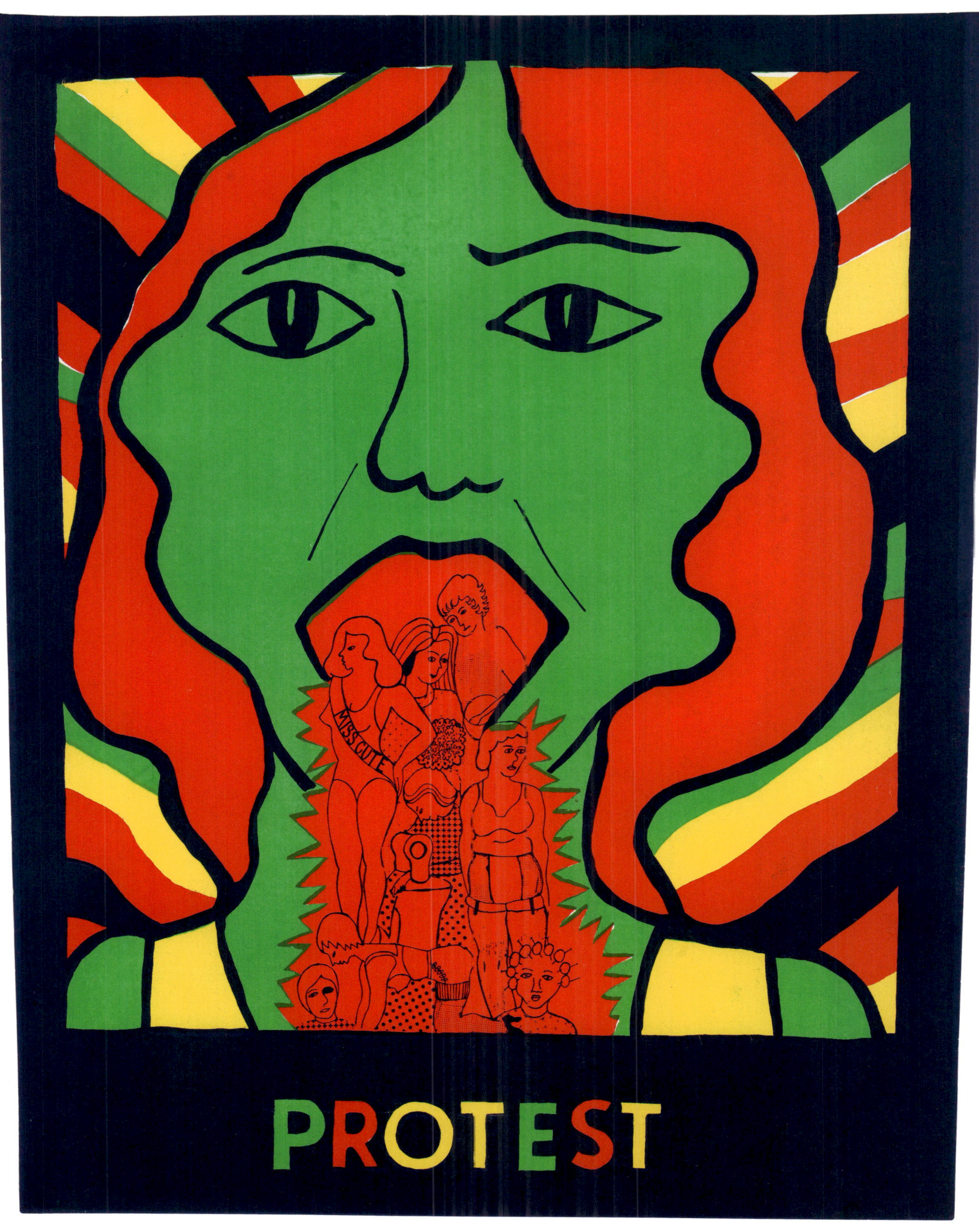

PROTEST, 1973 55 × 51 cm

Women Unite (*previous page*)
Women Unite was not in included in our
catalogues. With five different colours,
meaning five separate printings, the poster
was both time consuming and expensive to
print. Limited numbers however were printed
and were offered for sale at the national
conferences and other events.

Disc Jockey
One of three posters (along with *Protest* and
Women Unite) that were designed and printed
by Pru Stevenson at Camden Road before See
Red was founded and subsequently adopted
by the group.

Many women, in particular mothers of small
children, spent long hours and days at home on
their own with a radio as their companion and
link to the outside world. If you wished to listen
to pop music and the latest hits, you had to
endure the insidious and overtly sexist male disc
jockeys dominant at that time. The following
jingle was played every morning by the DJ
Jimmy Young:

> 'Keep young and beautiful, it's your duty to
> be beautiful, keep young and beautiful, if
> you want to be loved.'

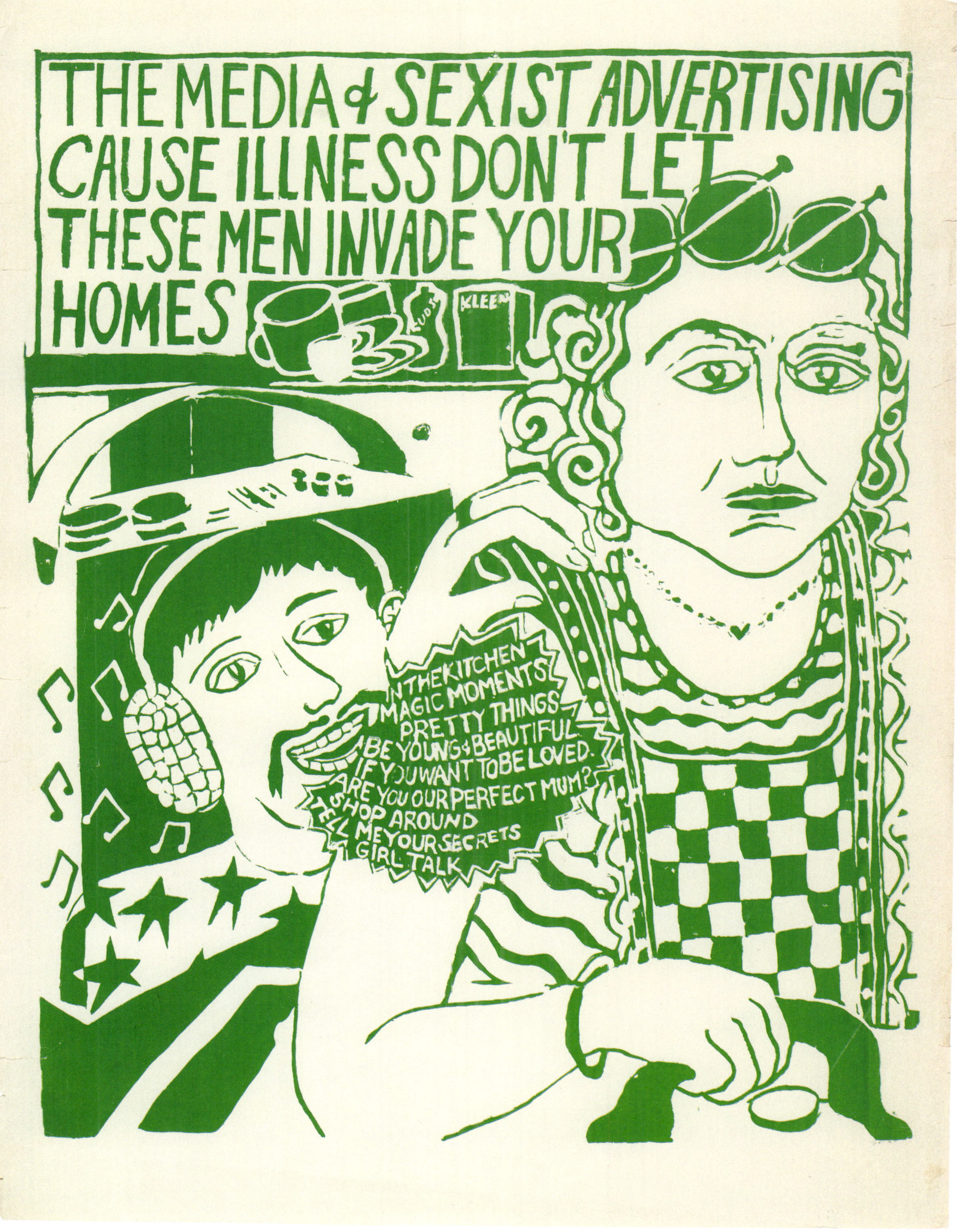

DISC JOCKEY, 1973 78.5 × 53.5 cm

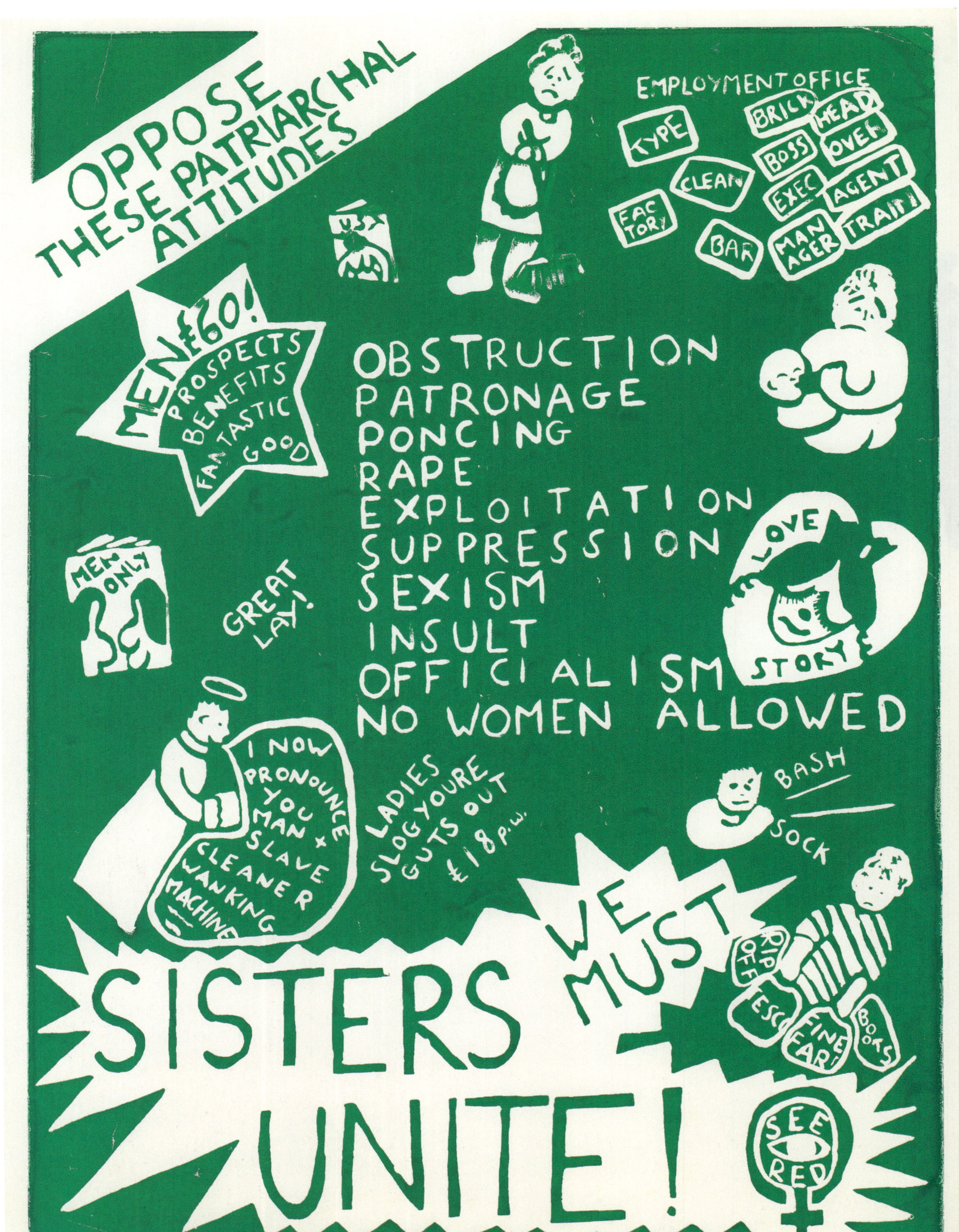

SISTERS UNITE, 1974 52 × 40 cm

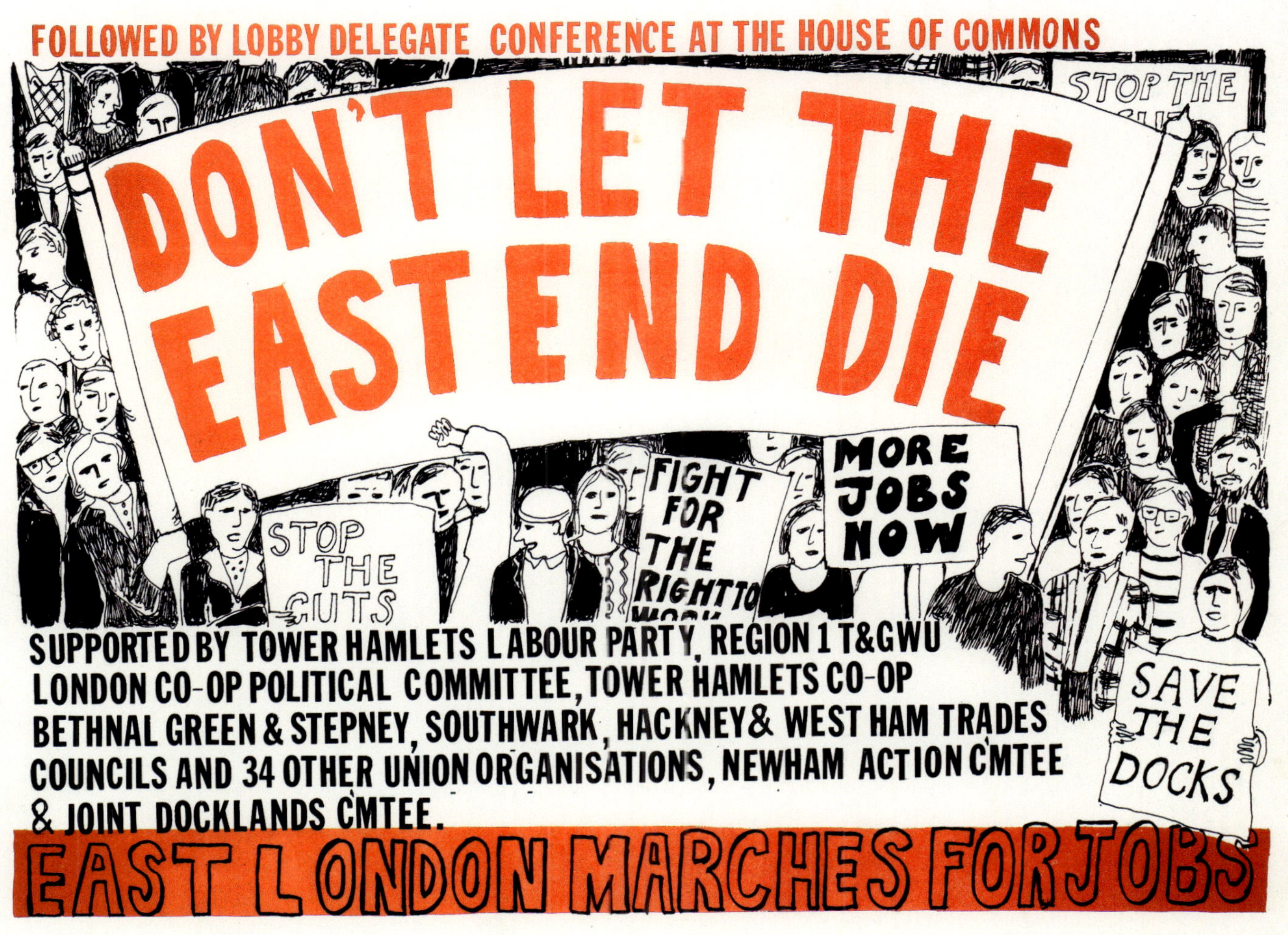

  DON'T LET THE EAST END DIE, 1974 61.5 × 43 cm

A Call To All Tenants

Some of us were involved with campaigns around housing. This poster was produced very quickly and simply with members of the local tenants' association.

In 1972 the then Conservative Government put forward proposals for legislative changes which would bring about significant rent increases in both the private and public rented sectors. Opposition to the proposed Housing Finance Act, especially amongst Council tenants, began to spread across the country, so that when the Act was passed and rent increases were introduced there were thousands of tenants in South Wales, the Midlands, the North of England, and in parts of London, committed to not paying the increase. By 1974 tenants in at least 80 local authority areas up and down the country, including Camden, were not paying the increase. Overall the fight against the Act played its part in the weakening of the Conservative Government and the return of Labour in 1974.

A Woman's Work Is Never Done

(*over the page*) Printed in red, to denote anger, the poster shows how women are doubly exploited — at work as cheap labour and as unpaid and unrecognised labour within the home — both to the benefit of capitalism.

'Women can't be independent without participating in the public workforce. That also means uniting in a fight for public childcare and for a restructuring of the workplace with women's equaility in mind, while insisting men share the housework and childcare on the home front so that women don't end up having to do it all.'

The Personal is Political by Carol Hanisch.

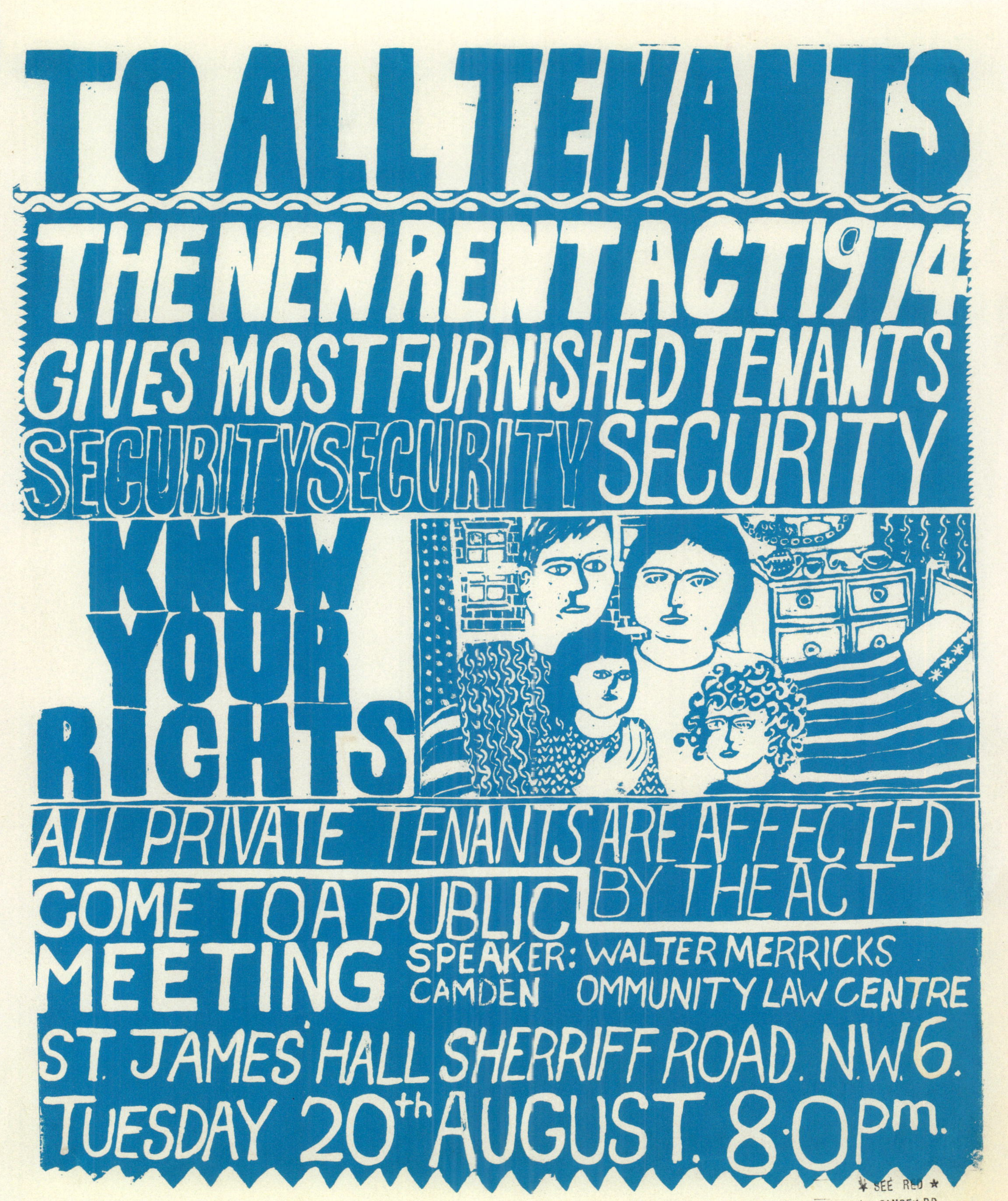

A CALL TO ALL TENANTS, 1974 47 × 25 cm

A WOMAN'S WORK IS NEVER DONE, 1974   51 × 66 cm

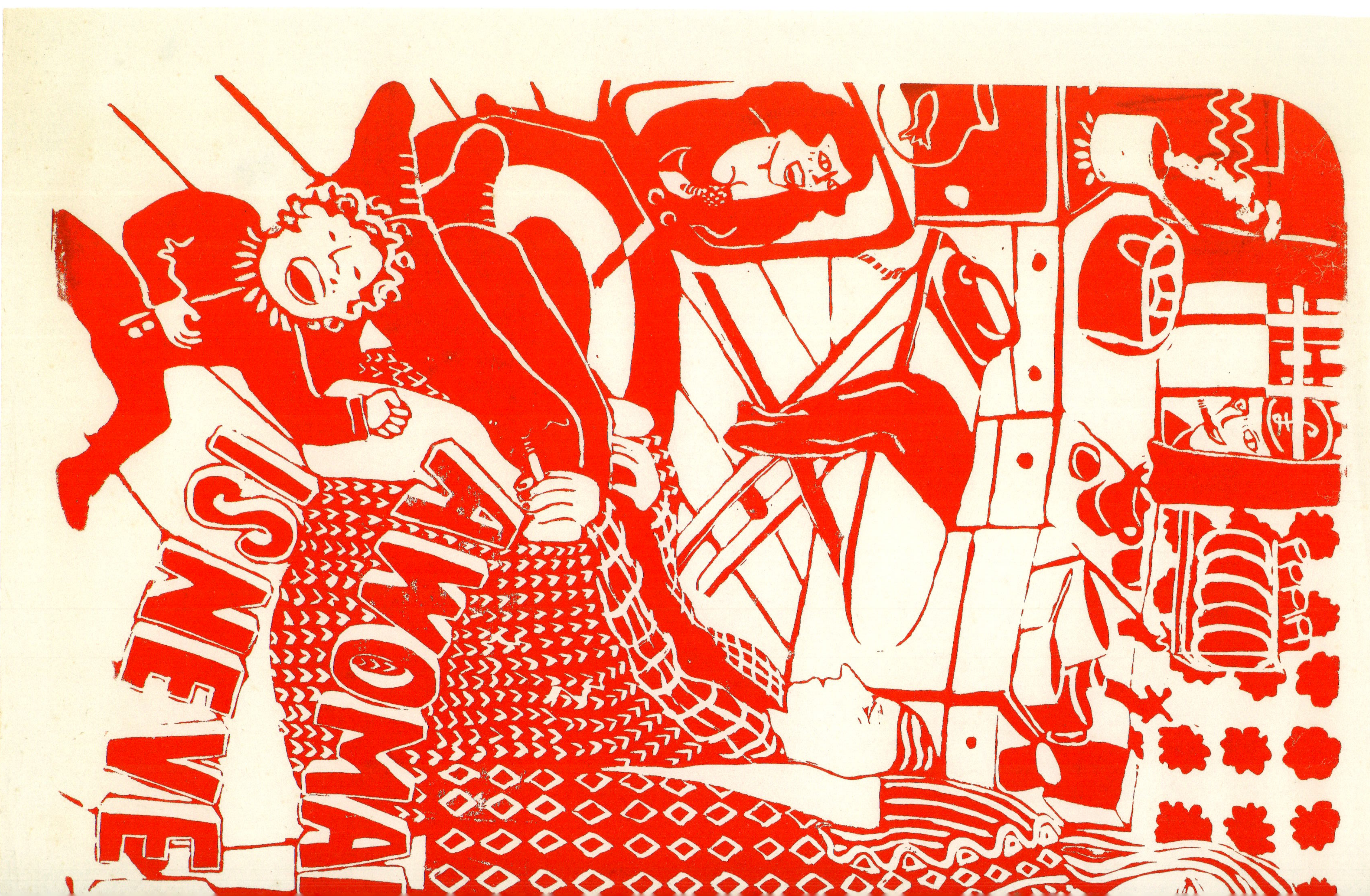

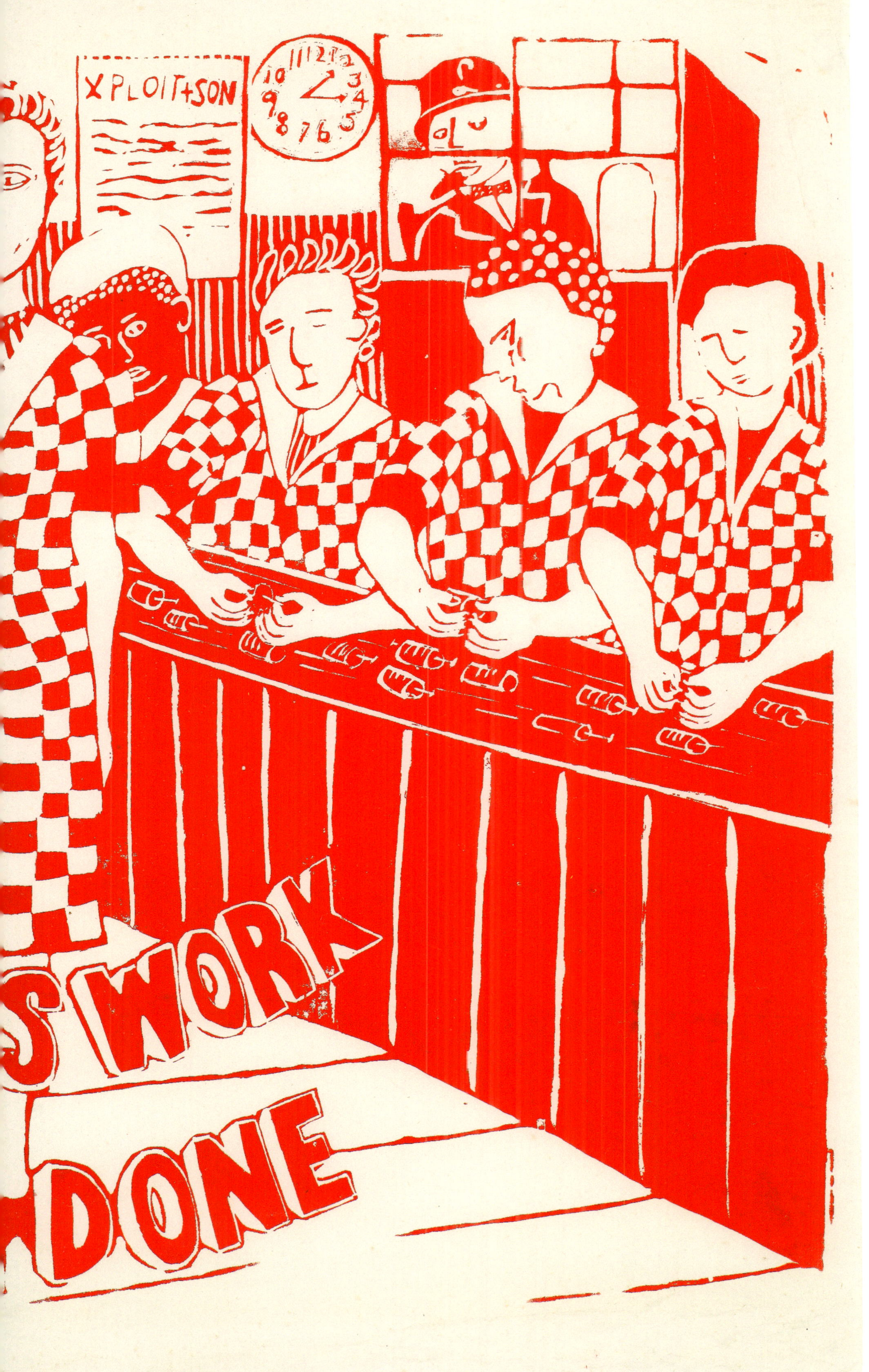
XPLOIT+SON
S WORK
DONE

Which One Are You?
An early See Red poster, made using
an actual, unretouched, Letraset art sheet
depicting women in various roles: wife,
girlfriend and mother, out to dinner with
hubby, shopping, etc. Letraset was used
widely by graphic designers at the time
and could be bought in individual sheets.
We just added the question, as we didn't
recognise these representations of
ourselves in these images.

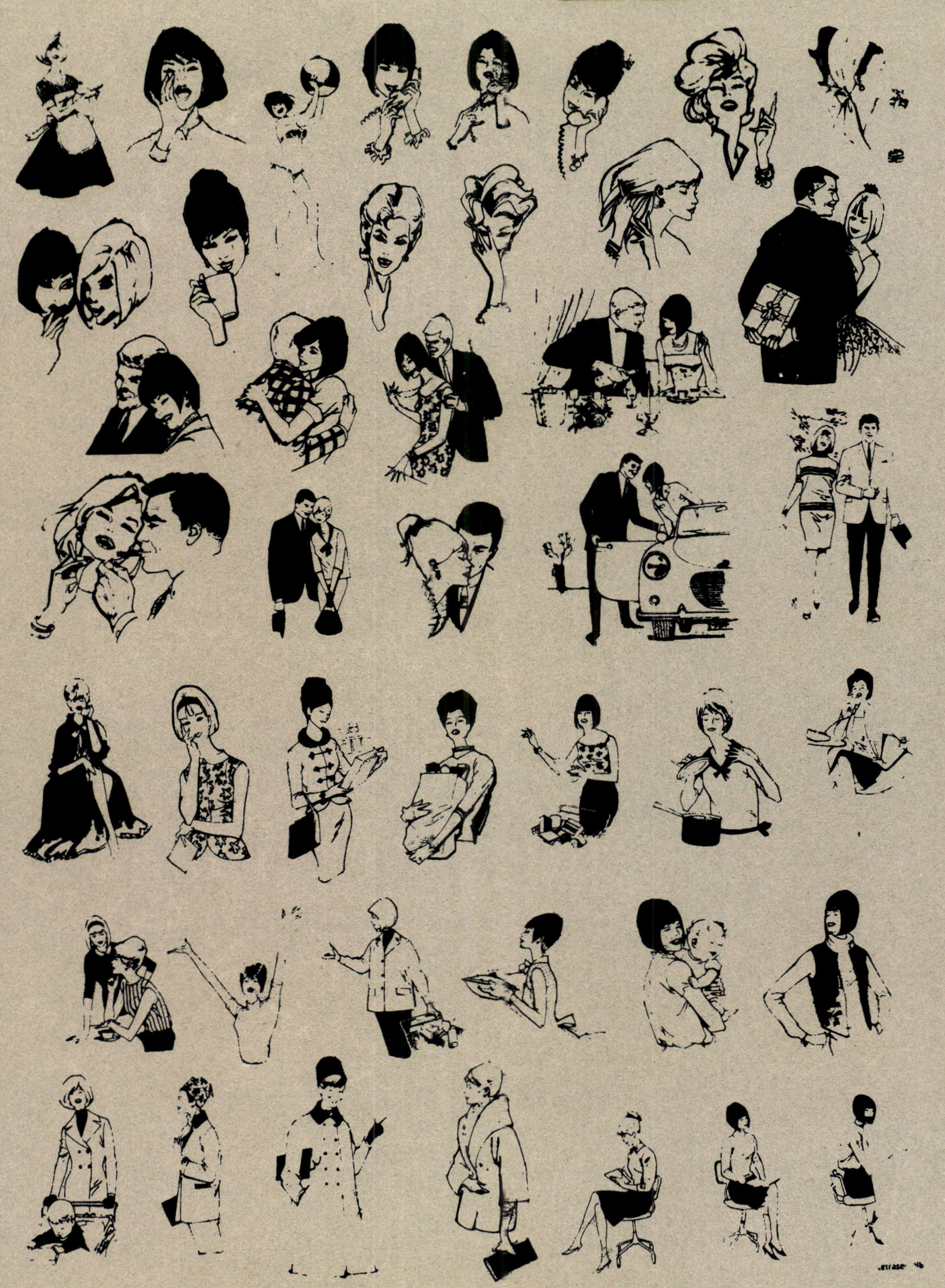

Which one are you?

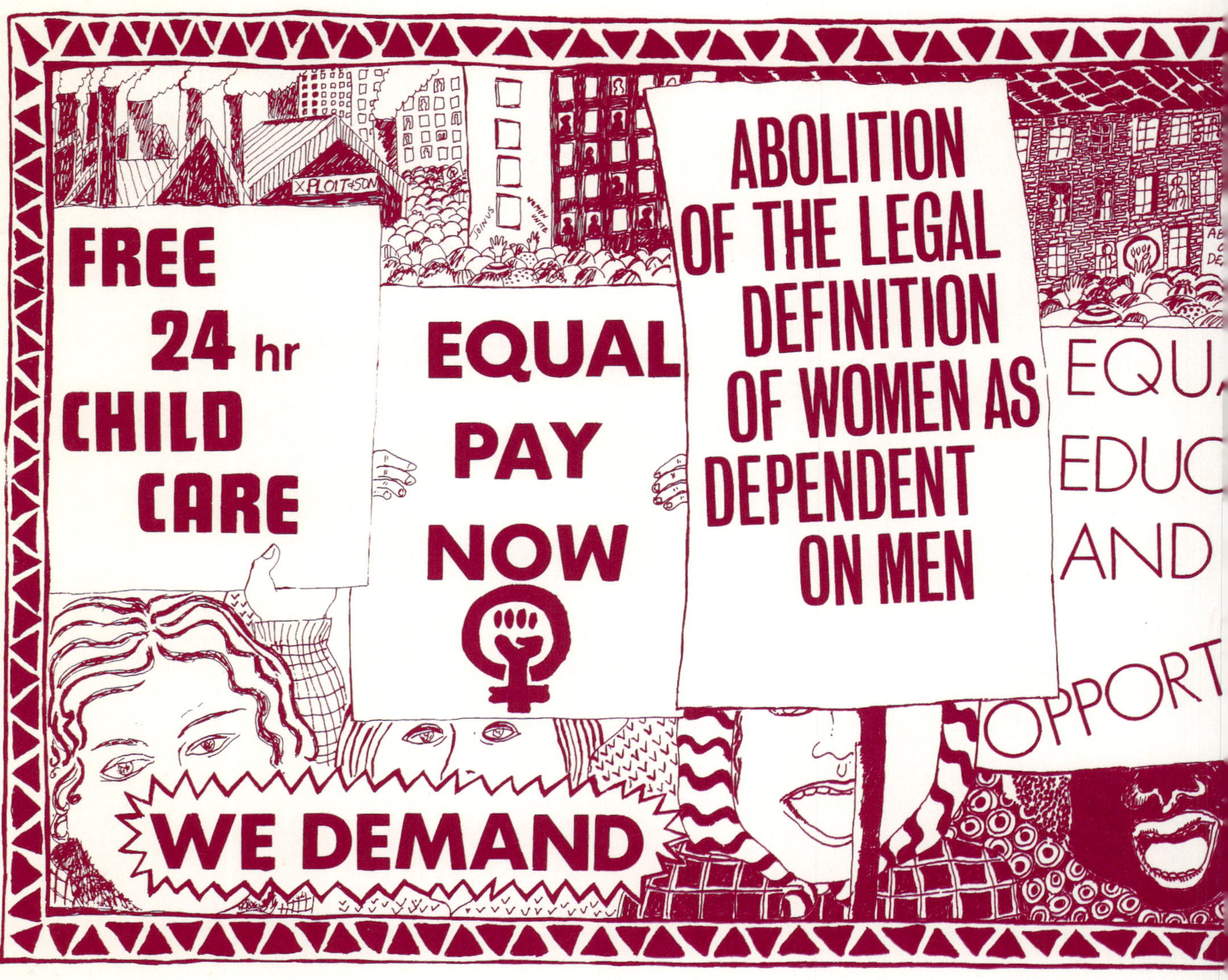

7 Demands

In March 1970, representatives from women's groups from around the country met at the first National Women's Liberation Conference at Ruskin College, Oxford to discuss the challenges facing women and the women's liberation movement and to work out a series of demands.

The following demands were passed the next year at the NWLM conference in Skegness:

1. Equal pay
2. Equal Education and Job Opportunities
3. Free Contraception and Abortion on Demand
4. Free 24-hour Nurseries

These demands were printed on banners and on a petition handed to the Prime Minister on 6 March 1971 when 4,000 marched through London on the movement's First International Women's Day march. The NWLM conference held in Edinburgh 1974 passed and added:

5. Legal and Financial Independence for all Women
6. The Right to Self Defined Sexuality. An End to Descrimination Against Lesbians.

The national conference held in Birmingham 1978 passed and added:

7. Freedom for all Women From Intimidation by the Threat or Use of Violence or Sexual Coercion Regardless of Marital Status; and an End to the Laws, Assumptions and Institutions which Perpetuate Male Dominance and Aggression Against Women.

The movement's campaign was very successful: The Sex Discrimination Act was passed in 1975 outlawing sexual discrimination in the workplace. The Women's Aid Federation was formed in 1974 providing support and refuge for women and children experiencing domestic violence.

The Domestic Violence Act was passed in 1976 enabling married or cohabiting women to obtain a court order aimed at preventing further violence and to exclude her violent partner from the home.

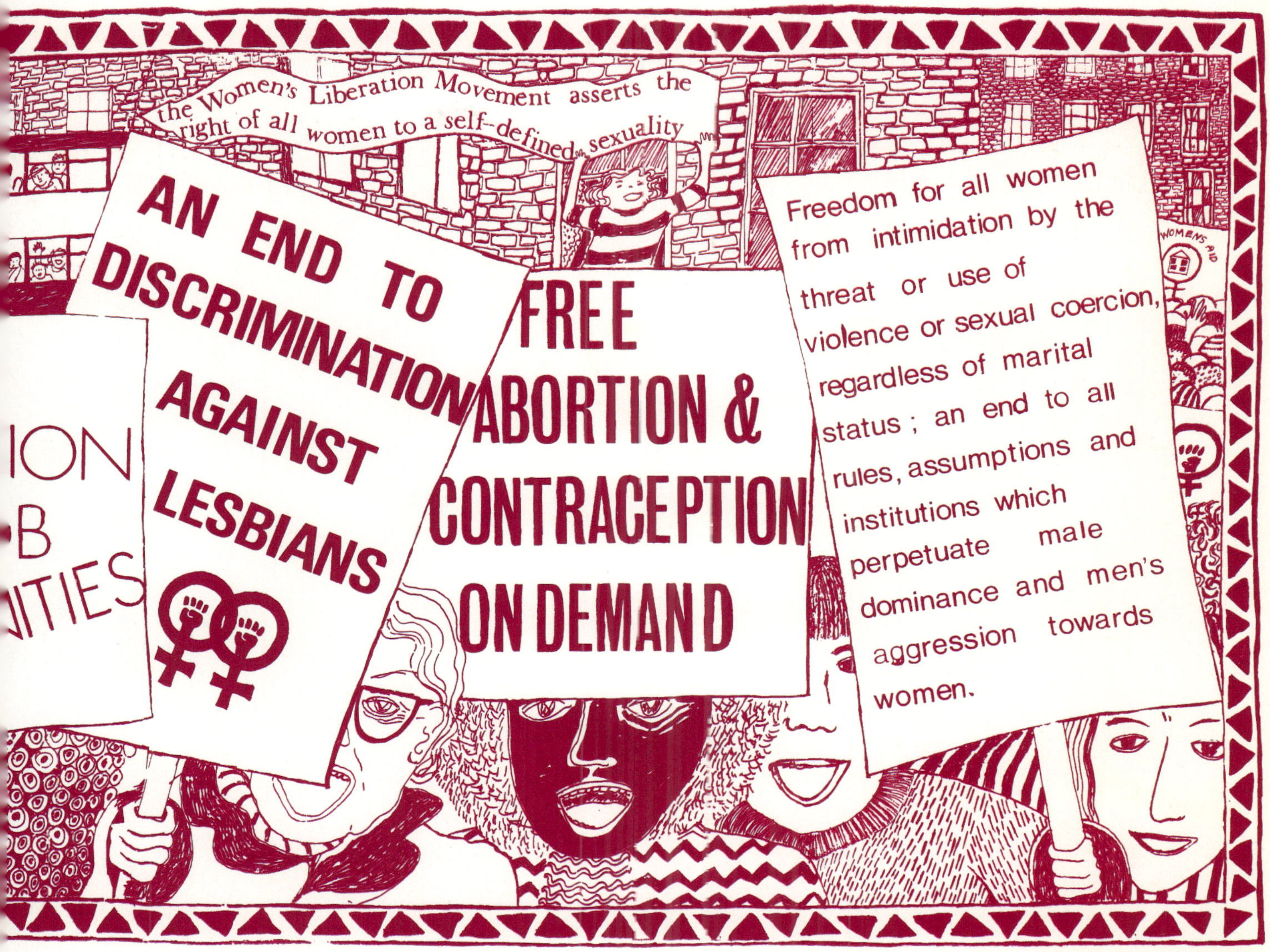

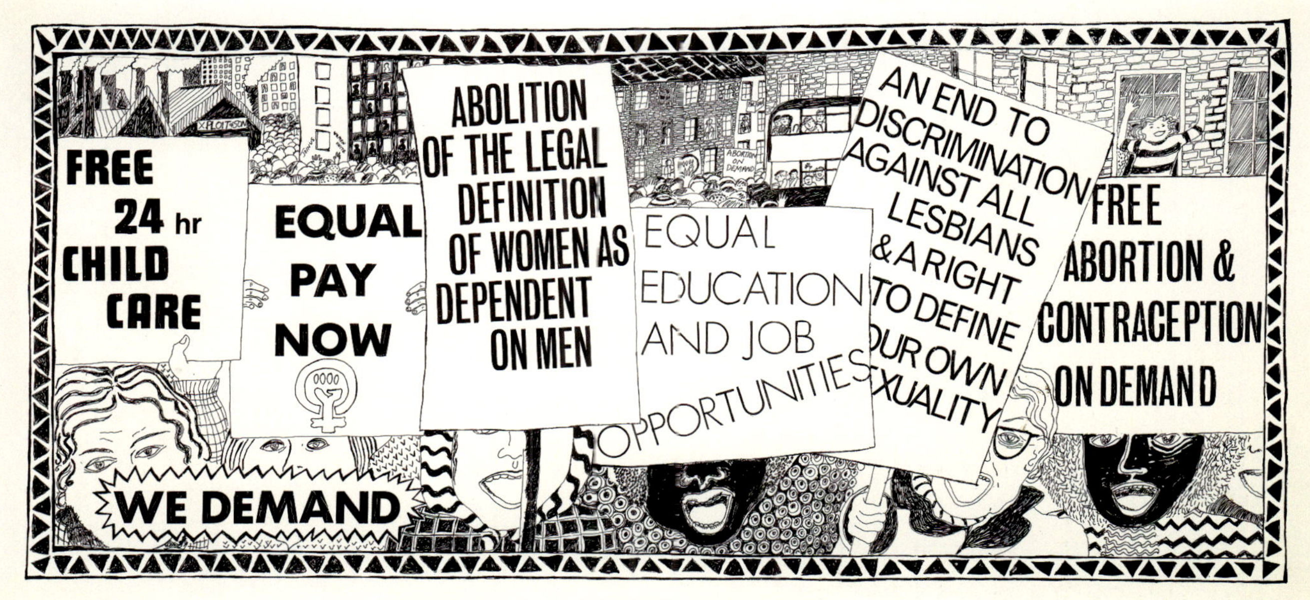

   7 DEMANDS, 1974 *33 × 79 cm*   6 DEMANDS, 1973 *29.5 × 63 cm*

Capitalism Also Depends On Domestic Labour

This poster explores a theme that is addressed in several of See Red's early posters: that domestic labour and family relationships are part of the way that society controls women and consolidates capitalist society. It illustrates how the political (work, labour, wages, etc) and the personal (home, domesticity, family, etc) are inextricably linked to support the successful functioning of capitalism.

Our design shows the influence of the Atelier Populaire with the jagged roofs and belching chimneys of the factory, and with the conveyor belt to carry workers from home to work and back again, always supported by women.

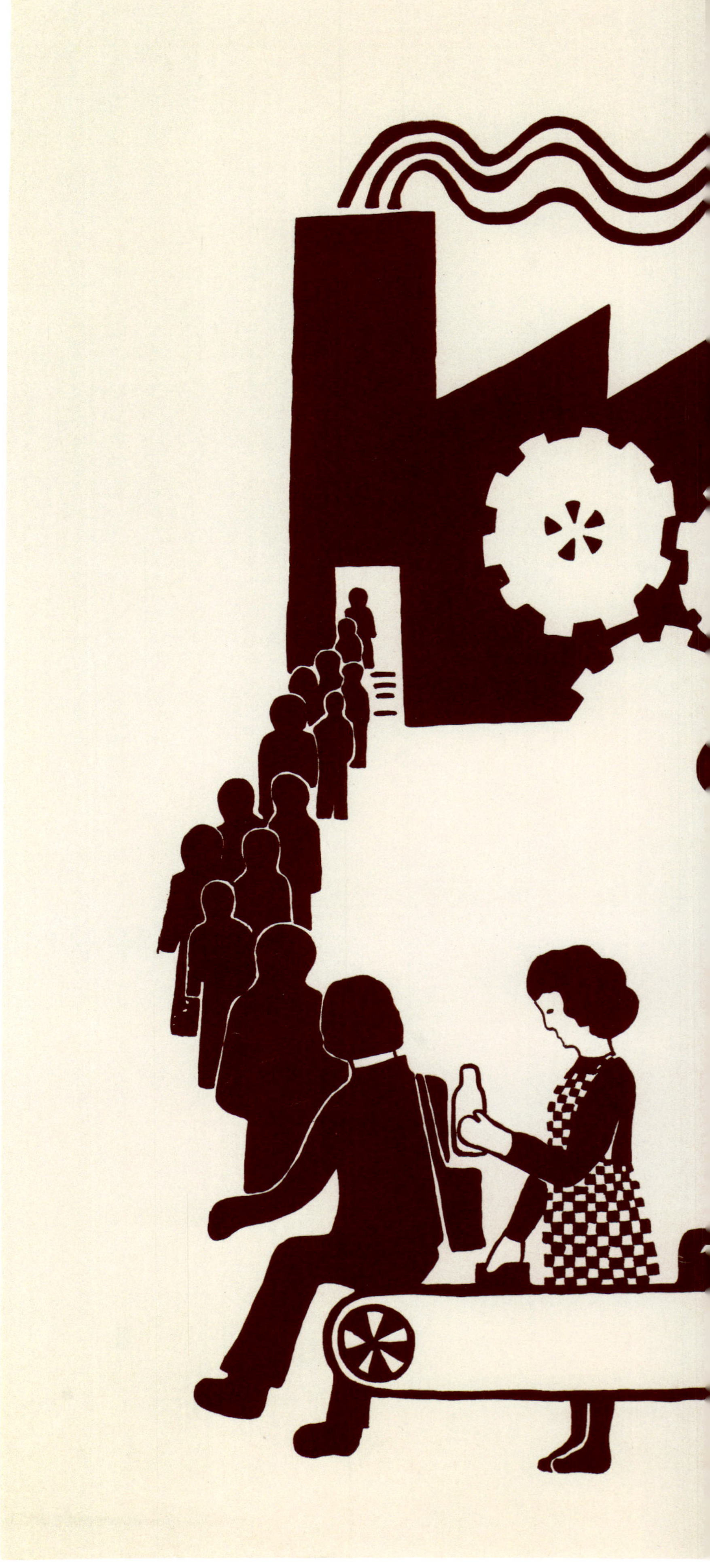

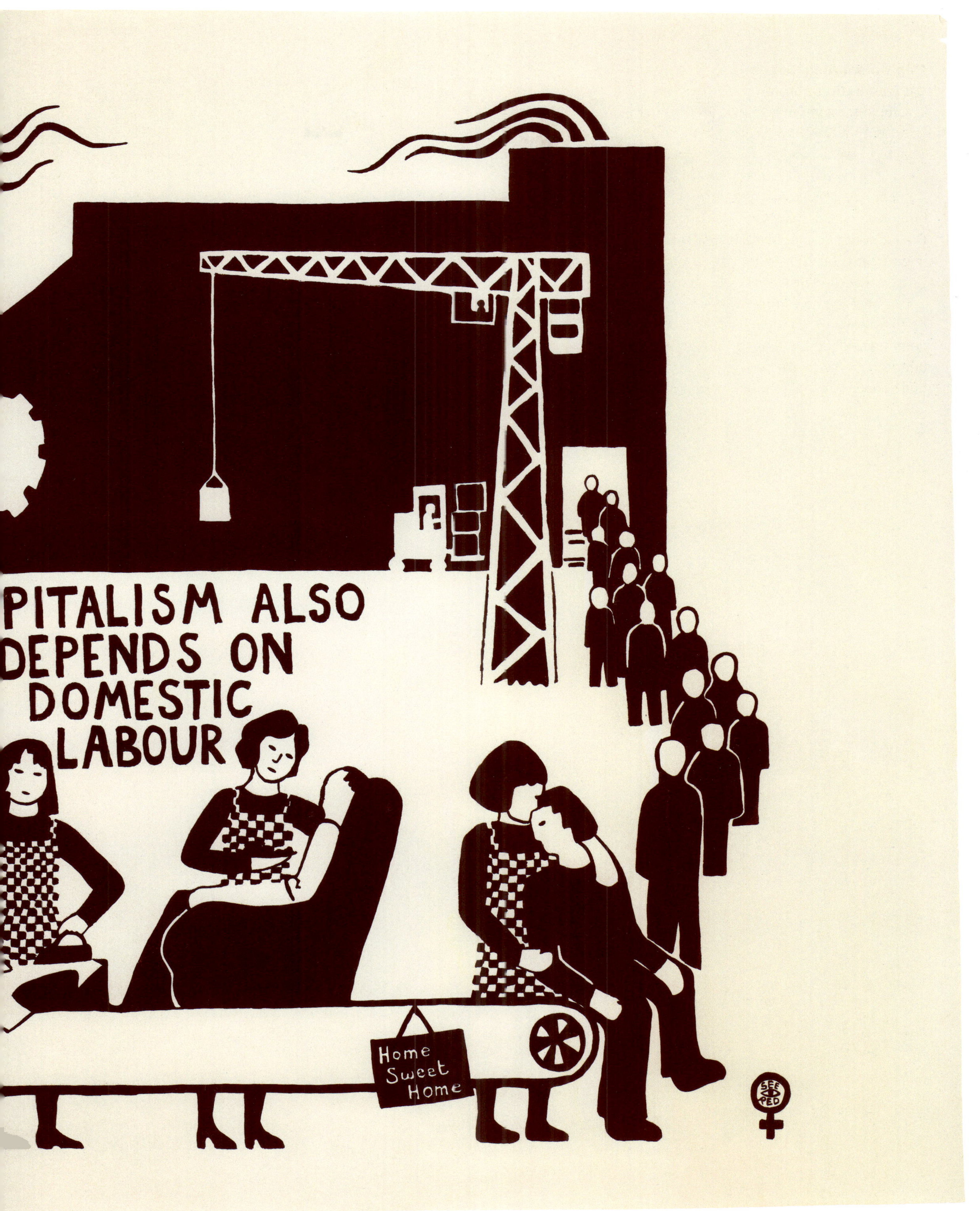

CAPITALISM ALSO DEPENDS ON DOMESTIC LABOUR, 1975 53.5 × 69 cm

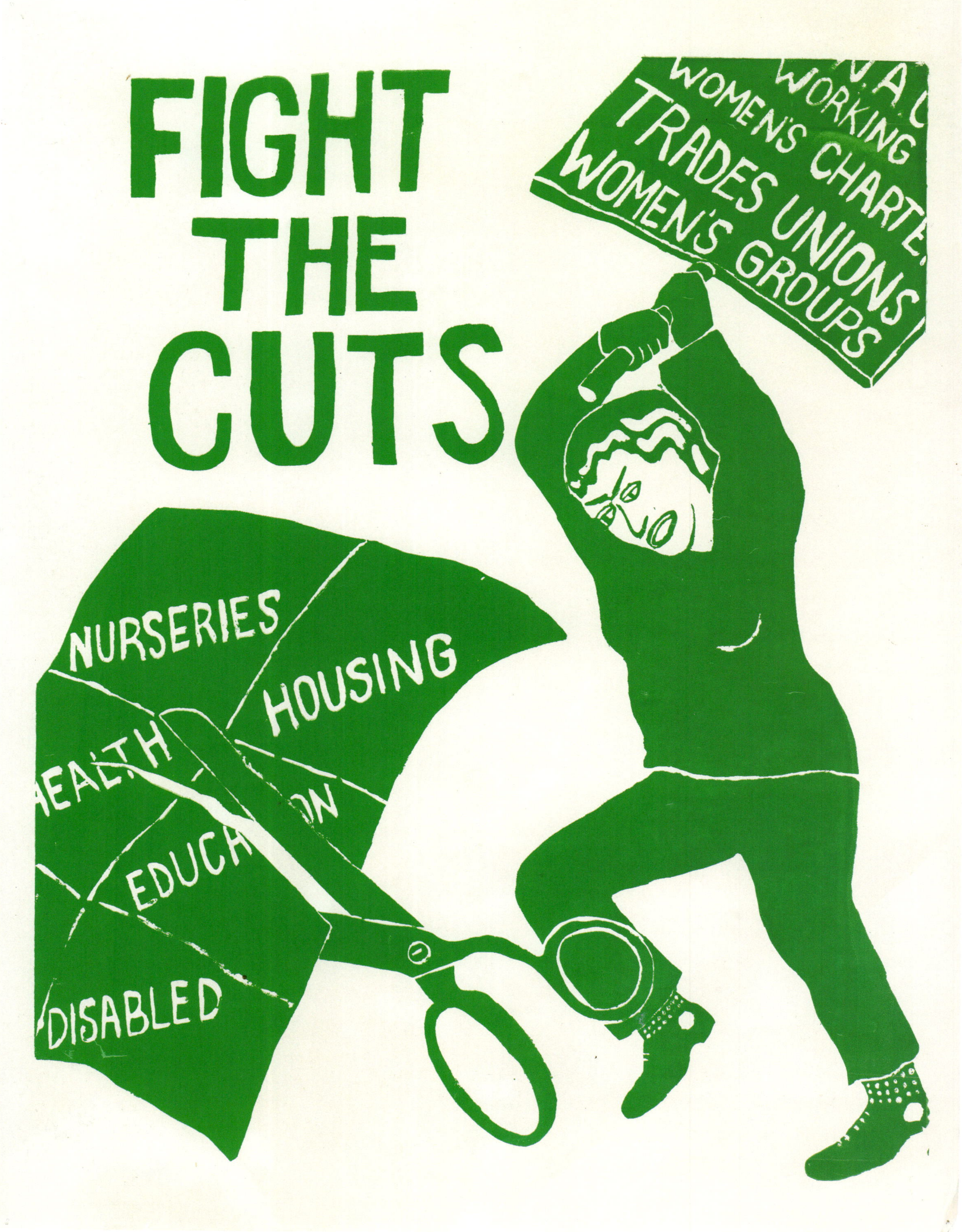

FIGHT THE CUTS, 1975 69.5 × 54 cm

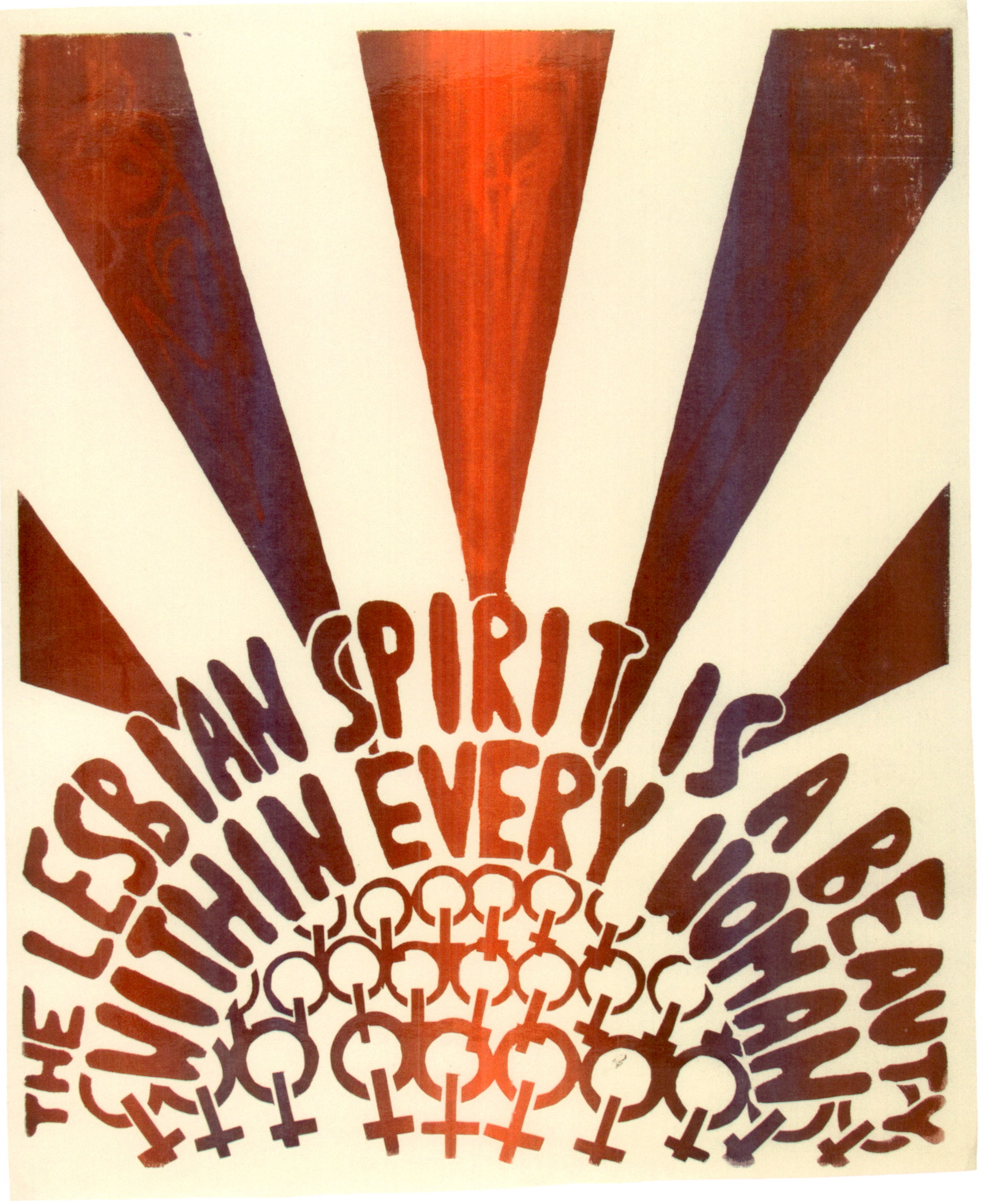

 LESBIAN SPIRIT, 1975 65 × 54 cm

Fight The Cuts (*previous page*)

One of a number of posters produced by the workshop, both general and commissioned, about government imposed cuts, in particular those affecting women.

Women Throw Off Our Double Burden

This small poster was produced for flyposting.

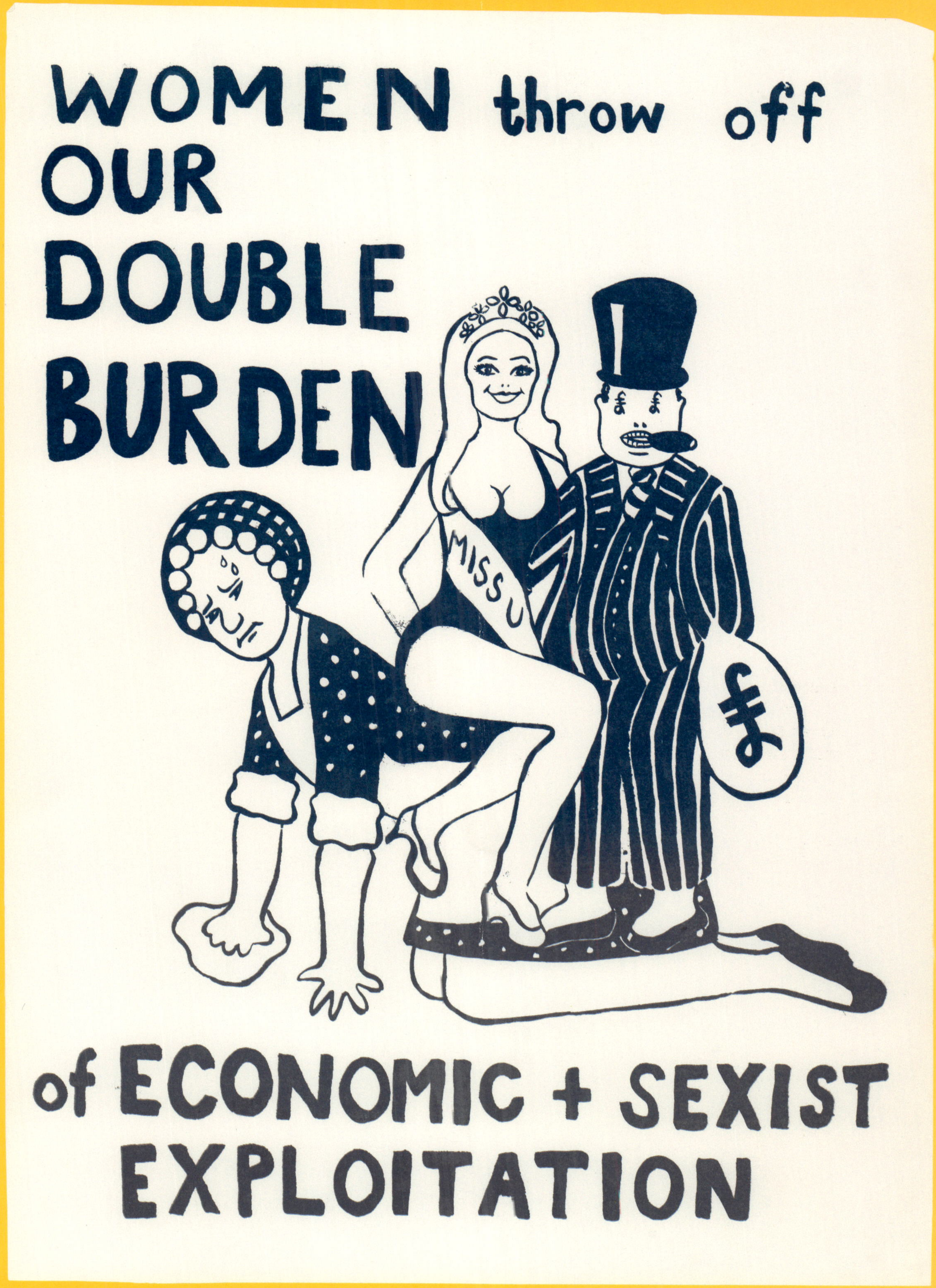

WOMEN THROW OFF OUR DOUBLE BURDEN, 1975   46.5 × 26.75 cm

Don't Break Down
In the 1970s, millions of tranquilisers were
prescribed by over-worked GPs and encouraged
by the multi-million pound pharmaceutical
industry to women dissatisfied and deeply
unhappy at the enforced narrowness of their
lives. The most common was Valium, which
was known as 'Mother's Little Helper' and
was highly addictive.

Feminists did not believe this dissatisfaction
was something that could be cured by taking
'happy pills'. They saw it as a political problem
to be solved through activism and changes
in society.

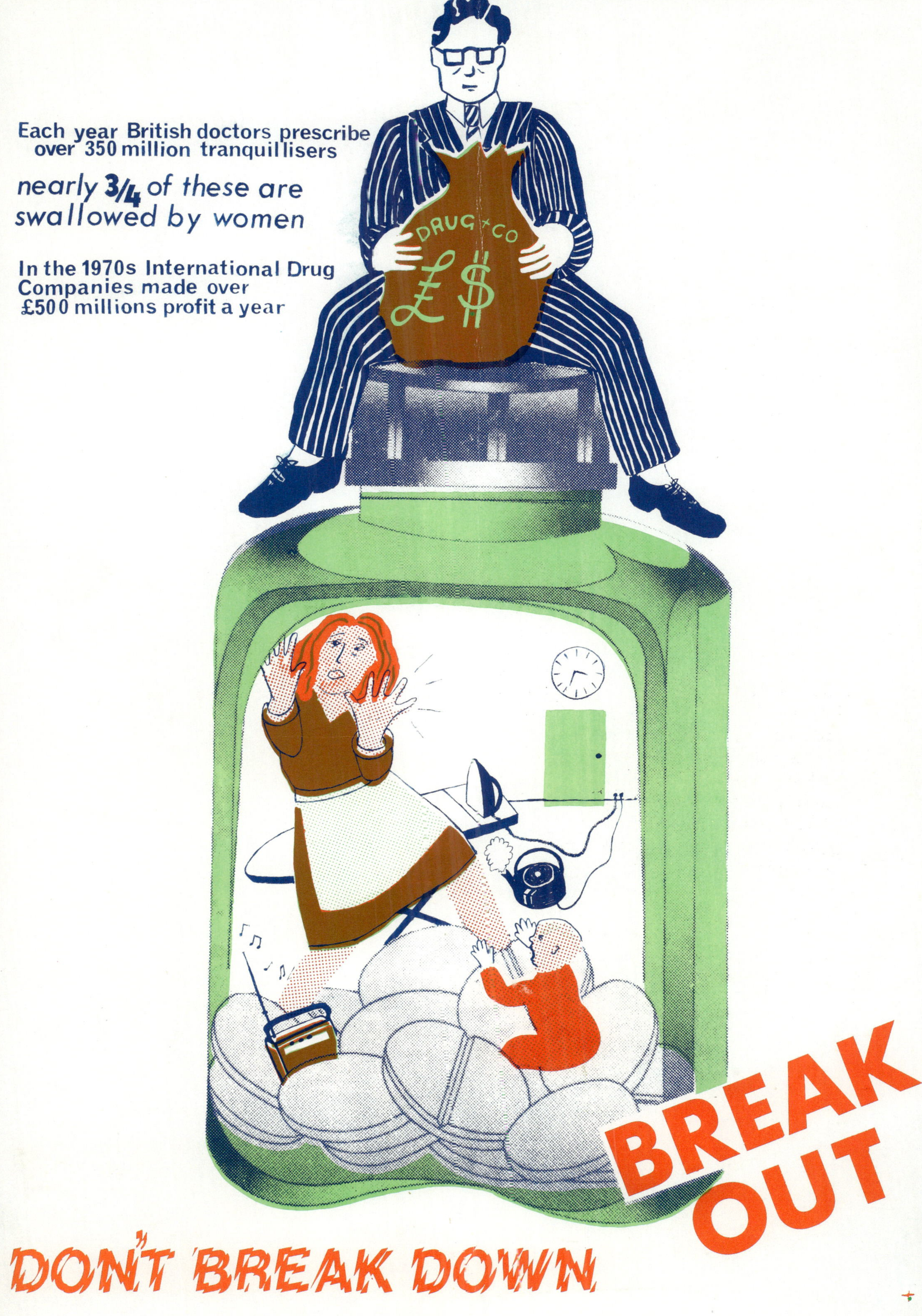

Each year British doctors prescribe
over 350 million tranquillisers

nearly 3/4 of these are
swallowed by women

In the 1970s International Drug
Companies made over
£500 millions profit a year

DRUG+CO
£ $

BREAK
OUT

DON'T BREAK DOWN

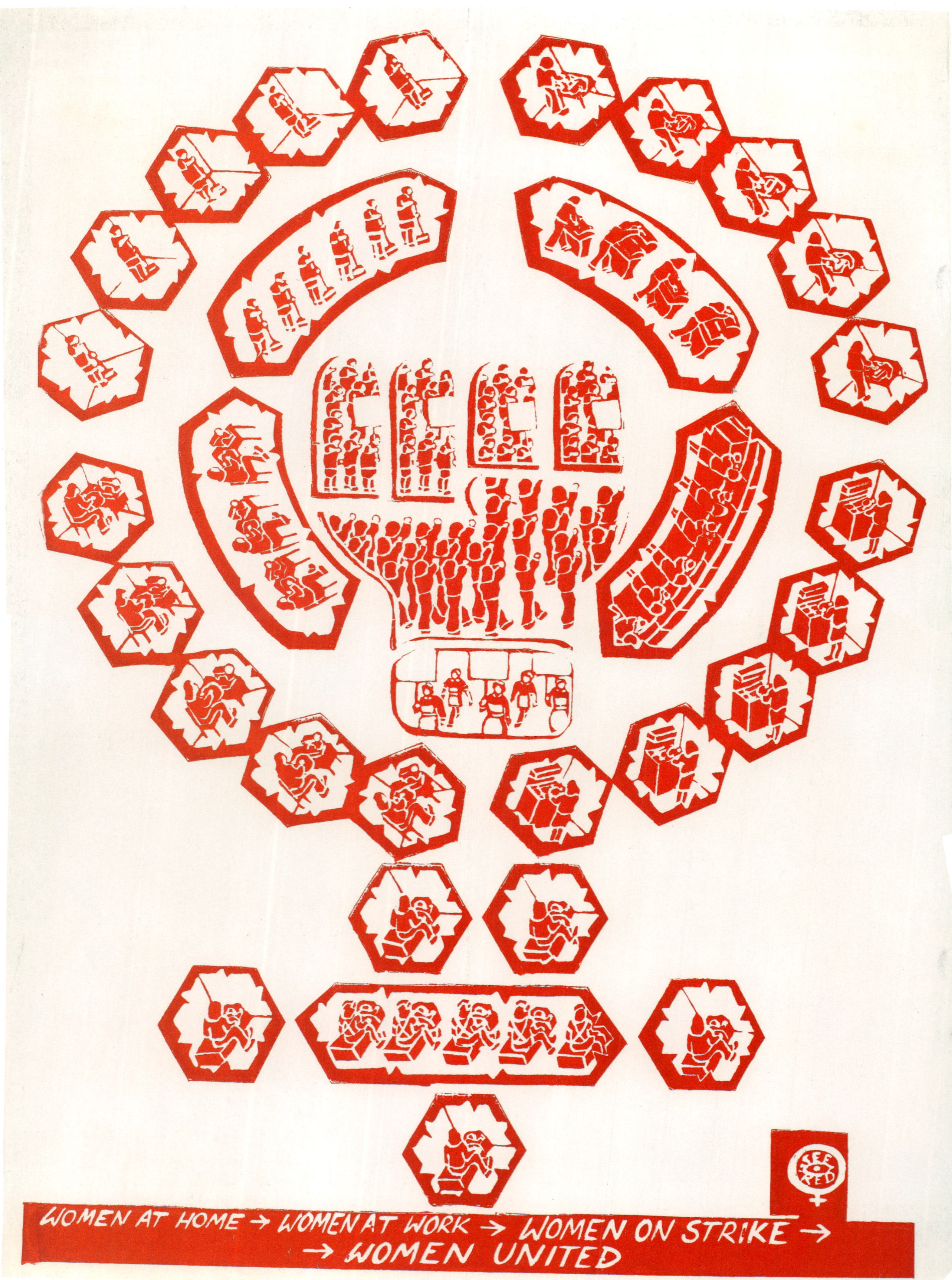

WOMEN UNITED, 1975 91 × 64 cm

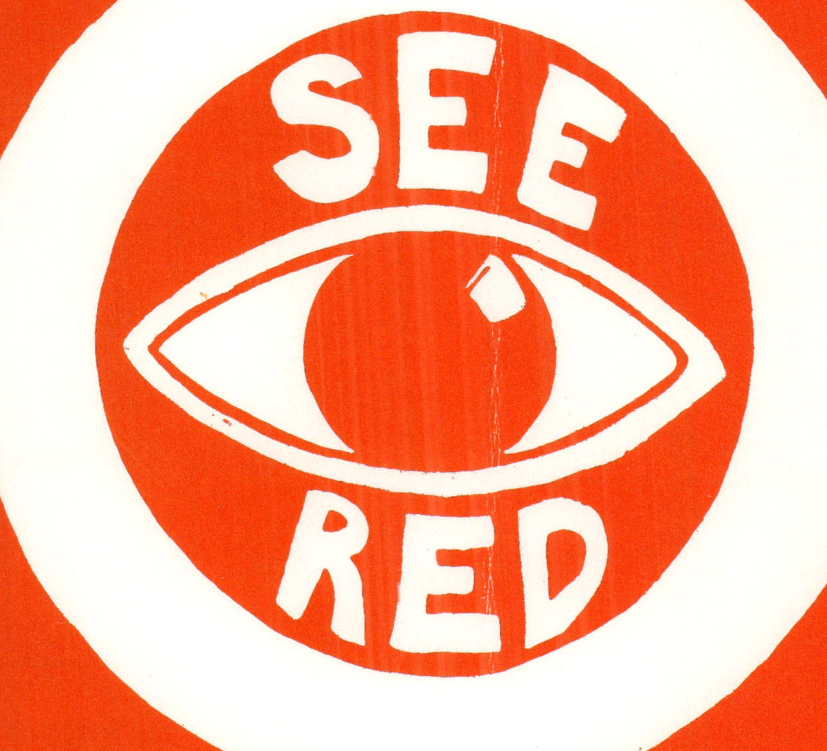

1976
SEE
RED
WOMENS
WORKSHOP
CALENDAR

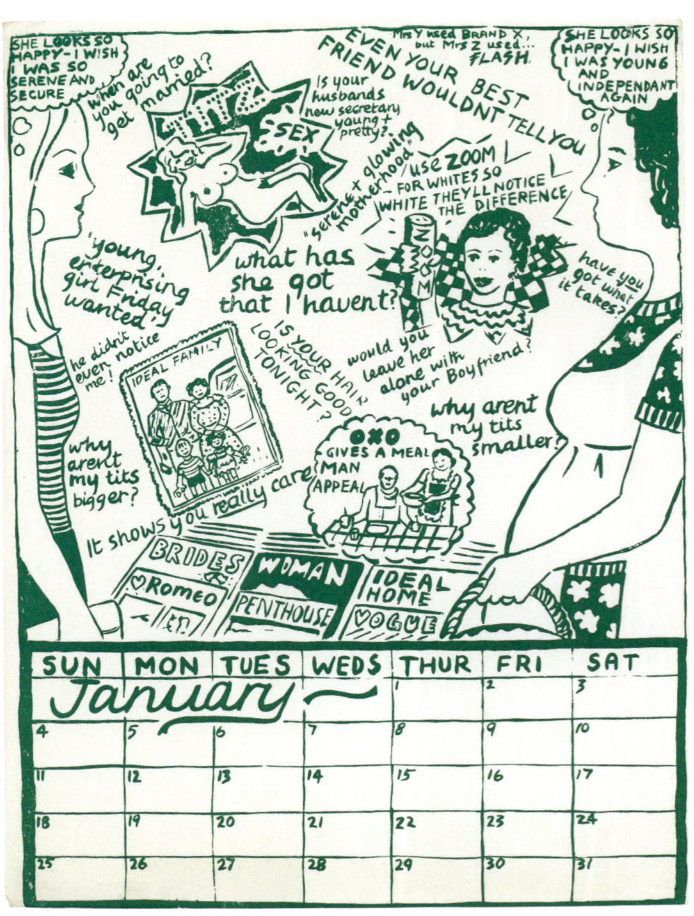

SUN	MON	TUES	WEDS	THUR	FRI	SAT
January				1	2	3
4	5	6	7	8	9	10
11	12	13	14	15	16	17
18	19	20	21	22	23	24
25	26	27	28	29	30	31

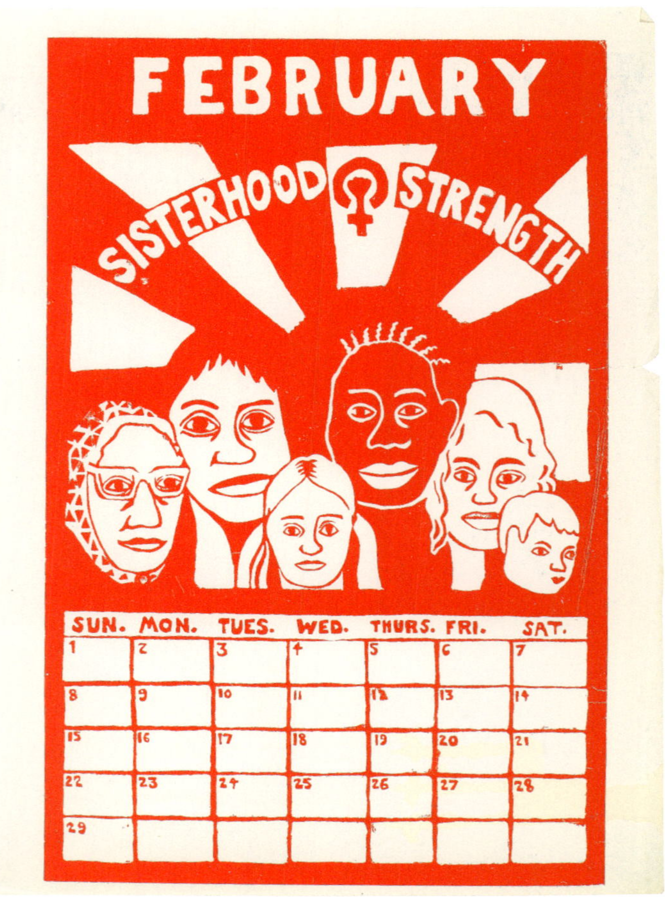

SUN.	MON.	TUES.	WED.	THURS.	FRI.	SAT.
1	2	3	4	5	6	7
8	9	10	11	12	13	14
15	16	17	18	19	20	21
22	23	24	25	26	27	28
29						

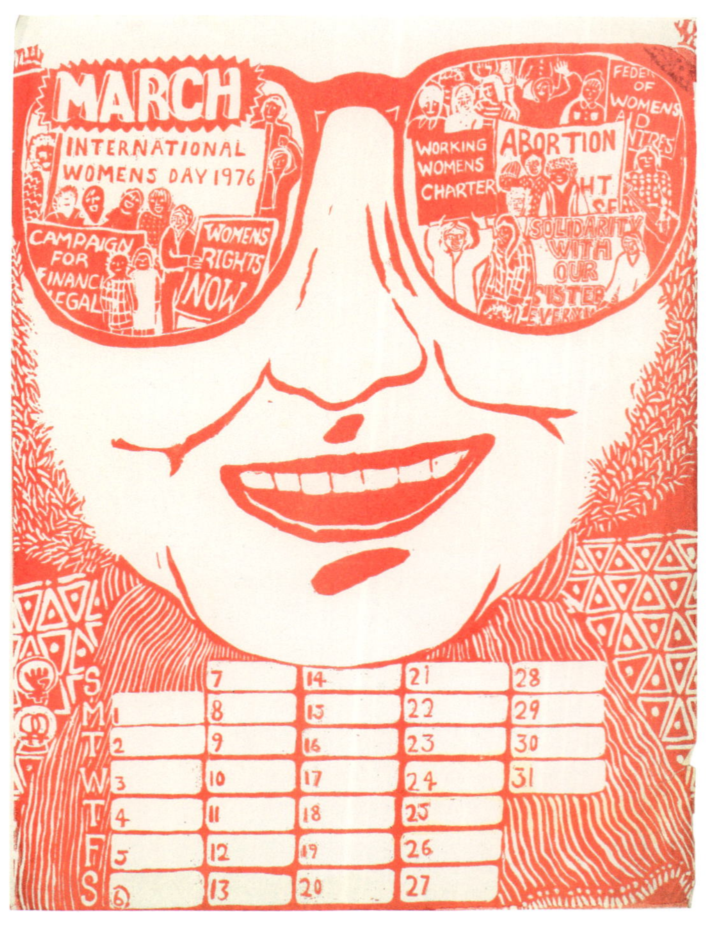

S	M	T	W	T	F	S
		2	3	4	5	6
7	8	9	10	11	12	13
14	15	16	17	18	19	20
21	22	23	24	25	26	27
28	29	30	31			

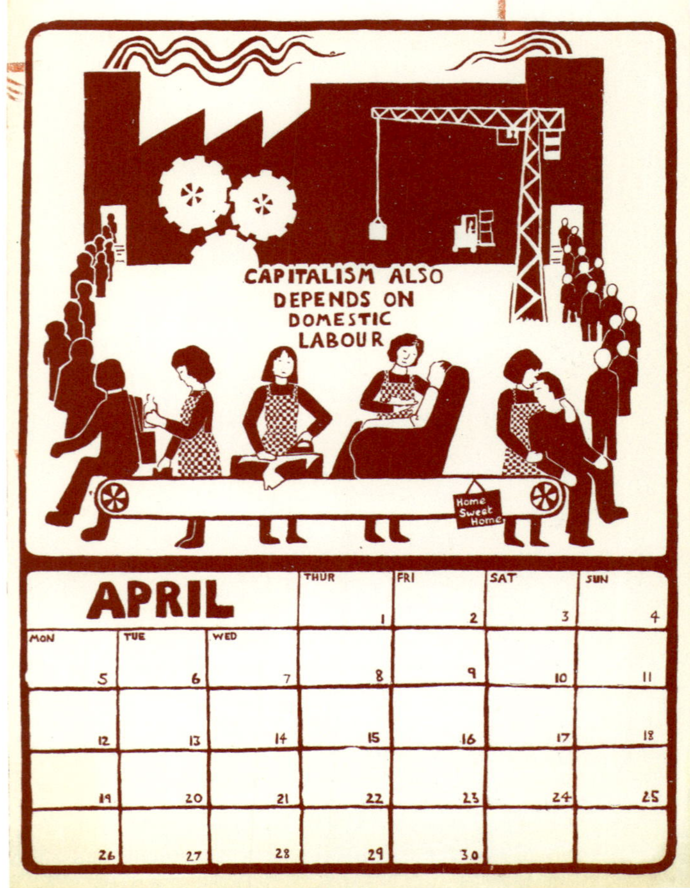

MON	TUE	WED	THUR	FRI	SAT	SUN
			1	2	3	4
5	6	7	8	9	10	11
12	13	14	15	16	17	18
19	20	21	22	23	24	25
26	27	28	29	30		

APRIL

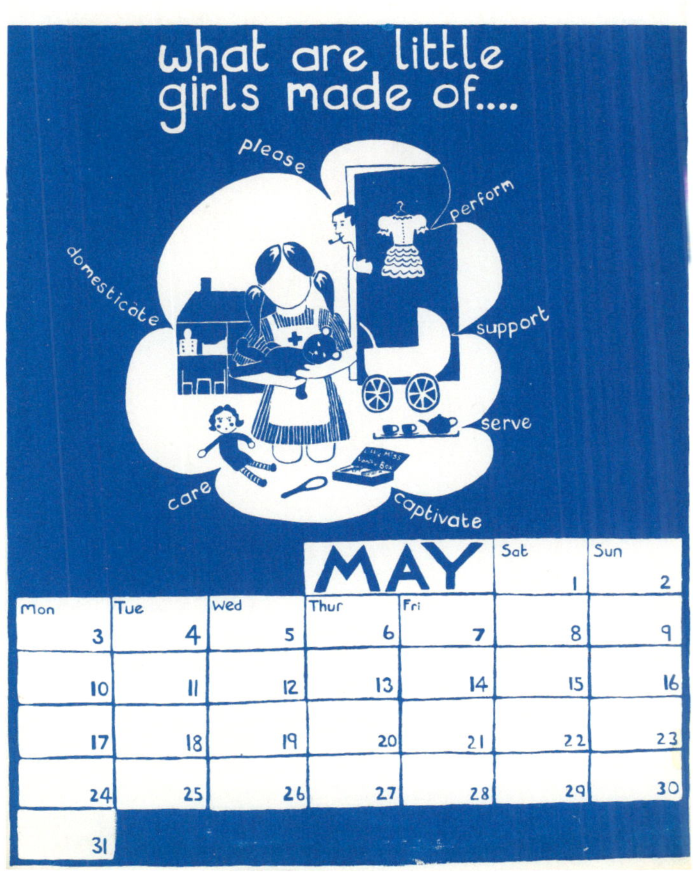

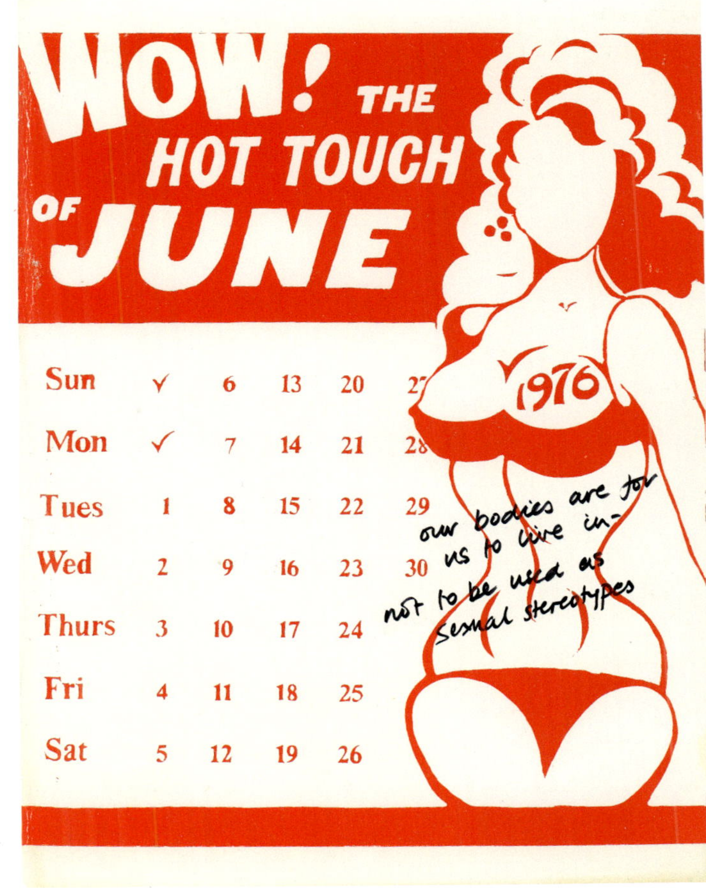

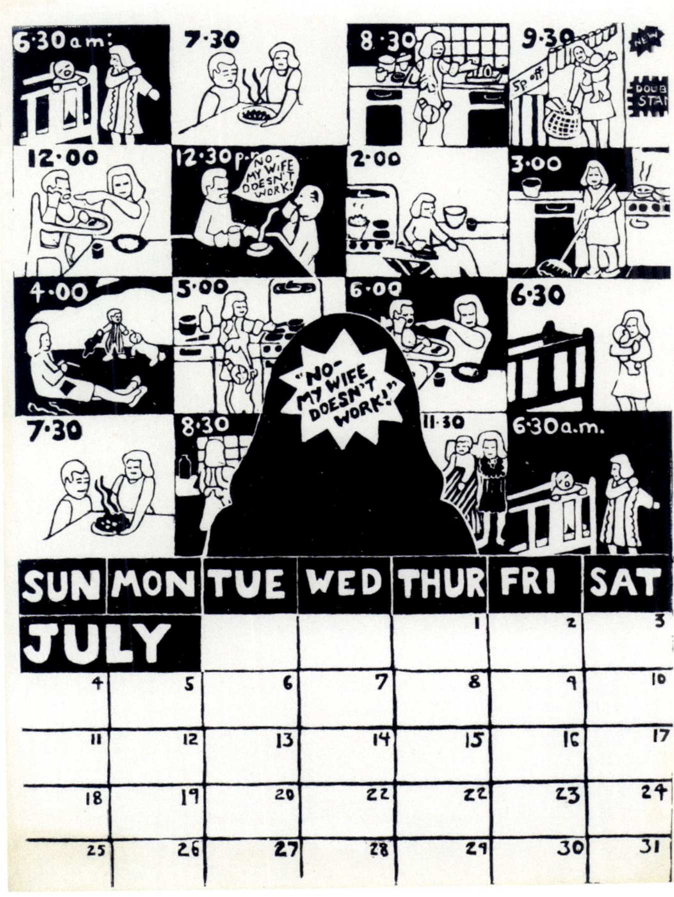

See Red Calendars

See Red produced calendars for the years 1976, 1977, 1978, 1980 and 1984.

The calendar format was a very useful way of trying out designs to see if they worked. The women in the group were brimming with a variety of ideas that we wanted to explore: it also gave us a chance to gauge the reaction to these themes. As the calendar pages were on walls for a month or two at a time, it was also a chance to use images and text that needed a longer look and had more detail to absorb. The calendars were extremely popular and we produced hundreds of copies, selling out every year.

   SEE RED CALENDAR, 1976 51 × 39 cm

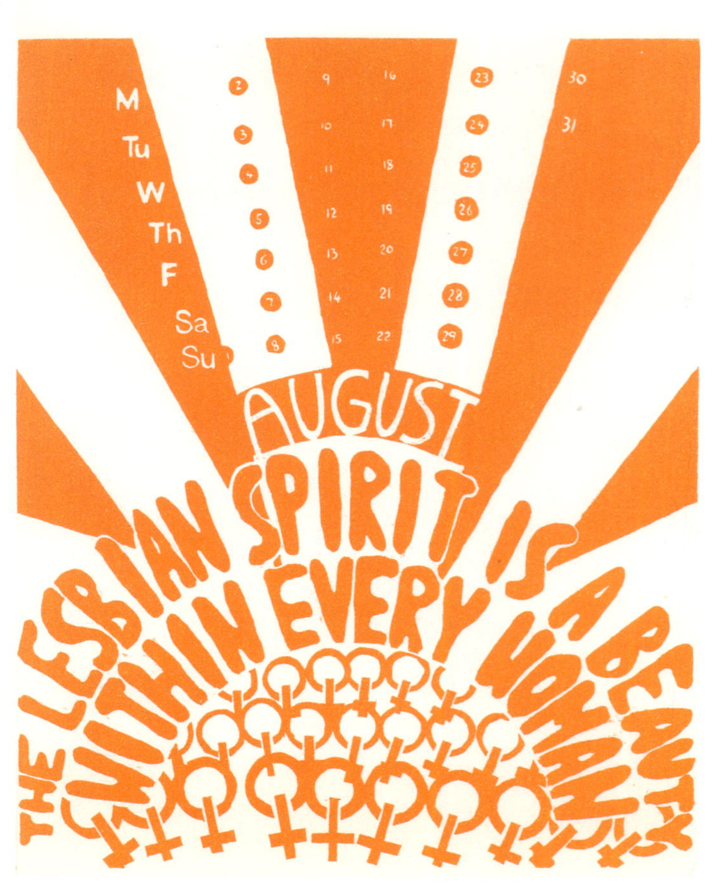

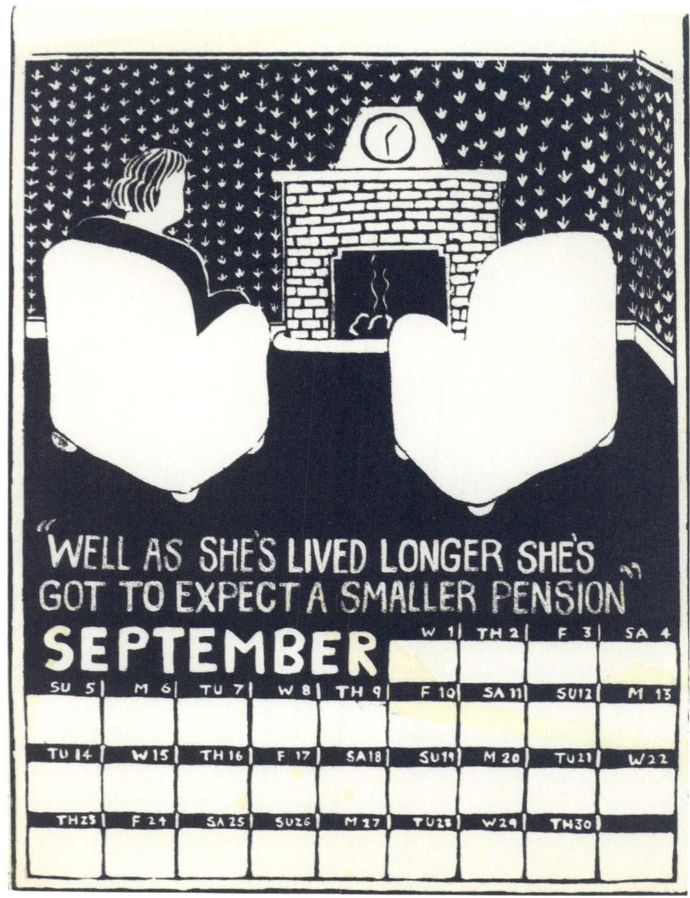

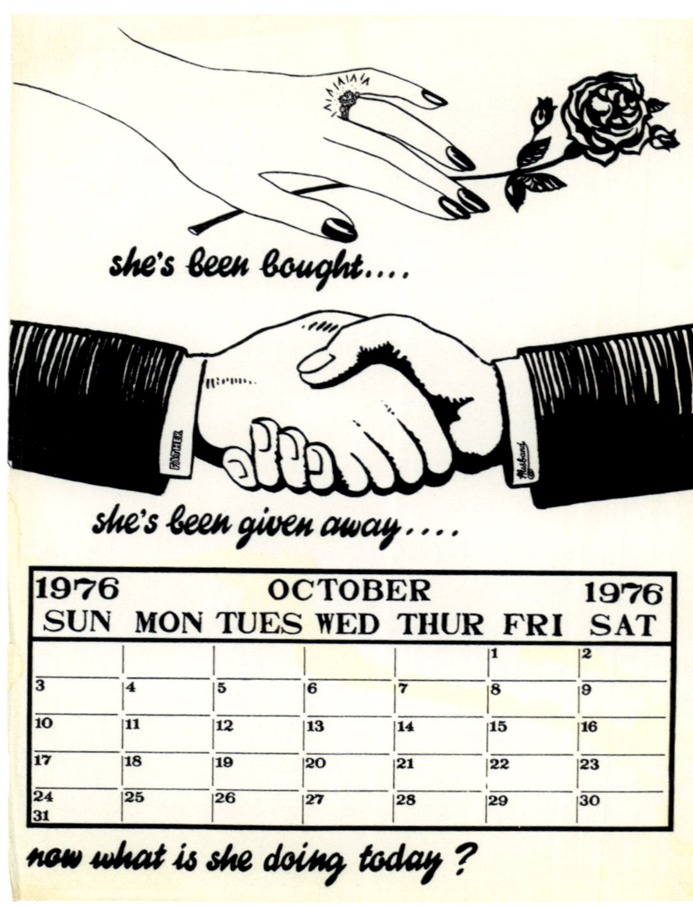

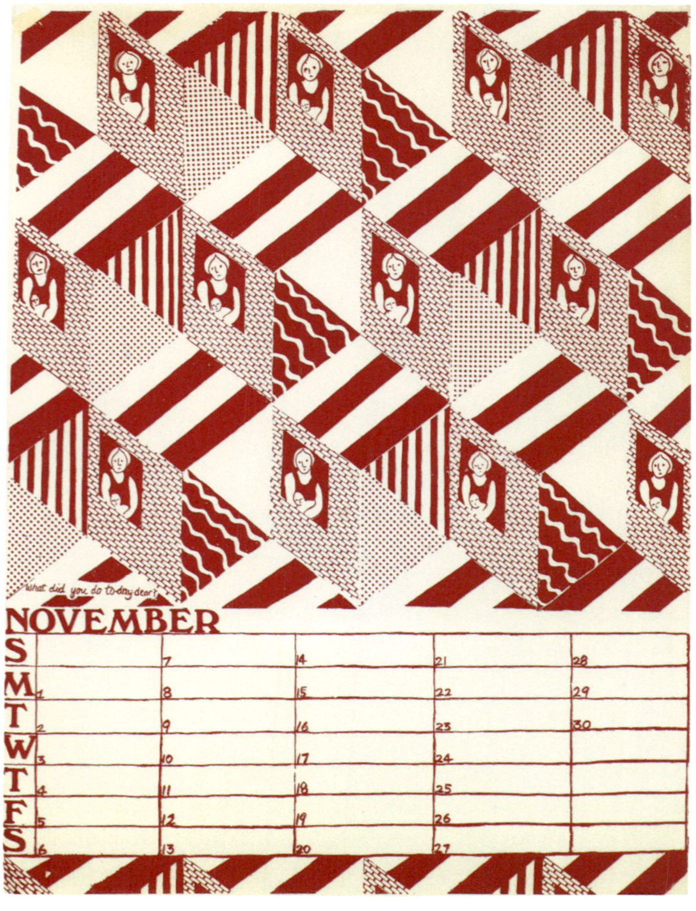

SEE RED CALENDAR, 1976 51 × 39 cm

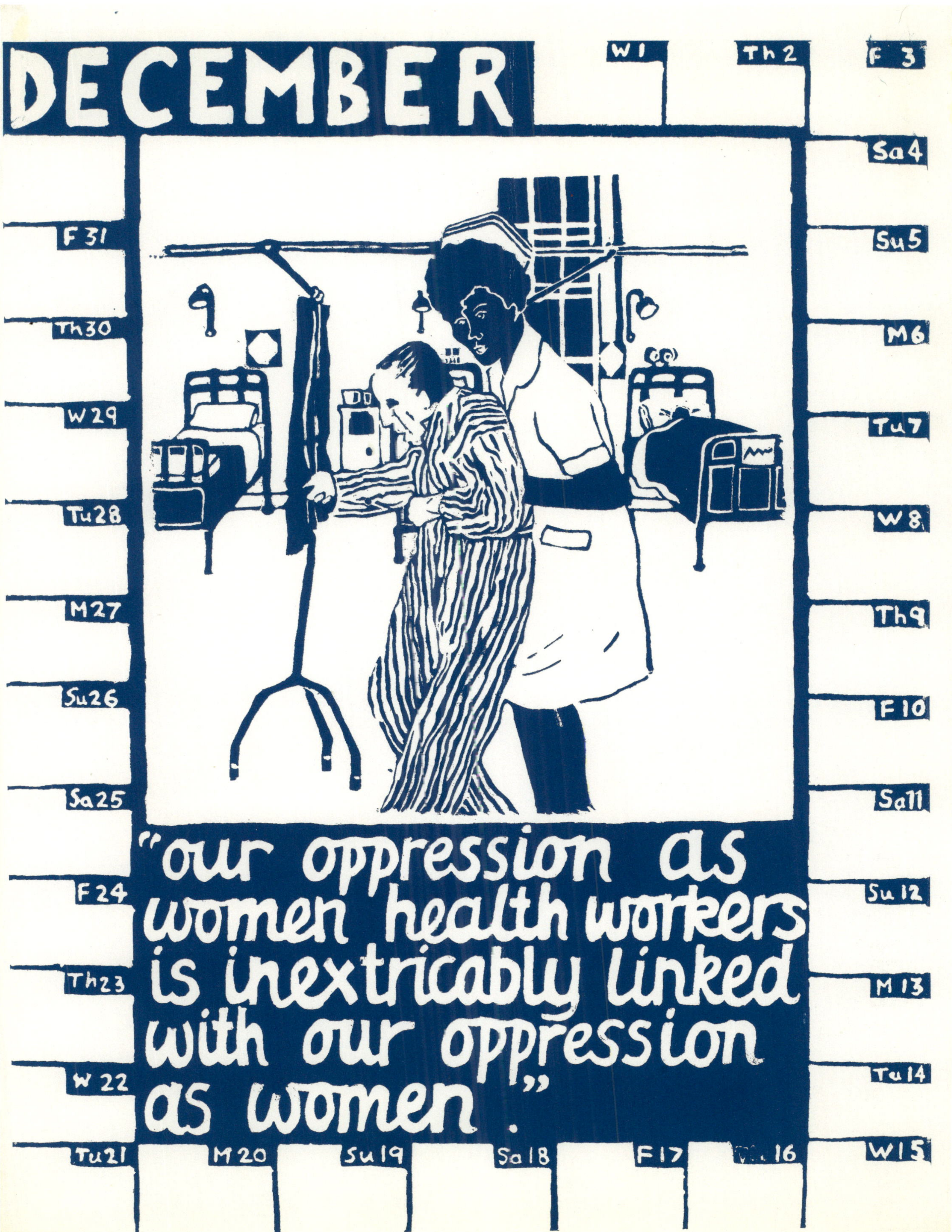

   SEE RED CALENDAR, 1976 51 × 39 cm

Fight For Safe Legal Abortion
A small poster for flyposting, advertising
a demo to defeat the Abortion Bill and fight
for safe legal abortion.

My Wife Doesn't Work (*over the page*)
Originally used in our first calendar, the
inspiration for this poster came from our personal
experiences of being wives and mothers.
It explores the reality faced by women trapped
in the home by using a series of boxes that
reference prison cells. The repetitive nature
of women's domestic life is detailed as a 24
hour job, even reaching into the bedroom.
Society promotes women's roles in supporting
husband and family with free housework and
childcare, at the same time as not giving it
equal value or recognition, with men
conditioned not to value women's work
in the home as 'real work'.

The aim of the poster was to encourage
women to start to question the monotony and
isolation of this role and to challenge the
inequality of prescribed gender roles in
marriage and parenthood. The question of
women's domestic labour was a recurring
theme in consciousness-raising groups and
in campaigns such as *Wages* For *Housework*.

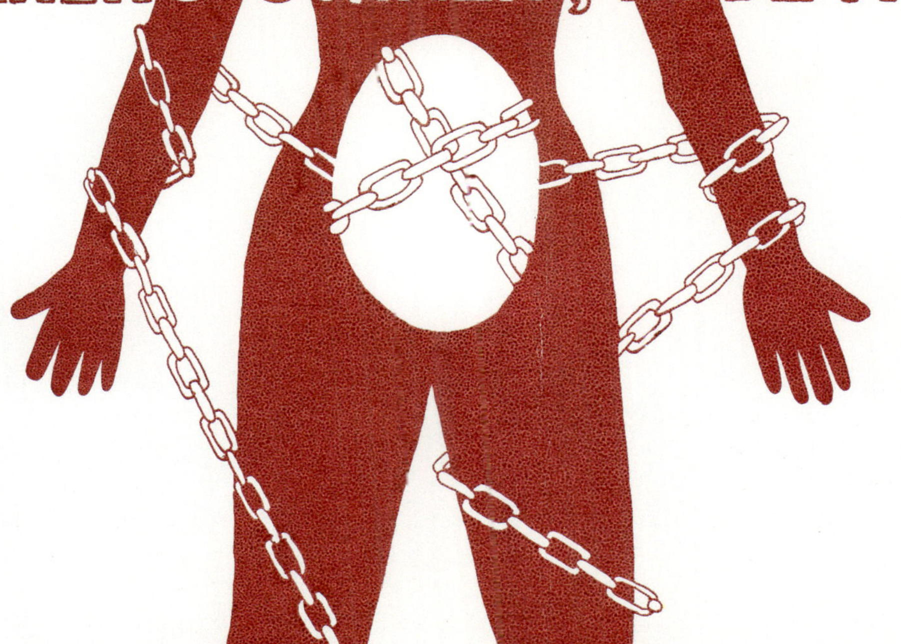

FIGHT FOR SAFE, LEGAL ABORTION, 1976 43 × 30.5 cm

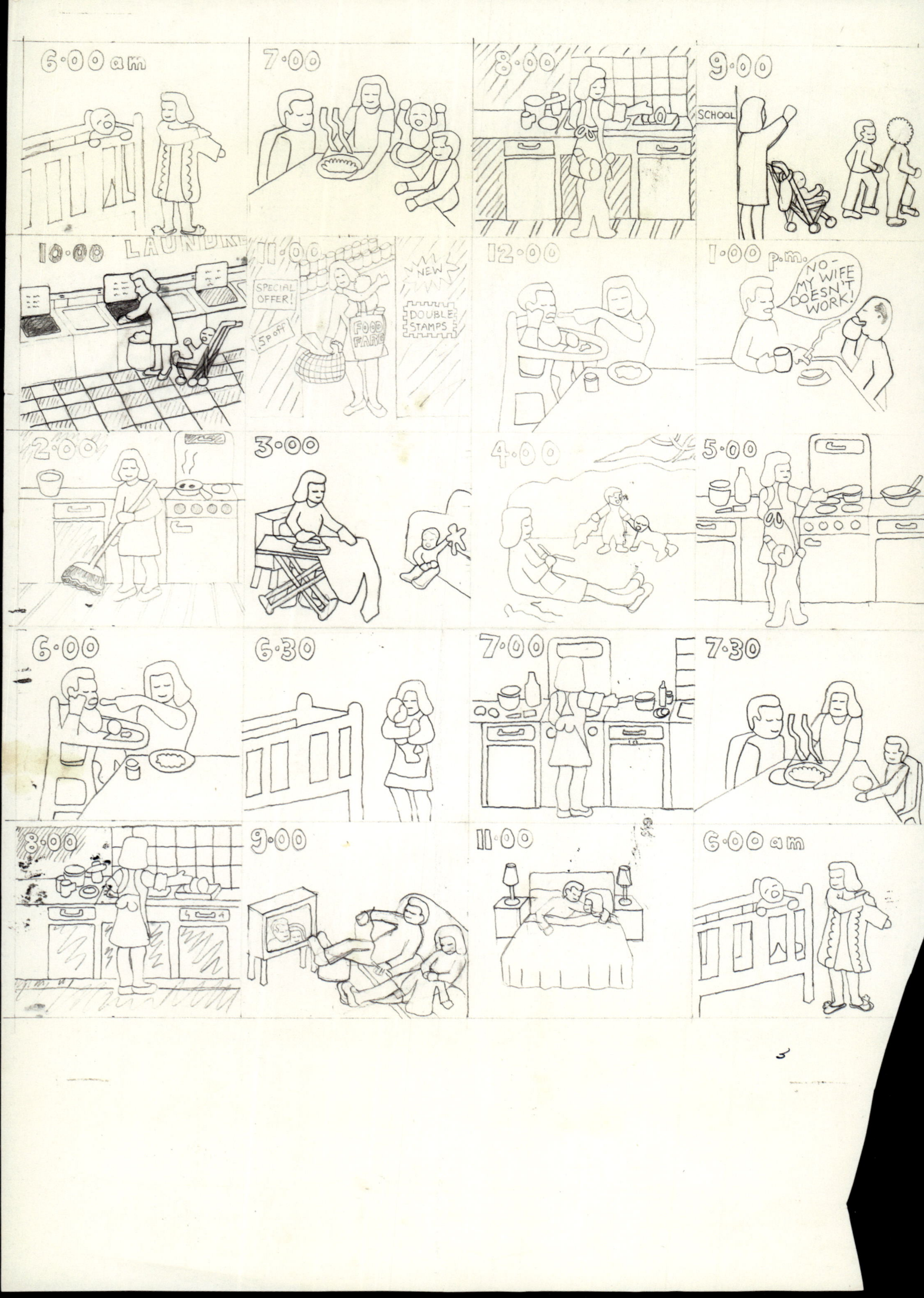

MY WIFE DOESN'T WORK, 1976 79 × 54 cm
Above: Preparatory Sketch

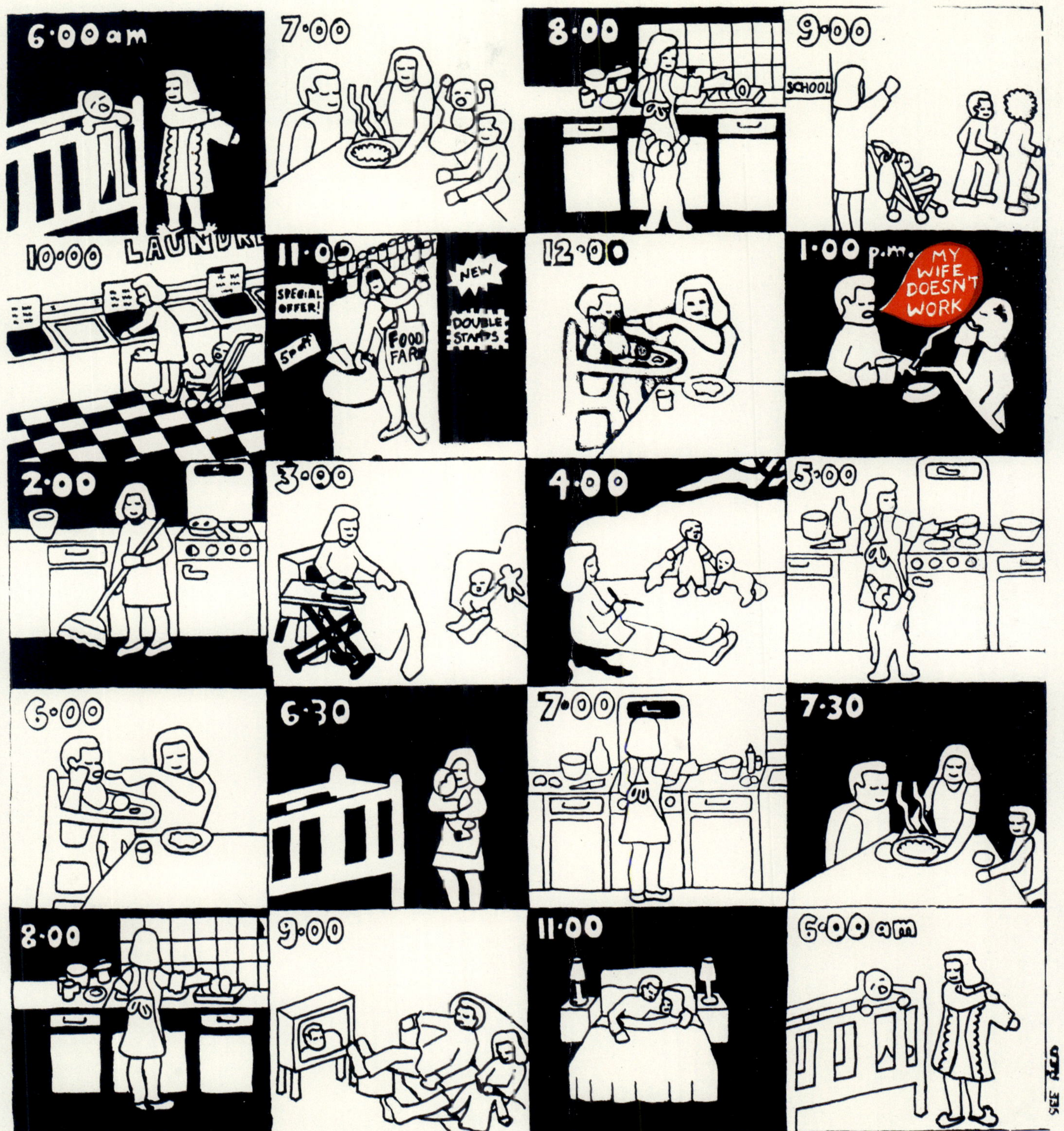

6:00 am
7:00
8:00
9:00
SCHOOL
10:00 LAUNDRE
11:00
SPECIAL OFFER!
5p off
FOOD FARE
NEW
DOUBLE STAMPS
12:00
1:00 p.m.
MY WIFE DOESN'T WORK
2:00
3:00
4:00
5:00
6:00
6:30
7:00
7:30
8:00
9:00
11:00
6:00 am

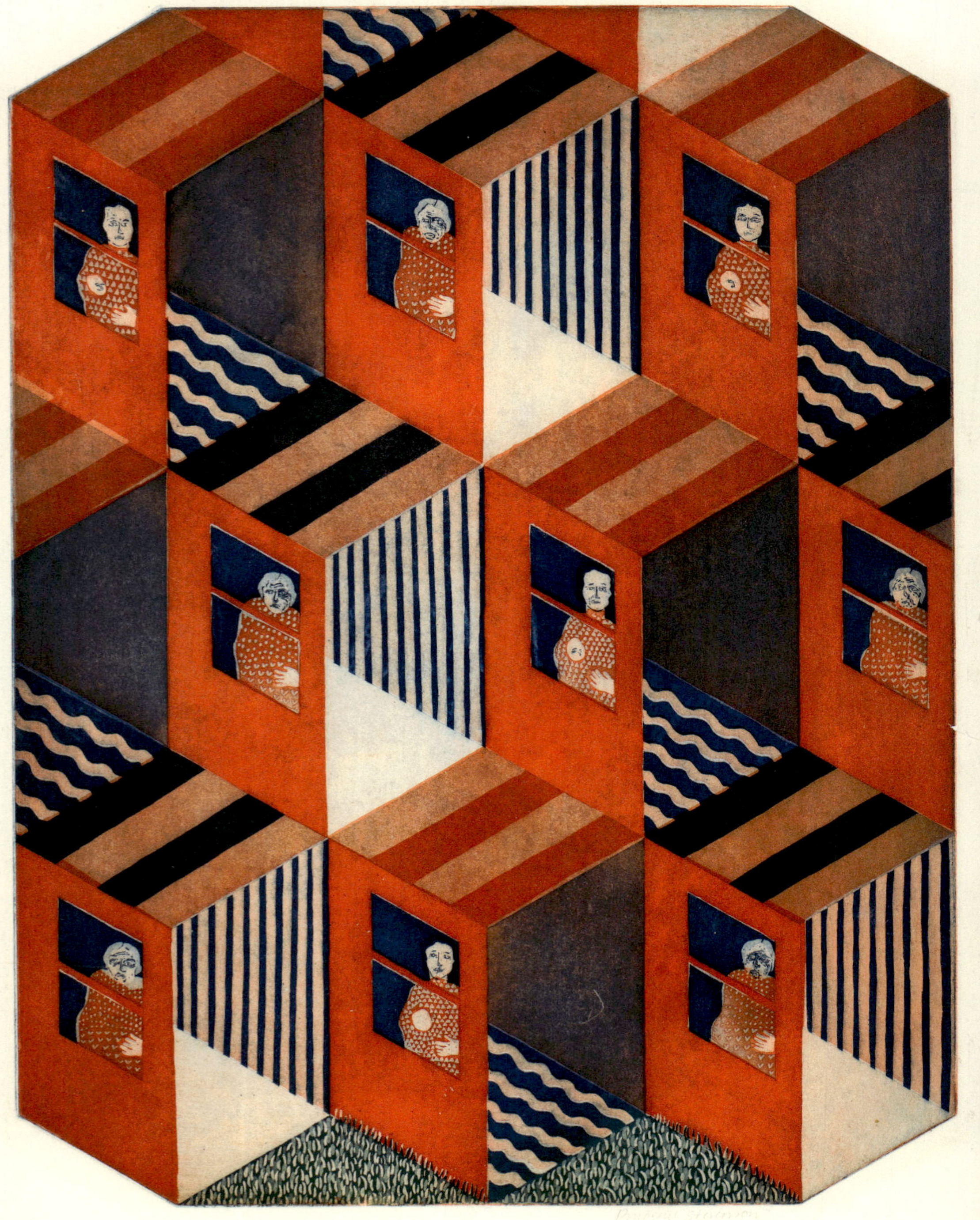

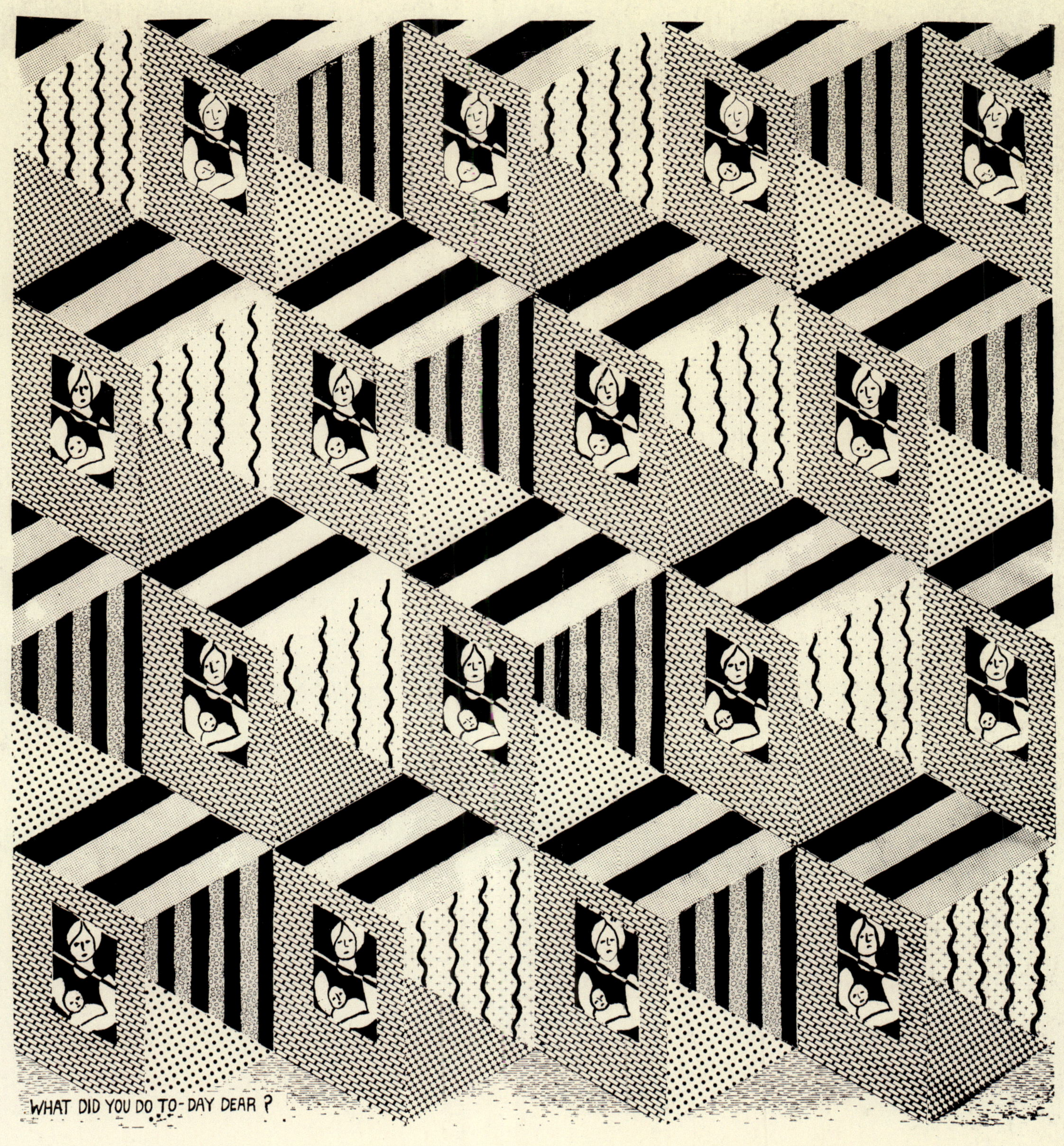

ALONE WE ARE POWERLESS...
TOGETHER WE ARE STRONG.

PRINT YOUR OWN PO[STER]

FRAME.. 2 lengths of hard wood 24"x2" + 2 leng[ths]

MESH.. Organdie, terylene: Organdie can be bo[ught]
department store. Cut piece 2" larger than frame[.]
tightly; this needs two people, one to staple o[n]

attach to base board or tabl[e]
hinges. Stick brown tape alo[ng]
by mesh and frame. this stops
through as well as determining

SQUEEGEE..

STENCIL.. newspaper or other thin paper to fit
work out wording & design. cut out with sharp b[lade]
Aim for blocks rather than lines

not

Hinge frame to base board; place stencil on cle[an]
end. pull squeegee across screen with stron[g]
to the screen & produce the first print. Hand[le]
when finished clean immediately with white spi[rit]
EXPERIMENT. try wallpaper paste mixed with powder
with wax crayon(remove with white spirit) a[nd]
remove with varnish remover.

Suppliers of screen materials: Ge[orge]
Shawheath. Cheshire. SERICOL 24 Pars[ons]
look up screen process printers in pho[ne]
they will sometimes give away end of [rolls]
phone us for advice + information

STER

38"x2"

. from any
retch

. pull mesh →

. ith lift off

. side angle made
. ink from seeping
. of print.

WOOD

rame
e

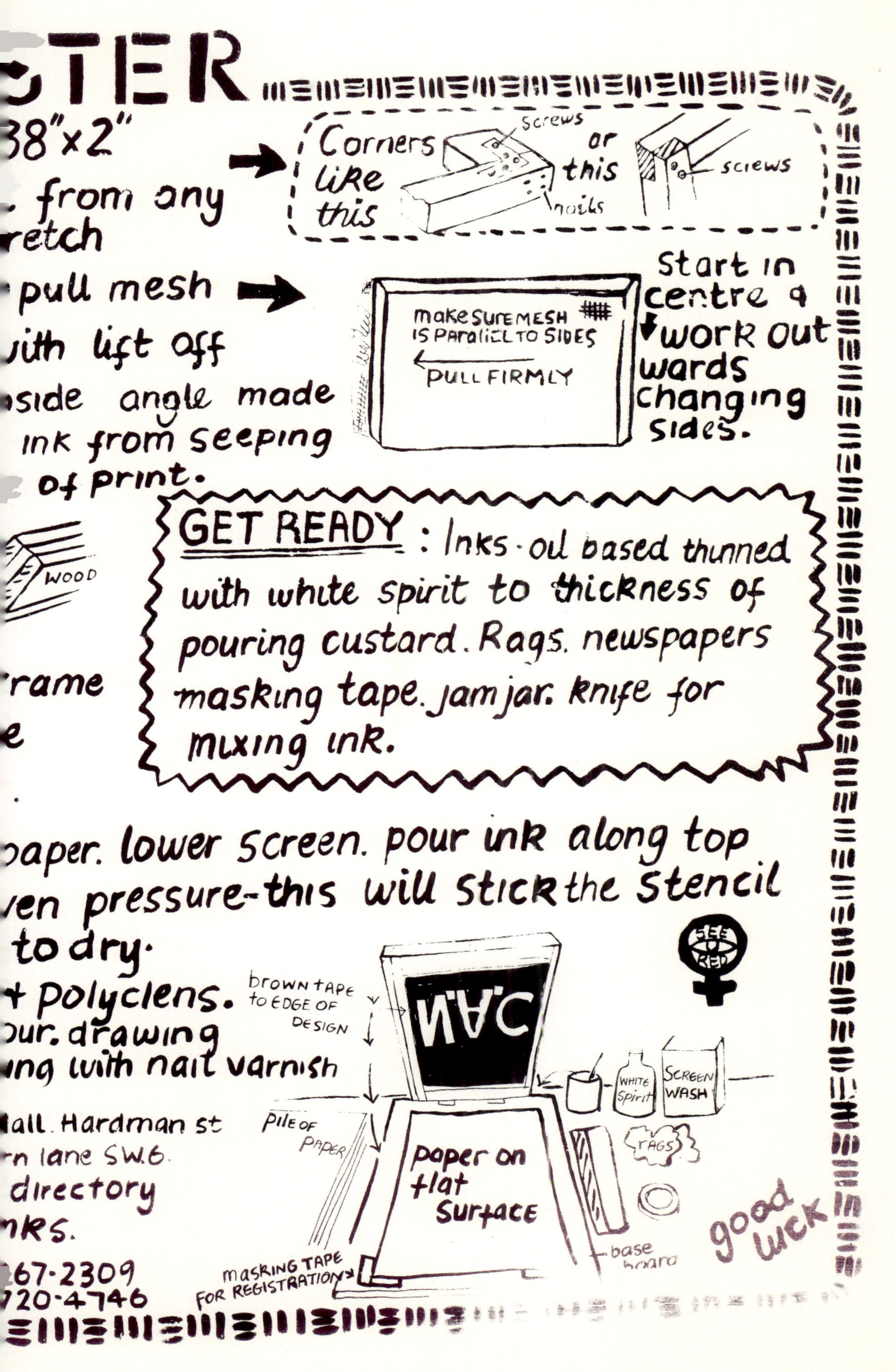

GET READY : Inks. oil based thinned with white spirit to thickness of pouring custard. Rags. newspapers masking tape. jam jar. knife for mixing ink.

paper. lower screen. pour ink along top
ven pressure- this will stick the stencil
to dry.
+ Polyclens.
our. drawing
ing with nail varnish

all. Hardman st
n lane S.W.6.
directory
nks.

67-2309
720-4746

The Ideal Couple
The only one of our posters entirely composed
of an illustration by an artist not part of the
group: Gay Preston.

Print Your Own Poster (*previous page*)
A do-it-yourself poster with simple instructions
showing how with the minimum of equipment
it is relatively easy to produce a run of posters.
Bought by youth clubs, schools, women's
groups, among others.

See Red Calendar 1977 (*over the page*)
April features the lyrics 'I've done what they
told me I've done what they said. Worked at
my job at home and in bed. But it's not too late
for my life to be fine now I know what's been
messing me up all the time.' May shows
Sojourner Truth, with the quote: 'I think that
twixt the black folk of the south and the
women of the north all talkin about rights that
the white men gonna give, gonna be in a pretty
fix soon. The man over there says women need
to be helped into carriages and lifted over
ditches and have the best places everywhere.
Nobody ever helped me into carriages or over
mud puddles, or give me any best place — and
ain't I a woman? The little man in the back
there said that women can't have as much
rights as men 'cos Christ weren't a woman.
Where did your Christ come from? From God
and a woman. Man didn't have nothing to do
with him.' December shows Joseph, saying
'Three more for supper, Mary'.

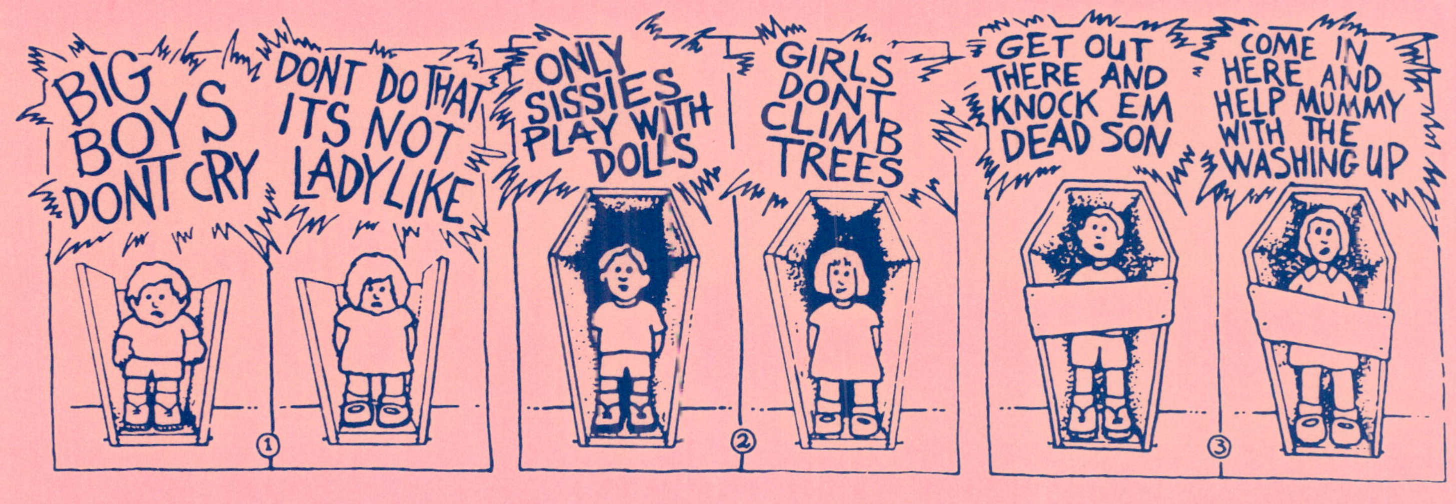

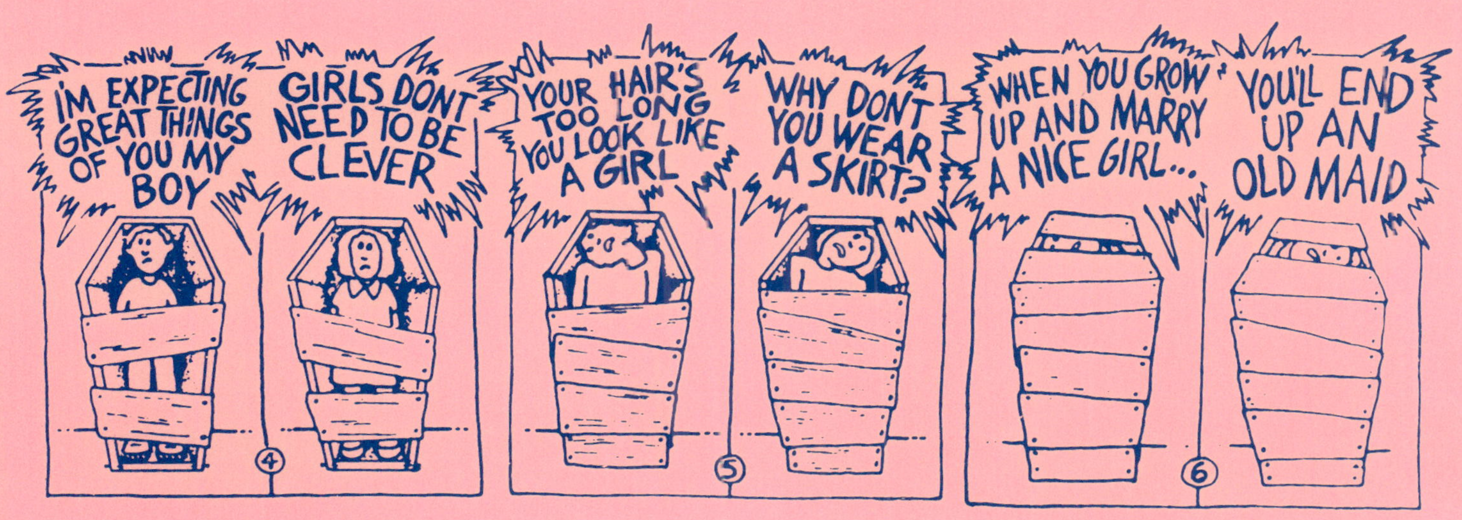

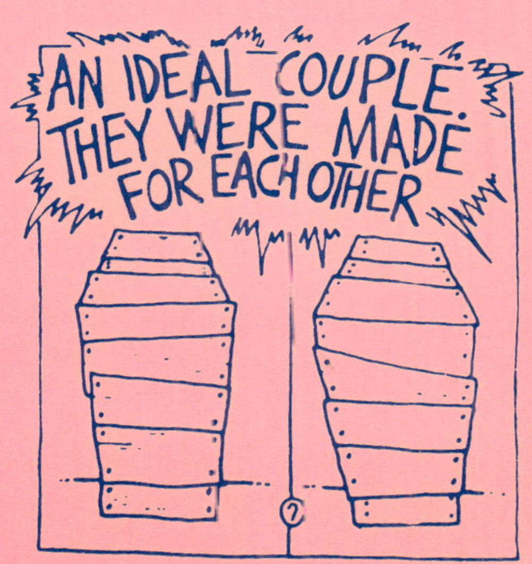

printed by See Red
designed by Guy Preston

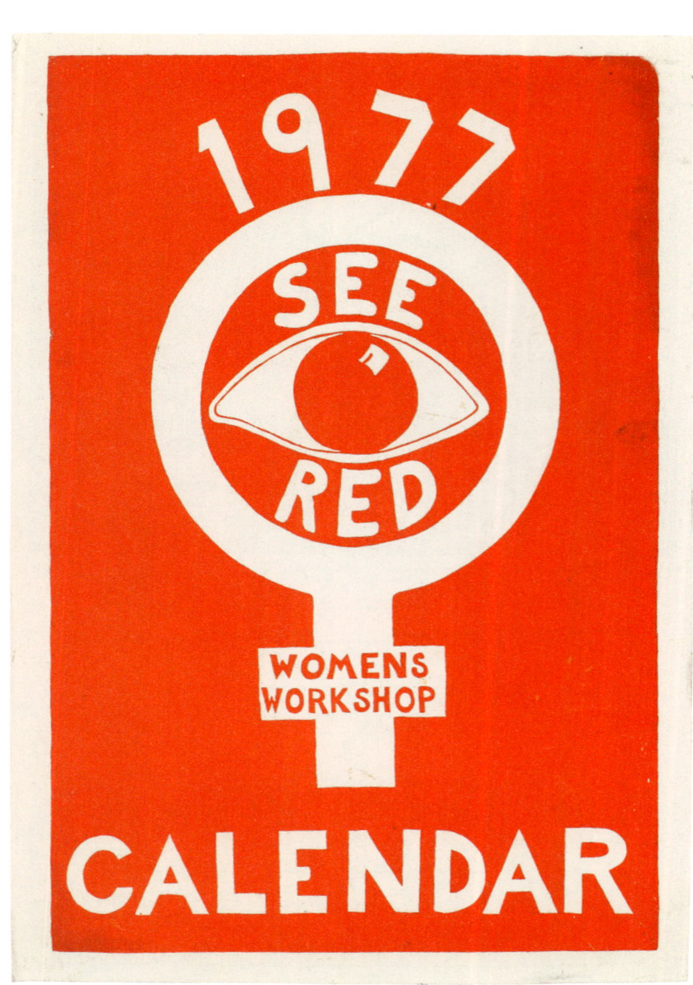

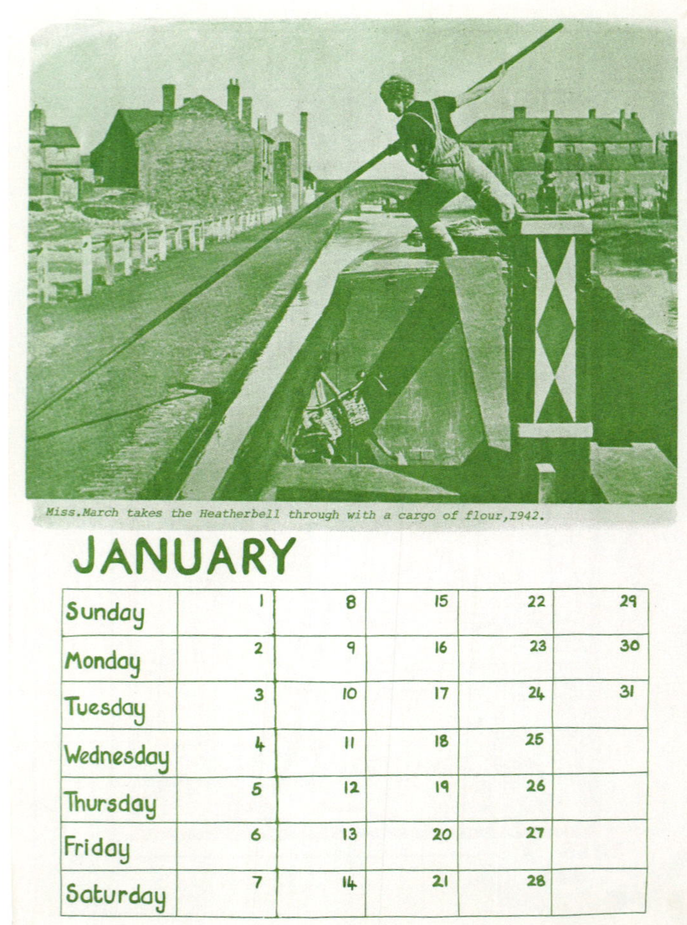

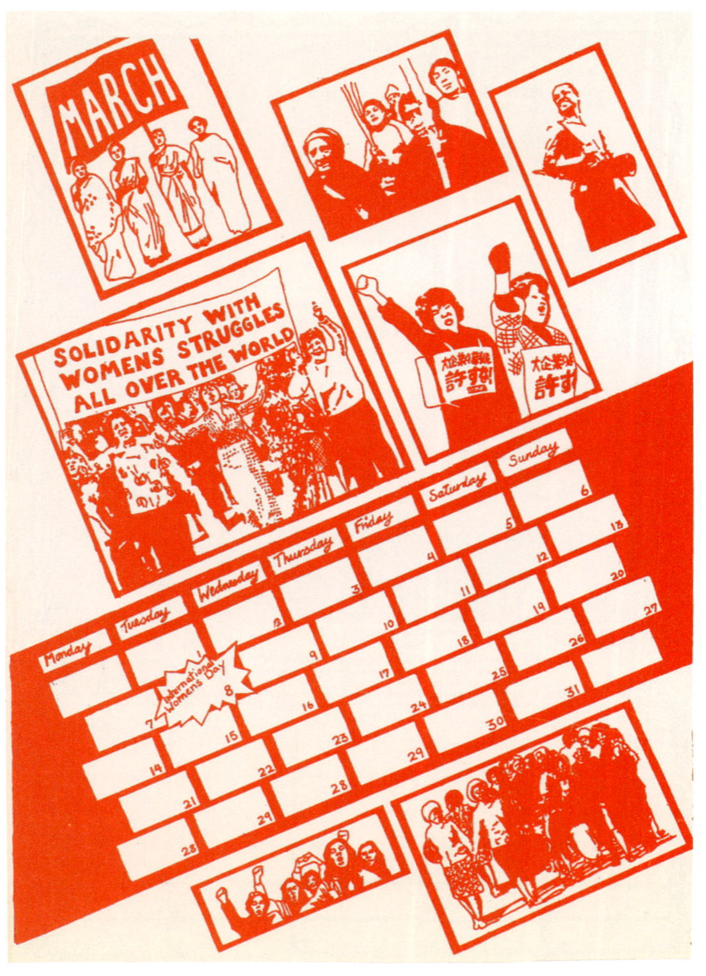

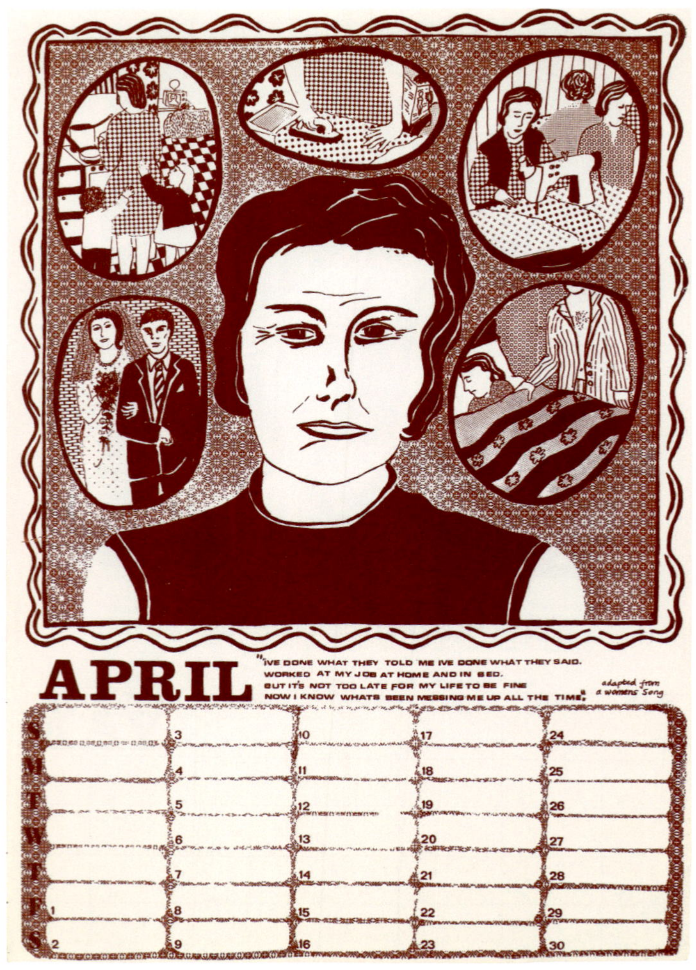

SEE RED CALENDAR, 1977 63.5 × 44.5 cm

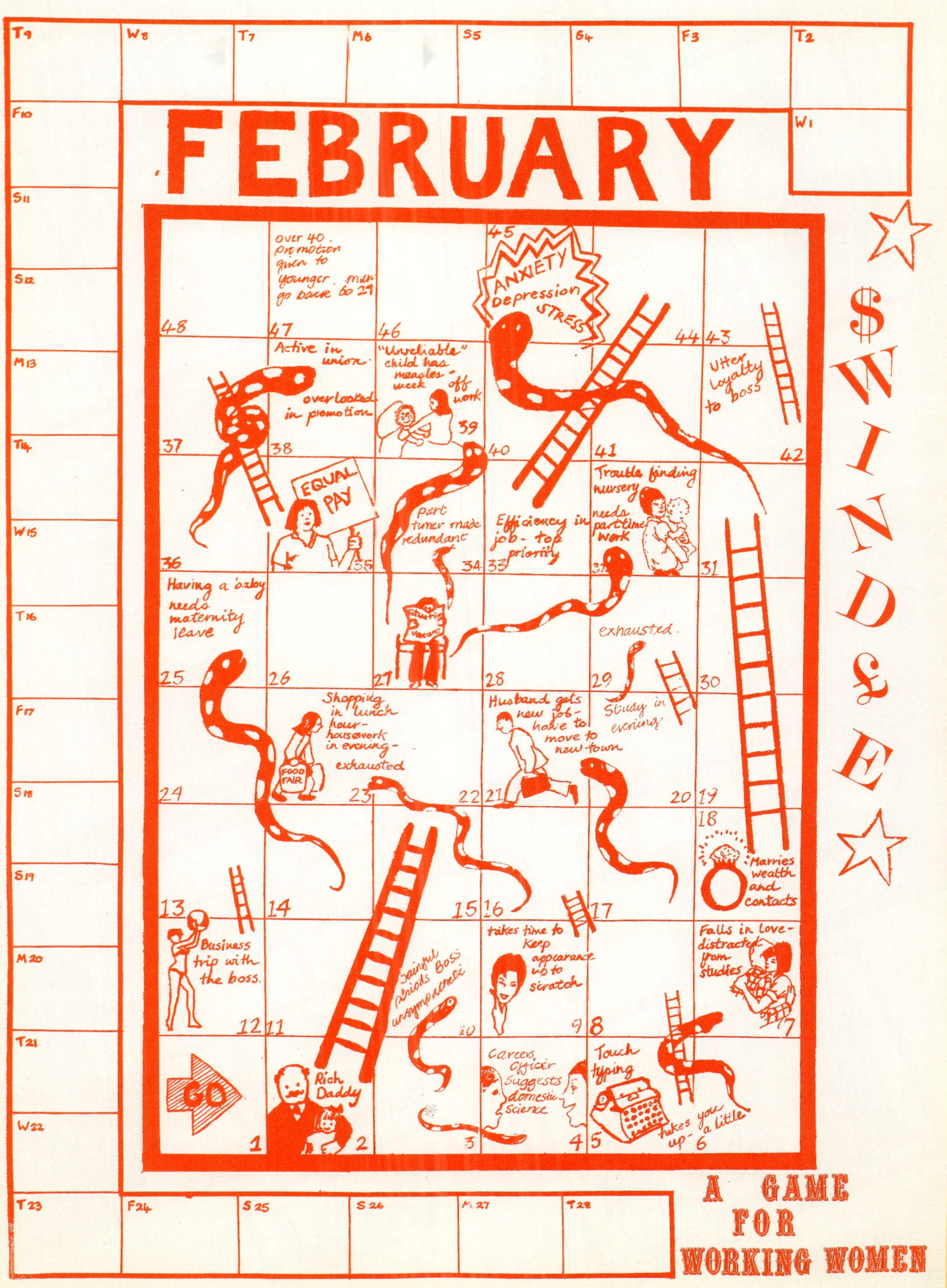

SEE RED CALENDAR, 1977 63.5 × 44.5 cm

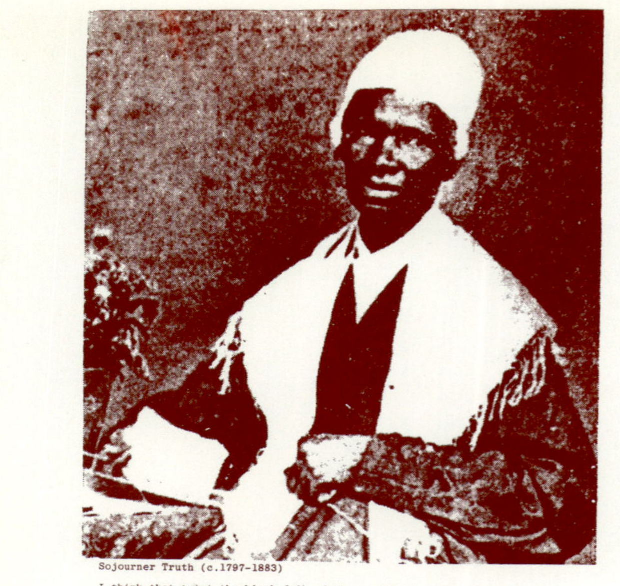

MON	TUES	WEDS	THURS	FRI	SAT	SUN
MAY						1
2	3	4	5	6	7	8
9	10	11	12	13	14	15
16	17	18	19	20	21	22
23/30	24/31	25	26	27	28	29

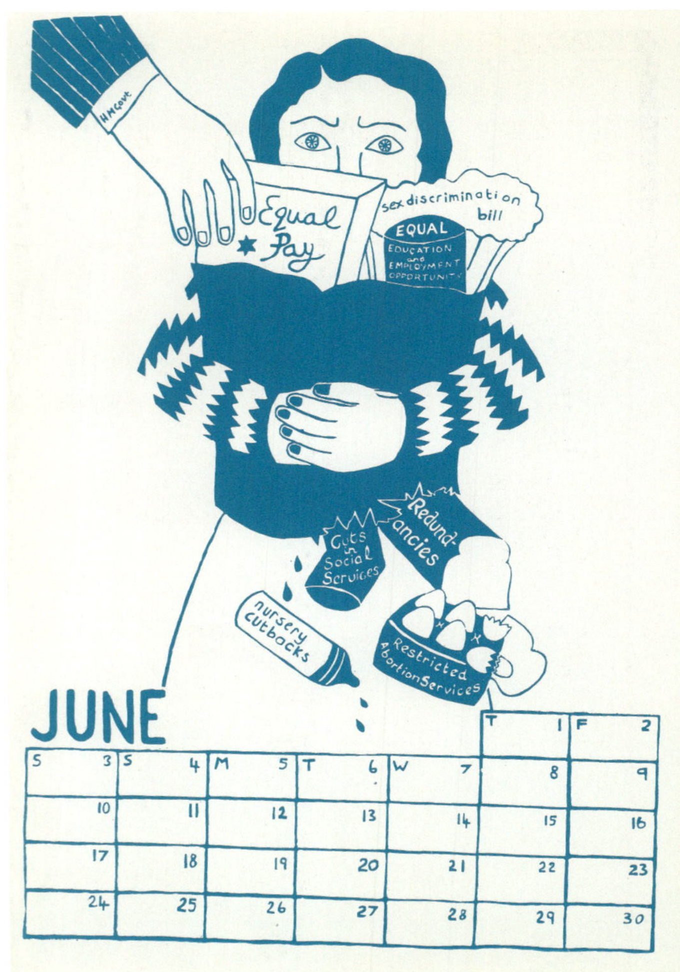

JUNE

S	S	M	T	W	T	F
					1	2
3	4	5	6	7	8	9
10	11	12	13	14	15	16
17	18	19	20	21	22	23
24	25	26	27	28	29	30

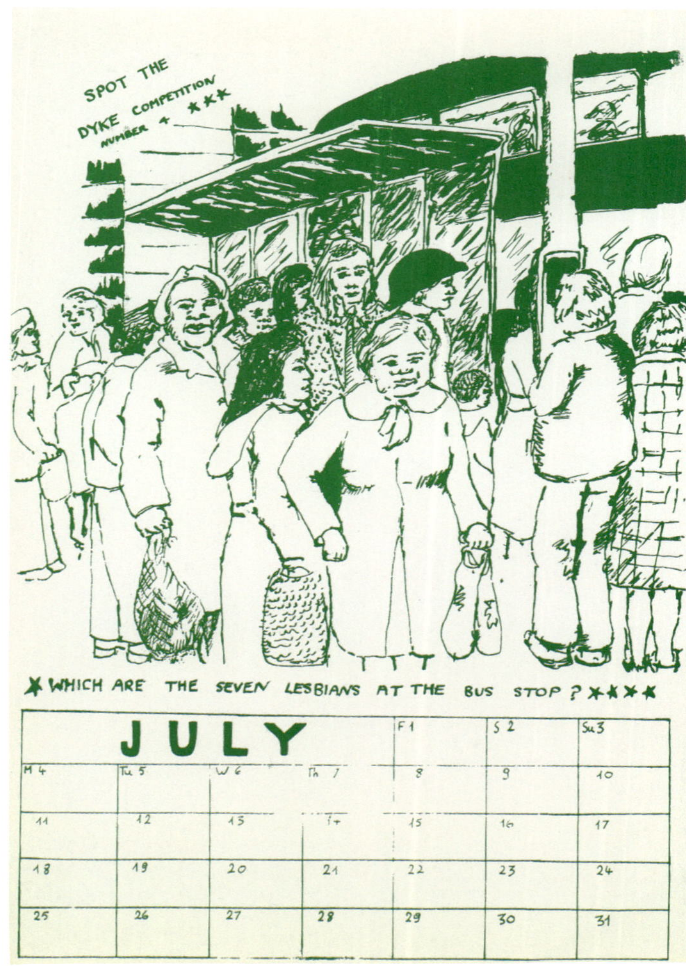

JULY

M	Tu	W	Th	F	S	Su
				1	2	3
4	5	6	7	8	9	10
11	12	13	14	15	16	17
18	19	20	21	22	23	24
25	26	27	28	29	30	31

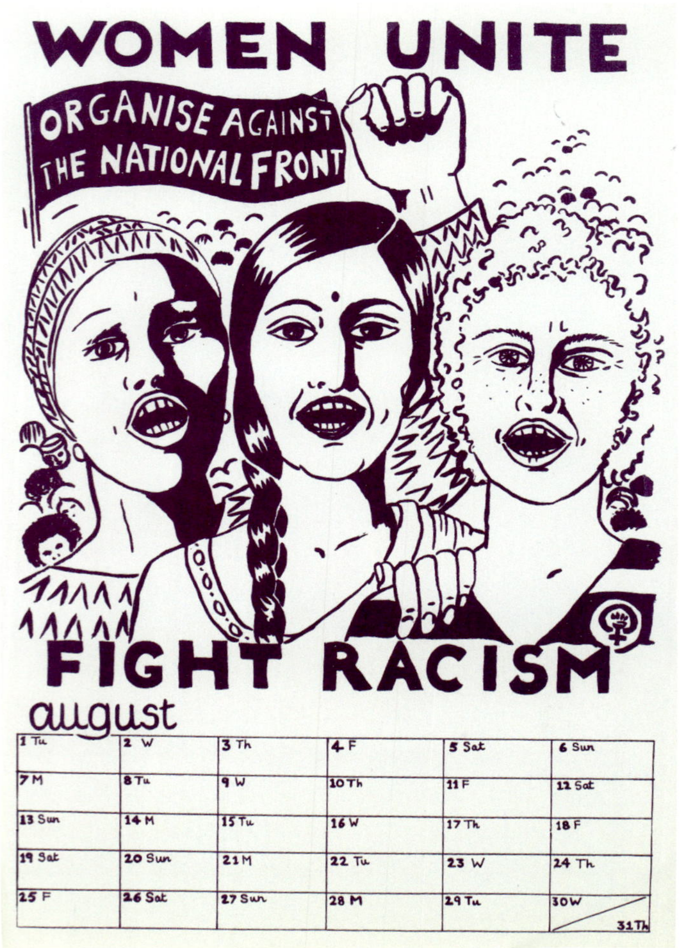

august

1 Tu	2 W	3 Th	4 F	5 Sat	6 Sun
7 M	8 Tu	9 W	10 Th	11 F	12 Sat
13 Sun	14 M	15 Tu	16 W	17 Th	18 F
19 Sat	20 Sun	21 M	22 Tu	23 W	24 Th
25 F	26 Sat	27 Sun	28 M	29 Tu	30 W
					31 Th

SEE RED CALENDAR, 1977 63.5 × 44.5 cm

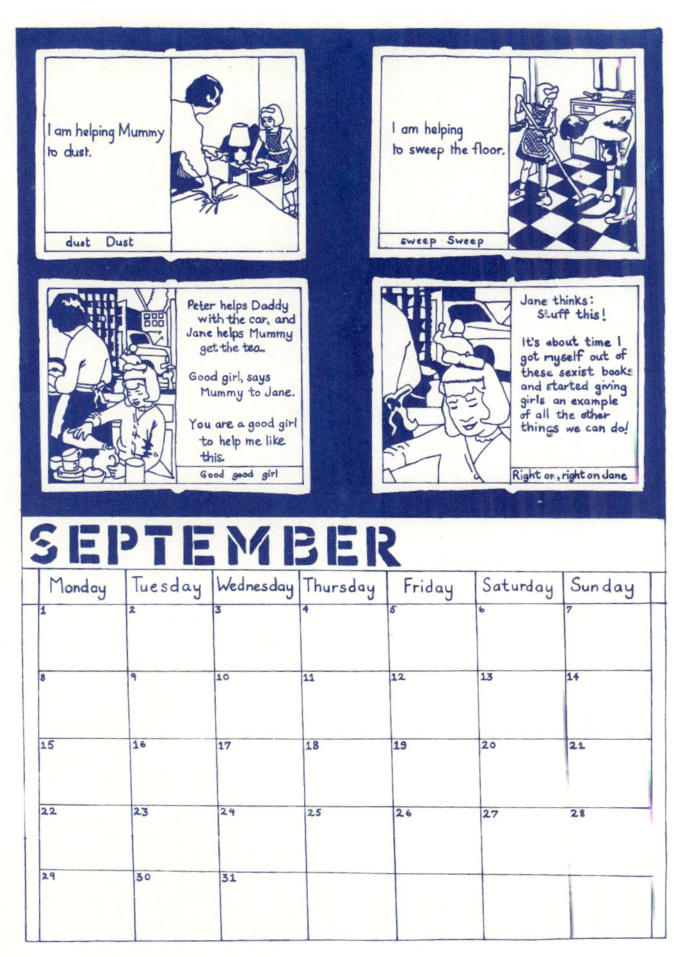

Monday	Tuesday	Wednesday	Thursday	Friday	Saturday	Sunday
1	2	3	4	5	6	7
8	9	10	11	12	13	14
15	16	17	18	19	20	21
22	23	24	25	26	27	28
29	30	31				

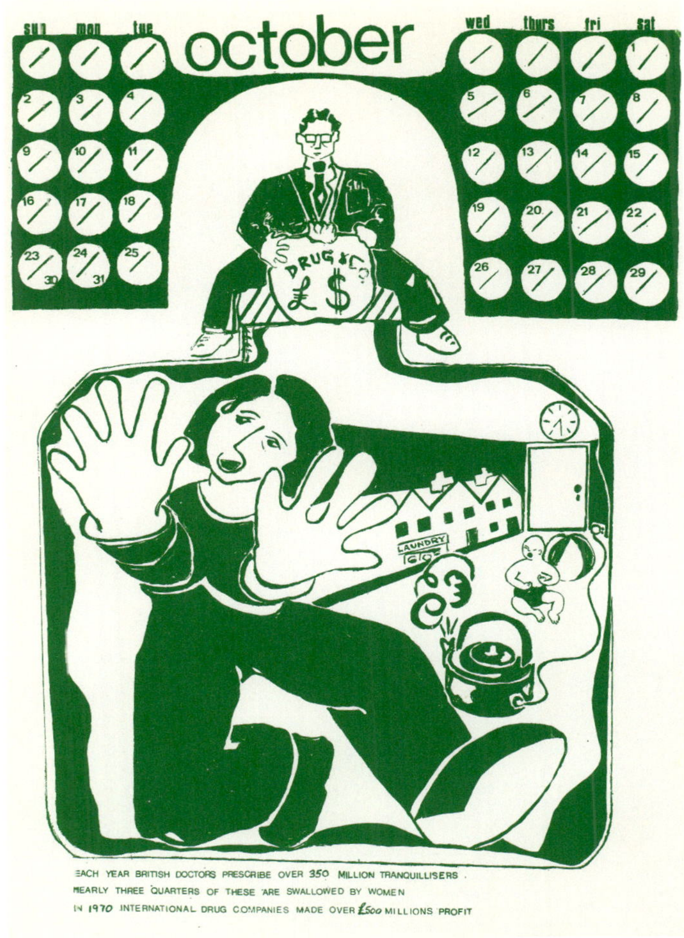

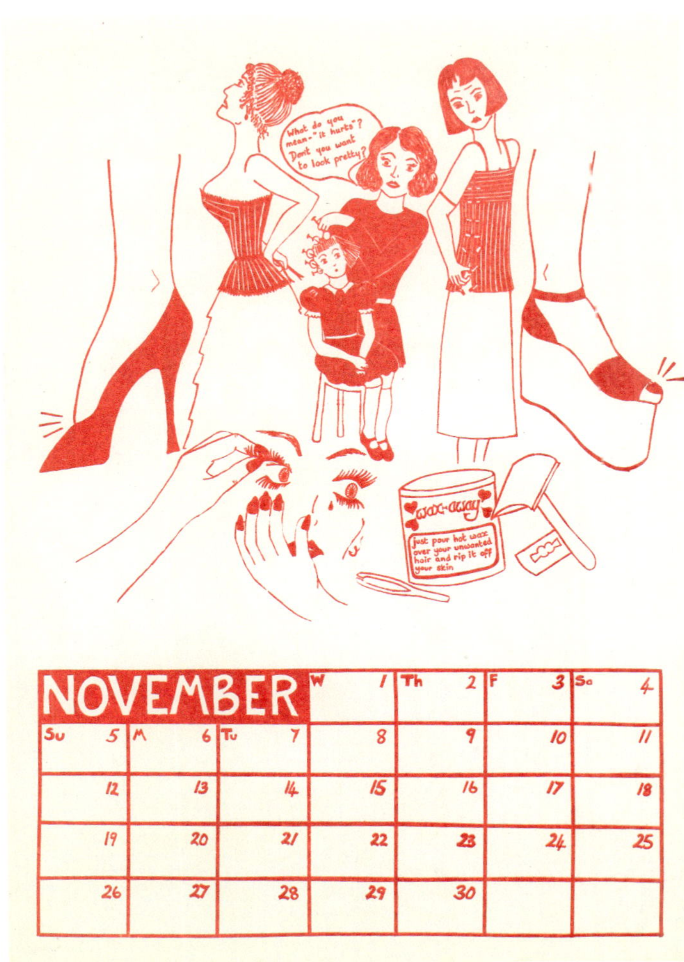

			W	1	Th	2	F	3	Sa	4
Su	5	M	6	Tu	7	8	9	10	11
12	13	14	15	16	17	18
19	20	21	22	23	24	25
26	27	28	29	30		

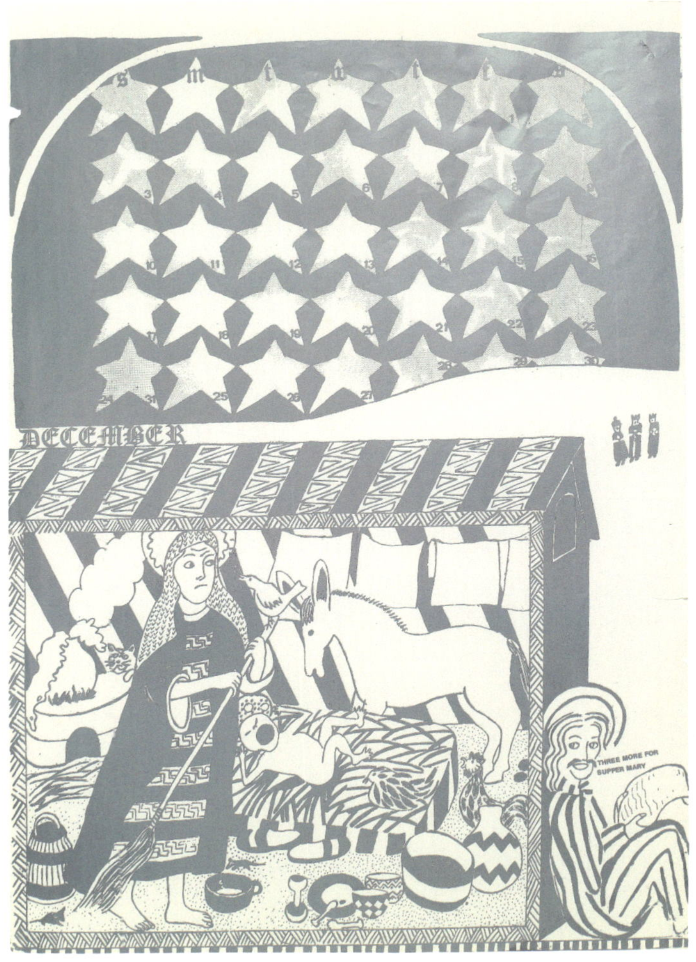

 SEE RED CALENDAR, 1977 63.5 × 44.5 cm

Take A Pill Mrs Brown
This poster picks up the issues of 'happy pills'
and big-pharma profiteering first explored in
Don't Break Down (page 54).

Sisters! Question Every Aspect Of Our Lives
(*over the page*) This poster started out as a page
in the 1977 calendar as a wordier illustration and
was then developed into a more visual design.

It showed how the media, the state,
housework and our sexual relationships, as
well as anxieties around our appearance, control
women by pitting us against each other and by
keeping us apart.

By focusing on the everyday sexism that
objectifies and oppresses women it aimed to
challenge the feelings of inadequacy that our
differences can raise.

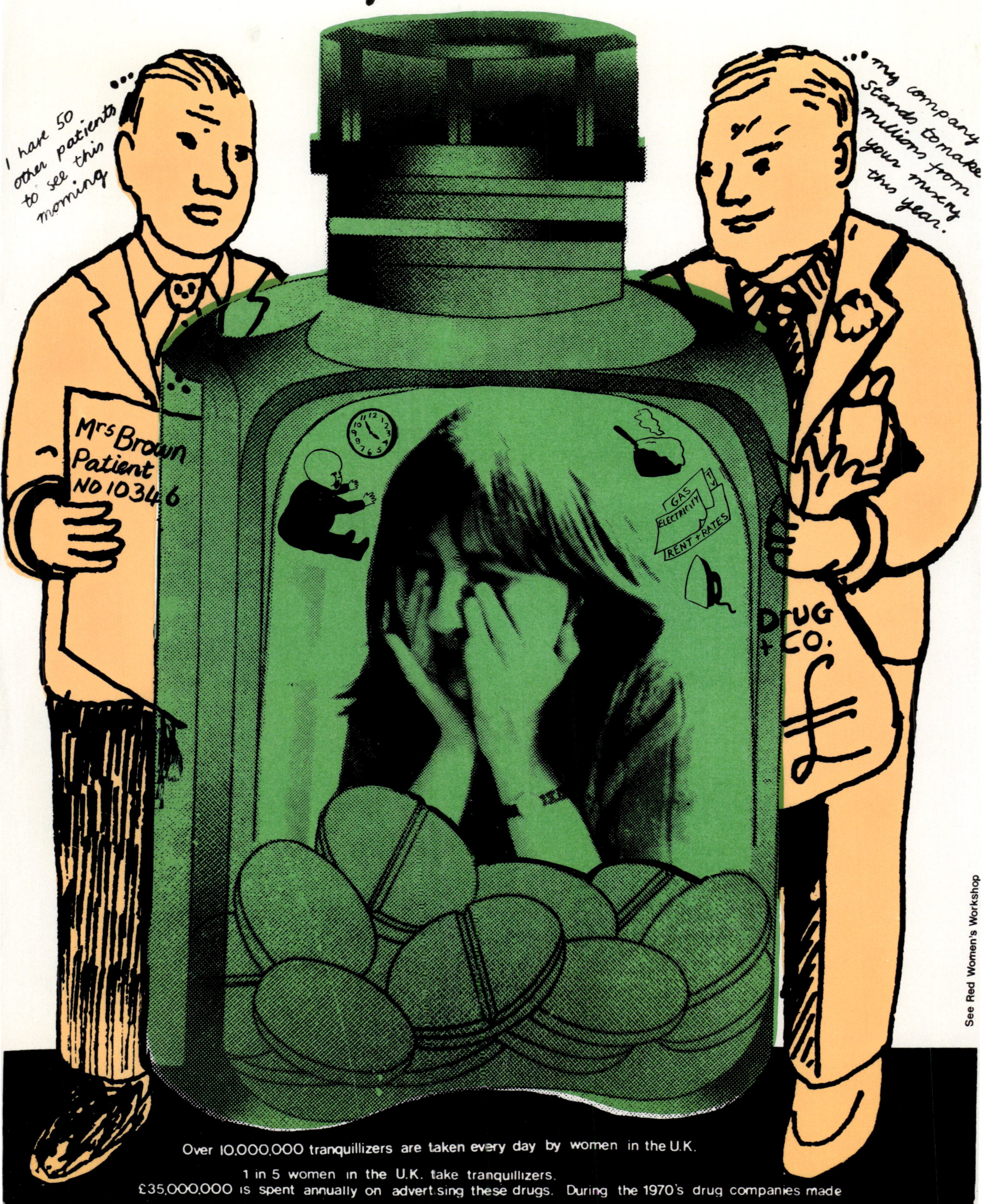
Take a pill Mrs Brown.
"...I have 50 other patients to see this morning"
"...my company stands to make millions from your misery this year."
Mrs Brown Patient NO 10346
GAS ELECTRICITY RENT + RATES
DRUG + CO. £
See Red Women's Workshop
Over 10,000,000 tranquillizers are taken every day by women in the U.K.
1 in 5 women in the U.K. take tranquillizers.
£35,000,000 is spent annually on advertising these drugs. During the 1970's drug companies made over £500,000,000 annually. Valium is the most profitable drug ever manufactured. It is addictive, stops being effective after 4 months, dulls concentration & causes dizziness, drowsiness and sometimes aggression. Doctors too easily prescribe them to patients whose problems they don't have time to deal with. Ask your doctor exactly what you are being prescribed.
DON'T LET THEM KEEP US BOTTLED UP.

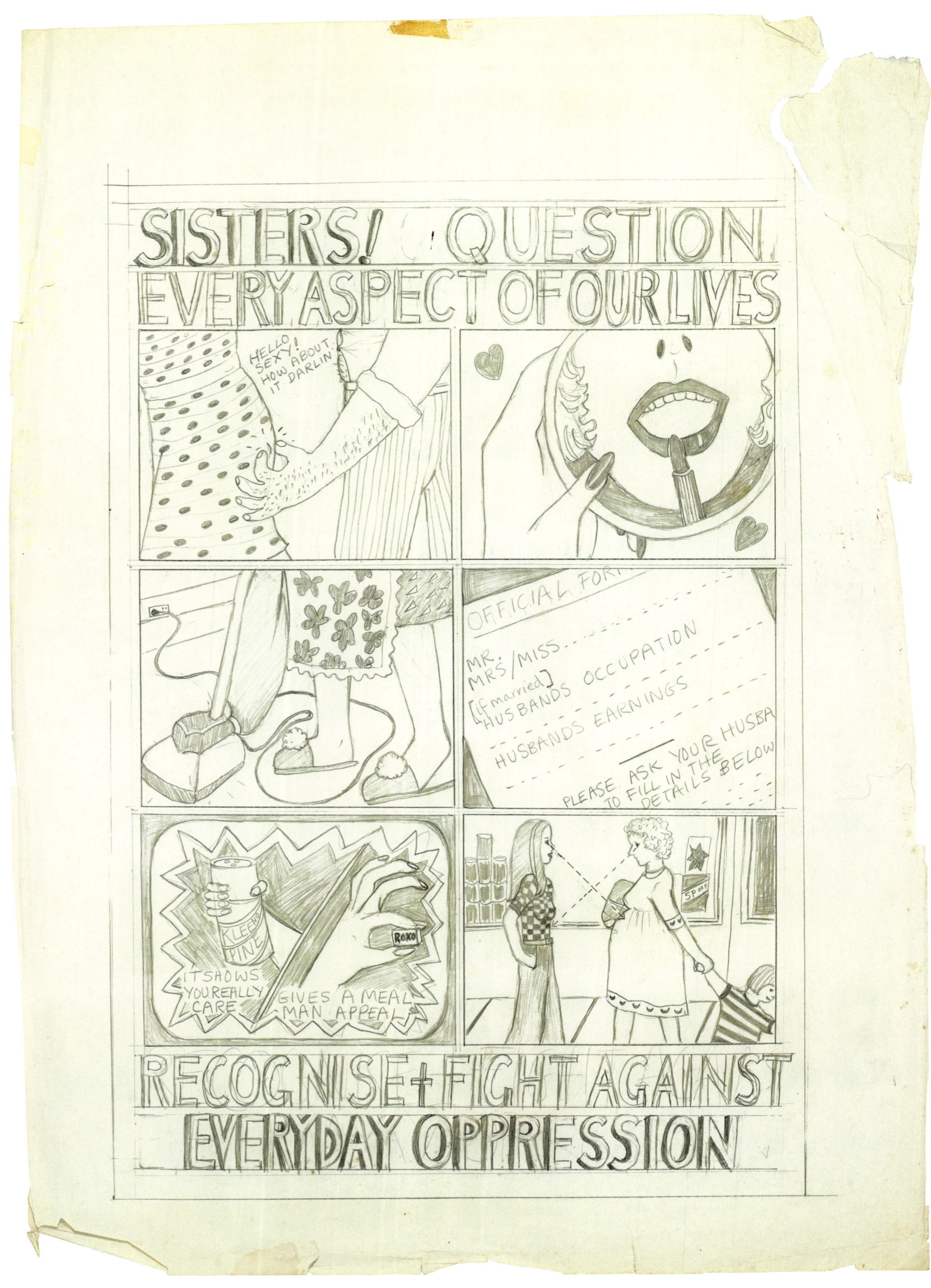

SISTERS! QUESTION EVERY ASPECT OF OUR LIVES, 1977 64 × 45 cm
Above: Preparatory sketch 78.5 × 57 cm

SISTERS! QUESTION EVERY ASPECT OF OUR LIVES

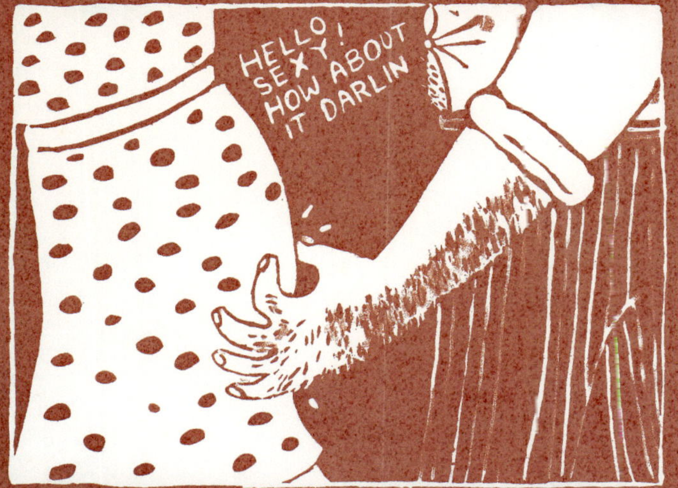

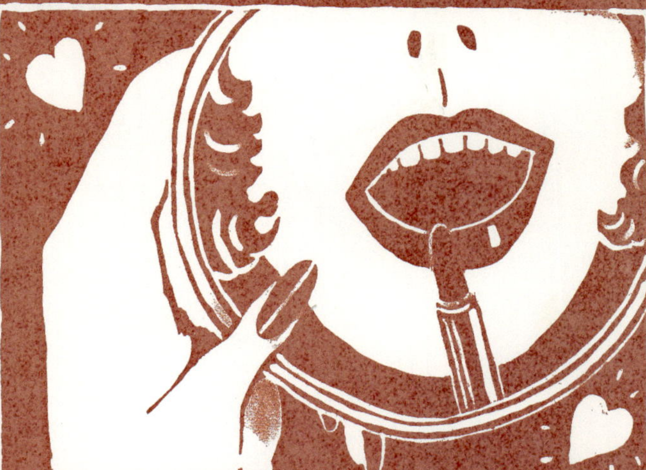

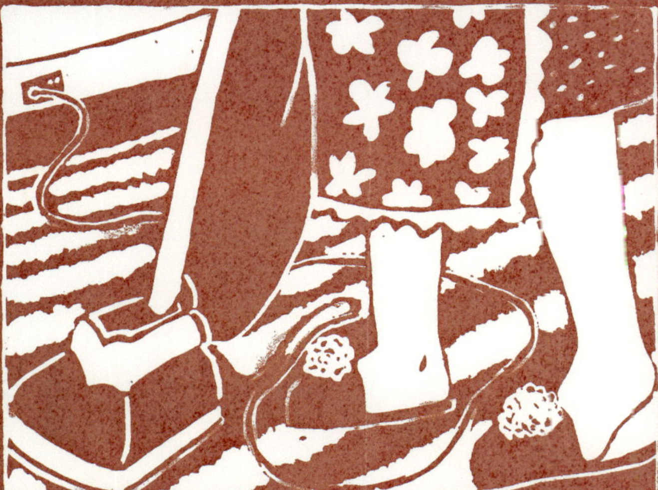

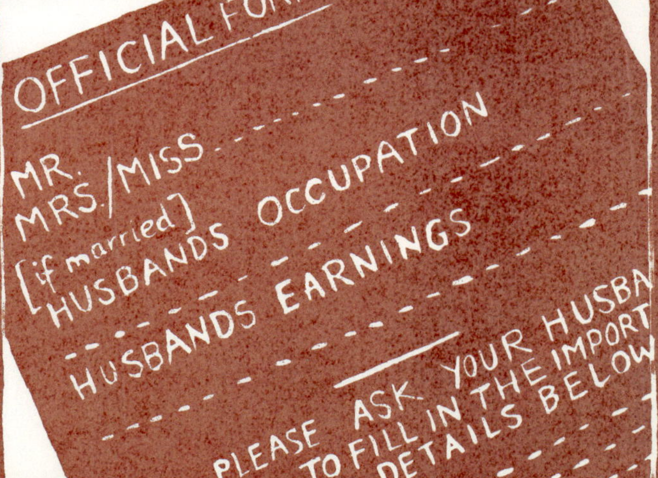
OFFICIAL FORM

MR.
MRS/MISS
[if married]
HUSBANDS OCCUPATION

HUSBANDS EARNINGS

PLEASE ASK YOUR HUSBAND
TO FILL IN THE IMPORTANT
DETAILS BELOW

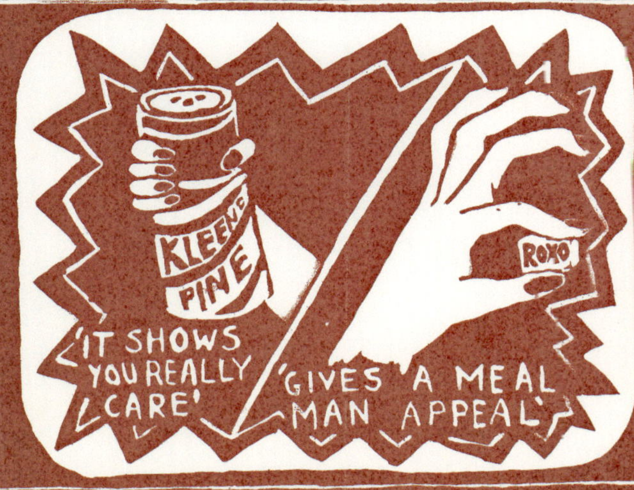

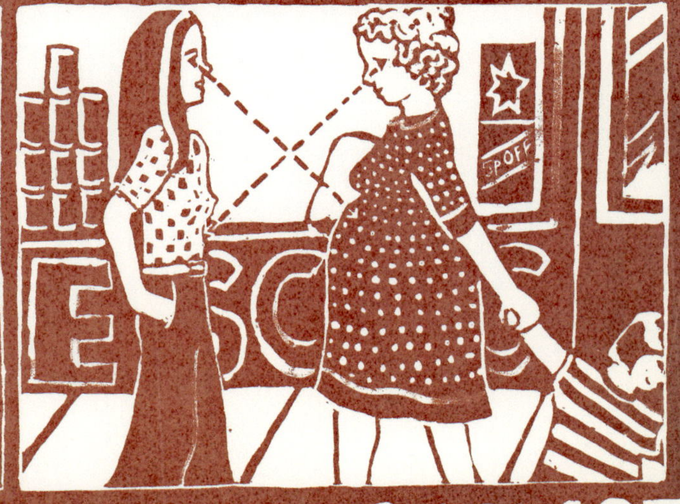

RECOGNISE + FIGHT AGAINST EVERYDAY OPPRESSION

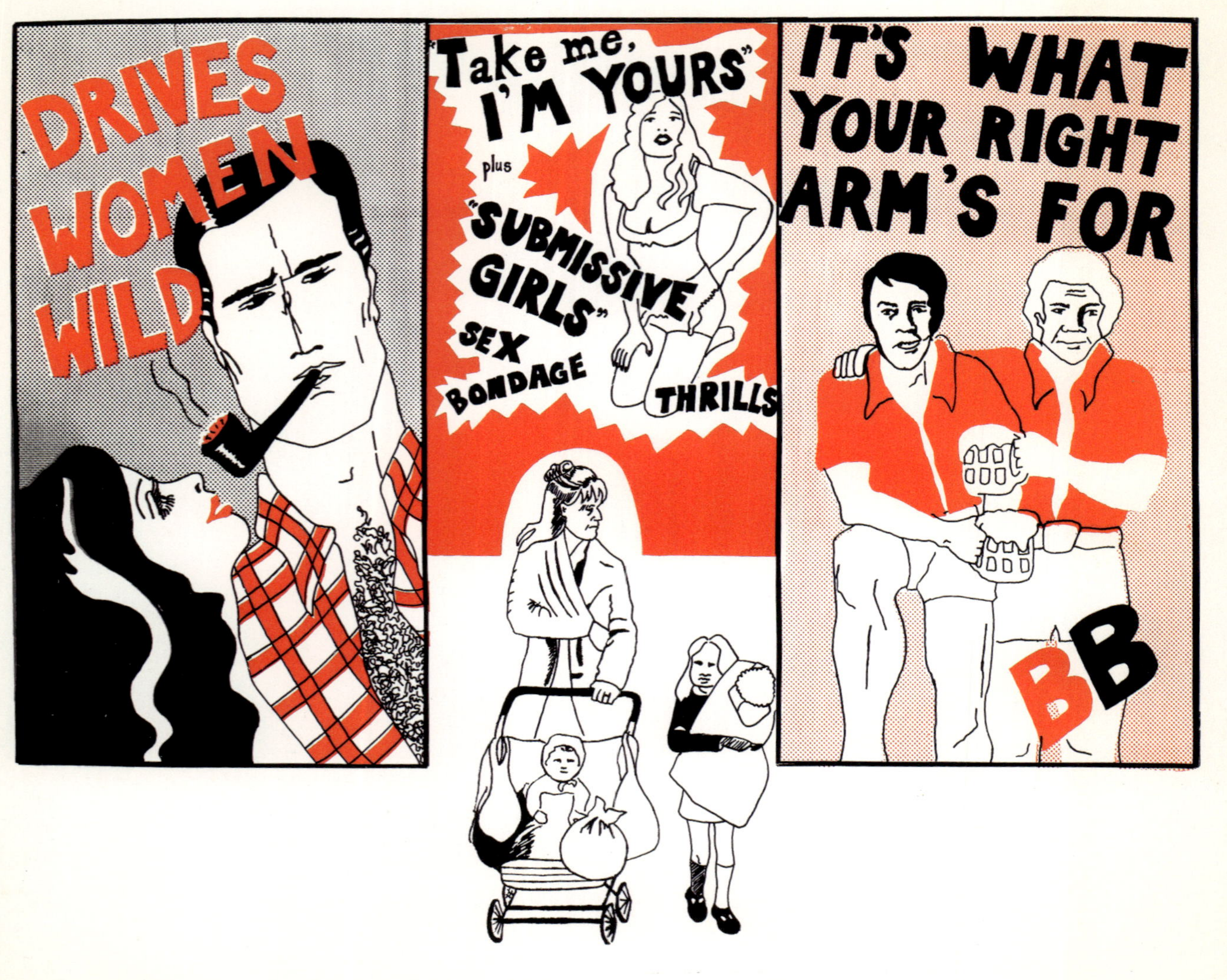

It's What Your Right Arm's For

This was an early attempt at describing the effects of the media, and its promotion of macho culture, on women. This poster was seen to be depressing and passive, showing a negative image of women and was discontinued as the Women's Liberation movement was focussing more on positive action: organisations such as Women's Aid were setting up refuges, 'Reclaim the night' was demonstrating around women's right to safety on the streets, self-defence classes for women were set up and positive action was acknowledged as the way forward.

Silver Jubilee (*facing page*)

A small poster printed for flyposting: the Queen's Silver Jubilee was promoted as a cause for national celebration and a huge amount of public money was spent on it. We used current statistics for homelessness and education to point out that whilst she could afford to celebrate her Jubilee, we couldn't.

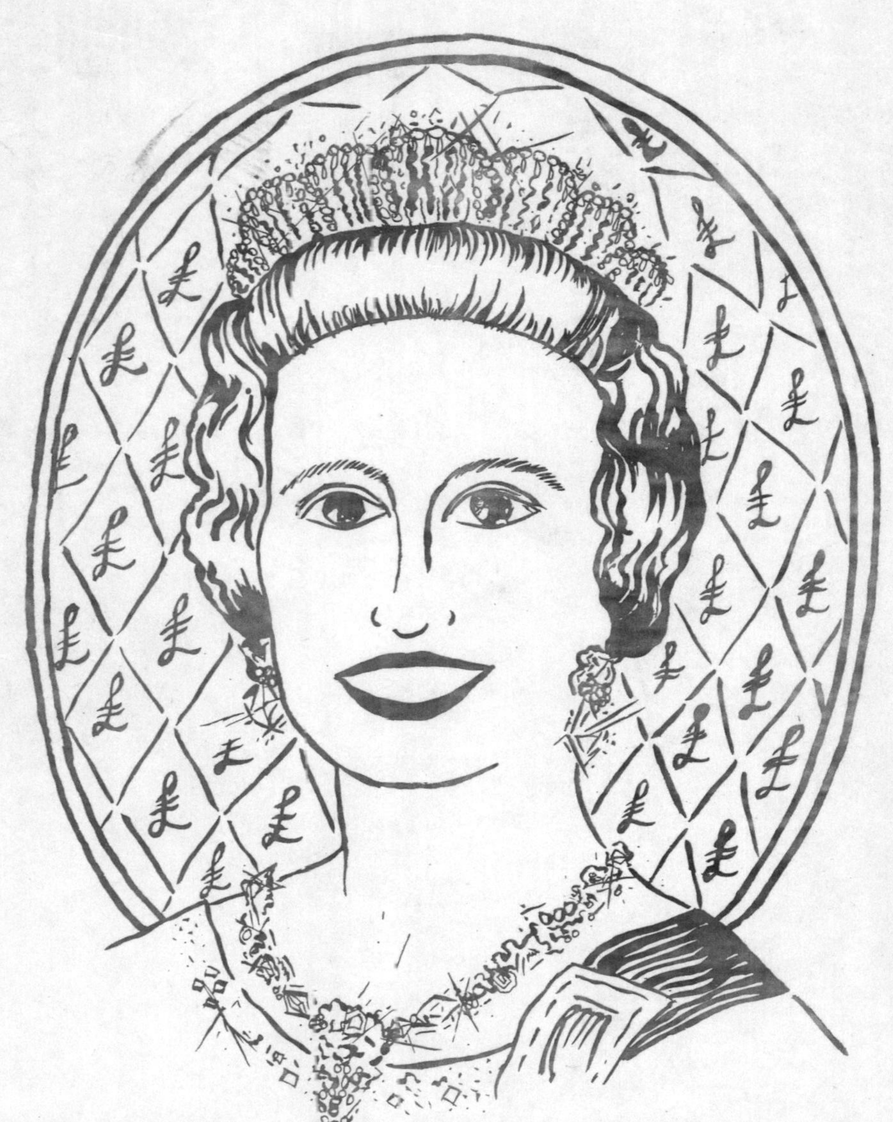

 SILVER JUBILEE, 1977 69.5 × 54 cm

SOCIALIST FEMINIST NATIONAL CONFERENCE

MARCH 24th + 25th

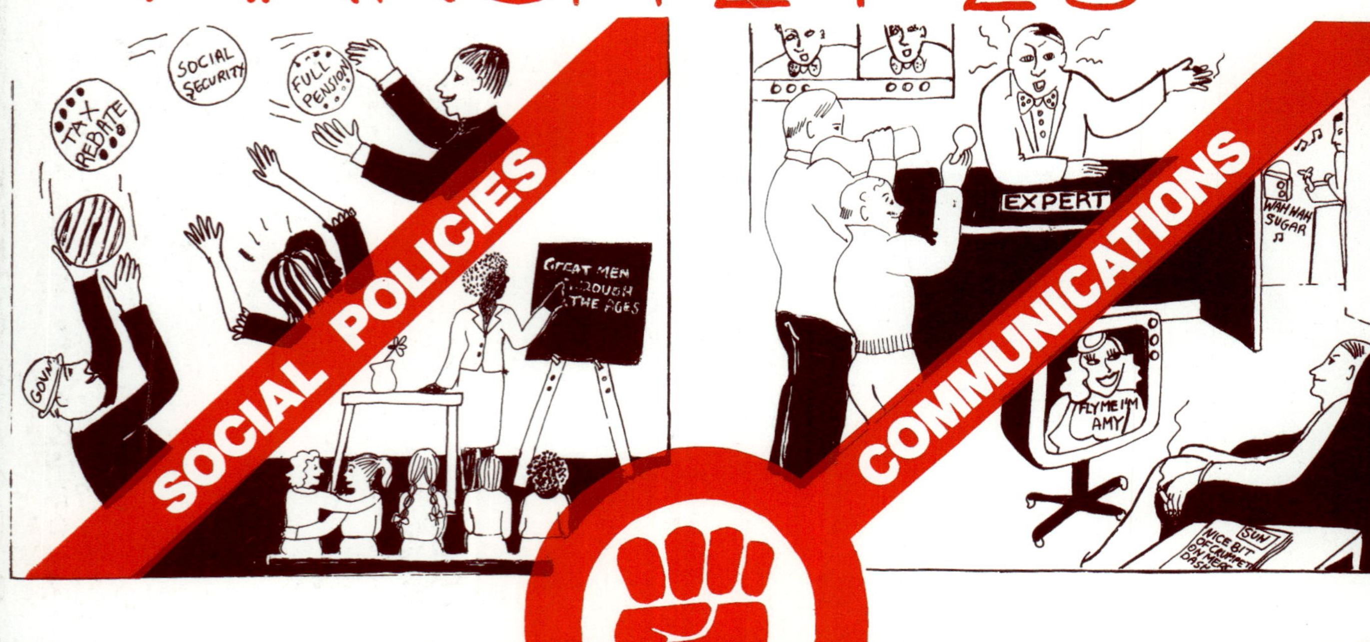

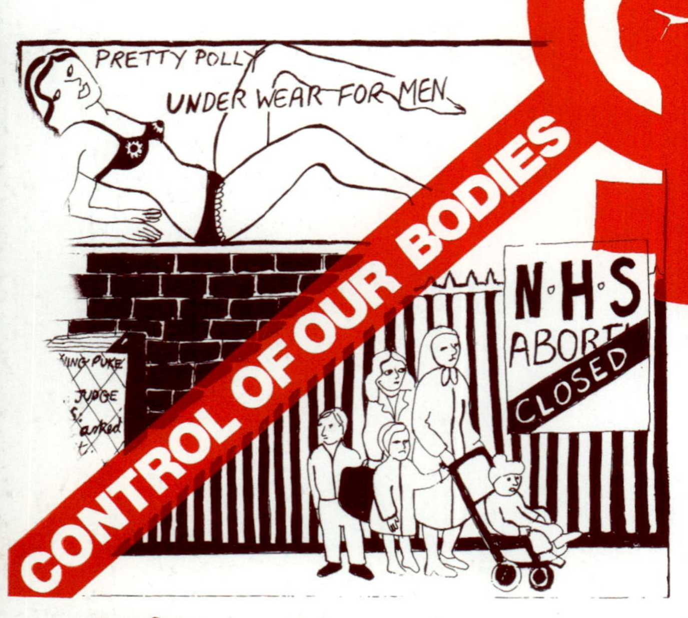

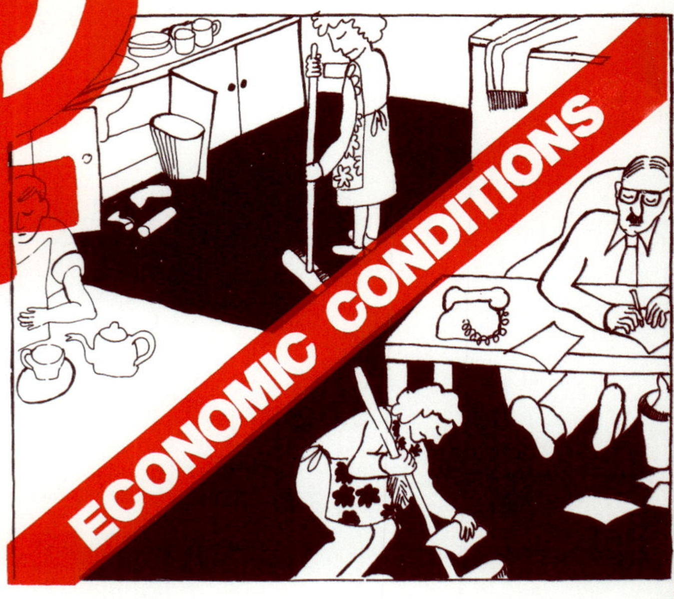

City University, St. John St.
ndon e.c.1, ⊖ Angel, creche

sfor papers: 27, Villa Rd,
London, s.w.8

address for registering: 39, Parkholme Rd
London, e.8

BLACK INFORMATION UNIT

The Hut,
50 St. Stephens Avenue,
tel: 743-7893   W. 12.

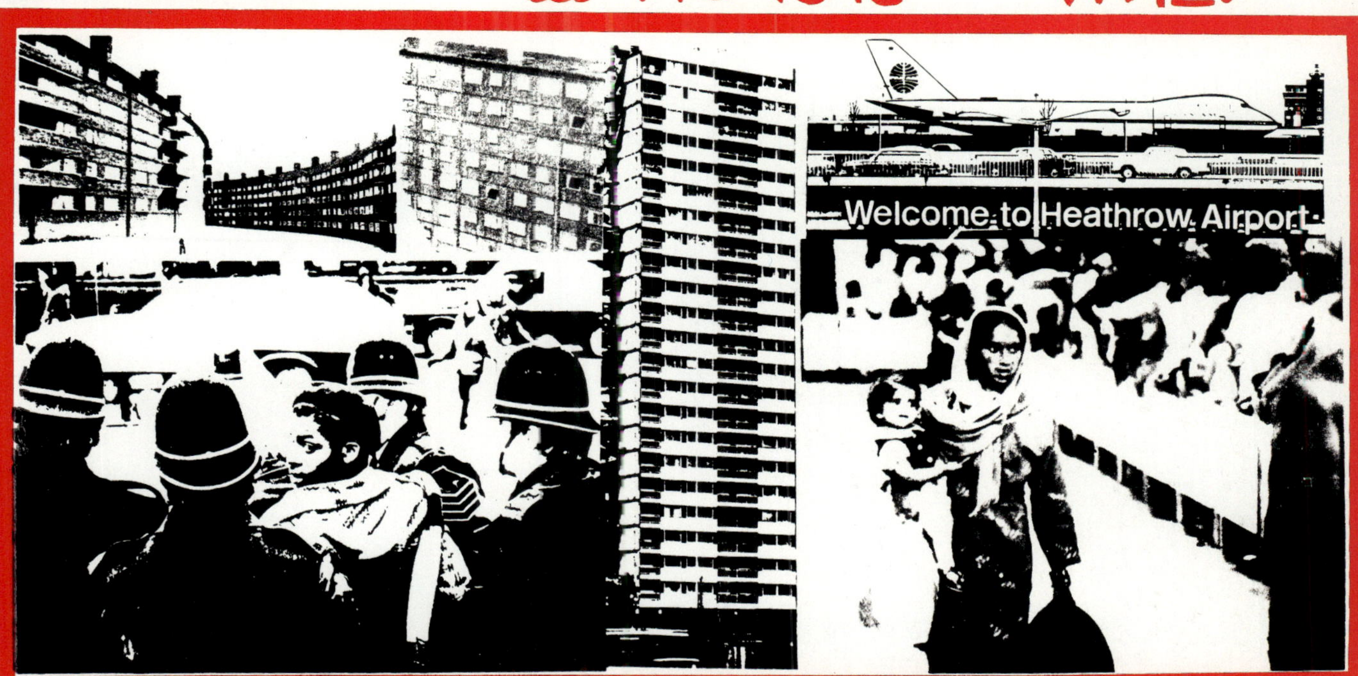

FREE INFORMATION AND ADVICE ON:

Immigration and Nationality
Police and Arrests
Single Homeless
Education etc.

OPEN: Monday, Friday, Saturdays : 10 - 1 pm
Wednesday: ALL DAY [10 - 8 pm]

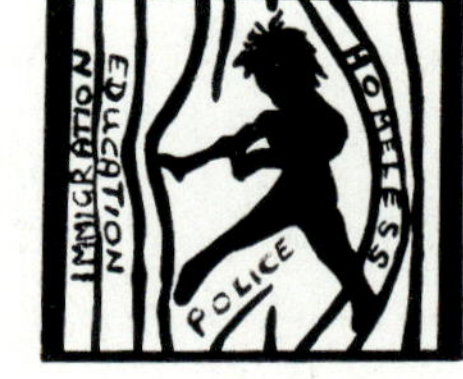

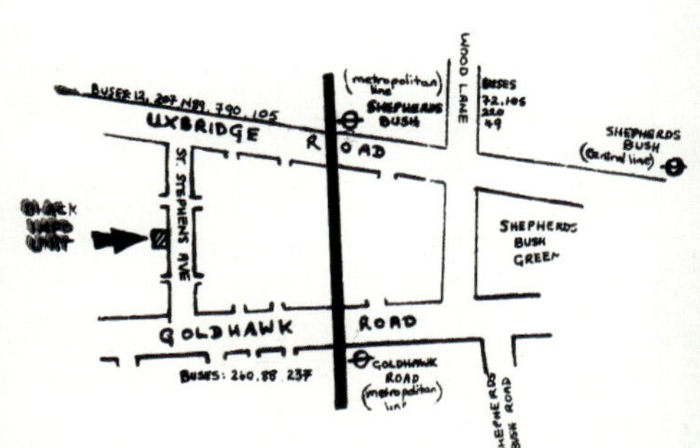

SPECIAL ADVICE SESSIONS

HOUSING . . . . WEDS 2 - 8
IMMIGRATION . . . . MON 10 - 1
. . . . WEDS 6 - 8

No Appointments Necessary

**Organise Against The National Front/
Don't Let Racism Divide Us** (*and next page*)
A hand-drawn version had been made for
the 1976 calendar and we went on to sell it
in a new form as a separate poster. Later, we
saw a photo by Syd Shelton taken at the 1977
Lewisham demonstration against the National
Front and changed the design to use this
image — it seemed the most active and relevant
illustration of our ideas. We wanted to show
that women were fully involved in these
protests and campaigns.

This process is typical of the way that we
used (with permission) the work of other
photographers, writers and poets in our posters
(e.g. Pat Mainardi, Nefertiti Gayle, Gay Preston)
as well as the way we adapted our work as we
went along.

In June 1982, the workshop was broken
into, with the National Front logo scrawled
onto the wall near the door (see page 25).

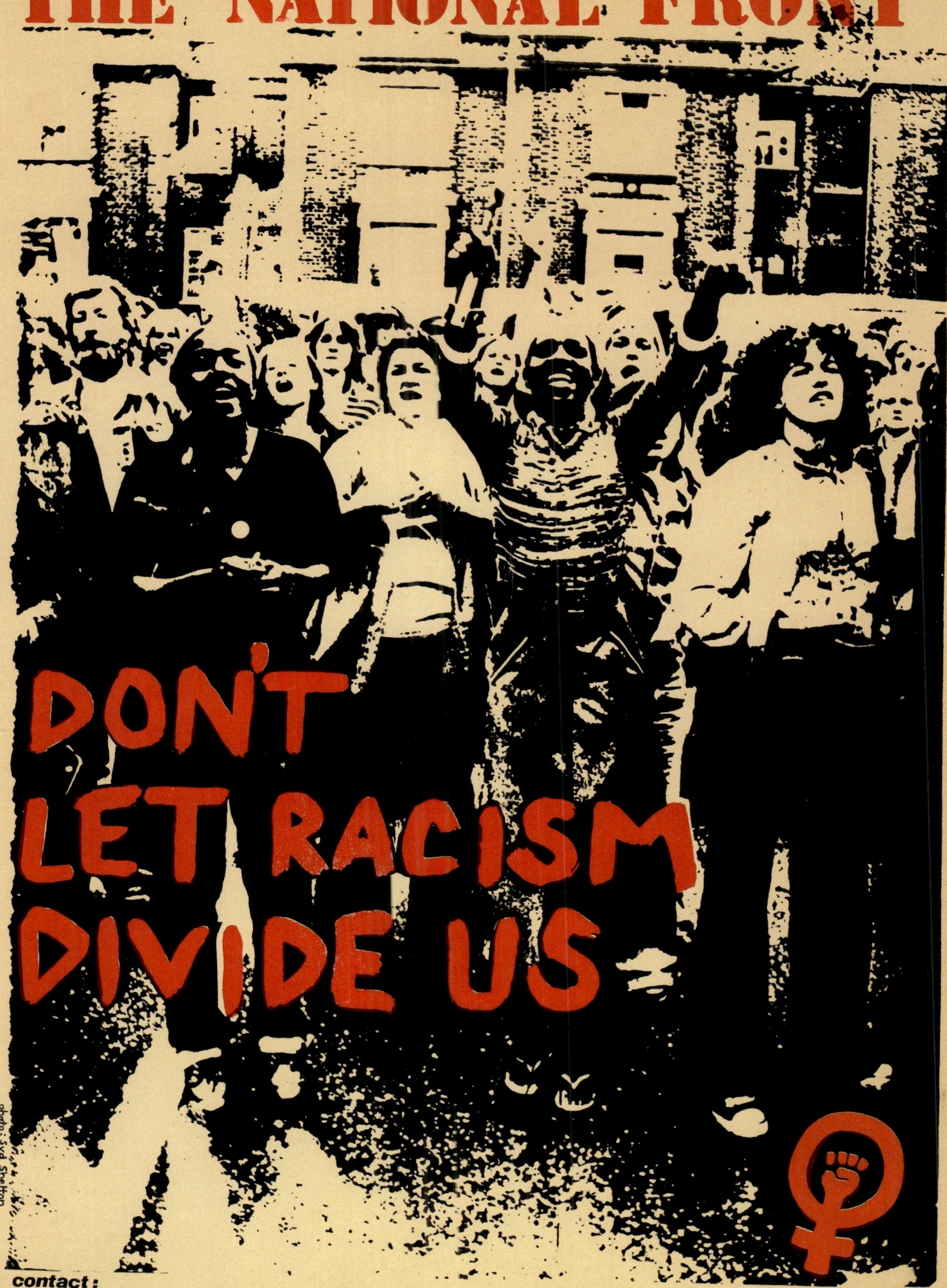

ORGANISE AGAINST THE NATIONAL FRONT
DON'T LET RACISM DIVIDE US
photo: Syd Shelton
contact:

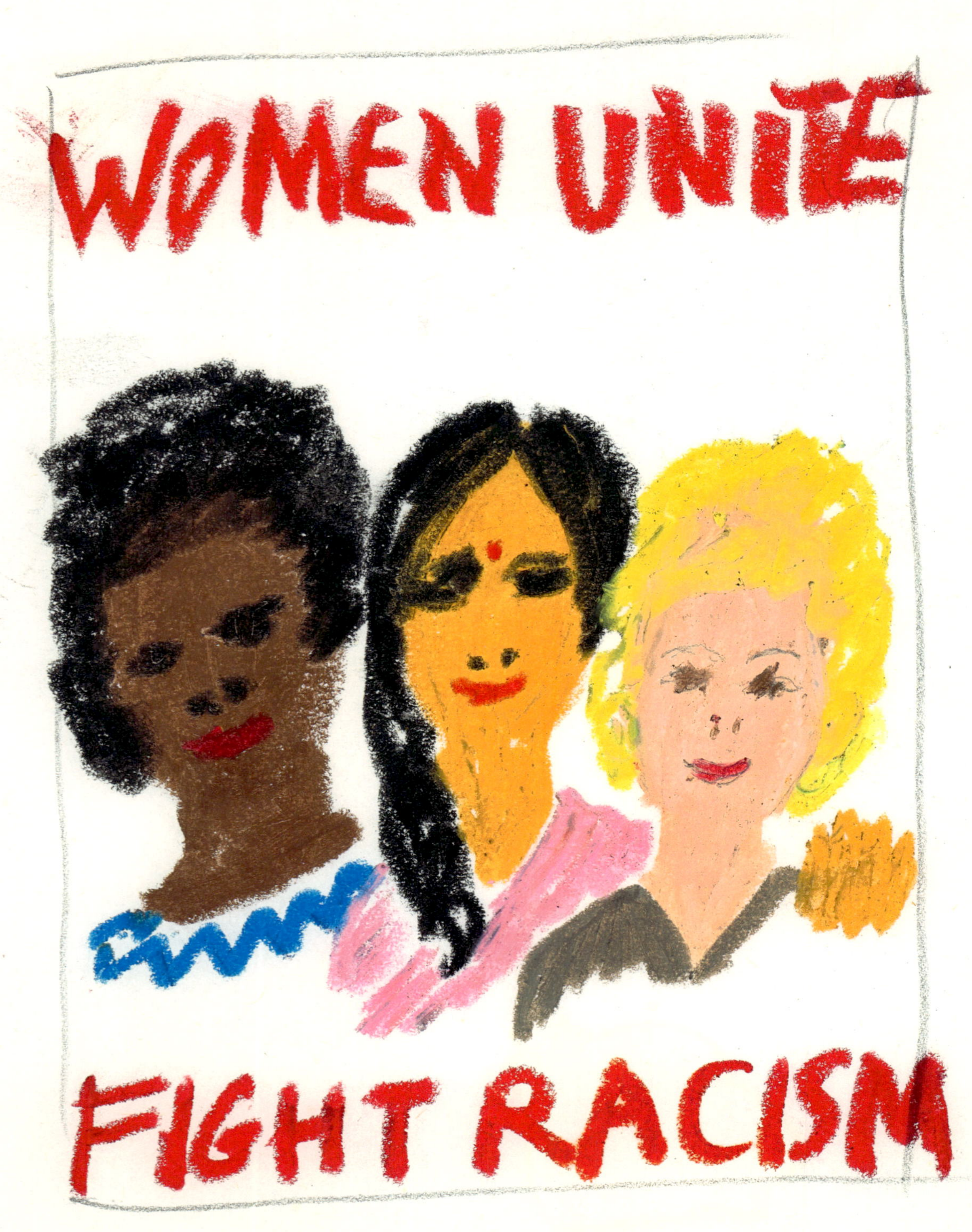

DON'T LET RACISM DIVIDE US, 1978 65 × 45 cm
Above: Preparatory sketch

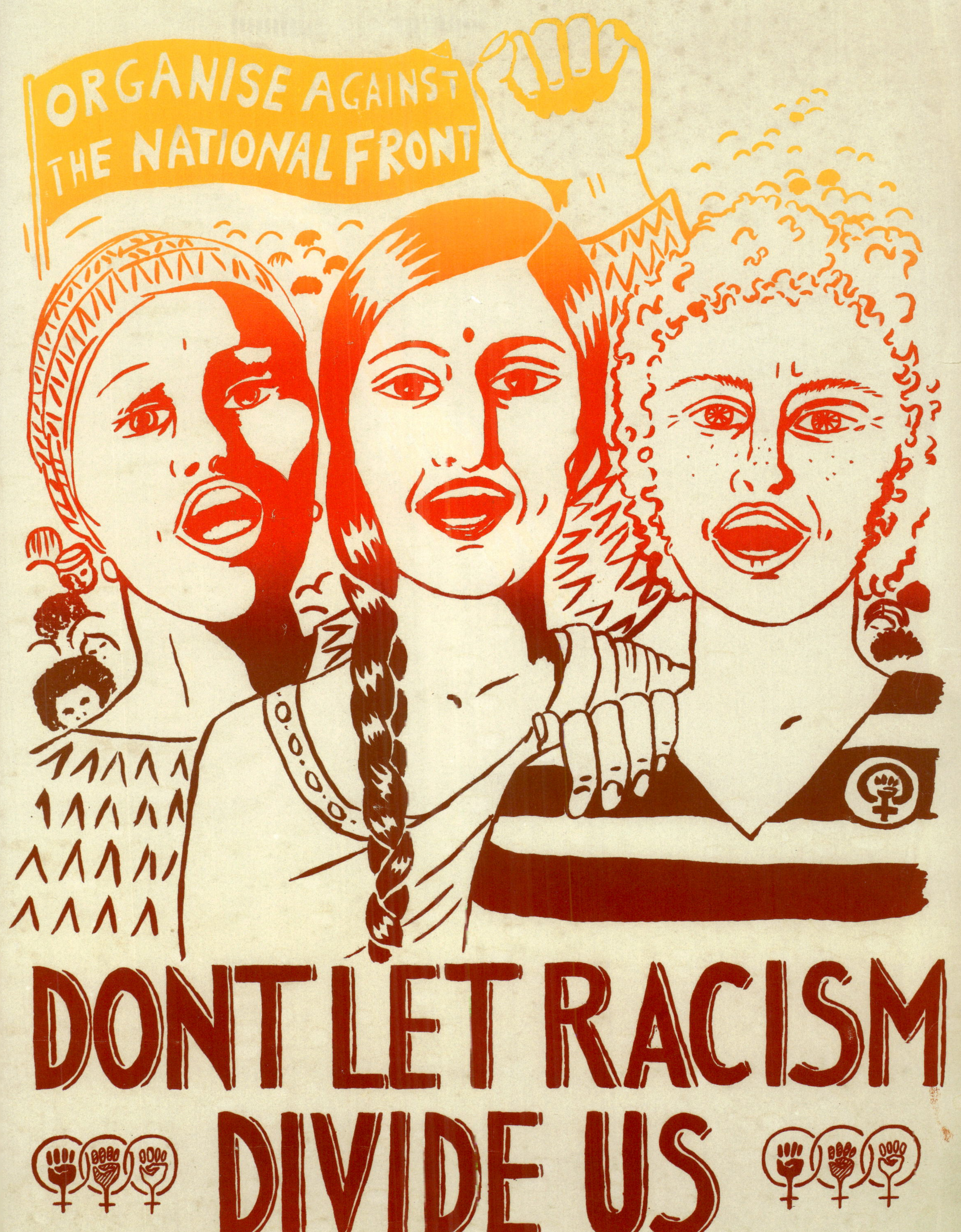

ORGANISE AGAINST THE NATIONAL FRONT
DONT LET RACISM DIVIDE US

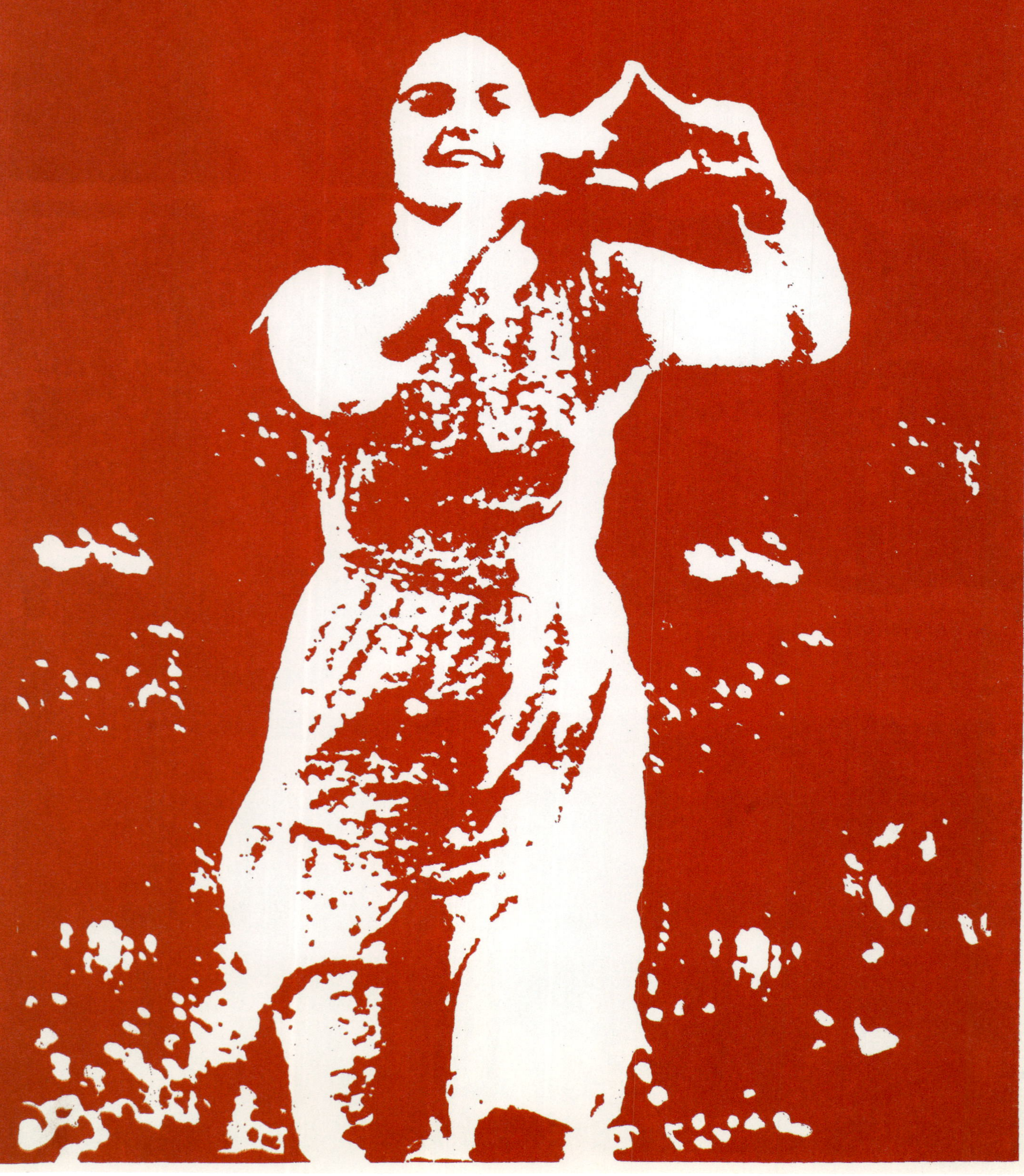
SEE RED
WOMEN'S WORKSHOP
CALENDAR 1978

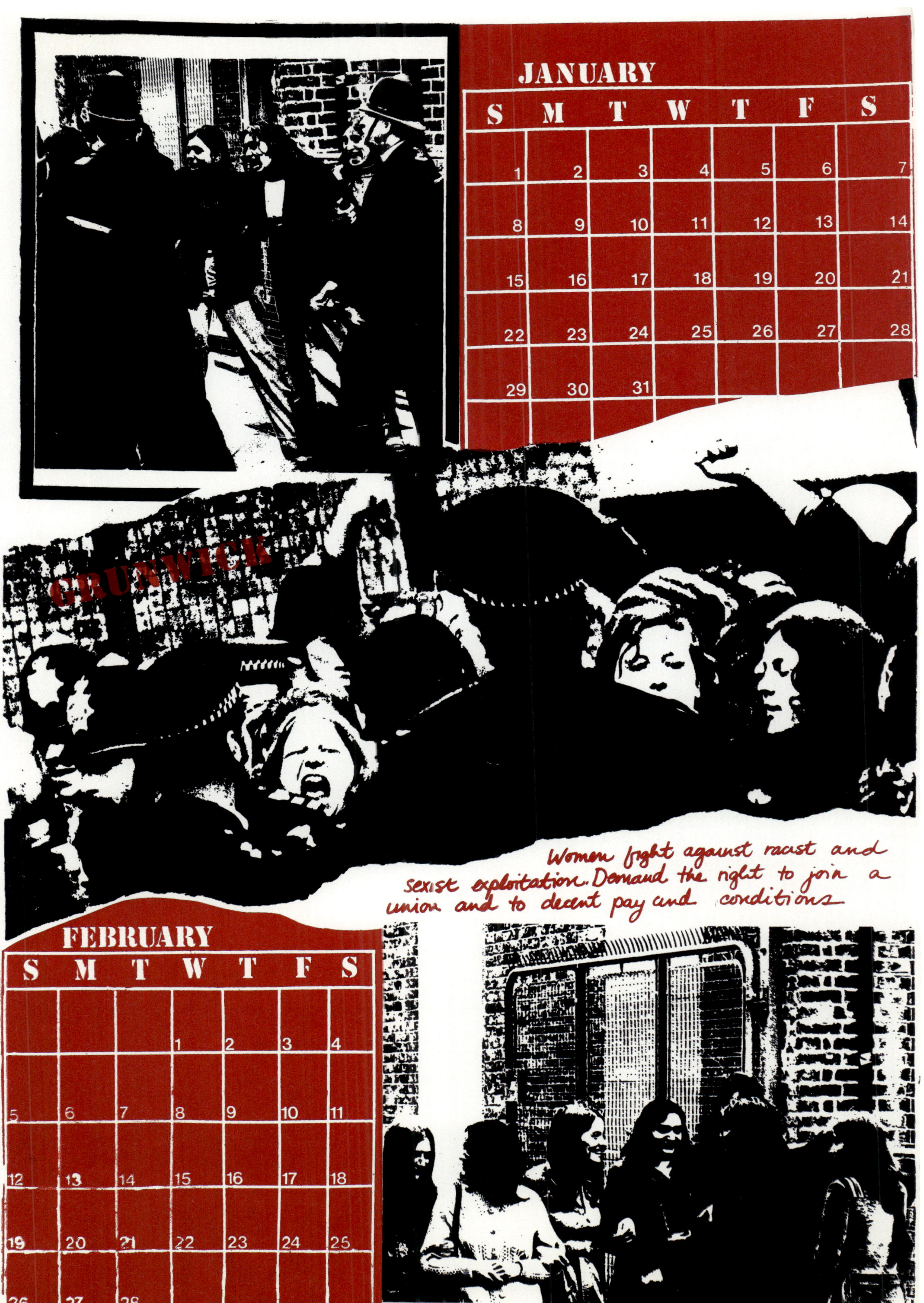

SEE RED CALENDAR, 1978 63 × 42.5 cm

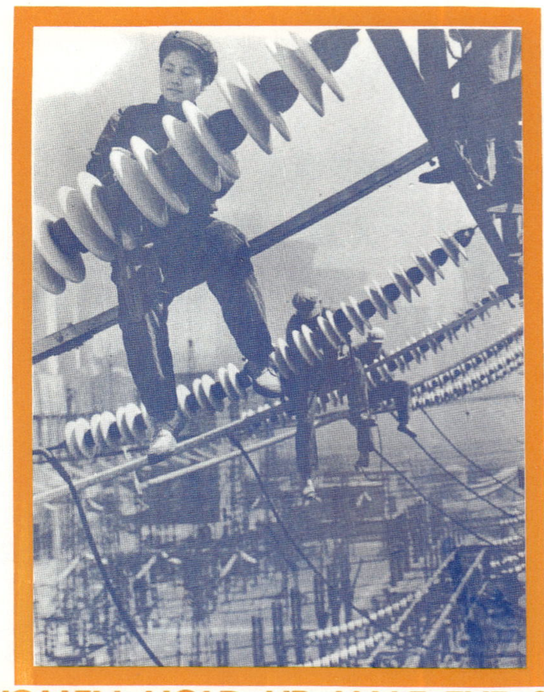

Sunday		5	12	19	26		2	9	16	23	30
Monday		6	13	20	27		3	10	17	24	
Tuesday		7	14	21	28		4	11	18	25	
Wed.	1	8	15	22	29		5	12	19	26	
Thursday	2	9	16	23	30		6	13	20	27	
Friday	3	10	17	24	31		7	14	21	28	
Sat.	4	11	18	25		1	8	15	22	29	

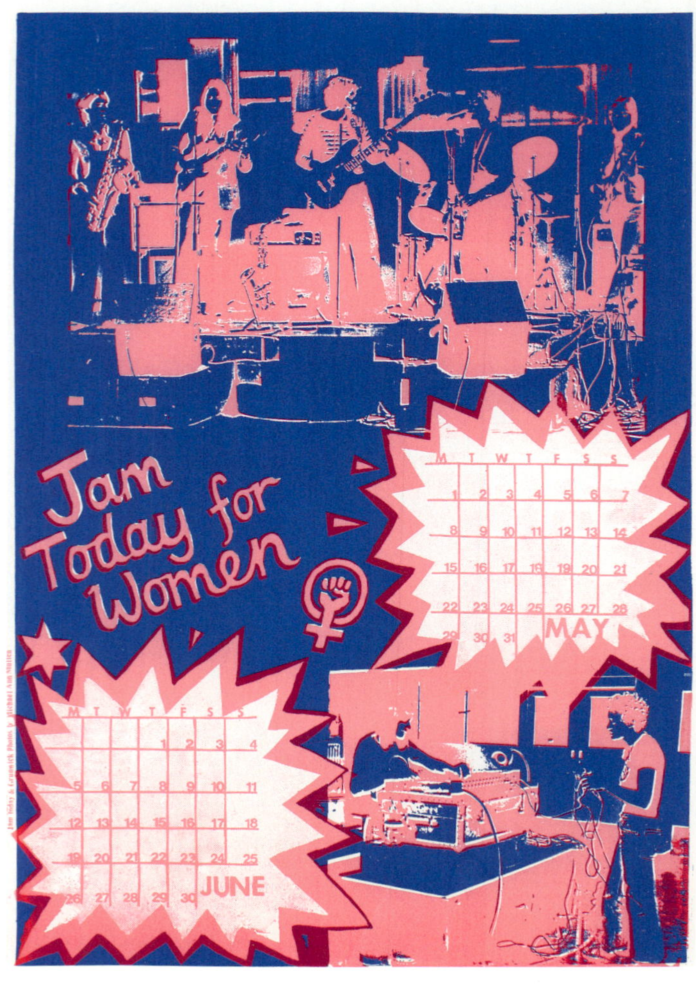

	Sat	Sun	Mon	Tue	Wed	Thur	Fri
	1	2	3	4	5	6	7
	8	9	10	11	12	13	14
	15	16	17	18	19	20	21
	22	23	24	25	26	27	28
	29	30	31				

Sat	Sun	Mon	Tue	Wed	Thur	Fri
			1	2	3	4
5	6	7	8	9	10	11
12	13	14	15	16	17	18
19	20	21	22	23	24	25
26	27	28	29	30	31	

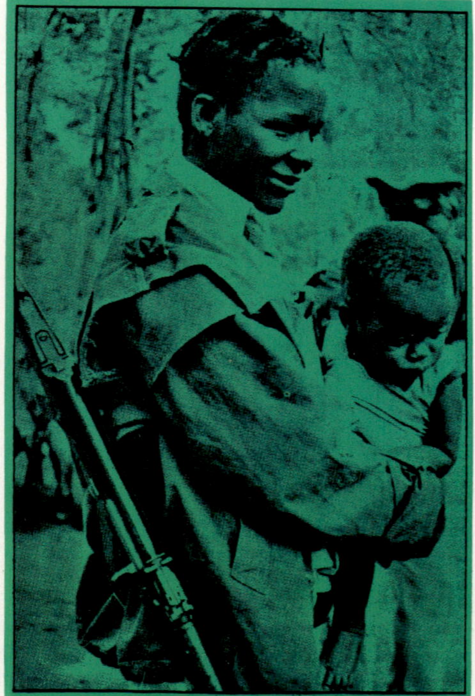

The Organization of Angolan Women (O. M. A.), the women's arm of the M. P. L. A., has developed into a strong, growing women's organization with a definite place in the Angolan struggle for liberation. O. M. A. militants know that without the liberation of women there can be no revolution, and equally that the liberation of women cannot come without the victory of the revolution they are helping to build.

"My direct involvement in combat made me more than ever convinced that women can in fact do many things......... I took part as an M. P. L. A. militant and as an O. M. A. militant who feels the domination of colonialism as well as men's domination over women....."

Maria Simao Paim

Mon	Tue	Wed	Thur	Fri	Sat	Sun	Mon	Tue	Wed	Thur	Fri	Sat	Sun
		1	2	3	4	5					1	2	3
6	7	8	9	10	11	12	4	5	6	7	8	9	10
13	14	15	16	17	18	19	11	12	13	14	15	16	17
20	21	22	23	24	25	26	18	19	20	21	22	23	24
27	28	29	30				25	26	27	28	29	30	31

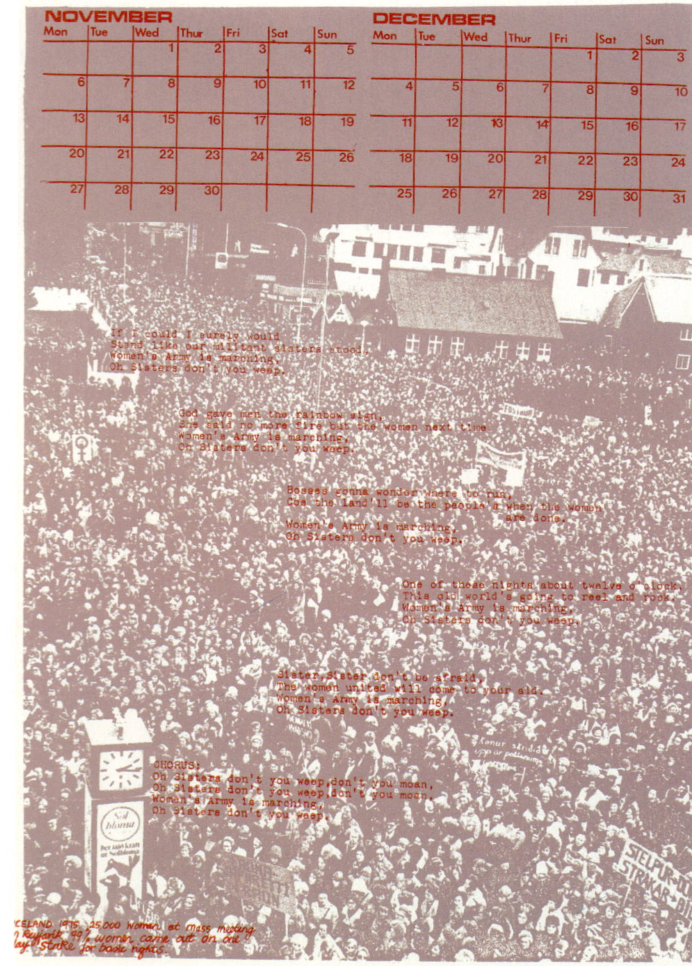

SEE RED CALENDAR, 1978 63 × 42.5 cm

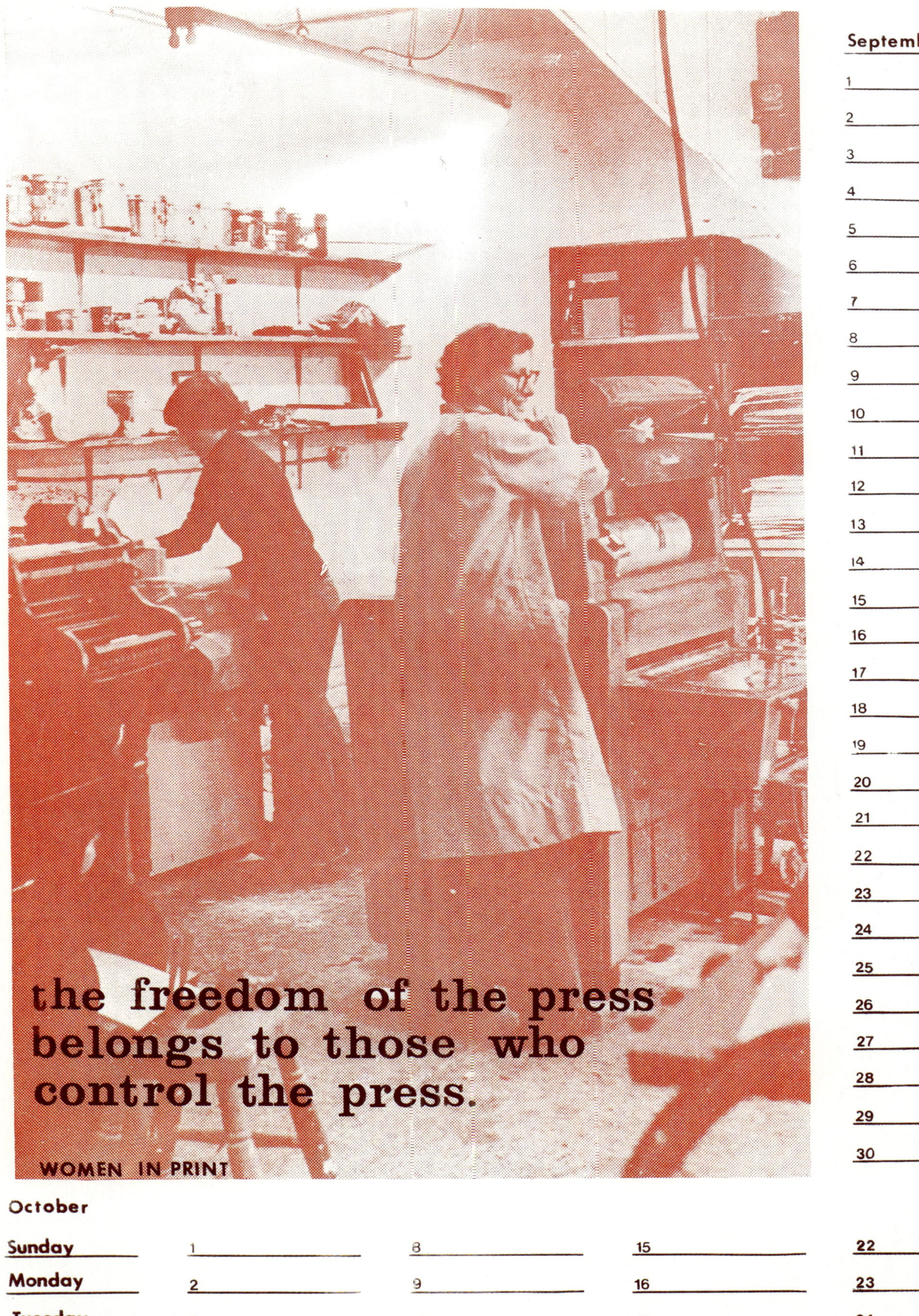

September	
1	F
2	Sa
3	Su
4	M
5	Tu
6	W
7	Th
8	F
9	Sa
10	Su
11	M
12	Tu
13	W
14	Th
15	F
16	Sa
17	Su
18	M
19	Tu
20	W
21	Th
22	F
23	Sa
24	Su
25	M
26	Tu
27	W
28	Th
29	F
30	Sa

October

Sunday	1	8	15	22 / 29
Monday	2	9	16	23 / 30
Tuesday	3	10	17	24 / 31
Wednesday	4	11	18	25
Thursday	5	12	19	26
Friday	6	13	20	27
Saturday	7	14	21	28

SEE RED CALENDAR, 1978 63 × 42.5 cm

Caption taken in part from an interview in
Spare Rib July 1975 with Mme Phan Thi Minh
a former resistance fighter in Danang, South
Vietman and then advisor to the provisional
Revolutionary Government's Foreign Minister.

> 'In the declaration of independence
> President Ho Chi Minh said, as he had
> said many times, that women are half of
> our people, and as long as women are not
> emancipated, are not free, the people
> are not free'.

Right On, Jane (*over the page*)
This poster started as a single colour illustration
in the 1977 calendar and became a very popular
poster with wide ranging appeal. It was a
reaction to the Ladybird Key Words Reading
Scheme series: as our children started to grow,
we were increasingly appalled by the 1950s
sexism in this series of books, and even more
so that they were still available in libraries and
promoted as reading material in schools.

In our poster, the first three frames present
images from one of these books, along with
the original text. Nothing has been changed,
other than the very deliberate choice of
primary colours in place of the four-colour,
'realistic' illustrations of the book.

The fourth picture is an enlargement from
the previous frame, and Jane's facial expression
has changed from quiet acquiescence to
quizzical anger, questioning her role in the story
and the book's sexism with the changed text.

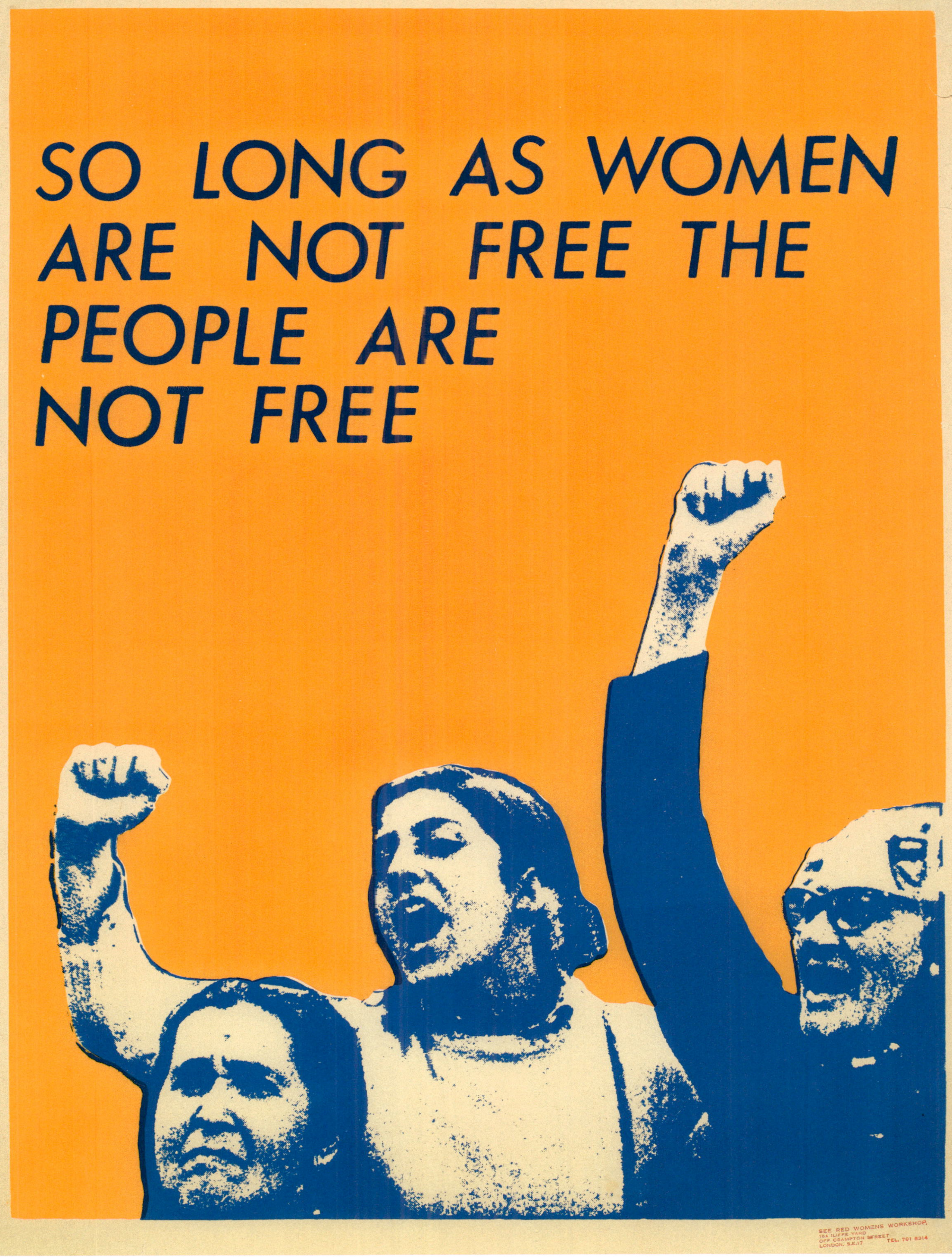

SO LONG AS WOMEN AFE NOT FREE, 1978 64 × 45 cm

RIGHT ON JANE, 1977/88 51 × 76 cm

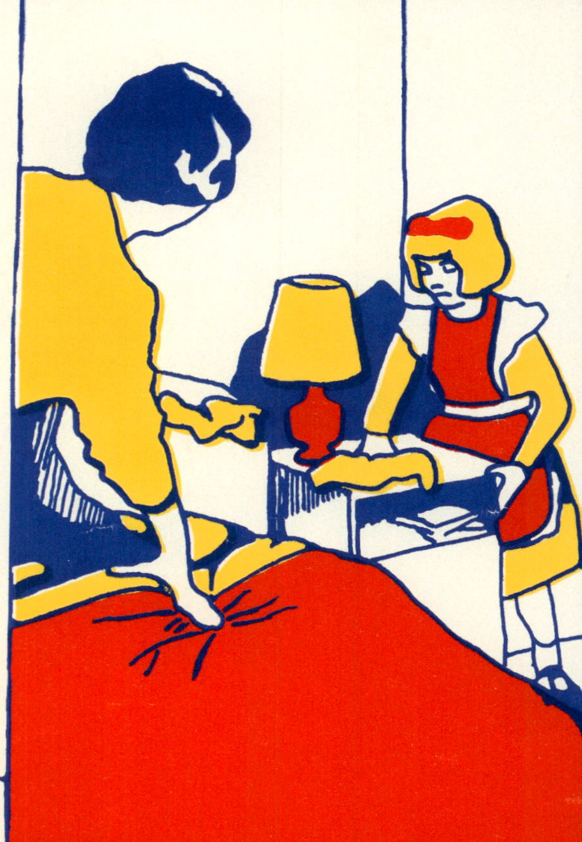

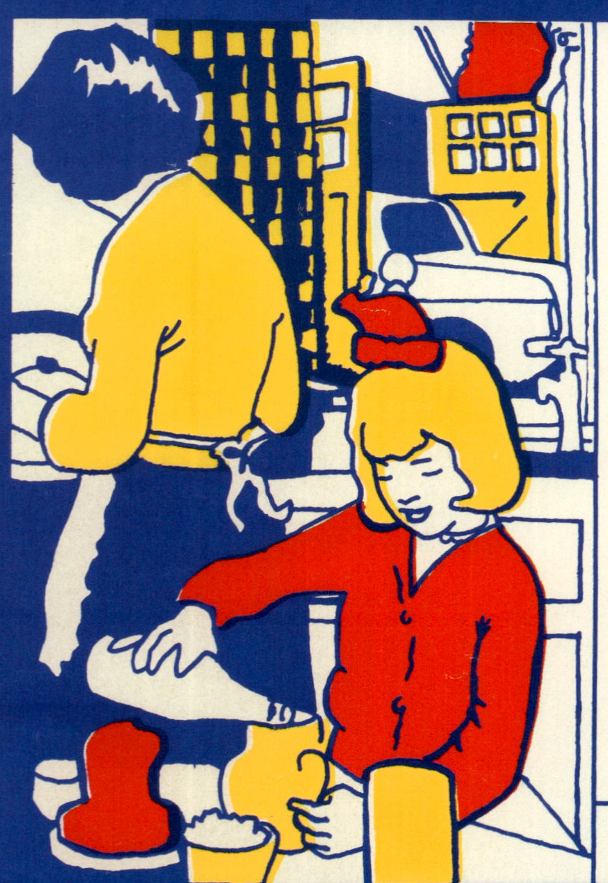

I am helping
to sweep the floor.

Sweep   sweep

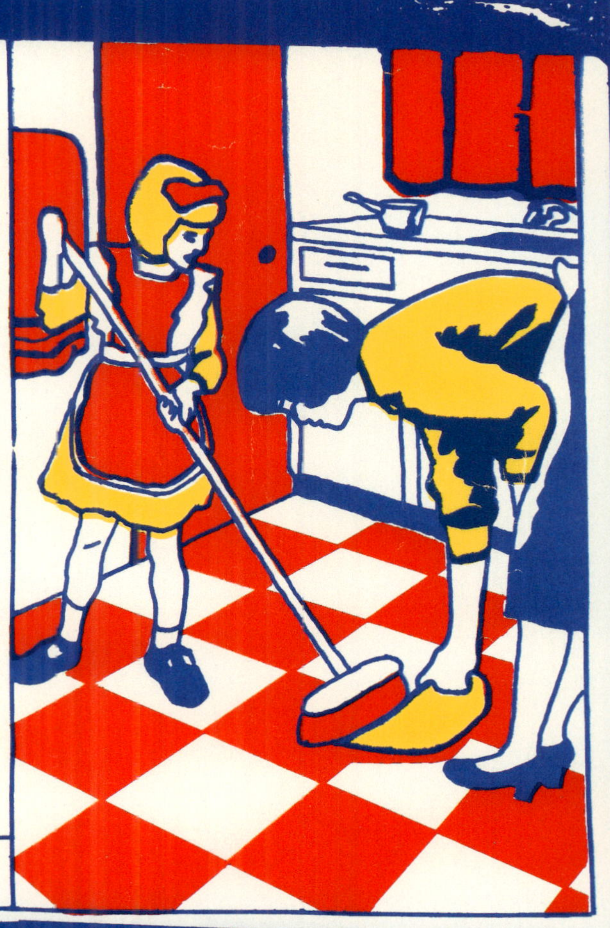

Jane thinks:
   Stuff this!

It's about time I
got myself out of
these sexist books
and started giving
girls an example
of all the other
things we can do!

Right on, right on Jane

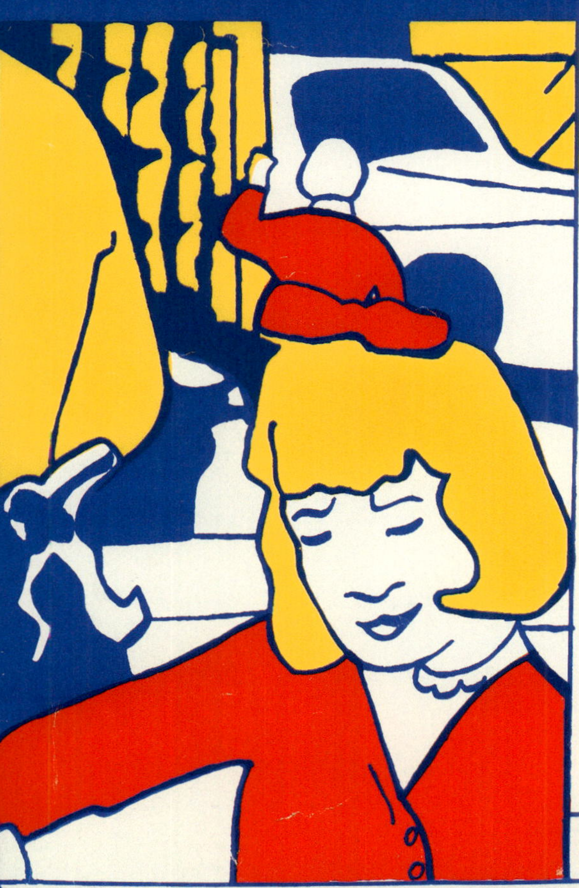

Bite The Hand
Despite the Equal Pay Act and the Sex
Discrimination Act, the actual effects of
government policies and practices meant
that cuts, closures and restrictions still
affected women and undercut positive
legislation.

Women Hold Up Half The Sky (*over the page*)
At the time all of us had posters produced
during the 1960s Chinese Cultural Revolution.
With strong and rousing images of women
engaged in heroic tasks they were a strong
influence. The title comes from a quotation
by Mao Tse Tung, and the words 'More than'
were inserted for a new version of the poster
in 1980.

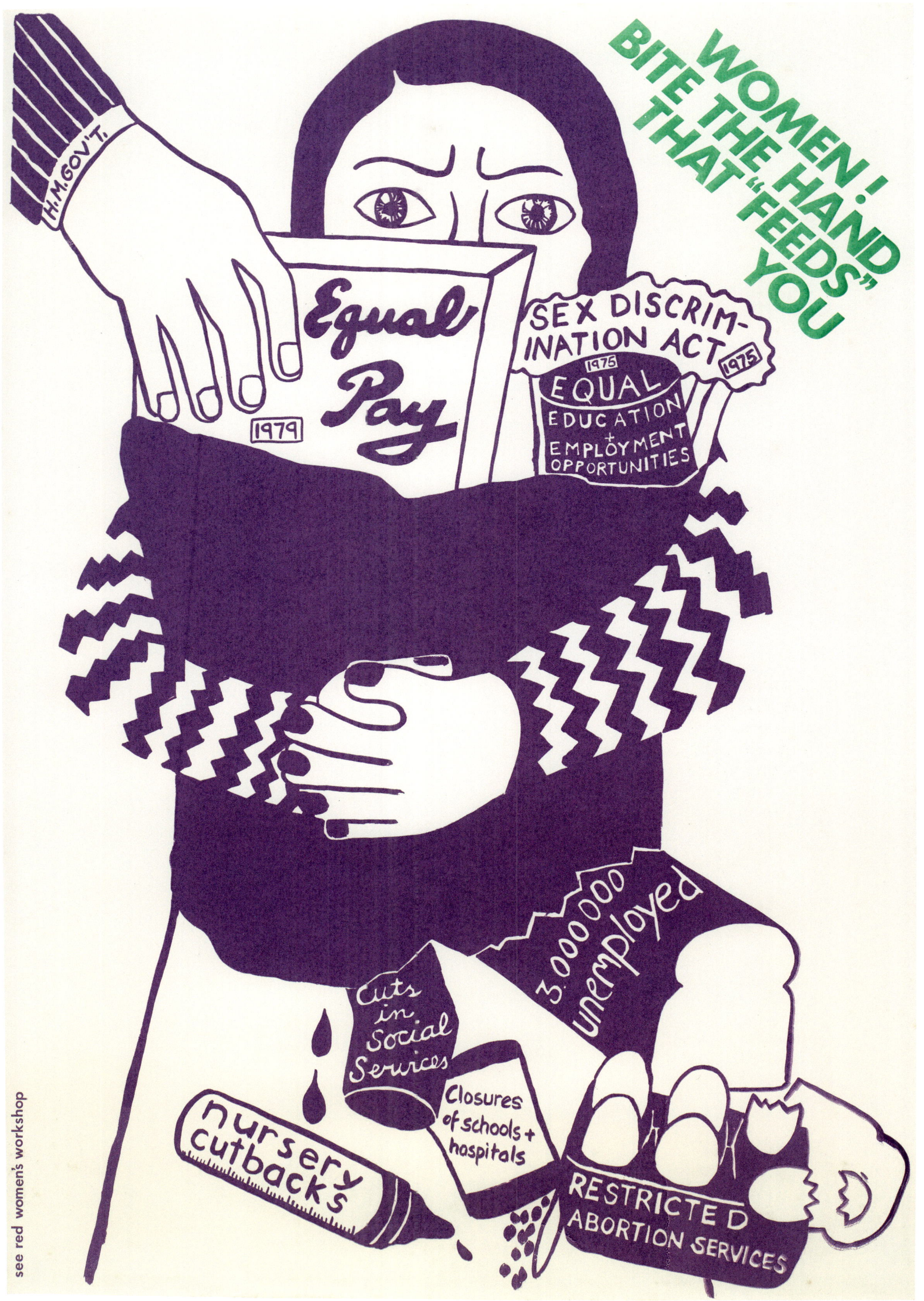

WOMEN!
BITE THE HAND
THAT "FEEDS"
YOU
H.M.GOV'T.
Equal Pay
1979
SEX DISCRIM-
INATION ACT
1975   1975
EQUAL
EDUCATION
+
EMPLOYMENT
OPPORTUNITIES
3,000,000 unemployed
Cuts in Social Services
Closures of schools + hospitals
nursery cutbacks
RESTRICTED ABORTION SERVICES
see red women's workshop

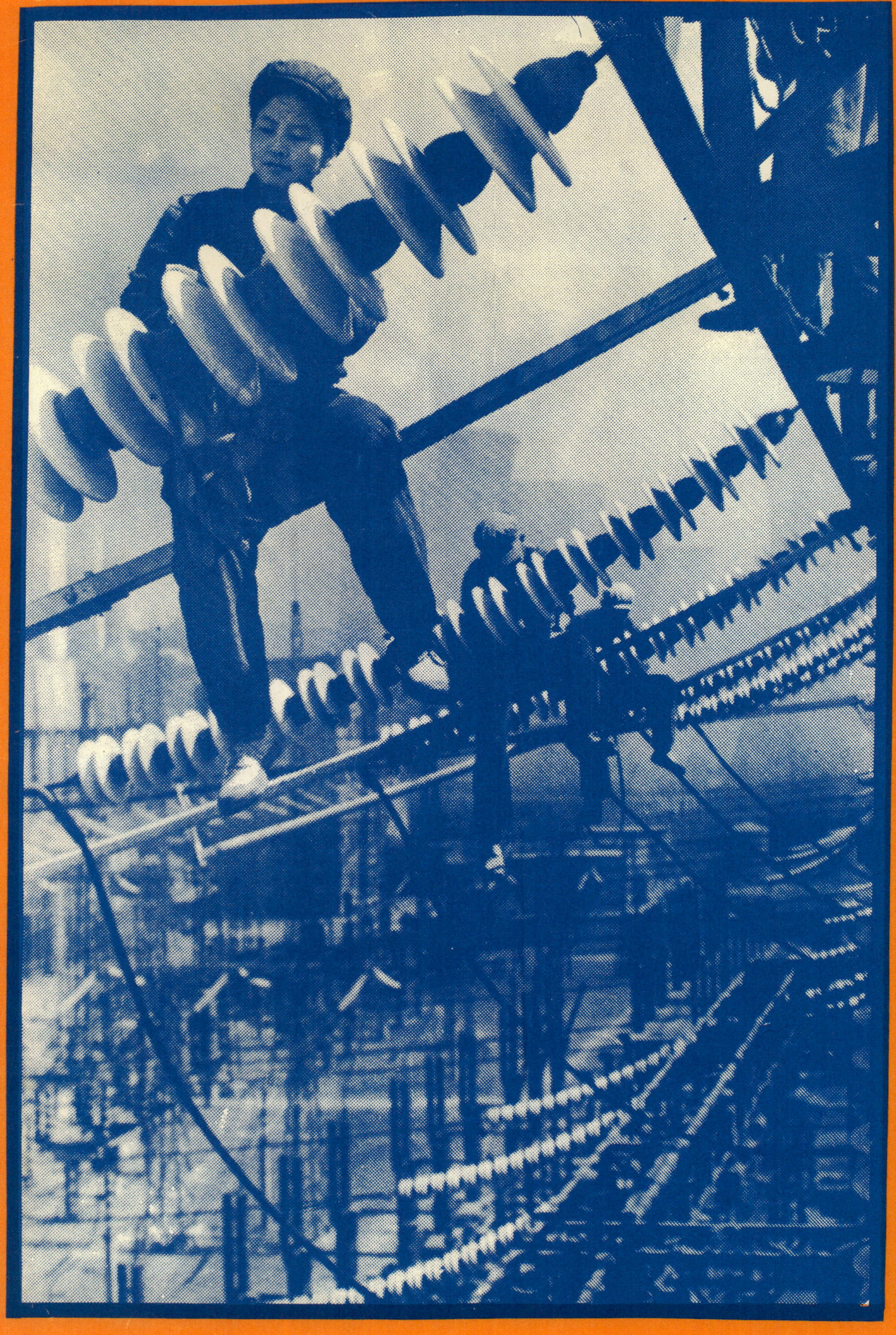

WOMEN HOLD UP HALF THE SKY, 1978 64 × 45 cm
facing page: WOMEN HOLD UP MORE THAN HALF THE SKY, 1986 64 × 45 cm

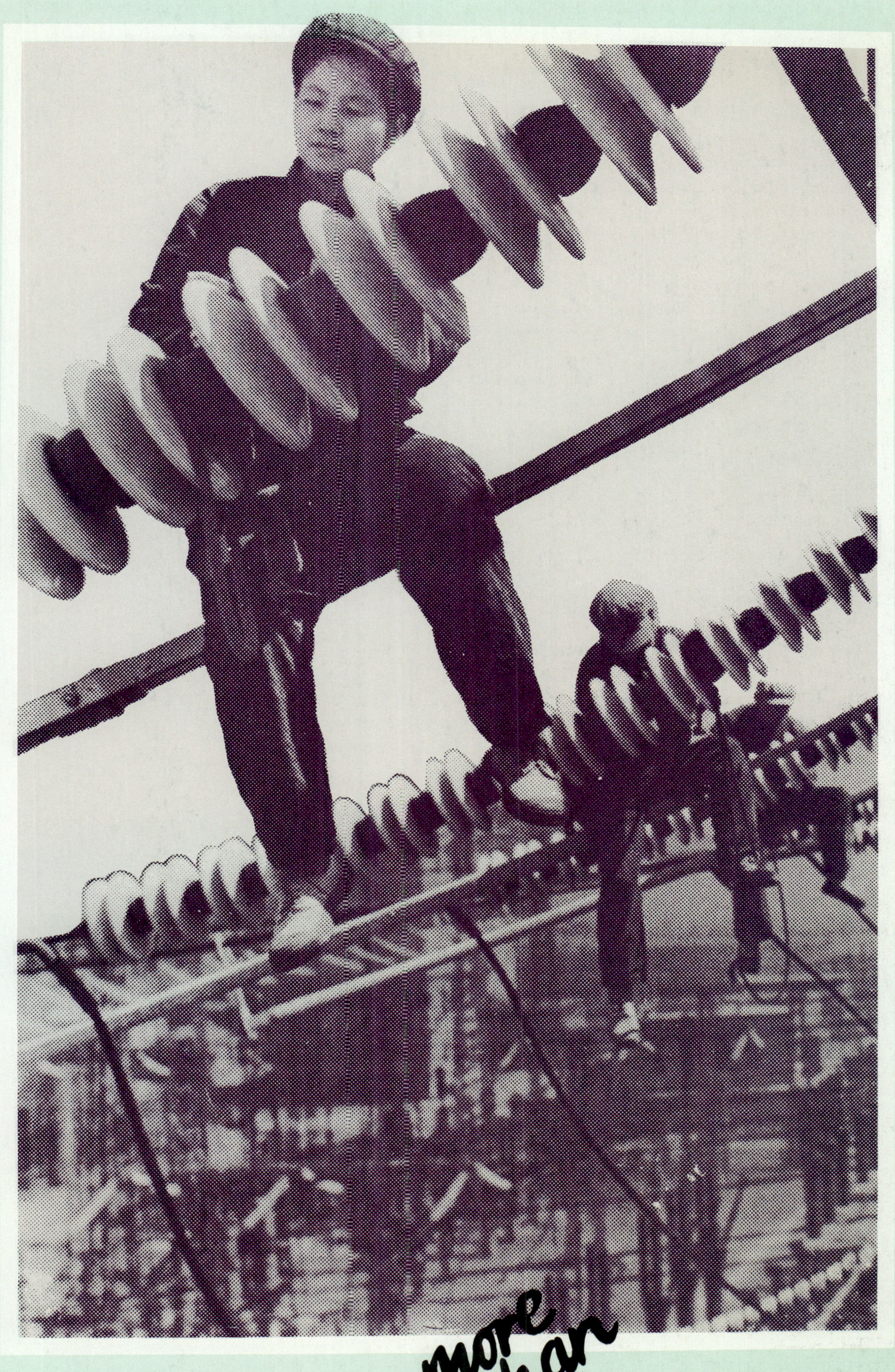

WOMEN HOLD UP ^{more than} HALF THE SKY

Old Age

Poem by Sonia Saxon.

We were young women when we designed and printed this poster in 1978. It is the only poster where regrettably we did not consult or work with women who had direct experience of the issues we wished to portray. The Women's Liberation Movement was essentially a young women's movement, sexism and racism were high on the agenda but not ageism and many older women felt 'rightly' that their concerns were not included and were ignored.

Many older women still feel side-lined and invisible. Two of us are now 'older' ourselves and are having to confront the many awful stereotypes presented by the media and society: the smiling and confused old dear, the grumbling obstinate old trout with the ubiquitous Zimmer frame or walking stick, the white-haired old woman with hearing aid, knitting by the fire-side.

Given the need to reject all of the stereotypes above and to be clear about how we choose to live our lives, the words of the poem in the poster, whilst sound, and the woman is sympathetic, she nonetheless comes across as tired and somewhat defeated. We would now produce a different image — more energetic, strong and positive, reflecting how many of us feel and would like to be seen.

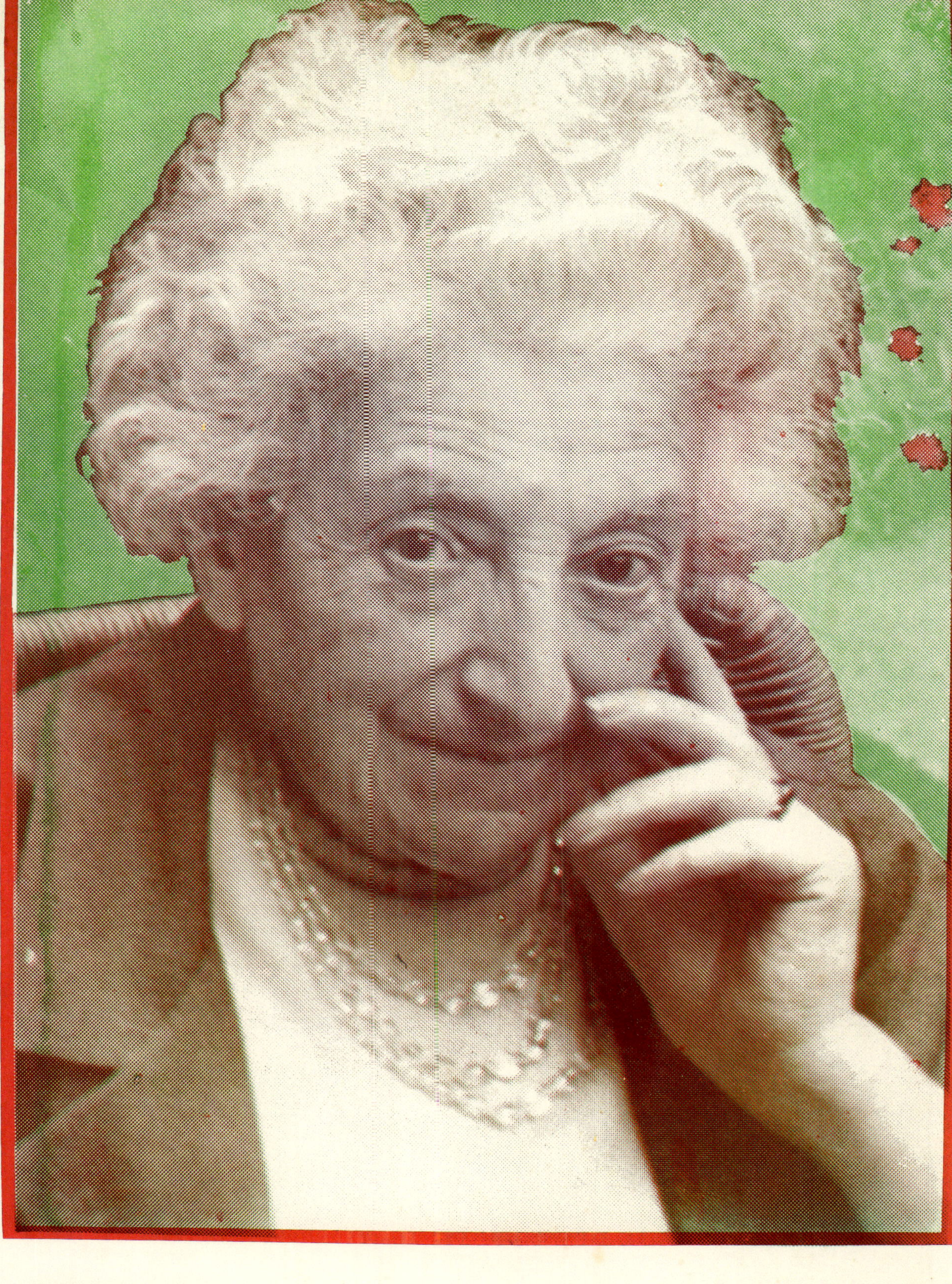

Old age isn't calm
Fires burn in bodies of old women
Flutes sing in their ears and they
  fall in love now and then
Old women dream of dancing in
  moonlight and of being held
Old women want you to hug them
  and to feel your warmth
I will not speak to you in
  platitudes — words of wisdom
"be like me"

I do not have a rocking chair — I
  have no pattern for younger
  women
I don't have a richer outlook on
  life (life is always confusing)
Except there is joy in struggle
And in leaping from change to
  change
But let the struggle be your own
  and let the changes be your own
Resist compromise — don't take
  anything lying down.

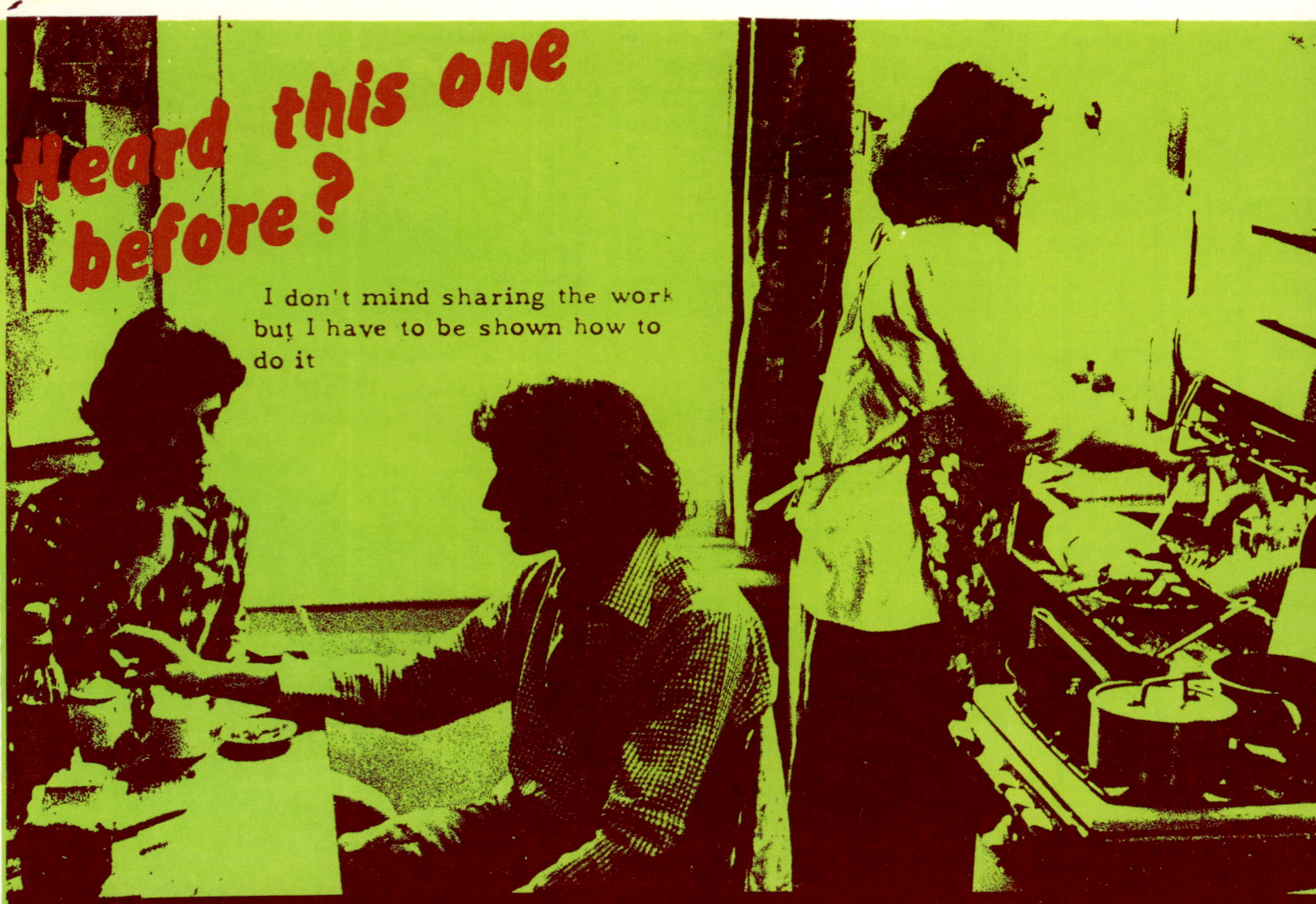
Heard this one before?
I don't mind sharing the work but I have to be shown how to do it
Meaning: I ask a lot of questions and you'll have to show me everything, every time I do it because I don't remember so good.
Also meaning: I can provoke innumerable scenes over the housework issue. Eventually, doin the housework yourself will be less painful to you than trying to get me to do half.

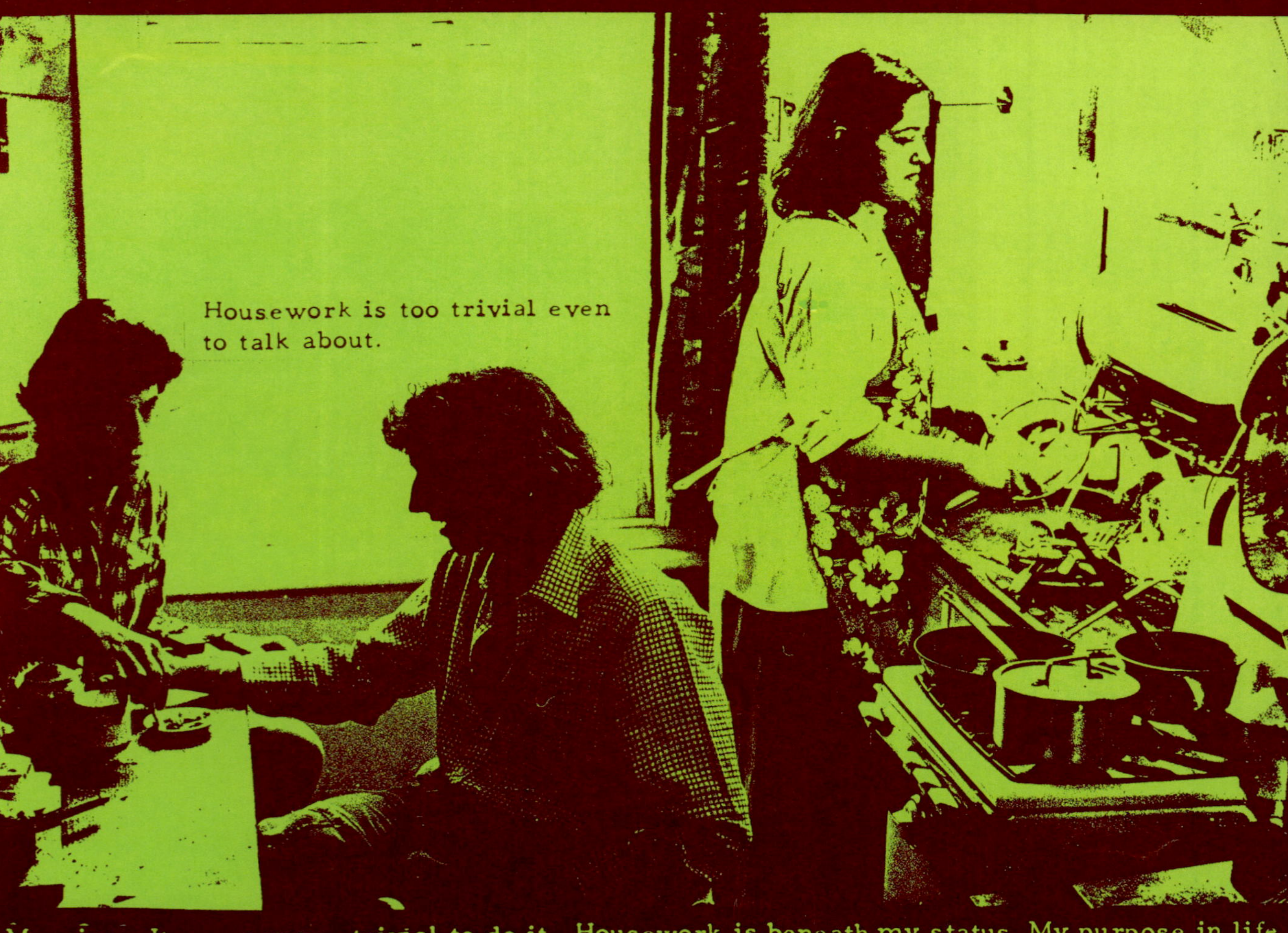
Housework is too trivial even to talk about.
Meaning: Its even more trivial to do it to deal with matters of significance Housework is beneath my status. My purpose in life to deal with matters of significance Yours is to deal with matters of insignificance. You sho do the housework.

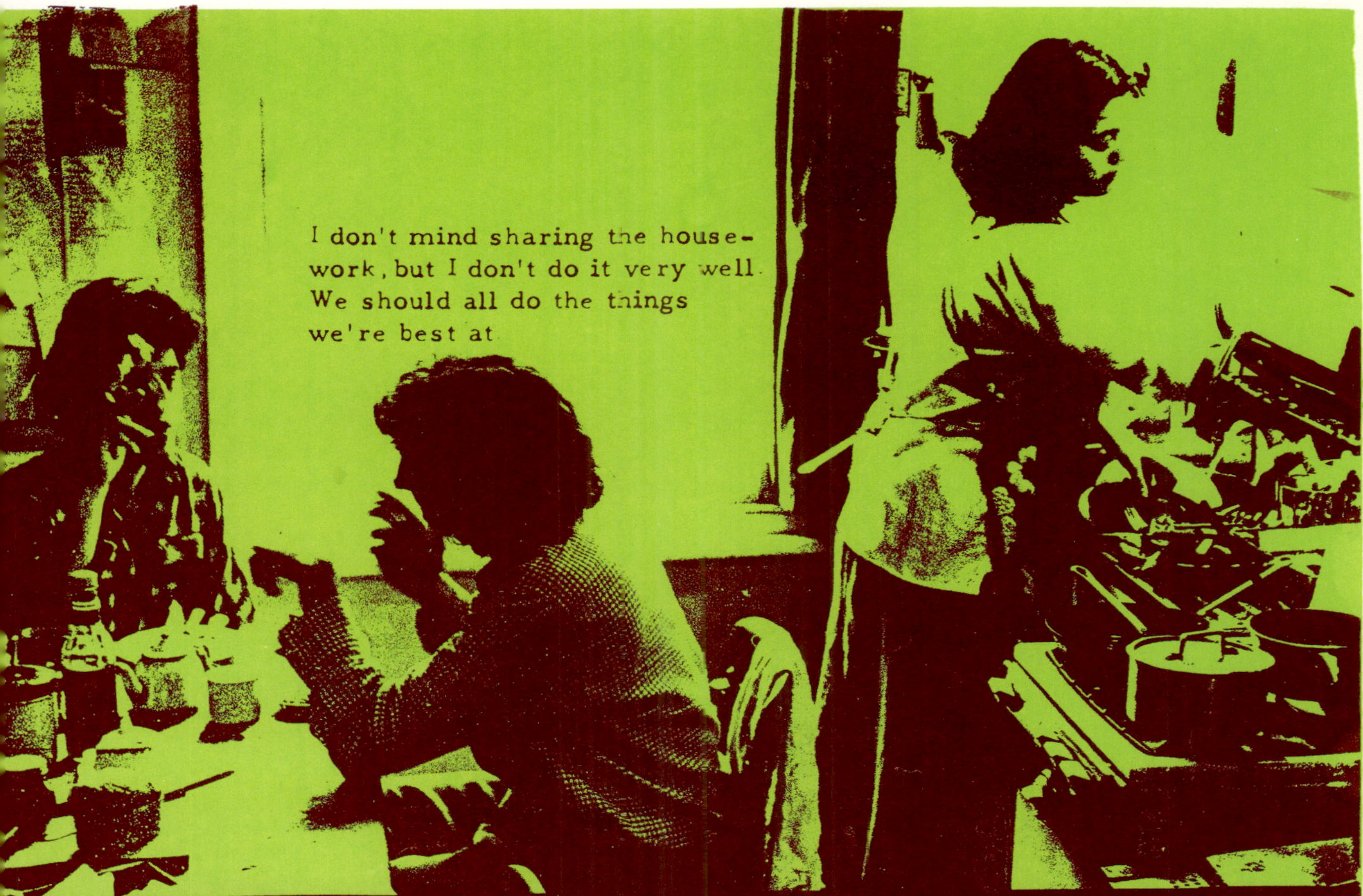

eaning; Unfortunately I'm no good at things like washing dishes and cooking. What I do best is little light carpentry, changing light bulbs, moving furniture (how often do you move furniture ?)
Also meaning; I don't like doing the stupid boring jobs, so you should do them.

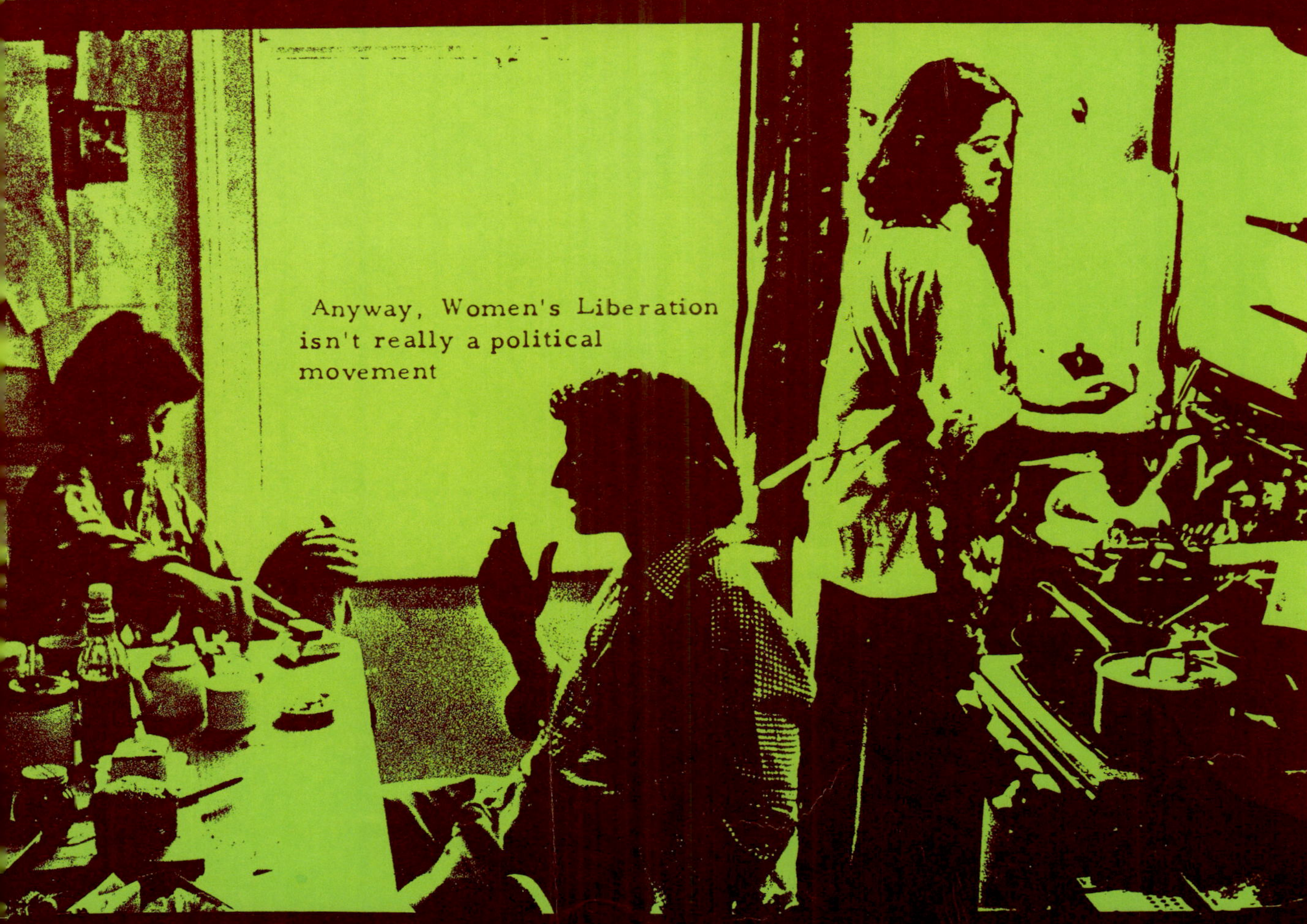

Meaning; I am only interested in how I am oppressed, not how I oppress others, therefore unemployment, the cuts etc are political Housework and Women's Liberation are not.
Also meaning; The revolution is coming too close to home.

Too right, brothers.

From: The Politics of Housework Pat Mainardi

Heard This One Before?

(*opposite and previous page*)
In our consciousness-raising groups, one
of the complaints that came up again and
again was about housework, and how
women — including those who went out to
work — were expected to take on all domestic
chores as well as childcare; how this was
seen as 'women's work'; and how men would
go to any lengths to avoid it and how grossly
unfair that was. Most men would not accept
that the way they conducted their lives was
a political act.

We had already made several posters
where we examined housework and women's
oppression, but these posters were the first
that challenged left-wing men who believed
that housework was women's work and that
women's liberation was a 'diversion from the
cause', and who didn't share in domestic
chores or childcare, even in collective
households.

Pat Mainardi's book *The Politics Of Housework*
provided the perfect text to highlight this point,
using a scathing and pointed humour. She went
through the many excuses that men give to
not do chores, and then deconstructed them
to expose the real meanings in the subtitles.

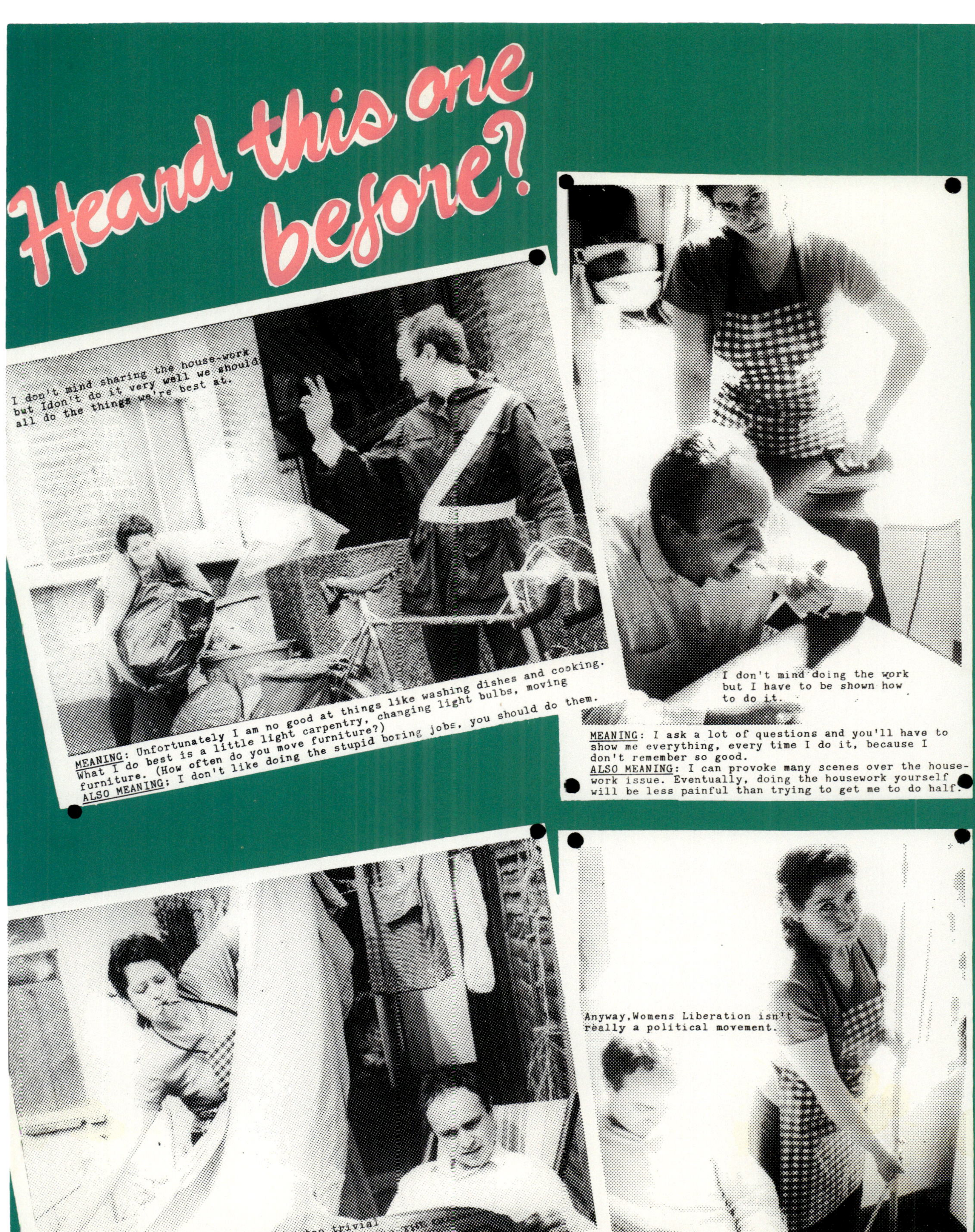

see red womens workshop

– from 'The Politics of Housework' by Pat Mainardi

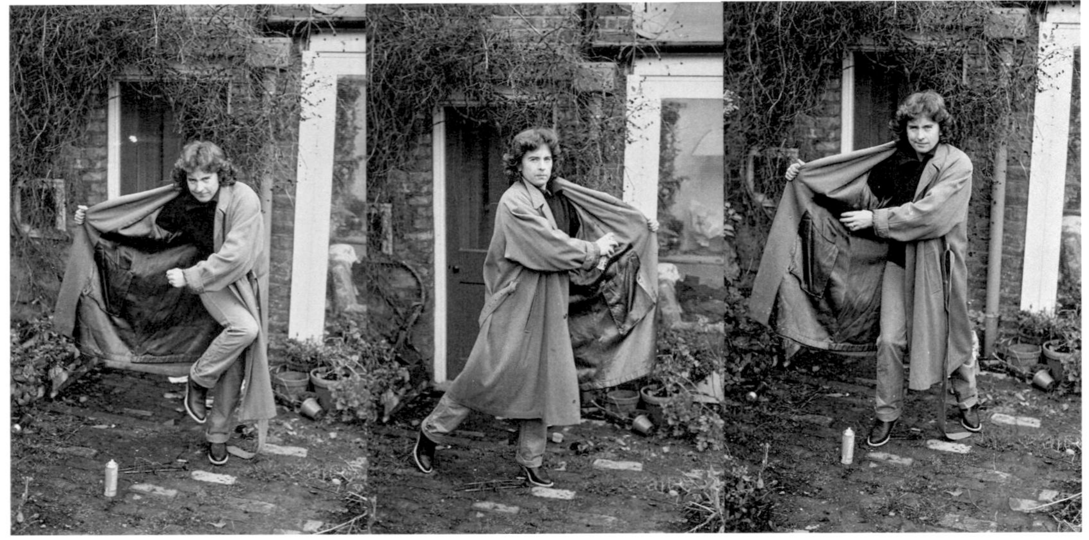

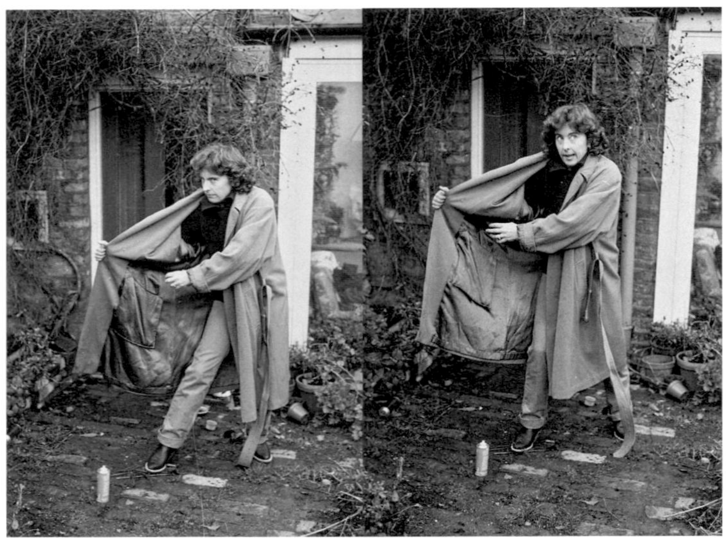

Lovable

Made in protest against the Polly Peck
advertisement for women's underwear.

The poster was inspired by feminist graffiti
prevalent at the time. Highly visible slogans
such as 'this degrades women' were sprayed
or plastered on many offending billboards
and notices.

The woman in the poster is about to spray
paint and stick notices on the advertisement
proclaiming 'this exploits women' or more
succinctly 'Sexist Crap' The caption 'Underneath
They're Are All Lovable' can only be spoken by
a man with his assumption of ownership of the
woman, which the poster challenges directly.

Underneath they're
all Lovable
oh, yeah?....
Spray on
Spray on
Spray on
THIS EXPLOITS WOMEN
SEXIST CRAP
This ad degrades women
Gigi.
with lace trimming. Matching briefs or French knickers
matching stickers   by AFFIRM c/o Women's Free Arts Alliance, 10, Cambridge Terrace Mews, London, NW1
SEE RED WOMEN'S WORKSHOP

Girls Are Powerful

Around this time, we also started to develop images that presented a positive and celebratory angle to Women's Liberation.

With this aim, we wanted to show that girls can do anything and are powerful in their own right. We took photos of girls and young women we knew: Pru's daughter Ottie swinging in an adventure playground; Nicki and Agnes, young apprentices at Women in Print; and young women taking photos and playing pool and table tennis on the young women's night at the youth club where Suzy worked.

Youth clubs for 12–18 year olds were predominately used by boys and young men until the advent of young women's youth work in the late 1970s. Young women began participating in activities such as pool, previously the domain of young men, and this was a new image to play with. Young women's groups, activities, events and projects grew and, despite some resistance, became an integral part of youth work, and the poster was also used in youth clubs to encourage young women to attend.

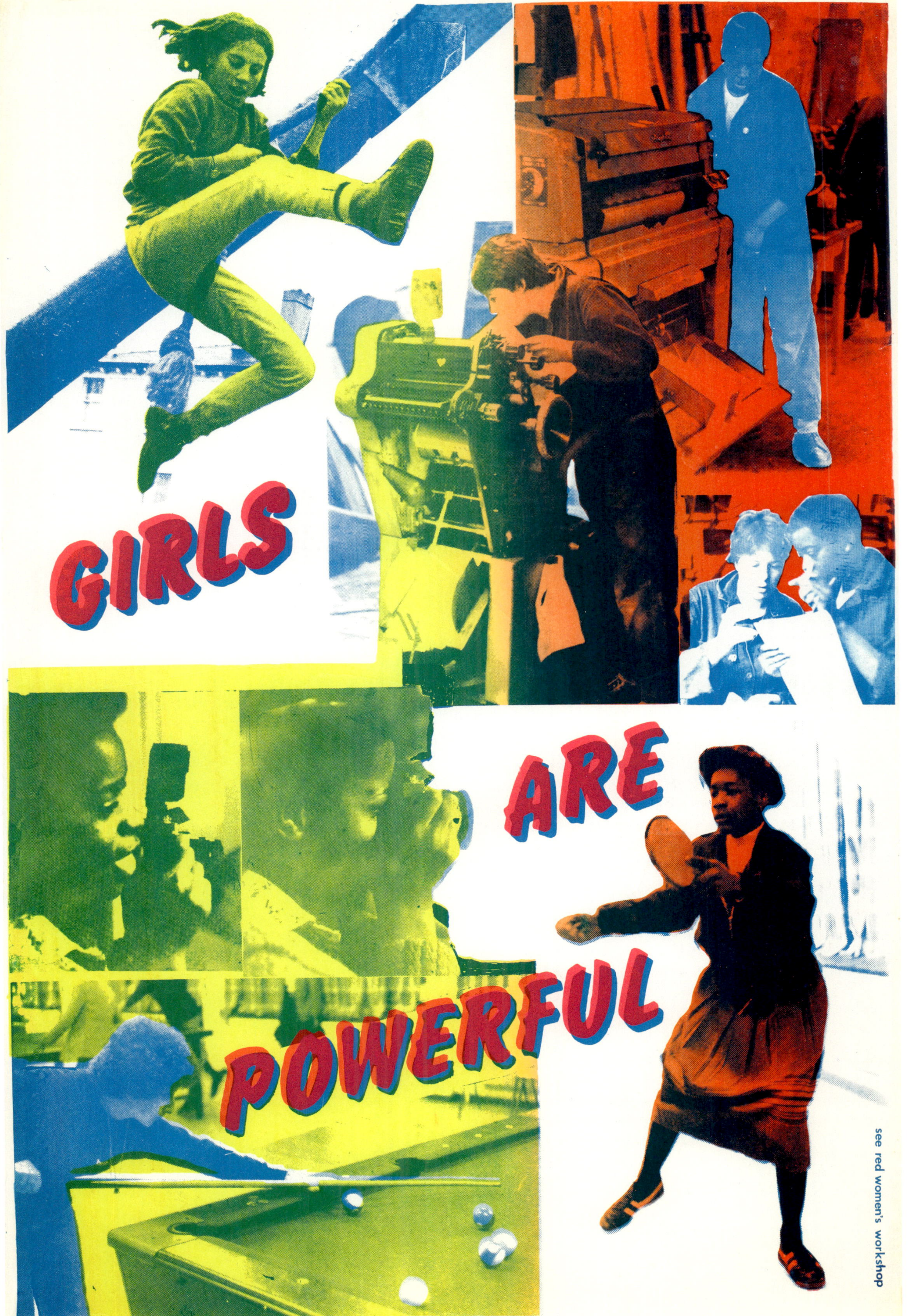

GIRLS
ARE
POWERFUL
see red women's workshop

Tough!

Although Margaret Thatcher was the first woman Prime Minister in the UK, she was already deeply unpopular with the left. She had first come to the attention of feminists as 'Maggie Thatcher, Milk Snatcher' after the earlier Conservative government had cut free school milk for the over-sevens. We wanted to do a poster that depicted her duplicity and deviousness, especially around issues that affected women.

One of us contacted the Conservative Central Office with a grovelling letter, praising her and asking if we could possibly have a high-quality photo of our leader. And we were quite surprised when this black and white picture duly arrived with a covering letter.

We drew the ornate frame around the picture by hand to represent all the ways that her policies discriminated against and actively harmed women and children using figures available at the time. The poster was revised in 1984, updating the information and using newspaper-style headlines in the frame rather than illustrations.

Miss March (*over the page*)

This is one of the posters showing women and girls in positions of strength made in response to comments that a number of the posters tended to be depressing.

Miss March is from a book called *Women Run a Boat: Life on Board a Canal Barge 'Heather Bell'* held by the Imperial War Museum. The full title of the photograph is: *Miss March Pushes off From the Bank to Send the Barge on its Way*, and was taken in 1942.

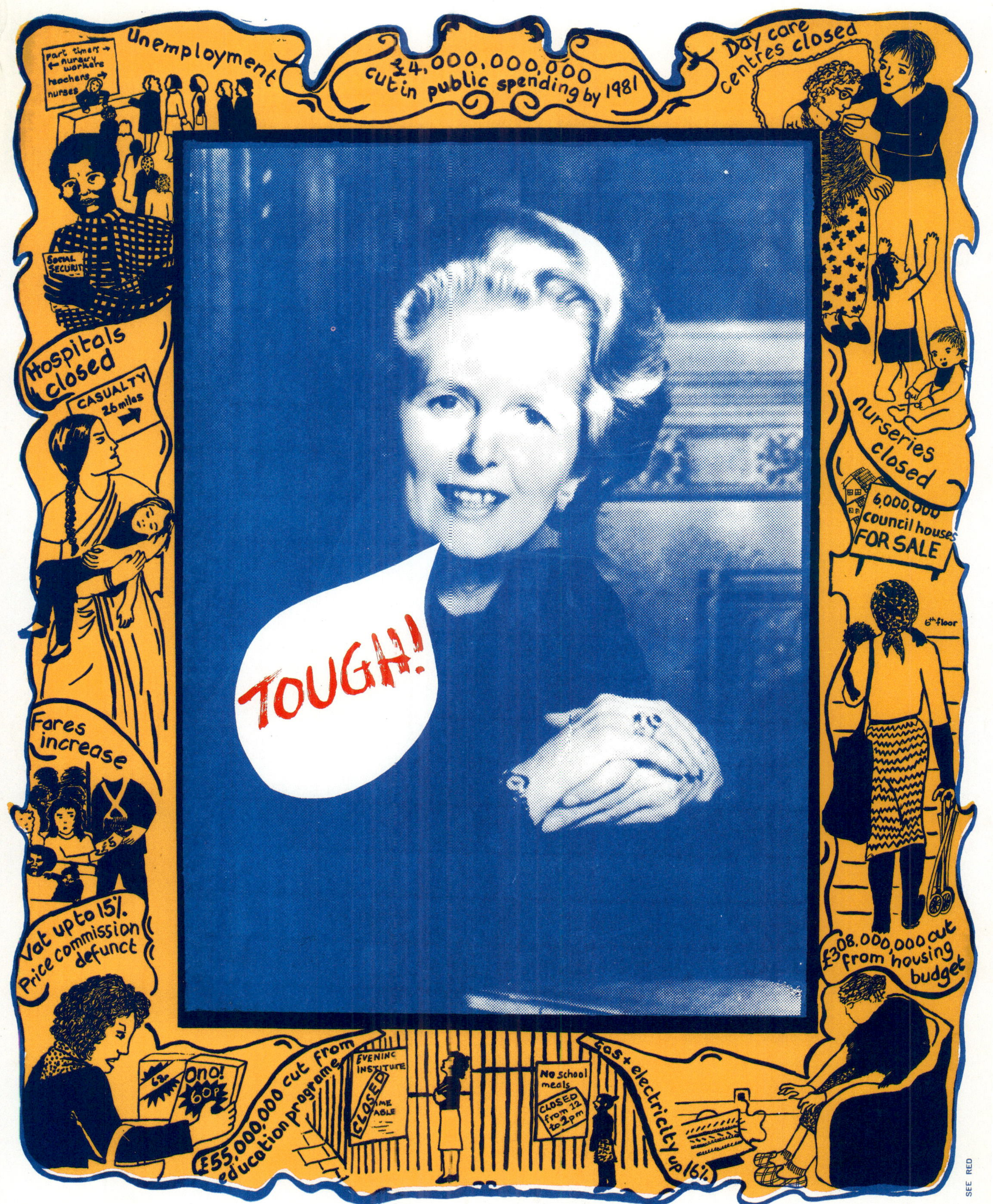

MY MESSAGE TO THE
WOMEN OF OUR NATION..
TOUGH!
Unemployment
part timers → nursery workers teachers nurses
£4,000,000,000 cut in public spending by 1981
Day care centres closed
SOCIAL SECURITY
Hospitals closed
CASUALTY 26 miles
nurseries closed
6,000,000 council houses FOR SALE
6th floor
Fares increase
£5
Vat up to 15%. Price commission defunct
£308,000,000 cut from housing budget
ono! 60p
£55,000,000 cut from education programe
EVENING INSTITUTE CLOSED TIME TABLE
No school meals CLOSED from 12 to 2pm
Gas + electricity up 16%
SEE RED

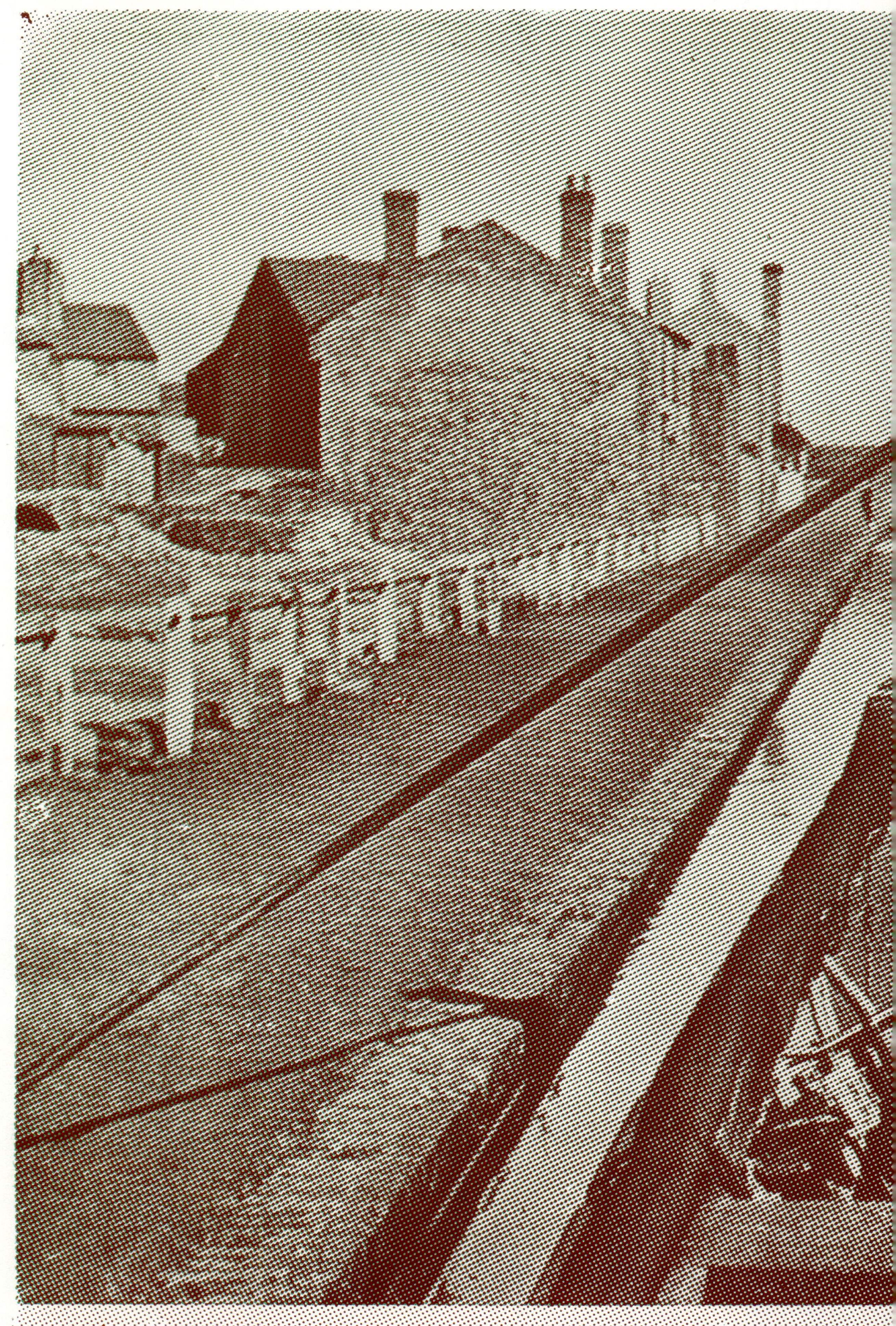

"Miss.March takes the Heatherbell through

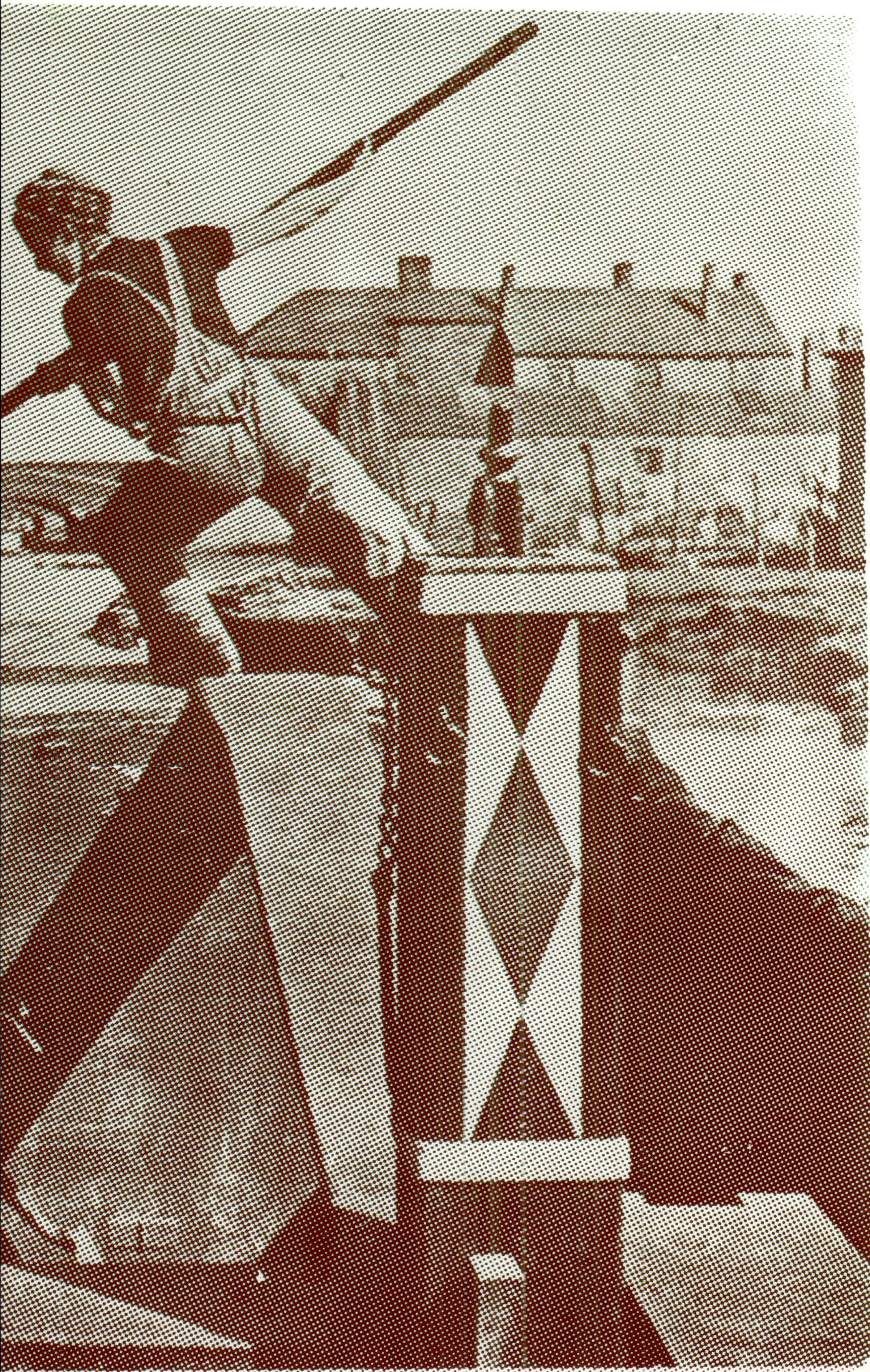

MISS MARCH, 1979 53 × 79 cm

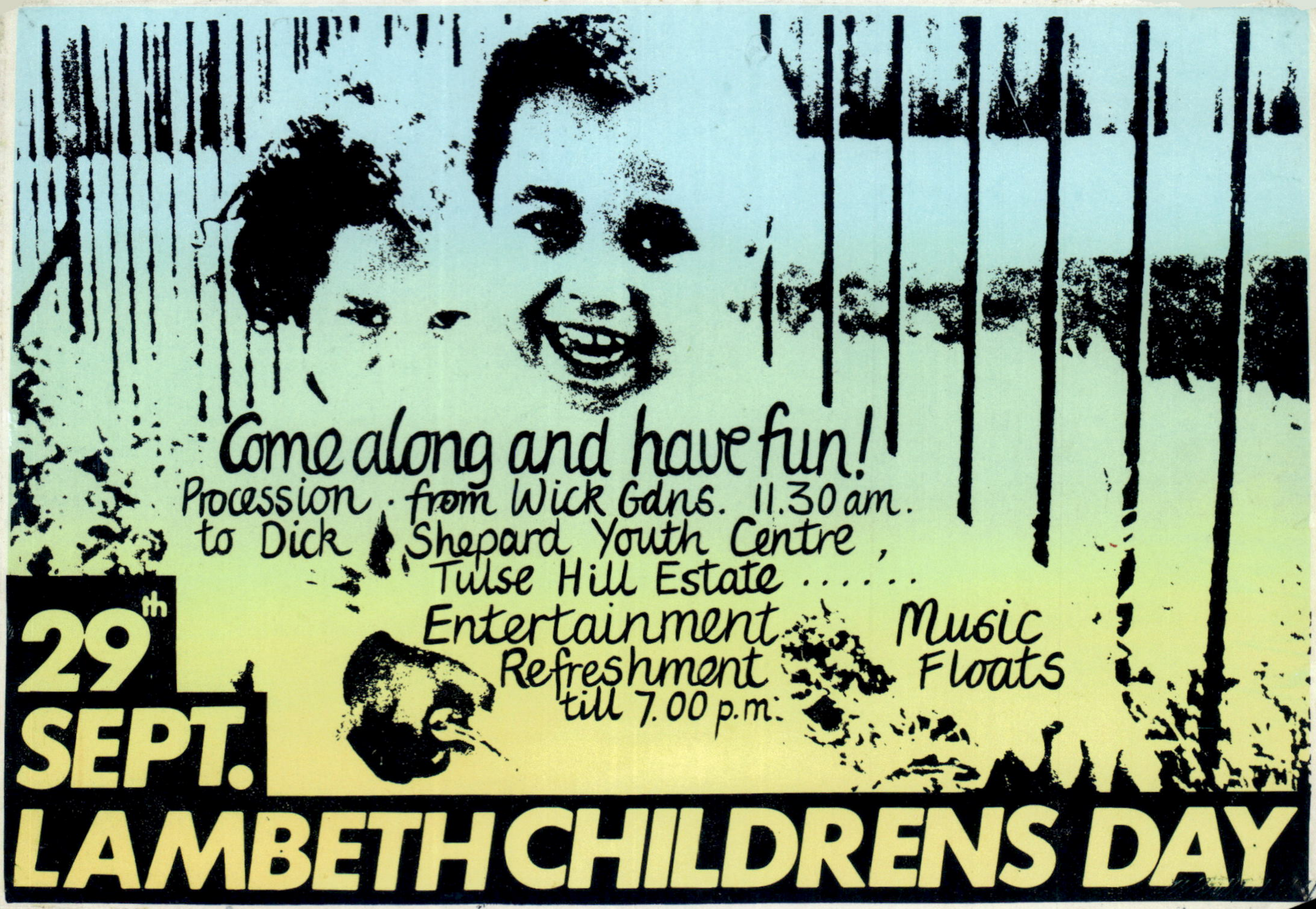

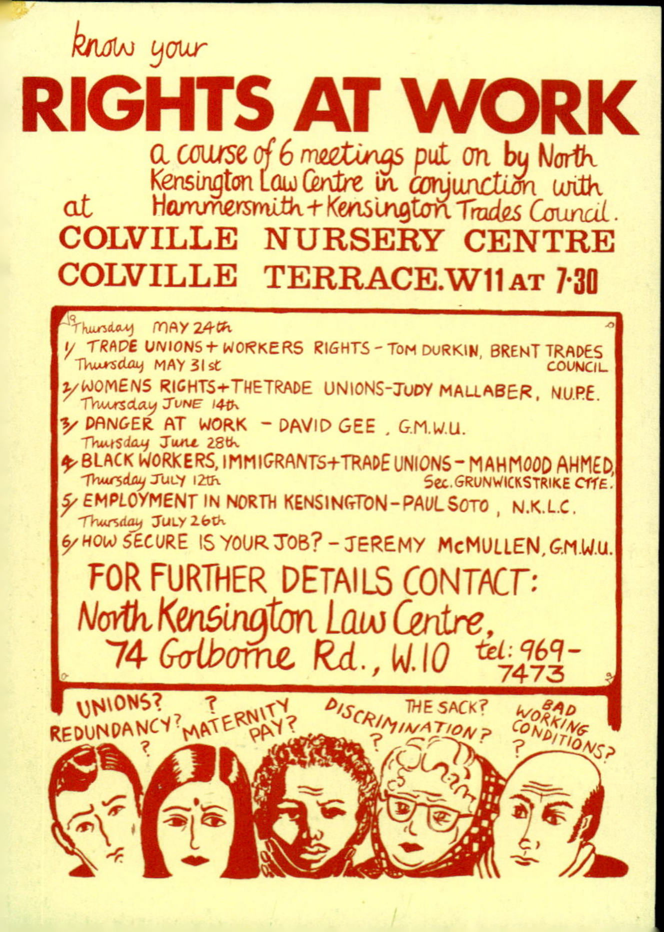

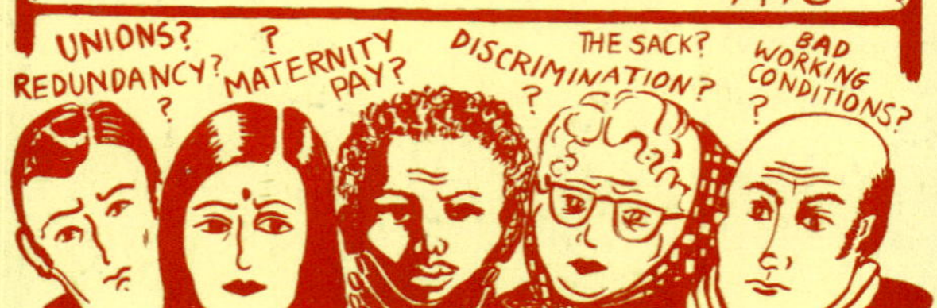

Feminist Disco (*facing page*)

Women-only discos became a significant part of feminist culture, providing much needed spaces where women could dance, drink and socialise liberated from the sexual norms and hassles of mixed heterosexual pubs and clubs. Events often took place in the upstairs rooms and cellars of pubs on unpopular nights, as well as community centres and town halls for the frequent benefit gigs. There was also a women's live music scene, with bands and singers such as the Feminist Improvising Group, The Fabulous Dirt Sisters, Carol Grimes, The Guest Stars, The Bright Girls, The Au Pairs, Maggie Nichols and many more. We printed several posters over the years for women's bands and cultural events. The blank silver star on this poster was for more information to be added in by hand when needed.

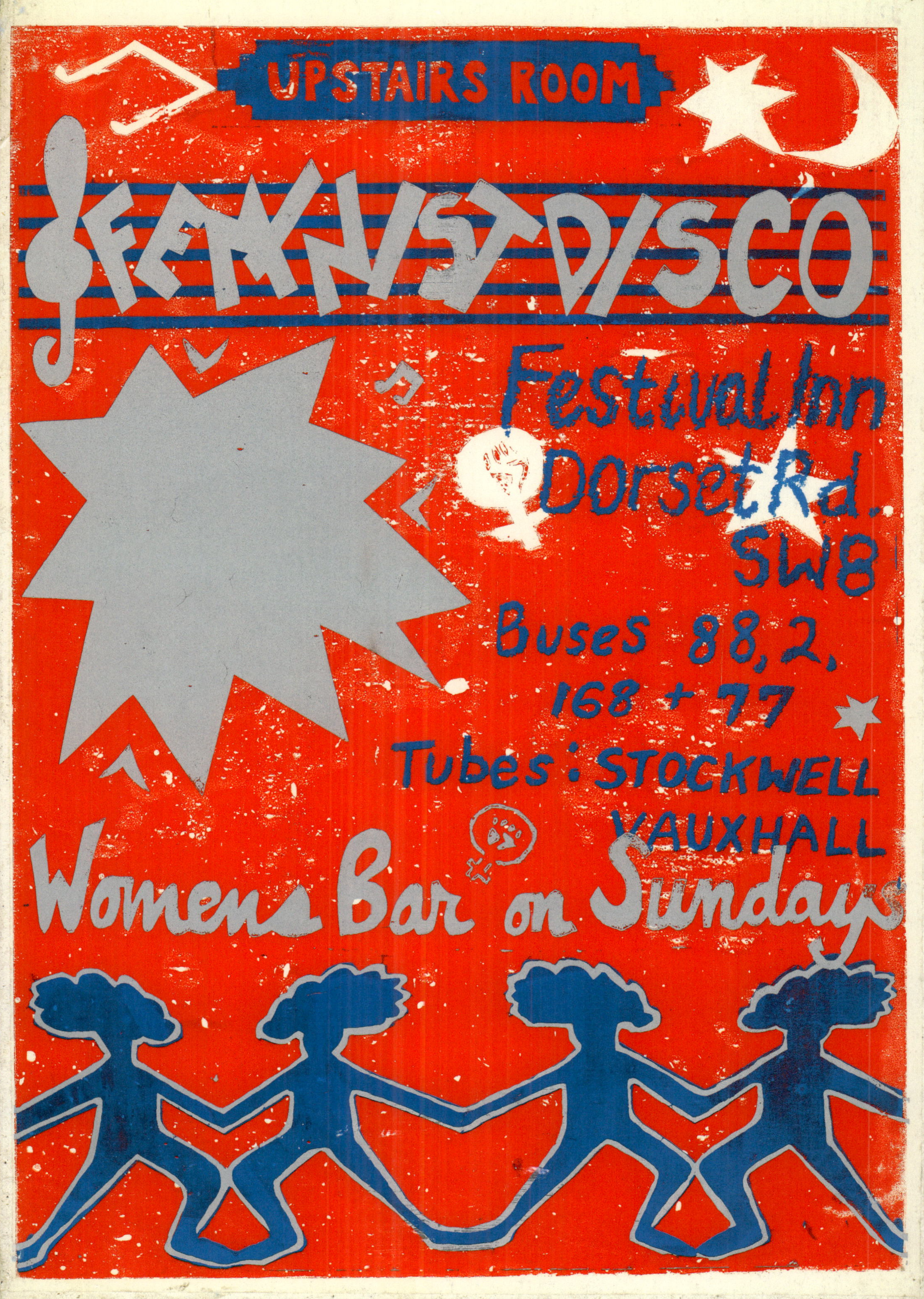

FEMINIST DISCO, 1980 64 × 44.5 cm

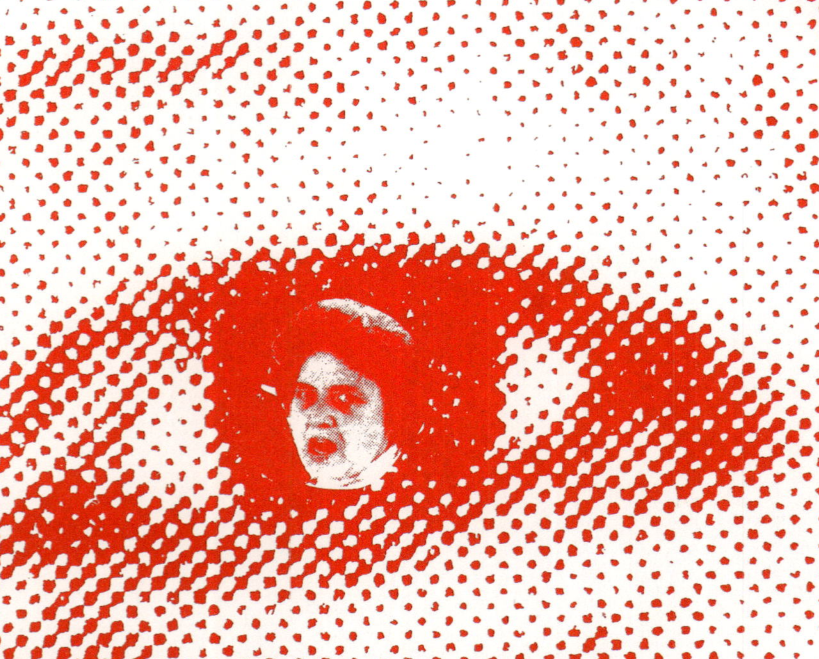
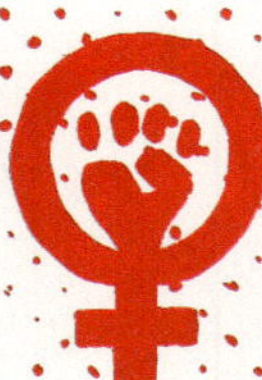
SEE RED WOMEN'S
CALENDAR 1980

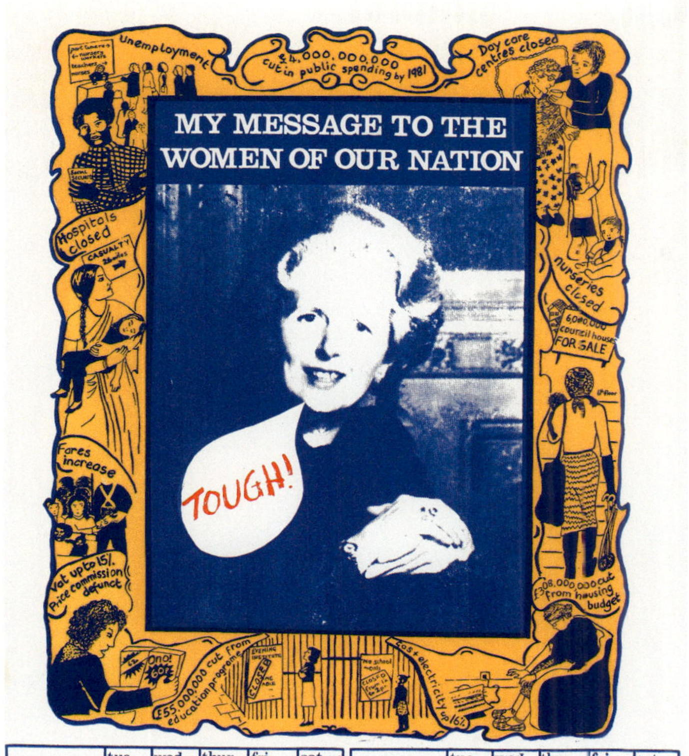

JANUARY	sun	mon	tue	wed	thur	fri	sat	FEBRUARY	sun	mon	tue	wed	thur	fri	sat

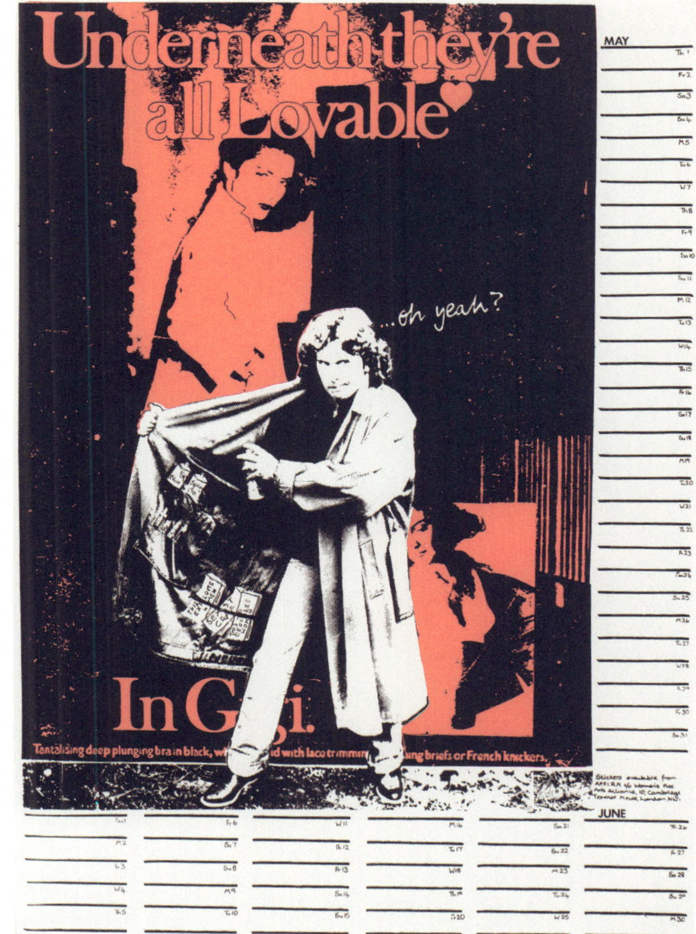

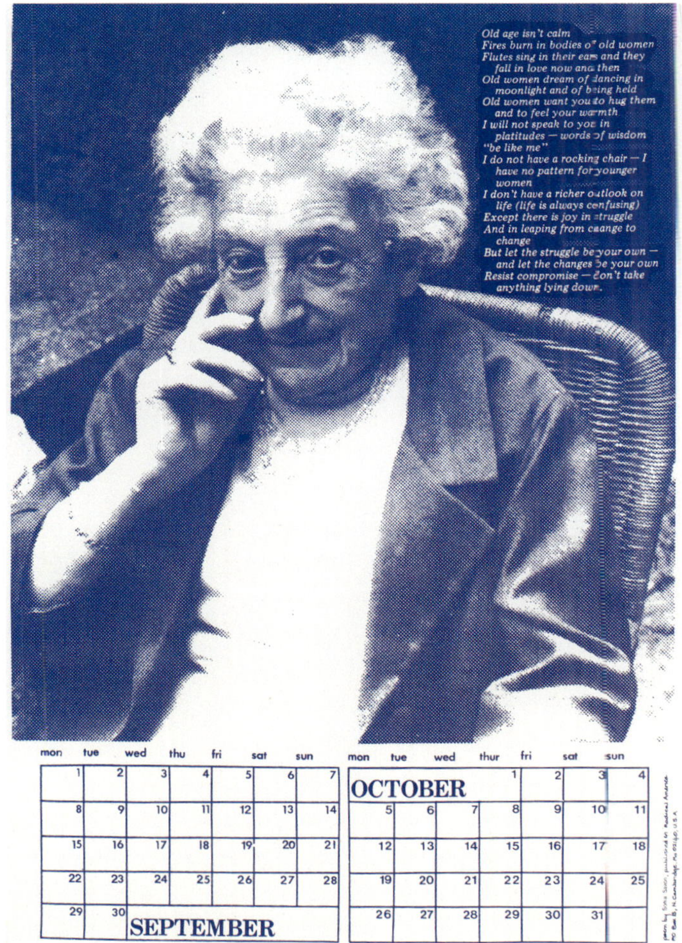

	mon	tue	wed	thu	fri	sat	sun	OCTOBER	mon	tue	wed	thur	fri	sat	sun

SEPTEMBER

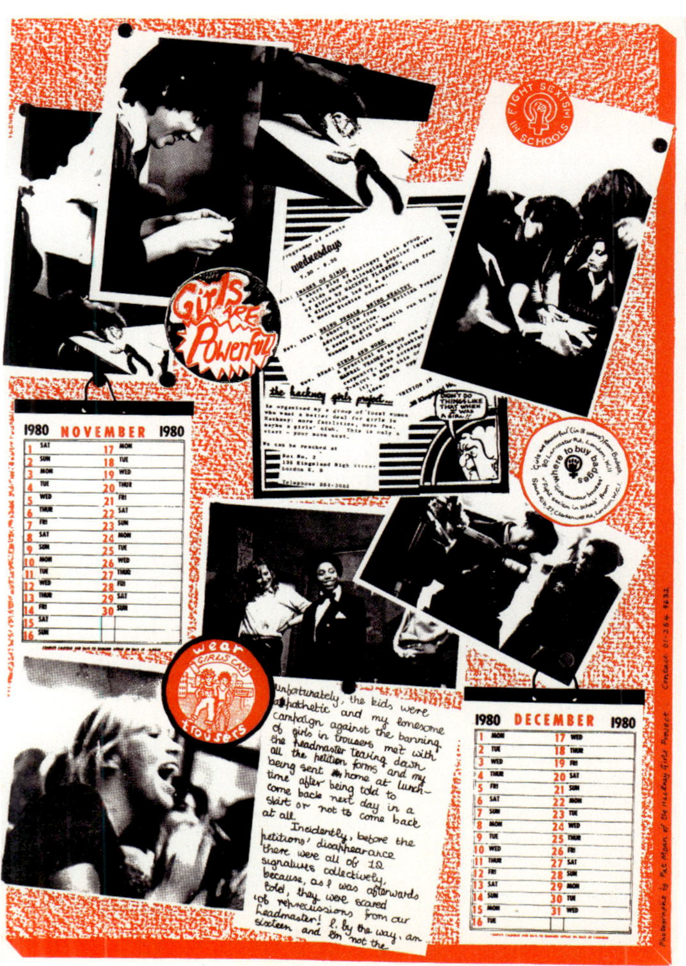

   SEE RED CALENDAR, 1980 *64 × 45 cm*

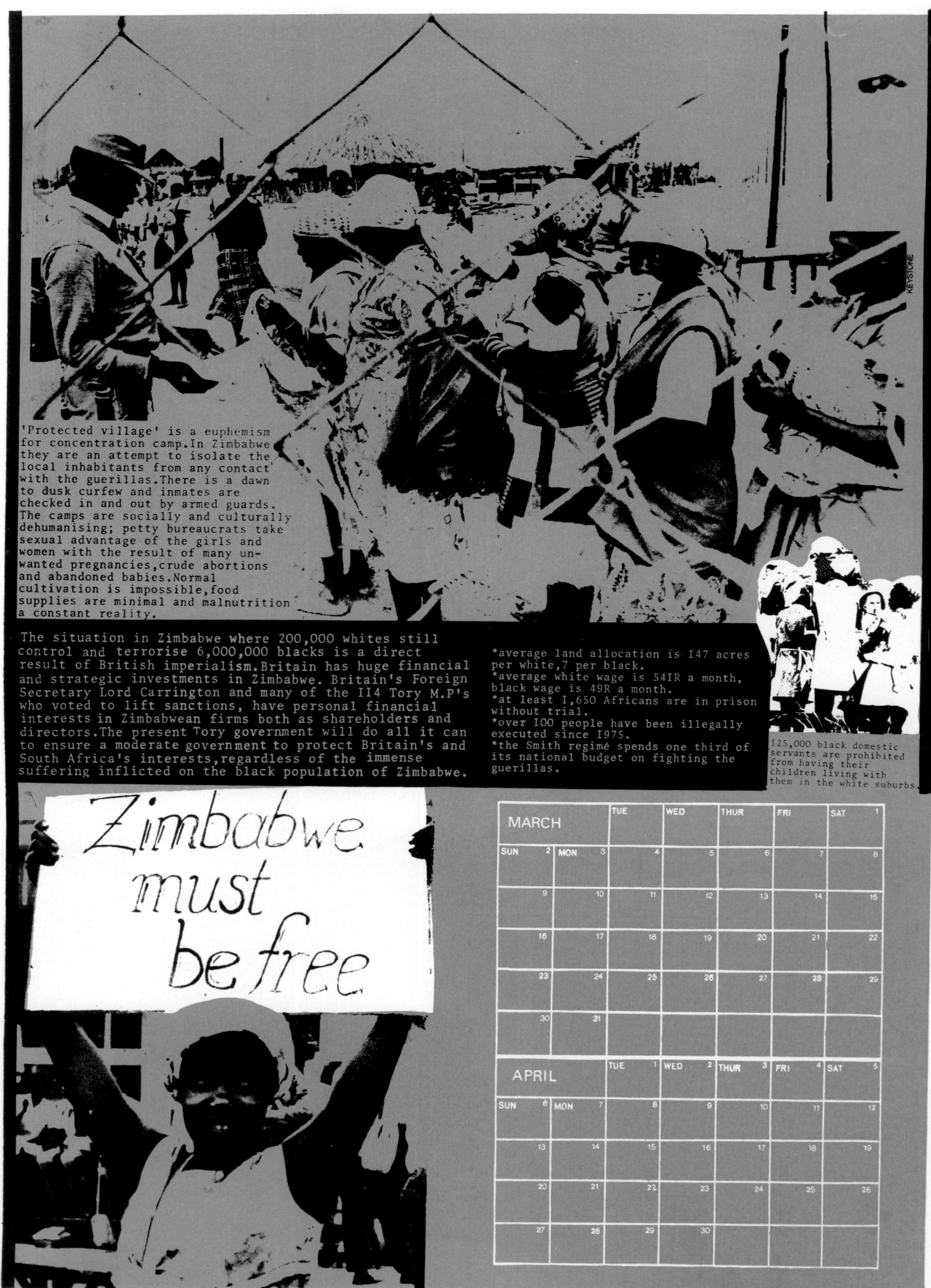

'Protected village' is a euphemism for concentration camp.In Zimbabwe they are an attempt to isolate the local inhabitants from any contact with the guerillas.There is a dawn to dusk curfew and inmates are checked in and out by armed guards. The camps are socially and culturally dehumanising; petty bureaucrats take sexual advantage of the girls and women with the result of many unwanted pregnancies,crude abortions and abandoned babies.Normal cultivation is impossible,food supplies are minimal and malnutrition a constant reality.

The situation in Zimbabwe where 200,000 whites still control and terrorise 6,000,000 blacks is a direct result of British imperialism.Britain has huge financial and strategic investments in Zimbabwe. Britain's Foreign Secretary Lord Carrington and many of the II4 Tory M.P's who voted to lift sanctions, have personal financial interests in Zimbabwean firms both as shareholders and directors.The present Tory government will do all it can to ensure a moderate government to protect Britain's and South Africa's interests,regardless of the immense suffering inflicted on the black population of Zimbabwe.

*average land allocation is I47 acres per white,7 per black.
*average white wage is 54IR a month, black wage is 49R a month.
*at least I,650 Africans are in prison without trial.
*over I00 people have been illegally executed since I975.
*the Smith regime spends one third of its national budget on fighting the guerillas.

I25,000 black domestic servants are prohibited from having their children living with them in the white suburbs.

MARCH		TUE	WED	THUR	FRI	SAT 1
SUN 2	MON 3	4	5	6	7	8
9	10	11	12	13	14	15
16	17	18	19	20	21	22
23	24	25	26	27	28	29
30	31					

APRIL		TUE 1	WED 2	THUR 3	FRI 4	SAT 5
SUN 6	MON 7	8	9	10	11	12
13	14	15	16	17	18	19
20	21	22	23	24	25	26
27	28	29	30			

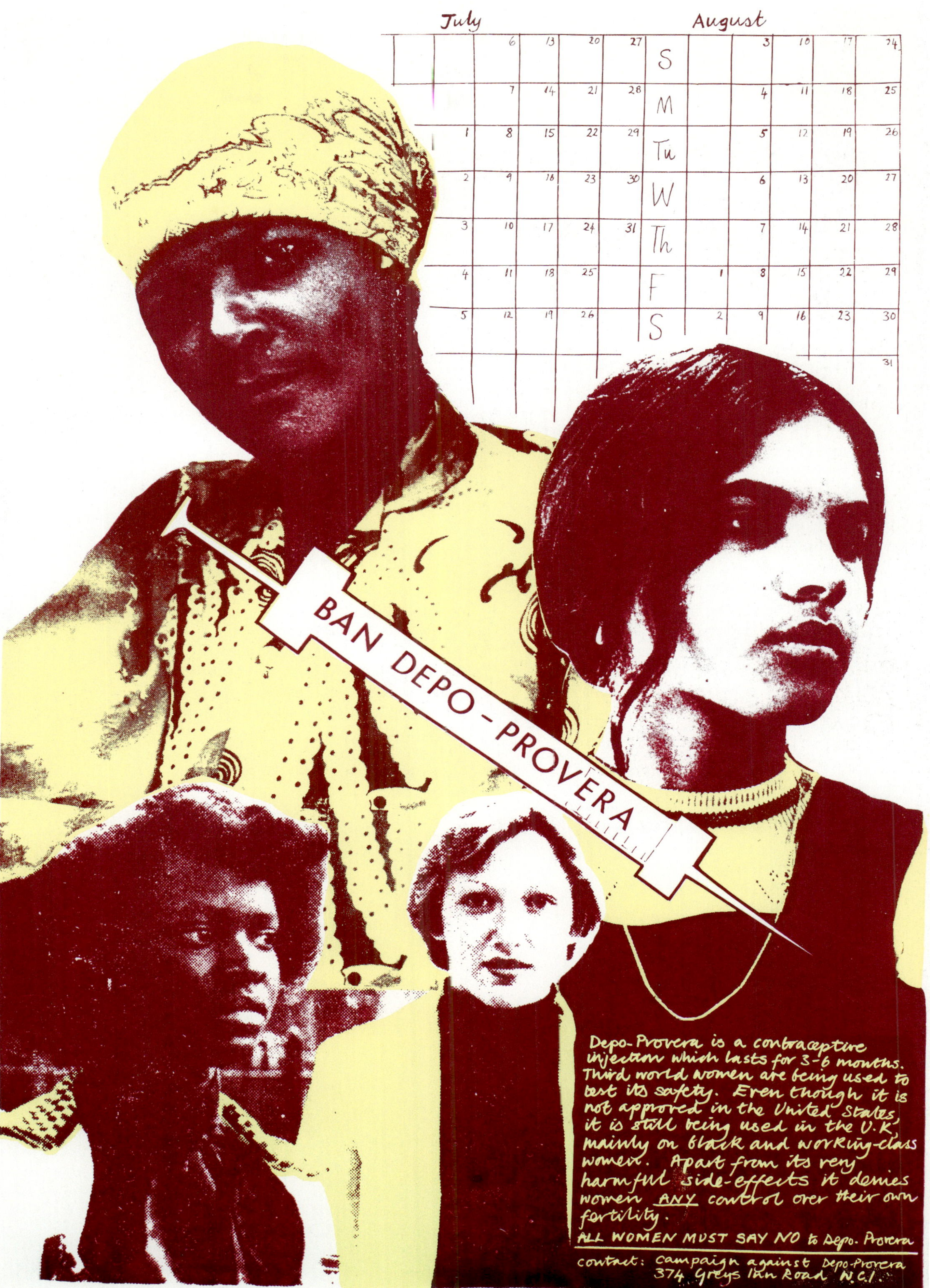

SEE RED CALENDAR, 1980 64 × 45 cm

A Colour It Yourself Alphabet
We were inspired to make this poster by
seeing posters aimed at children and young
people on our visit to women's and radical
print shops in the US. They produced posters
for children that could be used in schools
as well as the home, and which showed
positive images of girls engaged in
alternative activities.

Women Constitute ½ The Population
(*over the page*) photo: Charmian Reading.
Illustrating the facts about women from
the United Nations report 1980.

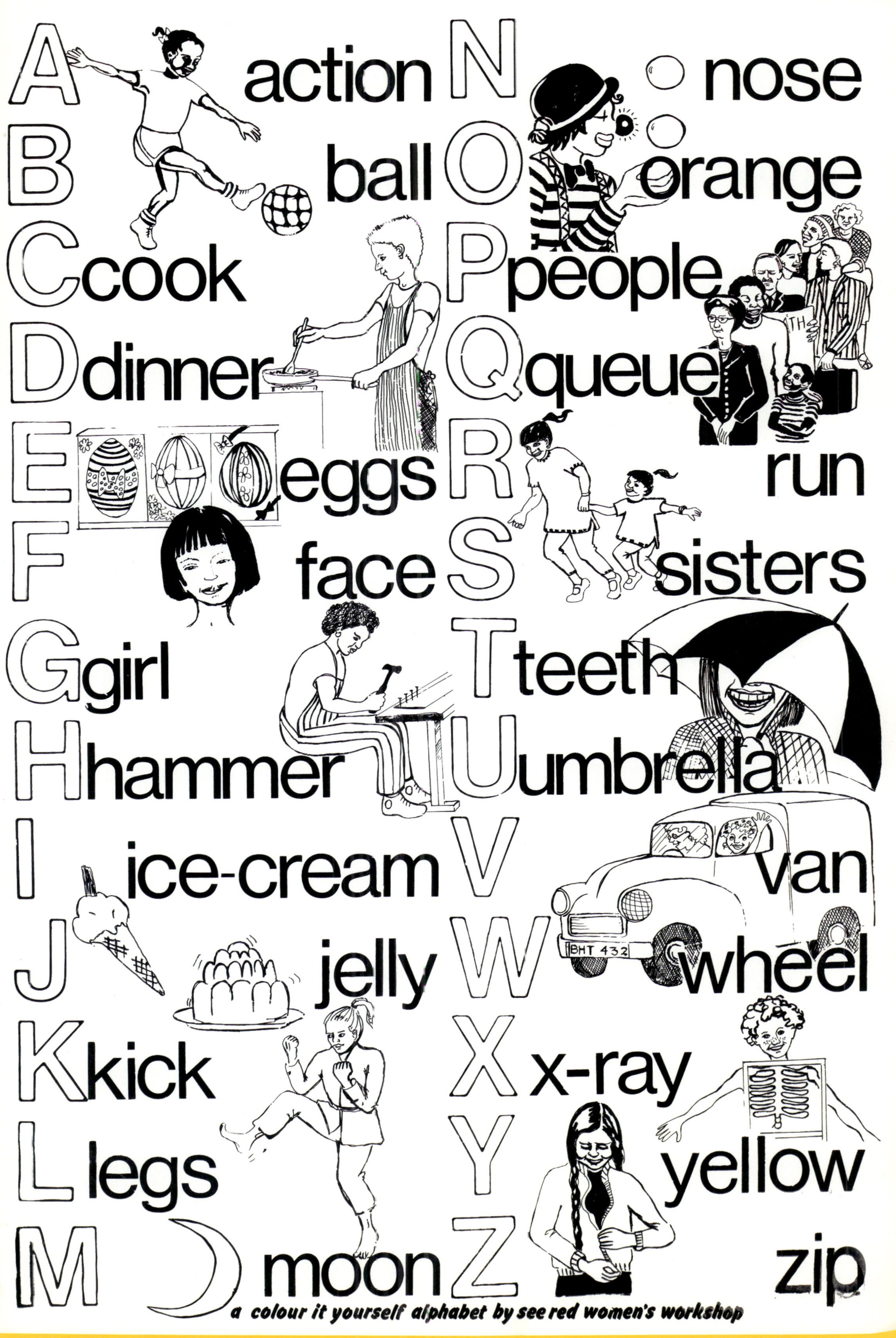
A
B
C cook
D dinner
E eggs
F face
G girl
H hammer
I ice-cream
J jelly
K kick
L legs
M moon
action
ball
N
O
P people
Q queue
R run
S sisters
T teeth
U umbrella
V van
W wheel
X x-ray
Y yellow
Z zip
nose
orange
a colour it yourself alphabet by see red women's workshop

Wom
constitute 1/2 the
perform nearly
receive 1/10 of th
and own l
of the worl

photos: Charmian Reading: L.N.S.

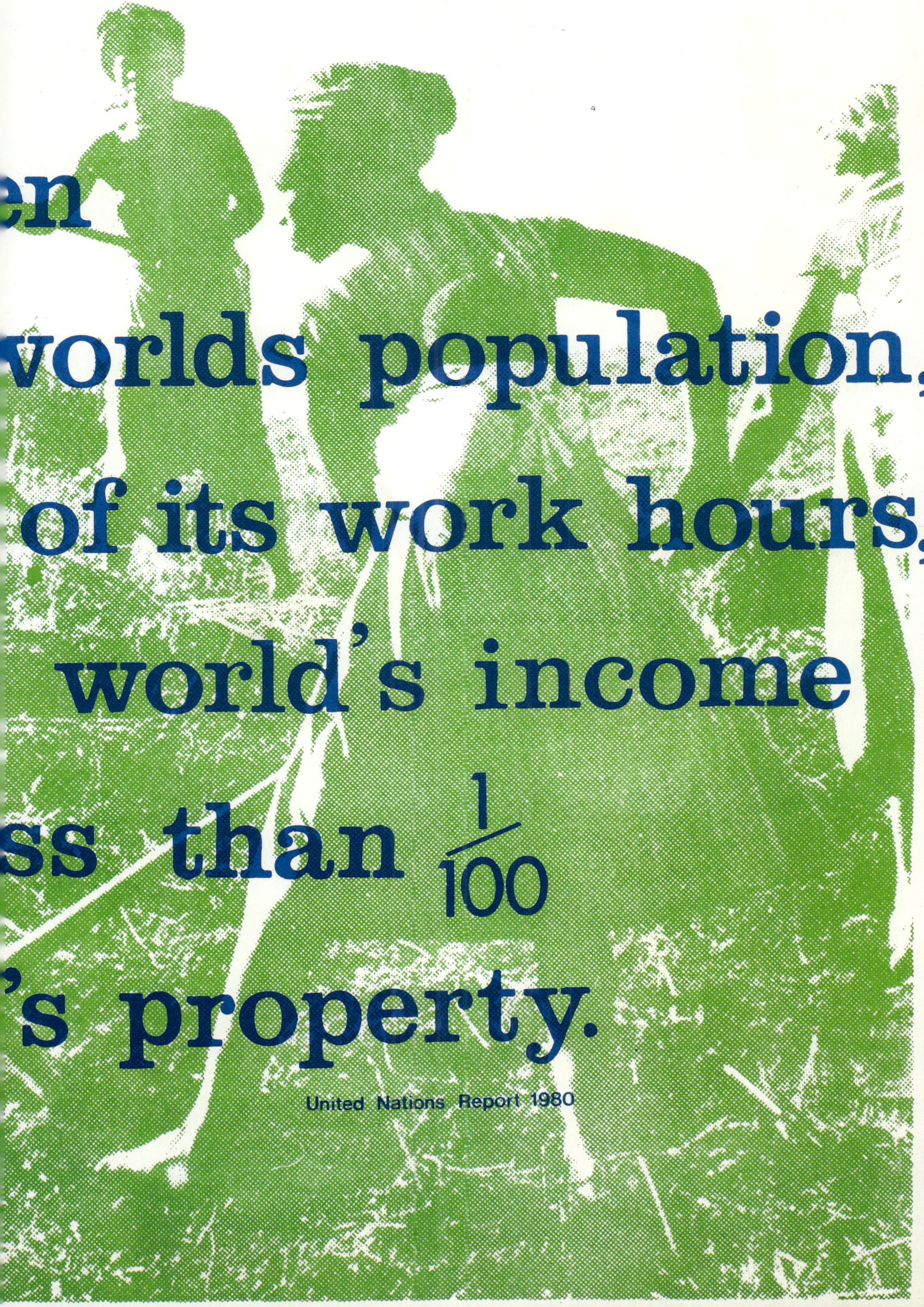

en

vorlds population,

of its work hours,

world's income

ss than $\frac{1}{100}$

's property.

United Nations Report 1980

See Red Women's Workshop

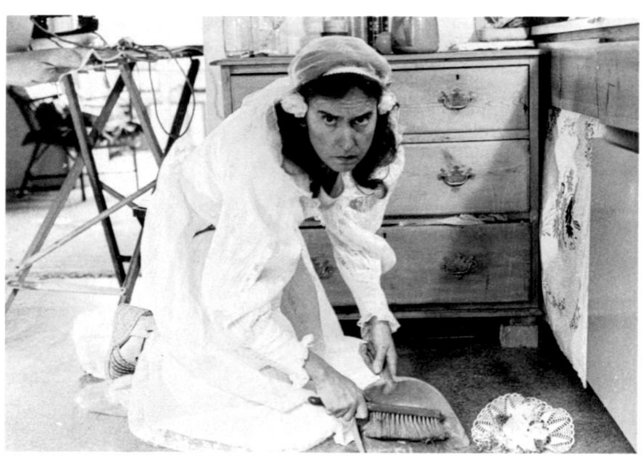

YBA Wife

Printed as part of the YBA wife and Don't Do it Di campaigns at the time of the marriage of Lady Diana Spencer and Prince Charles.

Traditionally, a married woman took her husband's name, promised to 'obey' him and often became economically and financially dependent on him.

The YBA Wife? campaign emerged from the campaign for Financial and Legal Independence and was approved as the Fifth Demand at the 1974 National Women's Liberation Conference.

> 'Why stop at legal and financial independence, why be a wife? ... it drew attention to the possibility that actually as women we don't have to be wives whether literally or symbolically and that was at its height at the time when poor Diana Spencer got married to Prince Charles.'
>
> Zoe Fairbairns, co founder of the YBA Wife campaign in *Sisterhood and After* (British Library)

IS there Life after Marriage?

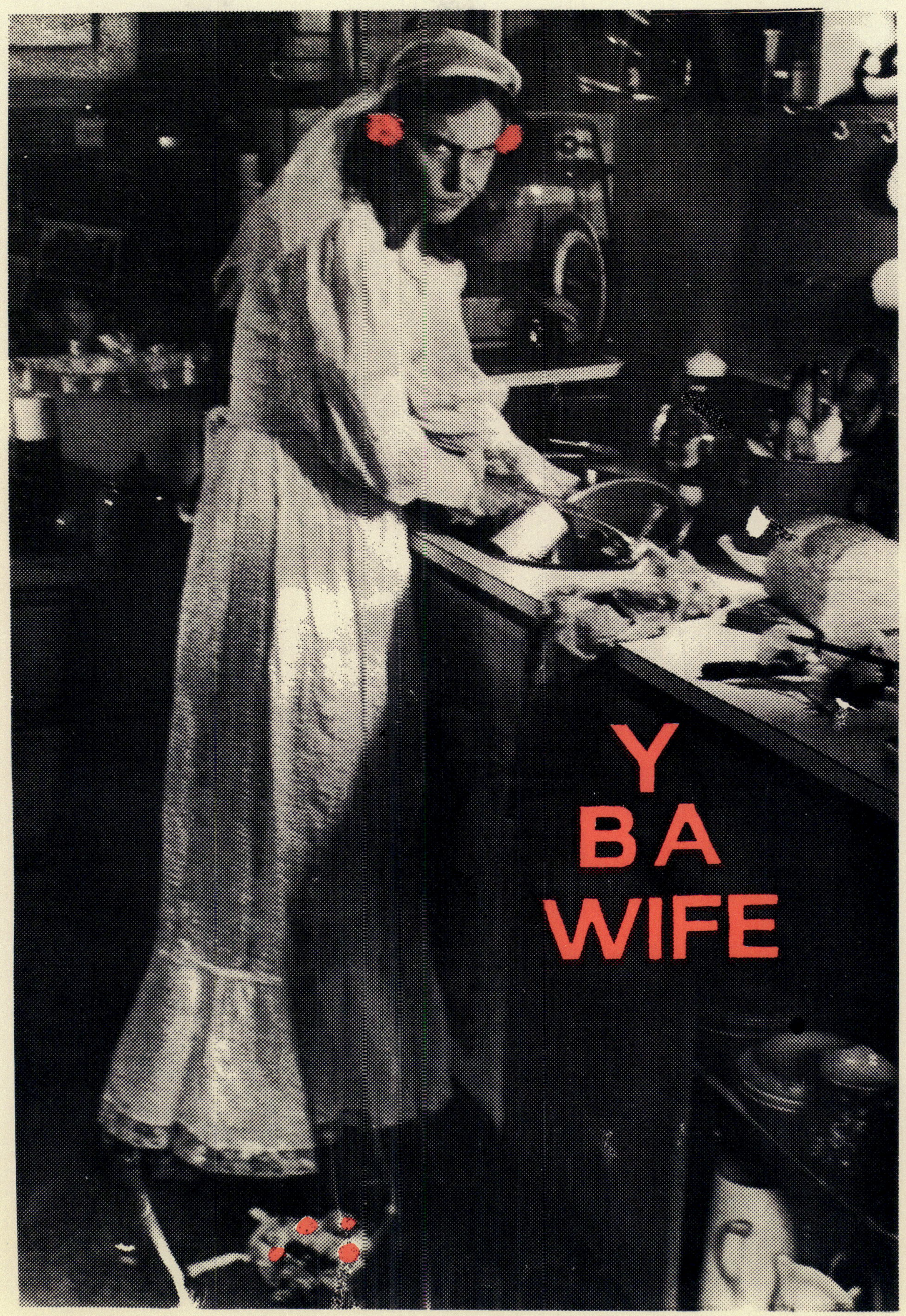

Support Our Sisters In Armagh Jail

Made in collaboration with the groups Women and Ireland and Women Against Imperialism in 1979-80.

In 1979 Armagh was the only women's prison in Ireland. At its height in 1975 the Irish republican women (most under the age of 25) numbered up to 120 but generally prison averaged around 60–70. In protest against the removal of their special category status and loss of privileges — deemed criminals rather than political prisoners — they refused to engage in any work or tasks. The women were very badly treated by a mostly male police force and prison officers, including: being locked up for 23 hours a day, having no ante-natal care, no books or radios, just two sanitary towels for three days a month, being allowed one 30 minute visit a month, and being subjected to sexual harrassment and beatings.

Initially feminists were divided in their support because of the women's membership of the IRA but later many came wholeheartedly to endorse the women's protest in part due to a letter smuggled out of the prison:

'It is a feminist issue in so far as we are women, even though we are treated like criminals. It is a feminist issue when the network of this jail is completely geared to male domination. The governor, the assistant governor, and the doctor are all males. We are subject to physical and mental abuse from the male screws who patrol our wing daily, continually peeping into our cells. If this is not a feminist issue, then we feel that the word feminist needs to be redefined to suit people who feel that 'feminist' applies to a certain section of women rather than encompassing women everywhere, regardless of politically held views.'

Armagh Prison closed in 1986.

**Three women's sexual health posters:
Our Body, Contraception, STIs** (*over the page*)

In 1980 we started work on a series of three women's sexual health posters: *Our Body*, *Contraception* and *Sexually Transmitted Infections* (STIs). Promoting and defining a new version of women's health became an integral part of the Women's Liberation movement and empowered women to have greater confidence in negotiating sexual relationships. From the mid 1970s, the publications *Our Bodies, Ourselves* by the Boston Women's Health Book Collective, and *Witches, Midwives and Nurses* by Barbara Ehrenreich and Deirdre English were essential and inspiring reading. Wordier than our usual posters, they came out of a need for alternative information for women about sexual and reproductive health issues that was accessible, respectful, and not full of medical jargon. This was a crucial part of empowering women to take charge of their own bodies. These posters were initially commissioned by a health promotion team in west London, and they were also distributed as See Red posters. All the information was up to date and double-checked by the Family Planning Association. *Contraception* lists different contraceptive methods with advantages and disadvantages clearly laid out.

The STI poster has an early mention of AIDS: it acknowledges that 'very little is known about its cause and how it is transmitted', that 'there has been a lot of scaremongering' about the illness and encouraging people to access health services if worried.

Our Body was specifically designed for use with young women: two See Red members used the sexual health posters at the youth clubs they worked at. We wanted to provide accurate and accessible information to counteract the lack of appropriately targeted health materials for young women.

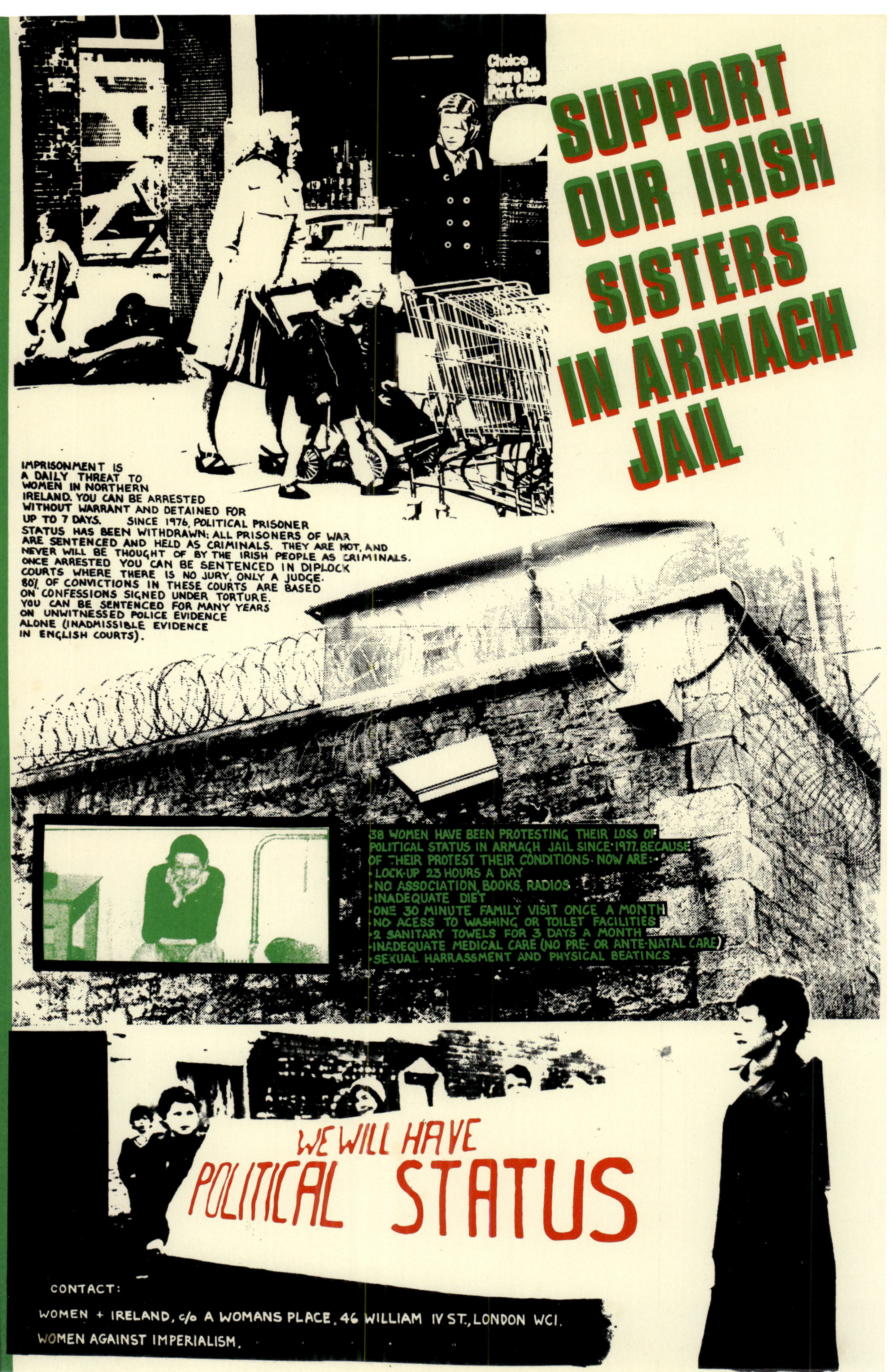

SUPPORT OUR IRISH SISTERS IN ARMAGH JAIL

IMPRISONMENT IS A DAILY THREAT TO WOMEN IN NORTHERN IRELAND. YOU CAN BE ARRESTED WITHOUT WARRANT AND DETAINED FOR UP TO 7 DAYS. SINCE 1976, POLITICAL PRISONER STATUS HAS BEEN WITHDRAWN; ALL PRISONERS OF WAR ARE SENTENCED AND HELD AS CRIMINALS. THEY ARE NOT, AND NEVER WILL BE THOUGHT OF BY THE IRISH PEOPLE AS CRIMINALS. ONCE ARRESTED YOU CAN BE SENTENCED IN DIPLOCK COURTS WHERE THERE IS NO JURY, ONLY A JUDGE. 80% OF CONVICTIONS IN THESE COURTS ARE BASED ON CONFESSIONS SIGNED UNDER TORTURE. YOU CAN BE SENTENCED FOR MANY YEARS ON UNWITNESSED POLICE EVIDENCE ALONE (INADMISSIBLE EVIDENCE IN ENGLISH COURTS).

38 WOMEN HAVE BEEN PROTESTING THEIR LOSS OF POLITICAL STATUS IN ARMAGH JAIL SINCE 1977. BECAUSE OF THEIR PROTEST THEIR CONDITIONS NOW ARE:
• LOCK-UP 23 HOURS A DAY
• NO ASSOCIATION, BOOKS, RADIOS
• INADEQUATE DIET
• ONE 30 MINUTE FAMILY VISIT ONCE A MONTH
• NO ACESS TO WASHING OR TOILET FACILITIES
• 2 SANITARY TOWELS FOR 3 DAYS A MONTH
• INADEQUATE MEDICAL CARE (NO PRE- OR ANTE-NATAL CARE)
• SEXUAL HARRASSMENT AND PHYSICAL BEATINGS

WE WILL HAVE POLITICAL STATUS

CONTACT:
WOMEN + IRELAND, c/o A WOMANS PLACE, 46 WILLIAM IV ST., LONDON WCI.
WOMEN AGAINST IMPERIALISM.

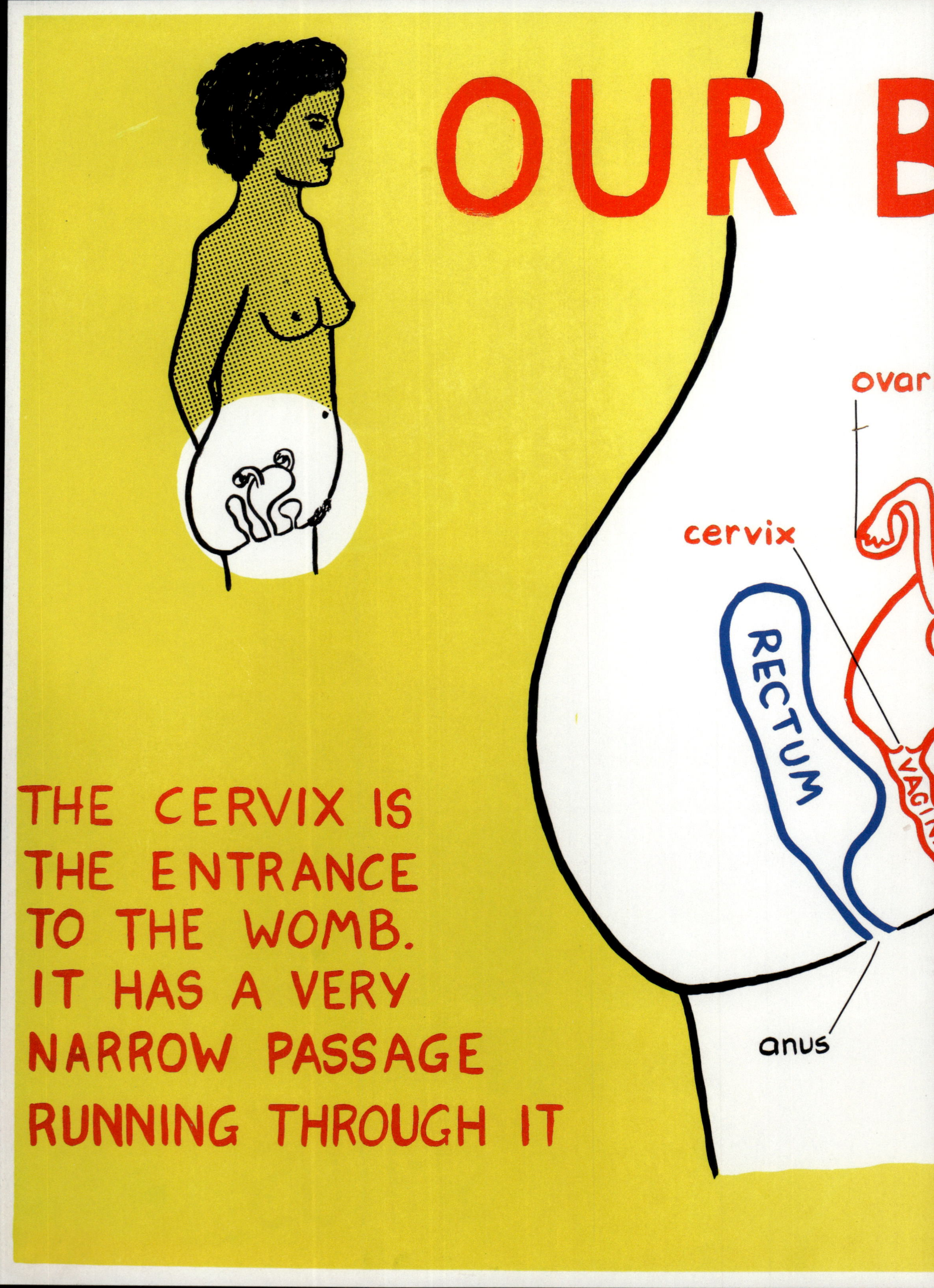

OUR BODY, 1980/81 51 × 76 cm

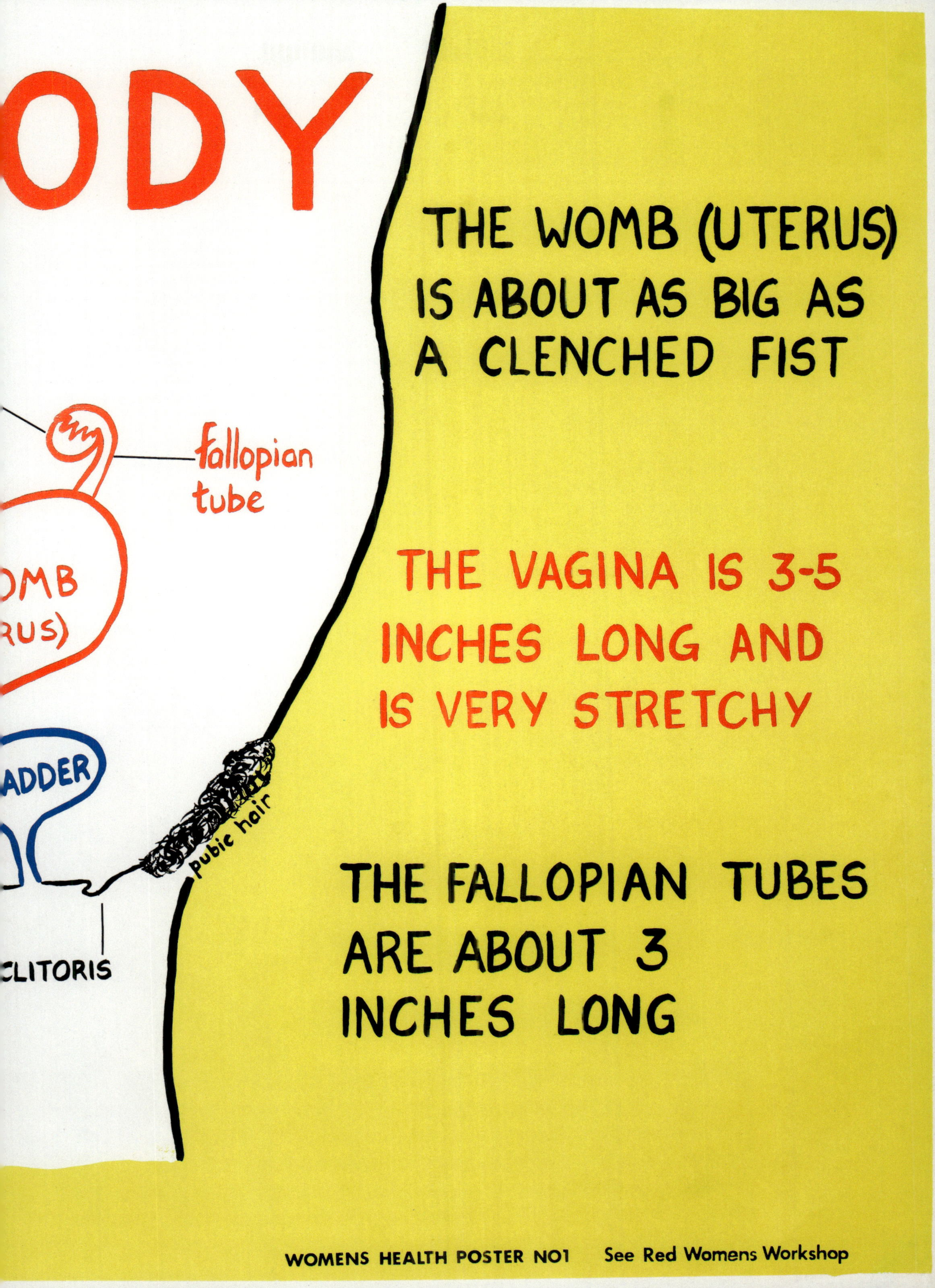

WOMENS HEALTH POSTER NO1   See Red Womens Workshop

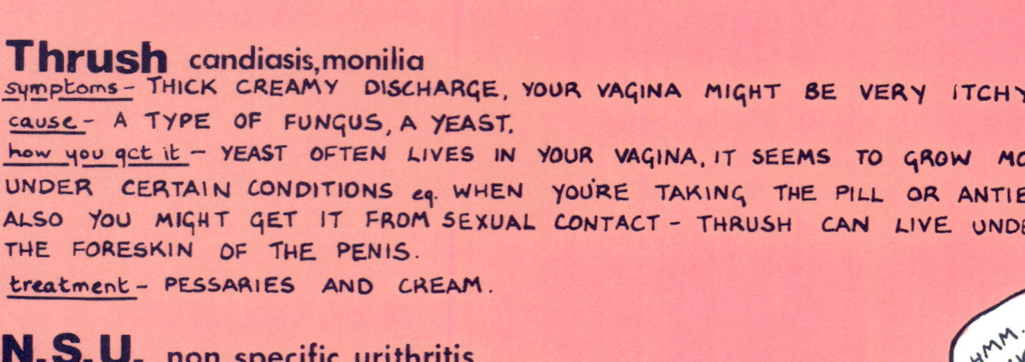

Thrush candiasis, monilia
symptoms- THICK CREAMY DISCHARGE, YOUR VAGINA MIGHT BE VERY ITCHY.
cause- A TYPE OF FUNGUS, A YEAST.
how you get it - YEAST OFTEN LIVES IN YOUR VAGINA, IT SEEMS TO GROW MORE UNDER CERTAIN CONDITIONS eg. WHEN YOU'RE TAKING THE PILL OR ANTIBIOTICS. ALSO YOU MIGHT GET IT FROM SEXUAL CONTACT - THRUSH CAN LIVE UNDER THE FORESKIN OF THE PENIS.
treatment- PESSARIES AND CREAM.

N.S.U. non specific urithritis
symptoms- A DISCHARGE; PAIN WHEN YOU URINATE.
cause- SOMETIMES AN ORGANISM CALLED CHLAMYDIA; THERE ARE OTHER CAUSES TOO.
how you get it- CLOSE SEXUAL CONTACT. WOMEN DON'T USUALLY HAVE SYMPTOMS BUT MAY PASS THE INFECTION ON.
treatment- ANTIBIOTICS.

Gonorrhea the clap, a dose
symptoms- DISCHARGE AND PAIN WHEN YOU URINATE. SOMETIMES IRRITATION AND DISCHARGE FROM YOUR ANUS. THESE FIRST SYMPTOMS APPEAR 3 DAYS - 3 WEEKS AFTER SEXUAL CONTACT. MEN USUALLY [BUT NOT ALWAYS] GET SYMPTOMS, BUT MANY WOMEN HAVE NO SYMPTOMS. IF YOU DON'T GET TREATMENT, THE INFECTION MIGHT SPREAD TO YOUR WOMB AND TUBES. IT MIGHT MAKE YOU STERILE
cause- BACTERIA CALLED GONOCOCCI
how you get it - CLOSE SEXUAL CONTACT
treatment- ANTIBIOTICS

Trichomoniasis
TV, trich, trikes
symptoms- A YELLOW DISCHARGE WITH A BAD SMELL
cause- AN ORGANISM CALLED TRICHOMONIASIS.
how you get it - CLOSE SEXUAL CONTACT. MEN DON'T USUALLY HAVE SYMPTOMS BUT MAY PASS THE INFECTION ON SOMETIMES YOU CAN GET IT FROM TOWELS ETC.
treatment- ANTIBIOTICS

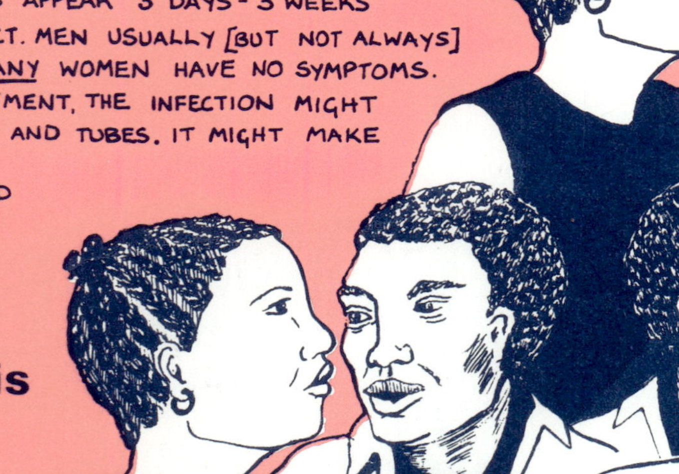

Genital Warts

symptoms - WARTS ON OR NEAR YOUR SEX ORGANS; THEY MAY ITCH. YOU GET THEM 1-9 MONTHS AFTER INFECTION.

cause - A VIRUS LIKE THE ONE WHICH CAUSES WARTS ON OTHER PARTS OF YOUR BODY.

how you get it - CLOSE SEXUAL CONTACT. CAN ALSO SPREAD FROM ORDINARY WARTS ON YOUR BODY.

treatment - OINTMENT: SOMETIMES A CHEMICAL PAINTED ON: OR THE WARTS ARE 'FROZEN' OFF.

Herpes

symptoms - PAINFUL ITCHY BLISTERS ON OR NEAR YOUR SEX ORGANS, 2-10 DAYS AFTER SEXUAL CONTACT. SOMETIMES TINGLING IN THE LEGS AND RUN-DOWN FEELING.

cause - A VIRUS CALLED HERPES 2; OR SOMETIMES HERPES 1 (WHICH CAUSES COLD SORES).

how you get it - CLOSE SEXUAL CONTACT.

treatment - SORENESS CAN BE HELPED BY PAINKILLERS, OINTMENT, HERBS AND DIET OUTBREAKS OF SORES CAN BE LESSENED BUT NOT COMPLETELY CURED.

Syphilis pox

symptoms - A PAINLESS SORE ON OR NEAR YOUR SEX ORGANS (YOU MAY NOT SEE THIS IF IT IS INSIDE YOU) APPEARING 10 DAYS TO 3 MONTHS AFTER SEXUAL CONTACT - USUALLY 3-4 WEEKS. IF YOU DON'T GET TREATMENT YOU MAY GET A RASH ON YOUR BODY WHICH DOESN'T ITCH. MUCH LATER ON (AFTER 5 YEARS OR SO) YOU COULD GET SERIOUS DAMAGE TO YOUR HEART, EYES, EARS AND CENTRAL NERVOUS SYSTEM.

cause - BACTERIA CALLED SPIROCHETE.

how you get it - CLOSE SEXUAL CONTACT.

treatment - ANTIBIOTICS

Crabs pubic lice, nits

symptoms - ITCHING IN YOUR PUBIC HAIR, EYEBROWS OR ARMPITS.

cause - TINY INSECTS SIMILAR TO HEAD LICE.

how you get it - CLOSE SEXUAL CONTACT, OR FROM BEDDING, TOWELS ETC.

treatment - POWDER AND SHAMPOO FROM THE CHEMIST OR FROM THE SPECIAL CLINIC.

A.I.D.S. Anti Immuno Deficiency Syndrome

VERY LITTLE IS KNOWN ABOUT IT'S CAUSE AND HOW IT IS TRANSMITTED.

symptoms - SUDDEN WEIGHT LOSS, PERSISTENT SWOLLEN GLANDS, SLIGHT FEVERS, DRY COUGH, AND DIARRHOEA   what happens - THE BODY'S IMMUNE SYSTEM BREAKS DOWN LEAVING IT DEFENCELESS AGAINST ANY INFECTIONS WHICH PROVE FATAL.

most at risk - ARE GAY/BISEXUAL MEN, INTRAVENOUS DRUG USERS, HAEMOPHILIACS. ALL OF THE SYMPTOMS ARE VERY VAGUE, SO THERE HAS BEEN A LOT OF SCARE-MONGERING. DON'T PANIC IF YOU THINK YOU HAVE IT - SEE A DOCTOR IMMEDIATELY.

[20·5·83 15 KNOWN CASES IN THE U.K.]

Cystitis

symptoms - FEELING YOU NEED TO GO TO THE TOILET VERY OFTEN. PAIN AND A BURNING SENSATION WHEN YOU GO

cause - INFECTION OR INFLAMMATION OF YOUR BLADDER.

how you get it - CAN BE CAUSED BY MANY INFECTIONS AND ILLNESSES. MAY HAPPEN AFTER SEX.

treatment - AS SOON AS IT STARTS DRINK LOTS OF WATER. TAKE 1 TEASPOON OF BICARBONATE OF SODA EVERY HOUR FOR THREE HOURS. WASH YOUR SEX ORGANS (NOT USING SOAP) AFTER GOING TO THE TOILET. GO TO THE SPECIAL CLINIC IF IT GOES ON - YOU MAY NEED ANTIBIOTICS.

see red women's workshop health poster no. 2

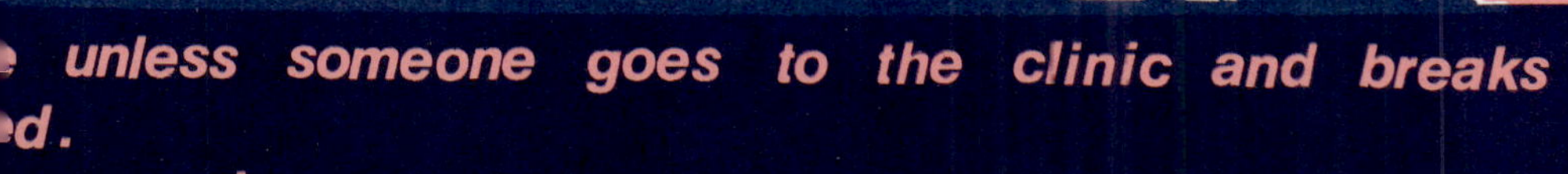

e unless someone goes to the clinic and breaks
d.

very important to go to the clinic. Treatment

Venereal diseases'
tion— you could just as easily have caught flu.
Tell your partner.

the pill

COMPLETELY **RELIABLE** IF PROPERLY USED. THE PILL CONTAINS HORMONES WHICH STOP EGGS BEING RELEASED FROM YOUR OVARIES. THERE ARE MANY KINDS- IF THE ONE YOU ARE PRESCRIBED DOESN'T SUIT YOU, ASK TO CHANGE. PILLS HAVE TO BE TAKEN REGULARLY - 1 A DAY FOR 3 WEEKS, THEN STOP FOR A WEEK. BE SURE YOU INSIST **ON A FULL MEDICAL CHECK-UP** BEFORE **STARTING** TO TAKE THE PILL- IF YOU HAVE THROMBOSIS IN THE **FAMILY,** OR JAUNDICE, EPILEPSY, DIABETES OR HIGH BLOOD PRESSURE YOU SHOULDN'T TAKE IT.

DISADVANTAGES-
WHILE YOUR BODY IS ADJUSTING TO THE PILL - TIREDNESS, WEIGHT GAIN, NAUSEA, HEADACHES, VAGINAL INFECTIONS. IF THESE GO ON FOR MORE THAN 1 OR 2 MONTHS GO BACK TO THE DOCTOR AND ASK HER TO FIND A KIND THAT SUITS YOU BETTER LONG TERM EFFECTS ARE NOT FULLY KNOWN.

ADVANTAGES-
MOST RELIABLE OF CONTRACEPTIVES, AND IS VERY CONVENIENT.

cap (DIAPHRAGM)

96% RELIABLE IF USED WITH SPERMICIDES.
A THIN SOFT RUBBER DISC YOU PUT IN YOURSELF BEFORE HAVING SEX, AND TAKE OUT 6 HOURS AFTER. (YOU MUST USE A SPERMICIDAL CREAM OR JELLY AS WELL). IT FITS INSIDE THE VAGINA CLOSING OFF THE ENTRANCE TO THE WOMB AND STOPPING SPERMS ENTERING. YOU GET THEM FROM A DOCTOR OR CLINIC AS THEY HAVE TO BE FITTED TO YOUR EXACT SIZE AND YOU MUST LEARN TO PUT IT IN PROPERLY YOURSELF.

DISADVANTAGES-
HAVING TO THINK ABOUT PUTTING YOUR CAP IN BEFORE SEX. SOME SPERMICIDES TASTE BAD, BUT TRY DIFFERENT ONES.

ADVANTAGES-
VERY SAFE METHOD (IF PROPERLY USED WITH SPERMICIDE) WHICH IS COMPLETELY UNDER YOUR CONTROL. NO RISK OF DAMAGING YOUR BODY WITH CHEMICALS.

coil

(INTER-UTERINE DEVICE: I.U.D.)
98% RELIABLE
SMALL COPPER OR PLASTIC DEVICE FITTED INSIDE THE UTERUS BY A DOCTOR, WHICH PREVENTS A FERTILISED EGG DEVELOPING INSIDE THE WOMB. THEY CAN STAY IN PLACE FOR SEVERAL YEARS- COPPER 7s HAVE TO BE CHANGED EVERY 2 YEARS.

DISADVANTAGES-
IT MAY CAUSE HEAVIER PERIODS AND INCREASE THE RISK OF INFECTION IN THE TUBES. ANY UNUSUAL PAINS SHOULD BE REPORTED TO YOUR DOCTOR. IT MAY BECOME DISLODGED, BUT YOU CAN CHECK WEEKLY TO MAKE SURE IT IS IN PLACE BY FEELING THE STRINGS.

ADVANTAGES-
THERE ARE NO CHEMICALS DISRUPTING YOUR BODY'S CYCLES. IF COMFORTABLY FITTED, ONCE IN PLACE, YOU DON'T KNOW ITS THERE.

CONTRACEPTION, 1980/81 51 × 76 cm

sheath
(DUREX, RUBBER, CONDOM)

96% RELIABLE IF PROPERLY USED. THE SHEATH IS MADE OF VERY THIN RUBBER AND FITS ONTO THE ERECT PENIS BEFORE HAVING SEX AND IS REMOVED AFTERWARDS. THE SHEATH COLLECTS THE SPERM AND PREVENTS THEM ENTERING THE WOMB.

DISADVANTAGES—
YOU HAVE TO BE VERY CAREFUL TO USE IT PROPERLY. THE MAN HAS TO WITHDRAW IMMEDIATELY AFTER HE HAS COME.

ADVANTAGES—

EASY TO BUY AND SIMPLE TO USE. CUTS DOWN ON SPREAD OF V.D.

depo-provera
do not us

THIS IS A CONTRACEPTIVE INJECTION WHICH LASTS 3-6 MONTHS. IT IS BANNED IN THE U.S.A, BUT IS STILL USED IN BRITAIN. BEWARE – IT IS ASSOCIATED WITH INCREASED RISK OF CANCER OF THE CERVIX; CAUSES IRREGULAR BLEEDING, POSSIBLE STERILITY AND LONGTERM INFERTILITY AFTERWARDS. MANY OTHER SIDE EFFECTS SUCH AS WEIGHT GAIN, HAIR LOSS, NAUSEA, DEPRESSION.

not safe

① WITHDRAWAL: THE MAN MAY NOT PULL OUT IN TIME TO PREVENT HIS SPERM FERTILISING THE EGG.
② RHYTHM METHOD: THERE ARE NO TIMES DURING THE MONTH WHEN IT IS 'SAFE' TO HAVE SEX, INCLUDING DURING A PERIOD.
③ DON'T RELY ON SPERMICIDES ALONE.
④ STANDING UP: THIS DOES NOT STOP THE SPERM SWIMMING UP TO MEET THE EGG.
⑤ DOUCHING: TRYING TO WASH THE SPERM OUT WITH WATER USUALLY TOO LATE AND CAN SPREAD INFECTION.

pregnancy

IF YOU ARE PREGNANT AND CAN'T TELL YOUR FAMILY, AND YOU DON'T WANT TO HAVE A BABY, YOU CAN HAVE AN ABORTION IF YOU DO DECIDE TO DO THIS IT IS VERY IMPORTANT THAT YOU GET SYMPATHETIC ADVICE. GO TO ONE OF THE PLACES LISTED HERE TAKE A FRIEND WITH YOU IF POSSIBLE TO GIVE YOU SUPPORT. AN EARLY ABORTION IS NOT UNCOMFORTABLE. DON'T TRY AND ABORT YOURSELF — GIN AND HOT BATHS ETC. DO NOT WORK AND ARE VERY DANGEROUS.

See Red Women's Workshop

ner St. London W1. 01 636 7866
n W1. 01 580 2991
Austy Manor, Wooton, Wawen,

es of these agencies.
questions --- it's your body.

Black Women Will Not Be Intimidated
(*opposite page*) Photos: L. Sparham,
L. Watson, M. Sheridan and M. Rusher

Celebration For Change (*over the page*)
Poem by Nefertiti (formerly Rosemarie) Gayle.
photo: M. Rusher

Although the women's movement aimed to
represent all women, it tended to be white-
dominated and often excluded black and Asian
women's history, issues and voices. In the 1970s,
black and Asian feminists began to organise
separately and establish their own distinct
identities, combining the struggle for racial
equality with the struggle for gender equality.

Black women set up local supplementary
schools and crèches, supported black
bookshops and black women writers, organised
black women's centres and conferences, and
mobilised against racism. Groups organised
around deportation and immigration issues, and
demonstrated in solidarity with black and Asian
womens' struggles internationally, including the
1976–78 Asian women workers' strike at the
Grunwick film processing laboratories, dubbed
'strikers in saris' by the media. Other groups
that were founded included: the Brixton Black
Women's Group, formed in 1973 to address
issues faced by black women and to offer
advice and support; the Southall Black Sisters,
formed in 1979 to support all black and Asian
women living in the UK through campaigns,
legal advice, information and counselling; and
the Asian Women's Refuge movement, which
began in Brent.

In 1978 the Organisation of Women of
Asian and African Descent (OWAAD), with
their newsletter *FOWAAD!*, was founded as
a UK-wide umbrella organisation supporting
smaller groups. It made a huge contribution
to placing the experience of black and Asian
women on the women's liberation agenda,
and campaigned on many issues such as the
'sus' campaigns, including racism in education
provision; domestic violence; exclusion of
children from school; industrial action by
black women; policing and defence policies;
and health and reproductive rights.

Kehinde James joined us in 1979 to portray
through posters the experiences of black women
in the UK: 'The message of *Black Women Will
Not Be Intimidated* is that in spite of racism,
sexism and discrimination, black women are
united, purposeful and committed and they
will keep campaigning and demonstrating
until they achieve fair and equal treatment
for themselves and their families.

'Carnival for Change is a way of saying,
yes we know black people love to celebrate,
but imagine what a difference it would make
if we also used the energy of carnival to make
a difference and change the world.

'In the 1980s many black women felt their
needs and priorities were very different and
more acute than those of white women, and
in many cases they were. Today my perspective
is more inclusive: discrimination and unequal
treatment, whatever form it takes and whoever
it is aimed at, is the same, it dehumanises
and harms.'

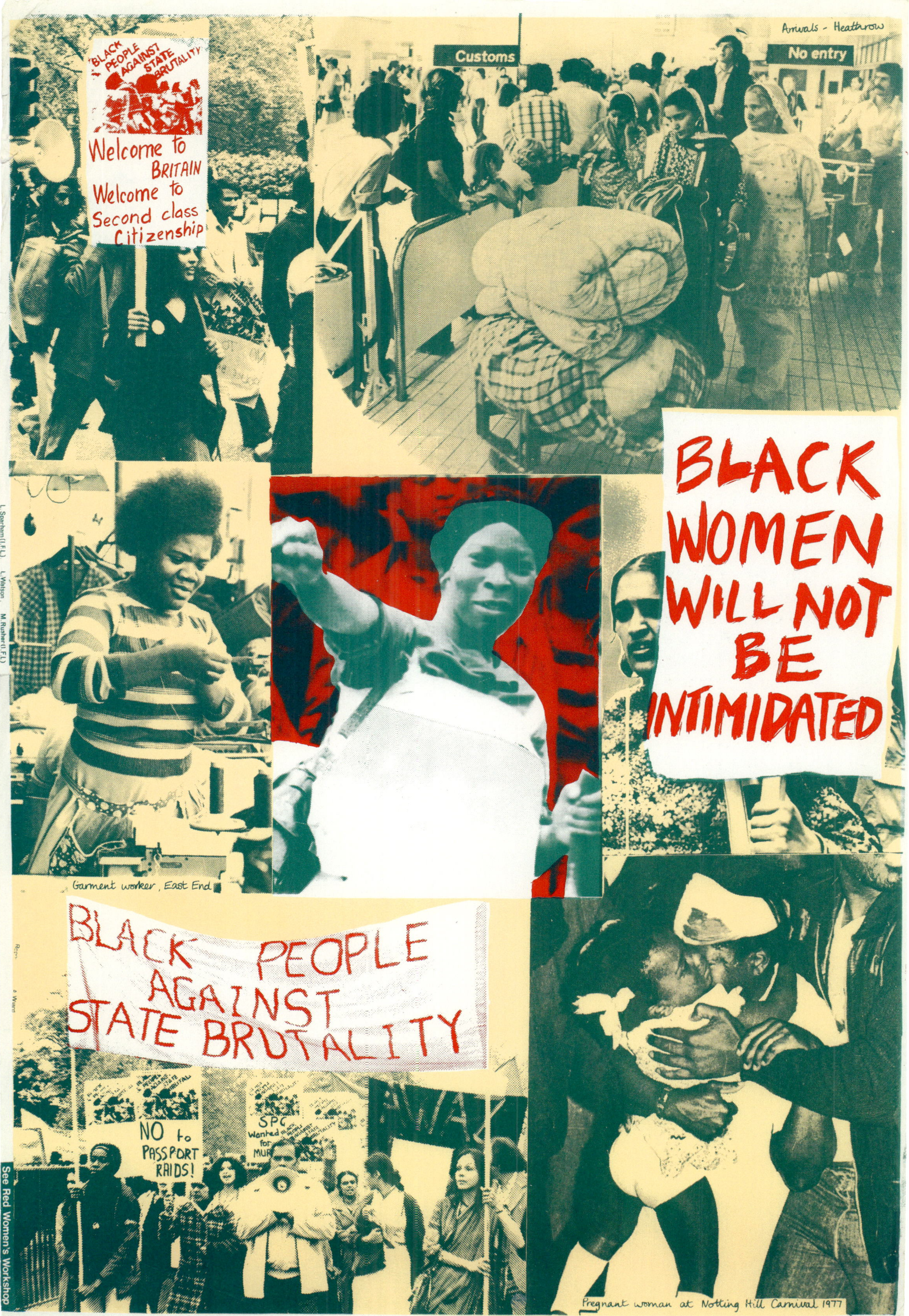
BLACK PEOPLE AGAINST STATE BRUTALITY
Welcome to BRITAIN
Welcome to Second class Citizenship
Arrivals - Heathrow
Customs
No entry
BLACK WOMEN WILL NOT BE INTIMIDATED
Garment worker, East End
L. Sperhent (I.F.L.)
L. Watson
M. Rutherd (I.F.L.)
BLACK PEOPLE AGAINST STATE BRUTALITY
NO to PASSPORT RAIDS!
SPG Wanted for MURDER
BWAL
See Red Women's Workshop
Pregnant woman at Notting Hill Carnival 1977
Report M. Sheridan (I.F.L.)

A CELEBRATION FOR CHANGE

Its carnival time
A celebration for change
Police brutality an
Margaret Thatcher reign
Hear pan beat
Jumping feet
Me black sisters laughing
An a prancing in the street.

Some in coloured garments
Marching in parade
Red, green an gold
In masks which are made.
See blue strangers lurking
For brothers who are bold
Oppressed people stand
Fighting, young an old.

Carnival is laughing
It must go on in strength
We are one people here to stay
We celebrate for change today
We are one people
We claim our rights
With unity an love we fight.

© Nefertiti Gayle

A CELEBRATION FOR CHANGE, 1981 45 × 64 cm

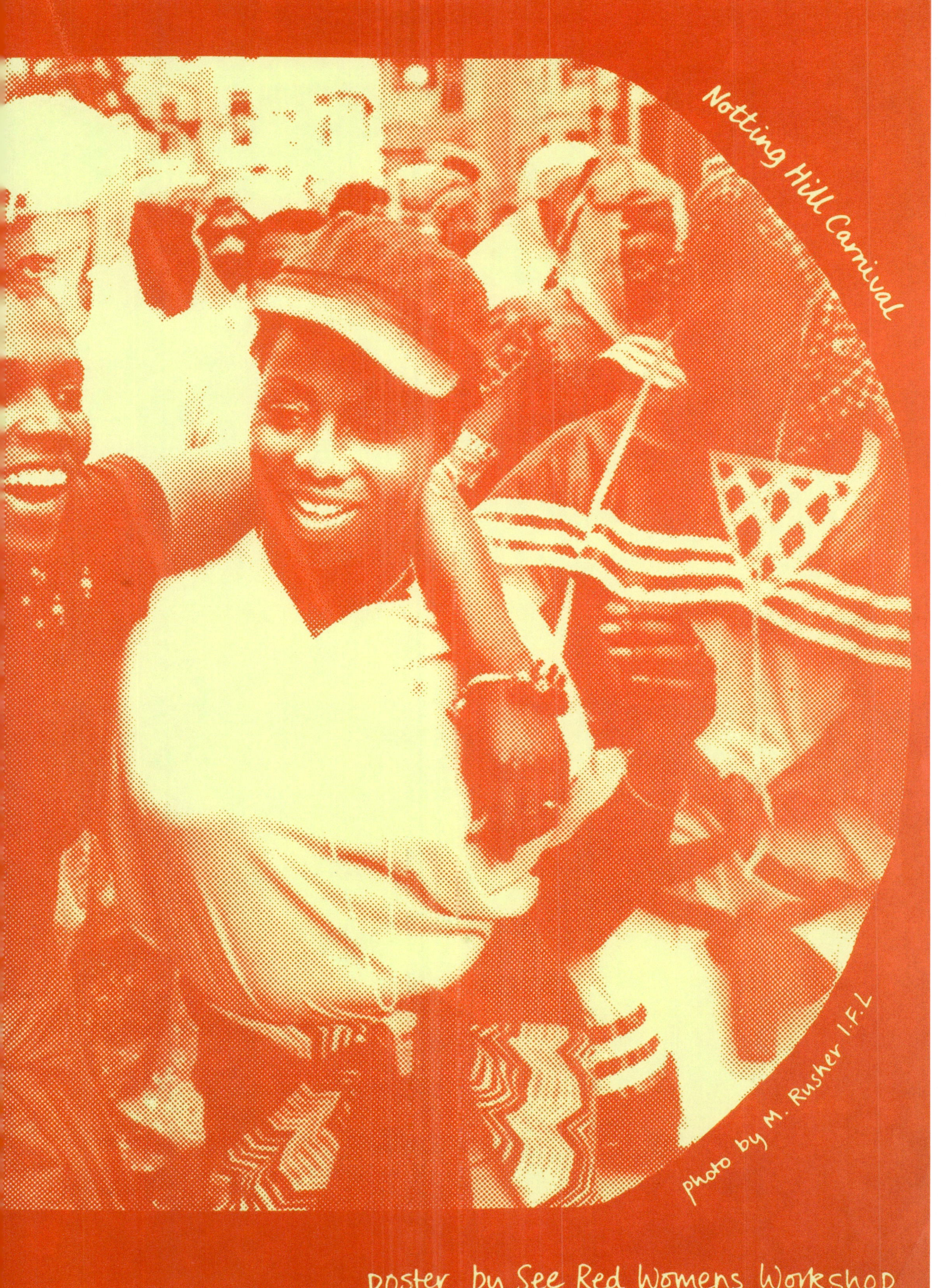

Notting Hill Carnival
photo by M. Rusher I.F.L
poster by See Red Womens Workshop

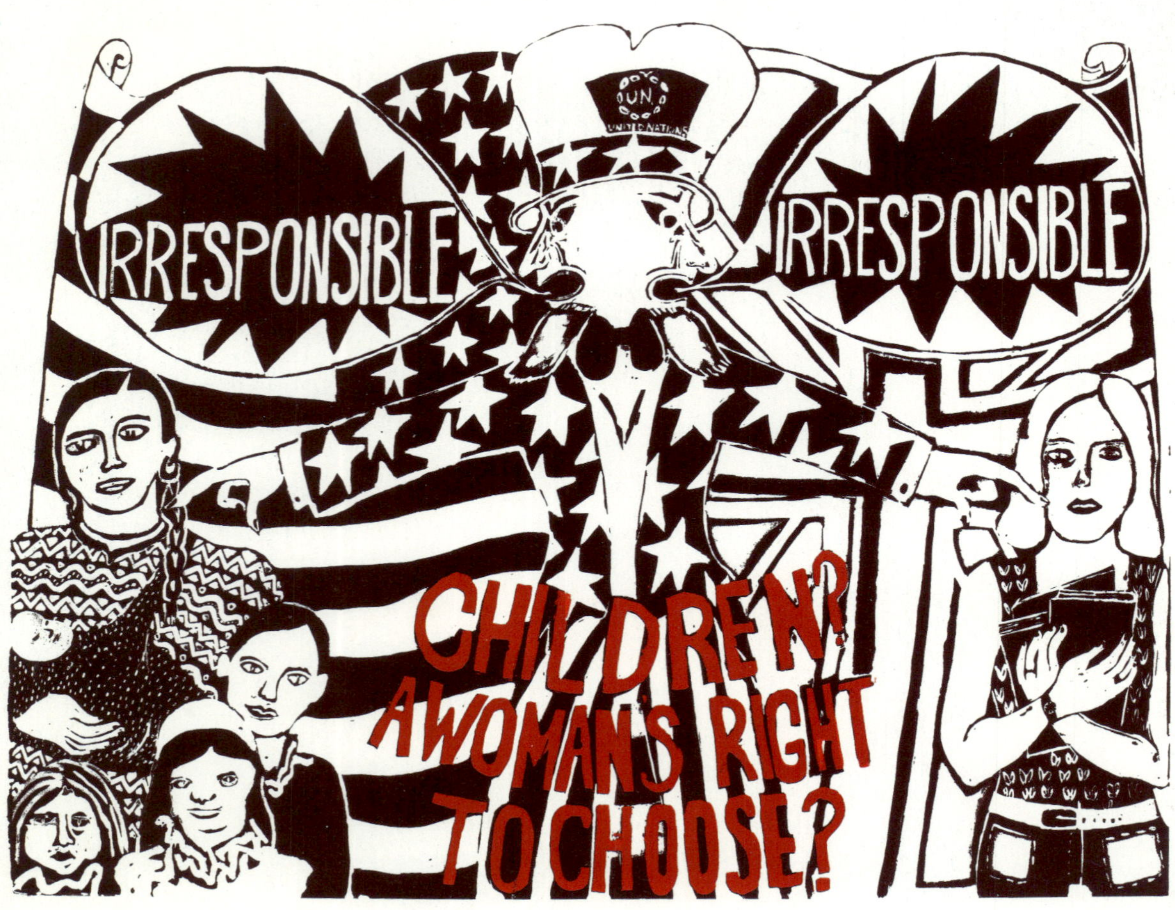

Children? A Woman's Right To Choose?
This poster, due to the illegibility of the wording, was not passed by the collective for production.

Participe De Nuestra Lucha!
Participate In Our Struggle!
Two political refugees, Magdalena from Colombia and Ginette from Chile, both living in the UK, came to See Red as apprentices. With advice from Amnesty International, the Chile Committee for Human Rights and the Latin American community in London, we made this poster concerning the thousands of women, men and children who were 'disappeared' during the right-wing military dictatorships which governed most of Latin America. All of them resorted to this barbaric act as a means of limiting opposition to their regimes.

An estimated 3,200 disappeared in Chile, 8,000 in El Salvador, and 13,000 in Argentina. Human rights organisations such as Grandmothers of Plaza de Mayo began as groups of women relatives looking for their missing loved ones. Their search still continues to this day.

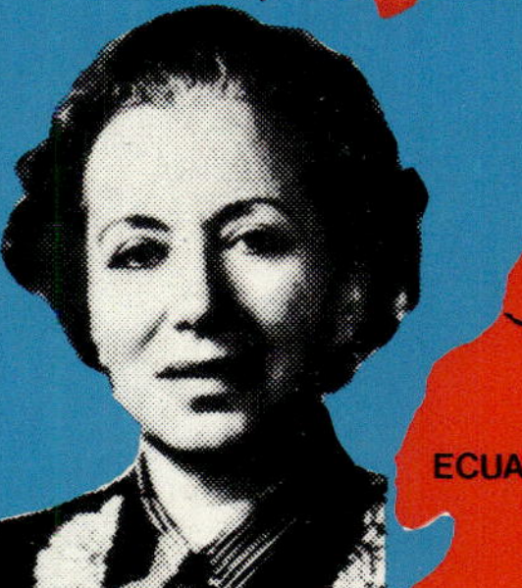

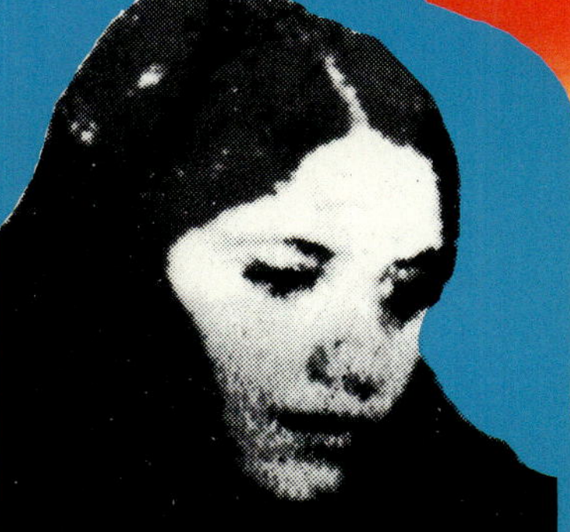

THOUSANDS OF
WOMEN & CHILDREN
ARE INVOLVED IN
THIS STRUGGLE

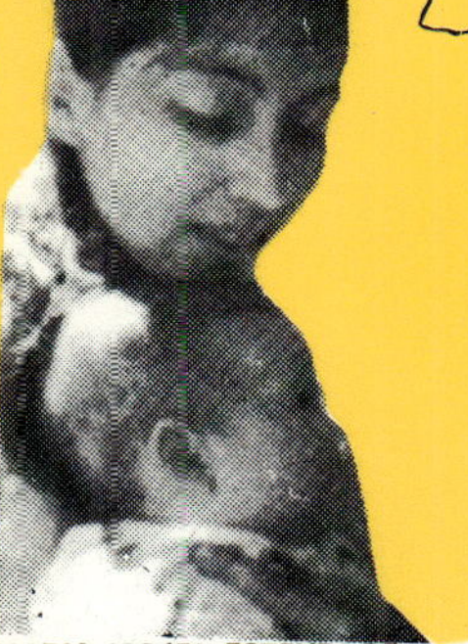

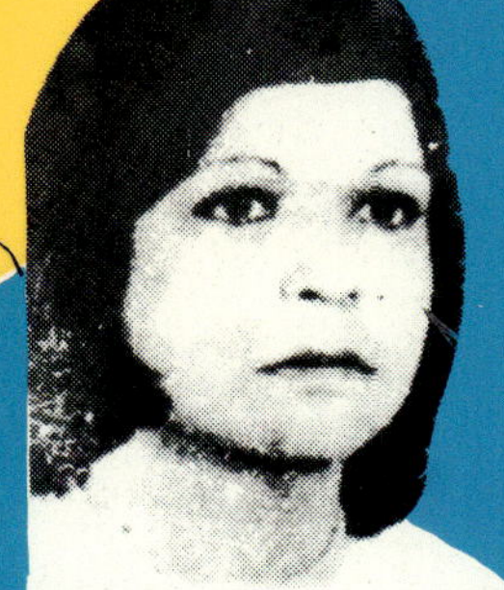

¡participe de nuestra lucha!

Lesbians Are Coming Out

Feminist image making in the early 1980s was a tricky business. The arguments of radical feminists such as Andrea Dworkin about pornography as violence against women in itself, with slogans like 'Porn is the theory, rape is the practice' were hotly debated, raising the question of how to represent women's sexuality. Arguments over producing 'lesbian' imagery at this time had escalated, as some feminists felt that photographs objectified women more than drawings. Some women argued that it was wrong to make any images of women loving women for fear of prurient male attention: something that our sisters at Women in Print had found when they produced a fundraising lesbian calendar for 1983.

So how to make a positive, inspiring feminist lesbian poster in this political climate? An earlier See Red poster, *A Lesbian Spirit Is Within Every Woman* seemed influenced by a more American hippy aesthetic and was felt not to speak to early 1980s lesbian politics in the UK. There was also still a good deal of hostility directed towards 'out' lesbians. The two lesbian collective members set to work and sought opinions from other lesbians, including those at Lenthall Road, a women's silkscreen workshop in Hackney. After much discussion we opted to use drawings rather than photographs and to include images of women which were not stereotyped to make the point that 'you can't always tell' and 'every woman can be'.

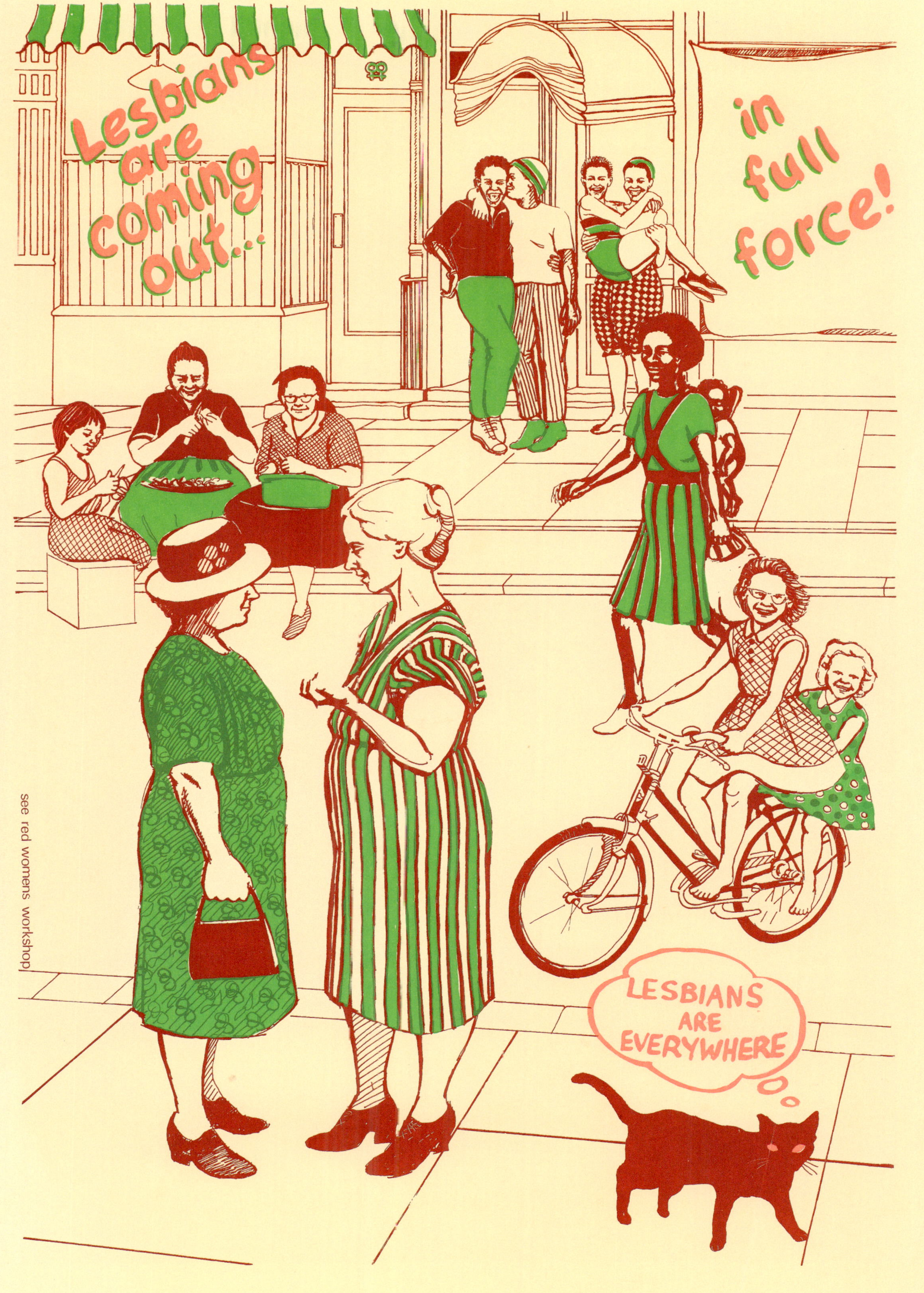

Lesbians are coming out...
in full force!
LESBIANS ARE EVERYWHERE
see red womens workshop

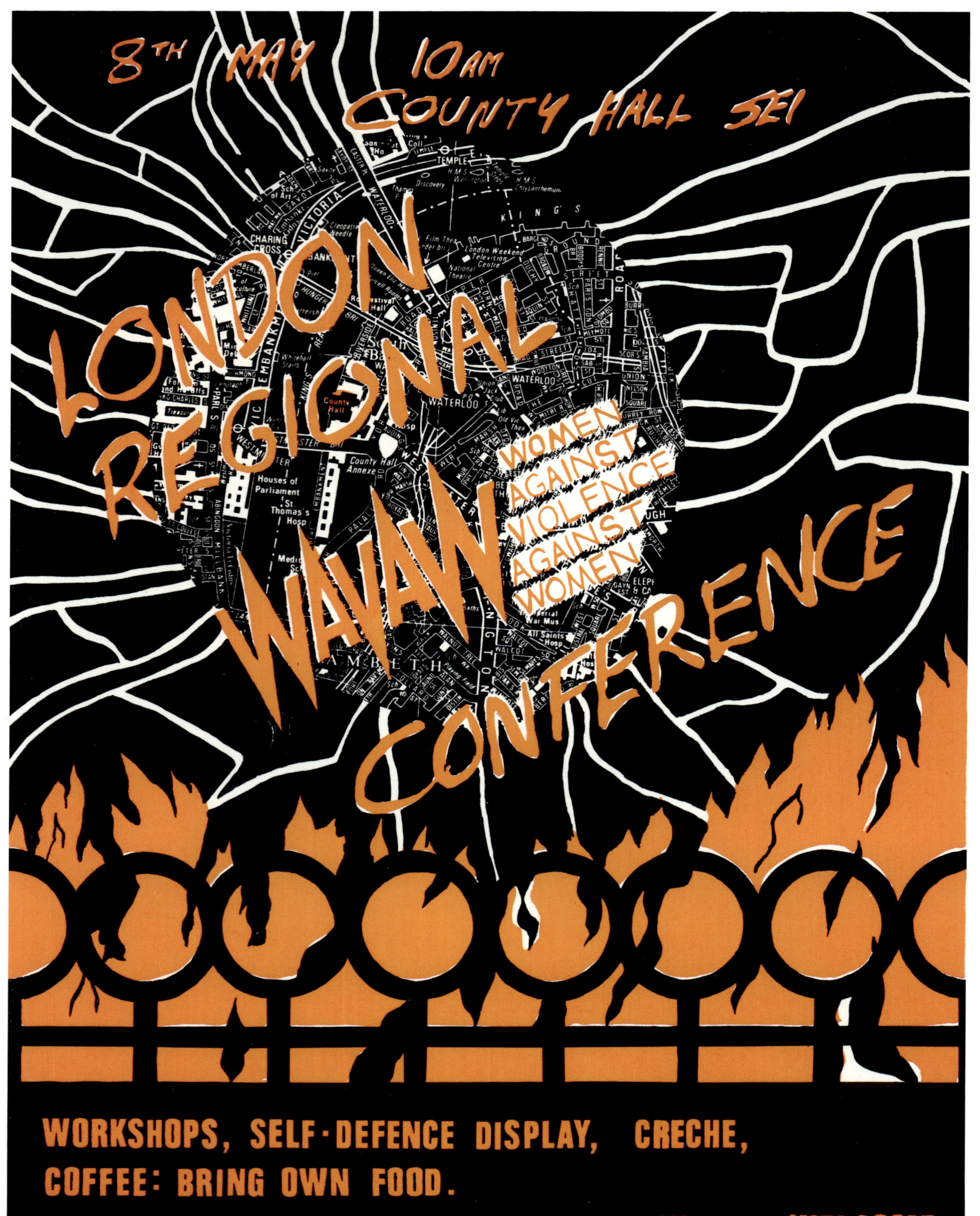

WAVAW CONFERENCE, 1982 51 × 38.5 cm

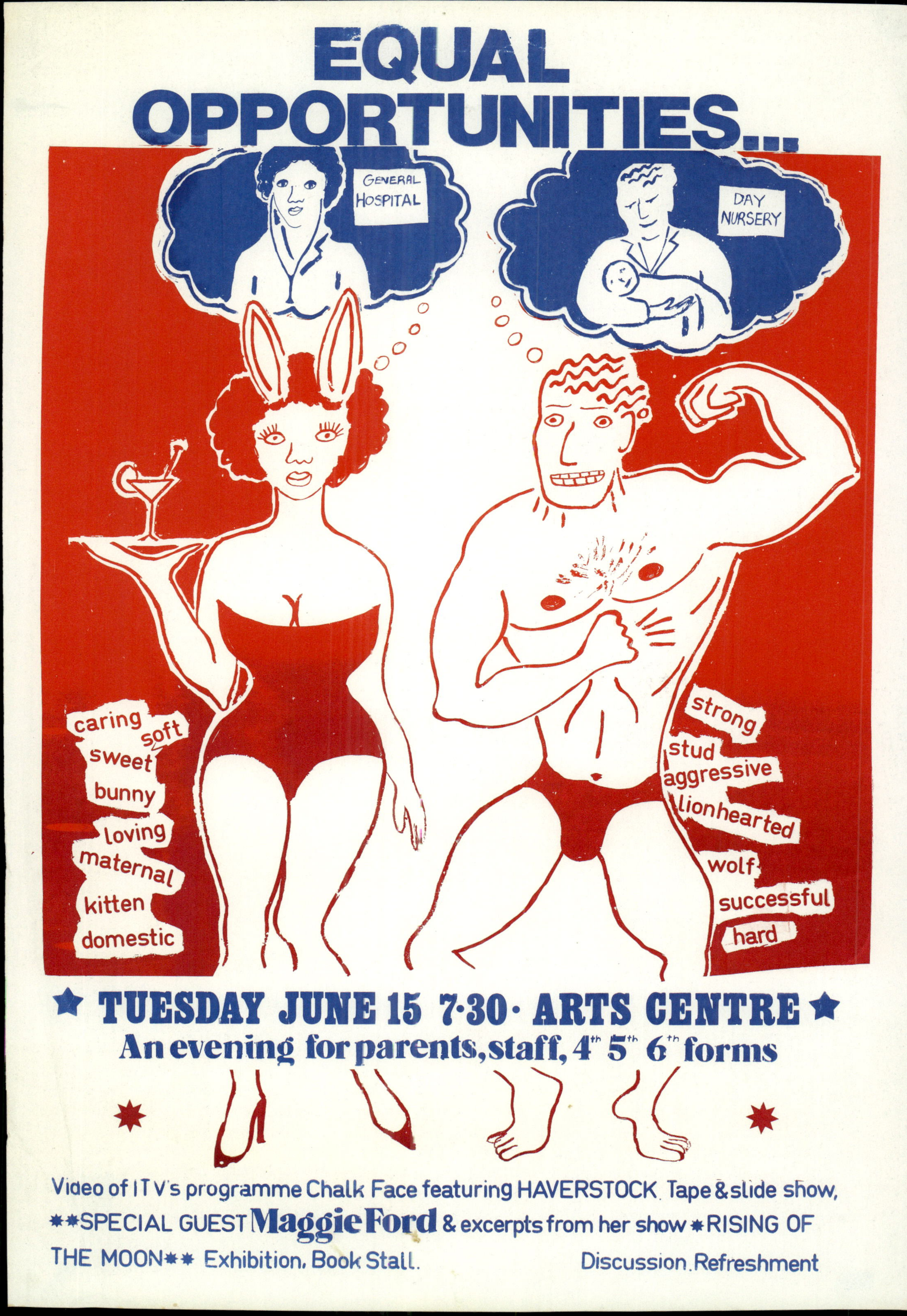

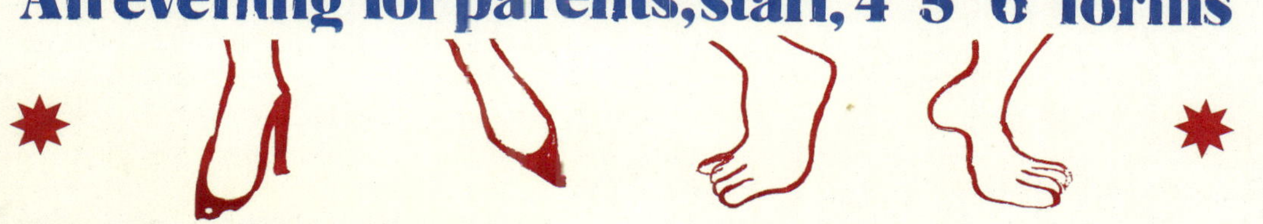

EQUAL OPPORTUNITIES, 1982   59 × 40.5 cm

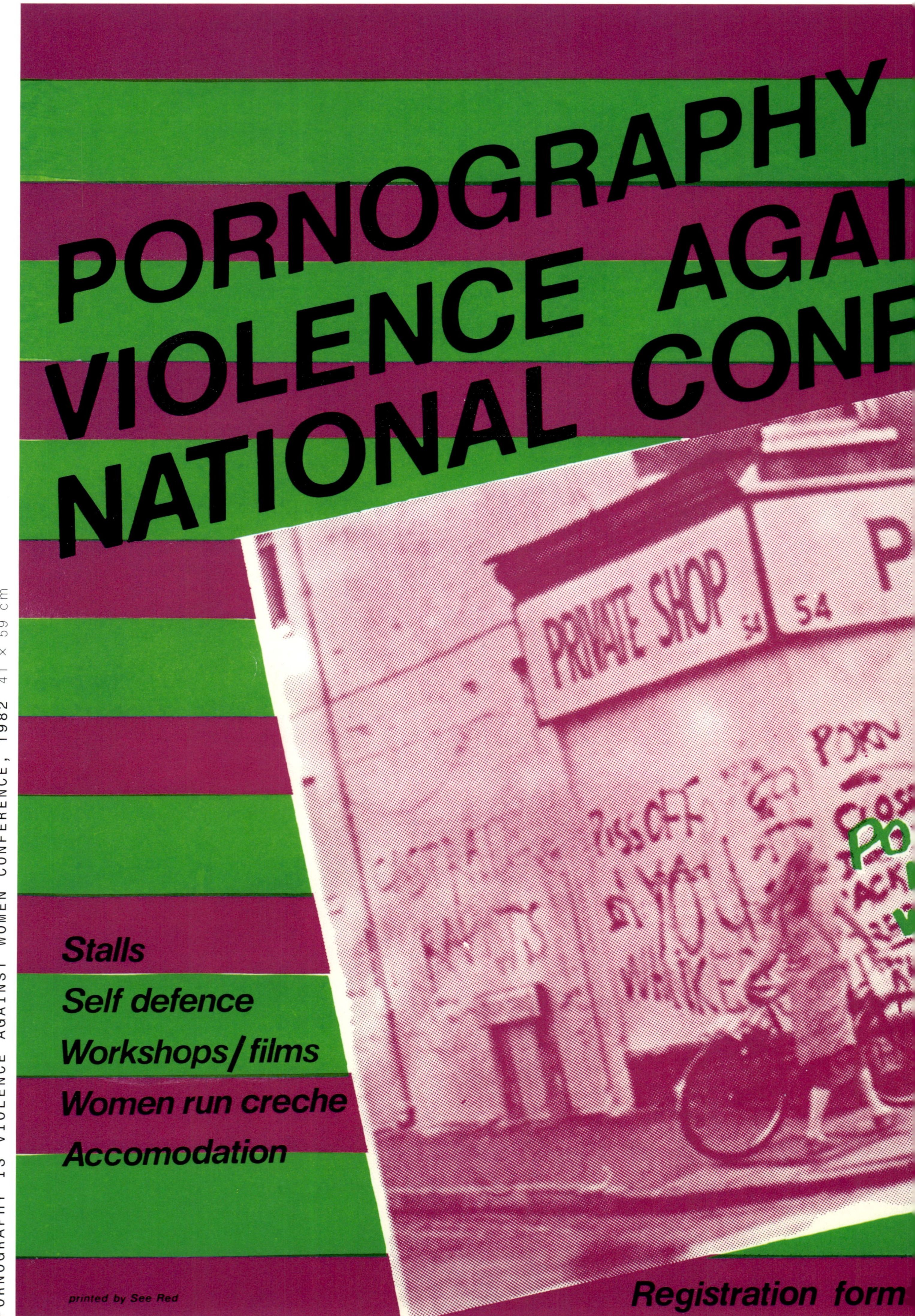

PORNOGRAPHY IS VIOLENCE AGAINST WOMEN CONFERENCE, 1982 41 × 59 cm

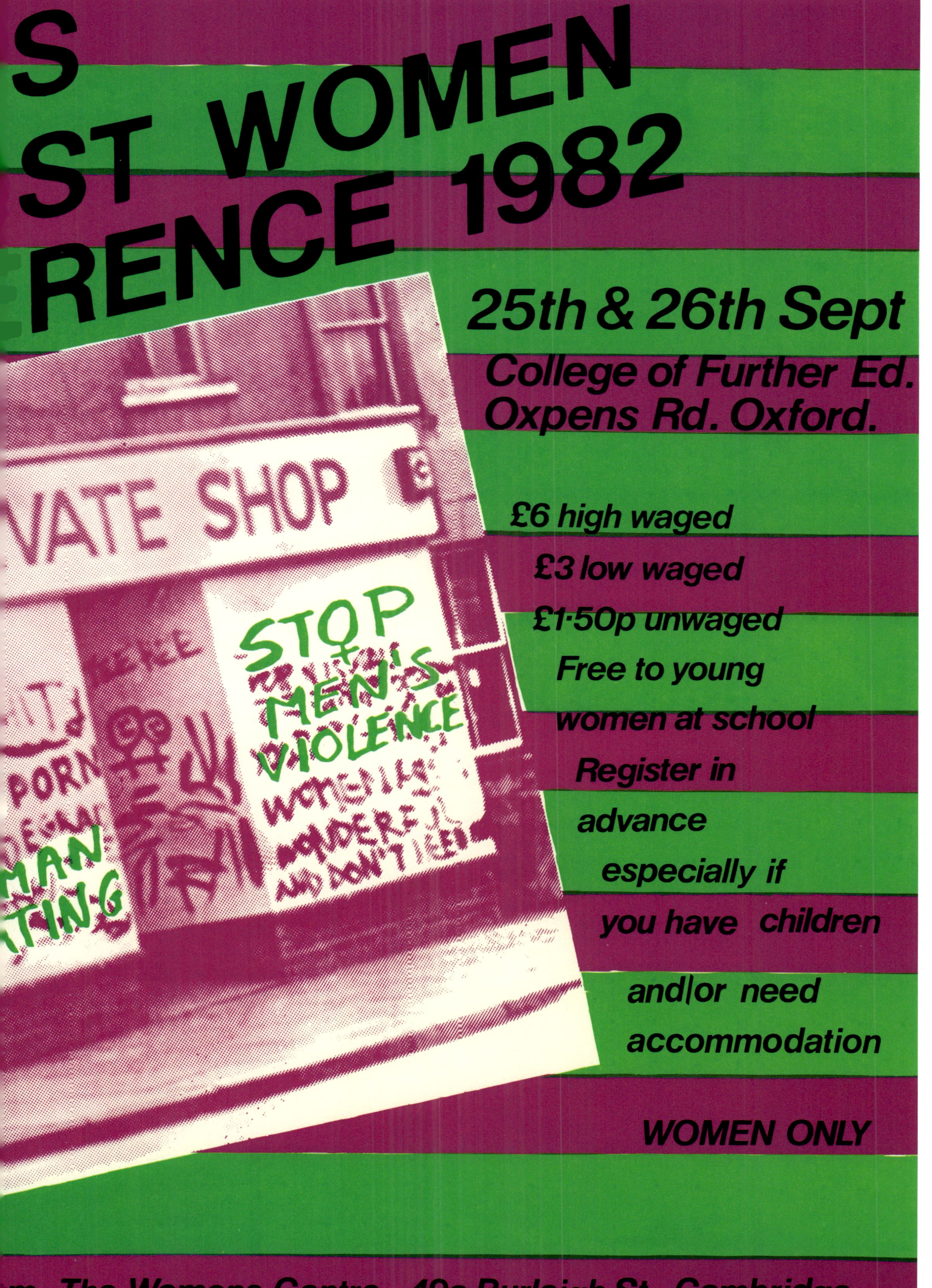
S
ST WOMEN
RENCE 1982
25th & 26th Sept
College of Further Ed.
Oxpens Rd. Oxford.
£6 high waged
£3 low waged
£1·50p unwaged
Free to young
women at school
Register in
advance
especially if
you have children
and/or need
accommodation
WOMEN ONLY
VATE SHOP
STOP
MEN'S
VIOLENCE
m The Womens Centre   49a Burleigh St   Cambridge

Underneath Every Woman's Curve

The influence of Women Against Violence
Against Women around this time is demonstrated
by the volume of material in *Spare Rib* and
Outwrite, and we wanted to address the issue
in a way that didn't disempower women. The
poster that emerged from our discussions
focused on women's self defence.

Self defence classes had become a feminist
demand to deal with attempts to curtail women's
freedoms in the wake of attacks such as those
of the Yorkshire Ripper. We had made an earlier
poster on the issue, which hadn't quite worked
and been dropped. This time around, help was
at hand with a new publication called *Squashed
Flies* (published in 1982) that provided a great
instructional diagram that we adapted. The
poster aimed to empower women with the
sense that they could resist effectively when
sexually harassed. It was deemed important
to stress that this was not only a possibility
for young women, so the poster shows an
older woman, veteran lesbian activist Jackie
Forster (1926–1998), with notes on strategies
she might use. In using her image, there was
also tacit recognition of the potential threat of
violence against lesbians. The other side of the
poster shows a rather stereotypical 'bloke' with
corresponding advice on how to fight back.

underneath every woman's 'curve' lies a muscle!

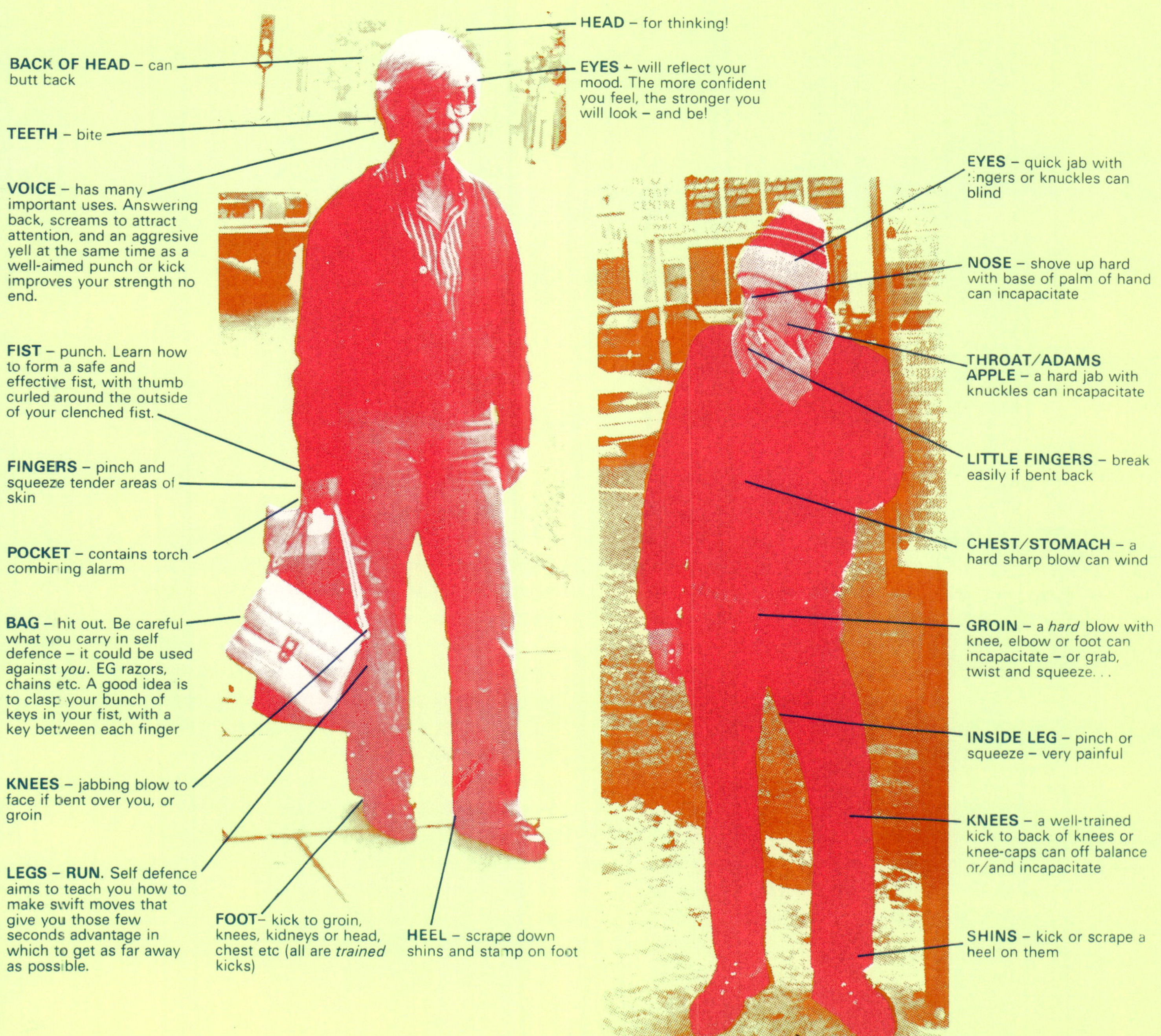

THIS POSTER IS JUST A USEFUL GUIDE & IS NOT A SUBSTITUTE FOR A SELF DEFENCE COURSE

Contacts for womens self defence

Birmingham: PO Box 558, B3 2HL

Manchester: Sally, 061 225 3915

London: Janet Hunt, 01 633 2742 or

Sheffield: WIRES, 0742 755290 & RCC, 0742 75522

Swansea: Anne Carrick, c/o Womens Centre, 58 Alexandra Rd, Swansea

Womens Karate Club, Camden Institute, Holmes Rd, Kentish Town, London, N5

see red womens workshop - with thanks to the booklet 'Squashed flies'

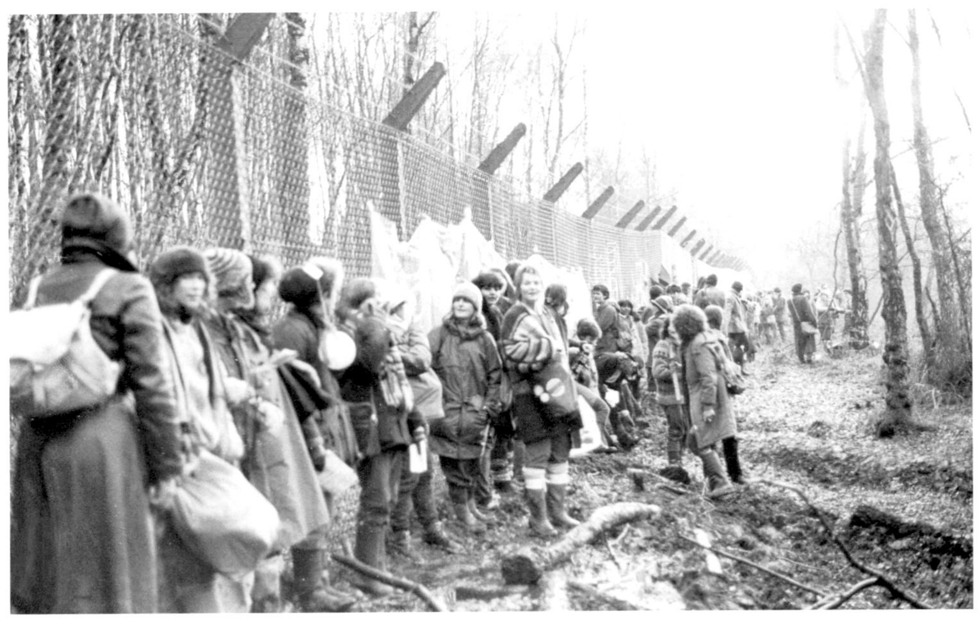

Support The Women's Peace Camps

The Greenham Common Women's Peace Camp was established outside the RAF base in Berkshire in September 1981, following the long march from Wales by the group 'Women For Life on Earth' who were demanding the reversal of a decision to site USAF cruise missiles at the base. Mass women's protests at the base, and the use of nonviolent resistance in confrontational situations, struck a chord with many who were uncomfortable with media images of women being dragged away. Police tactics and attacks from local men were often brutal and the women also attracted hostility in the mainstream press for their unfeminine appearance with headlines such as 'The ugly face of the girls of peace' (*The Sun*).

The See Red poster combines images of 'the fence' with photographs by feminist photographer Pam Isherwood in a design that shows these strategies for resistance by women of all ages and backgrounds. Their tactics included: attaching 'soft' personal objects and messages to the fence, 'embracing the base' (completely surrounding the fence with people holding hands) and using bolt-cutters to break through the fence in nightime direct actions.

See Red members had gone to Greenham to join the protests and some became very involved, setting up workshops to make common ground between women in anti-imperialist struggles and the peace movement.

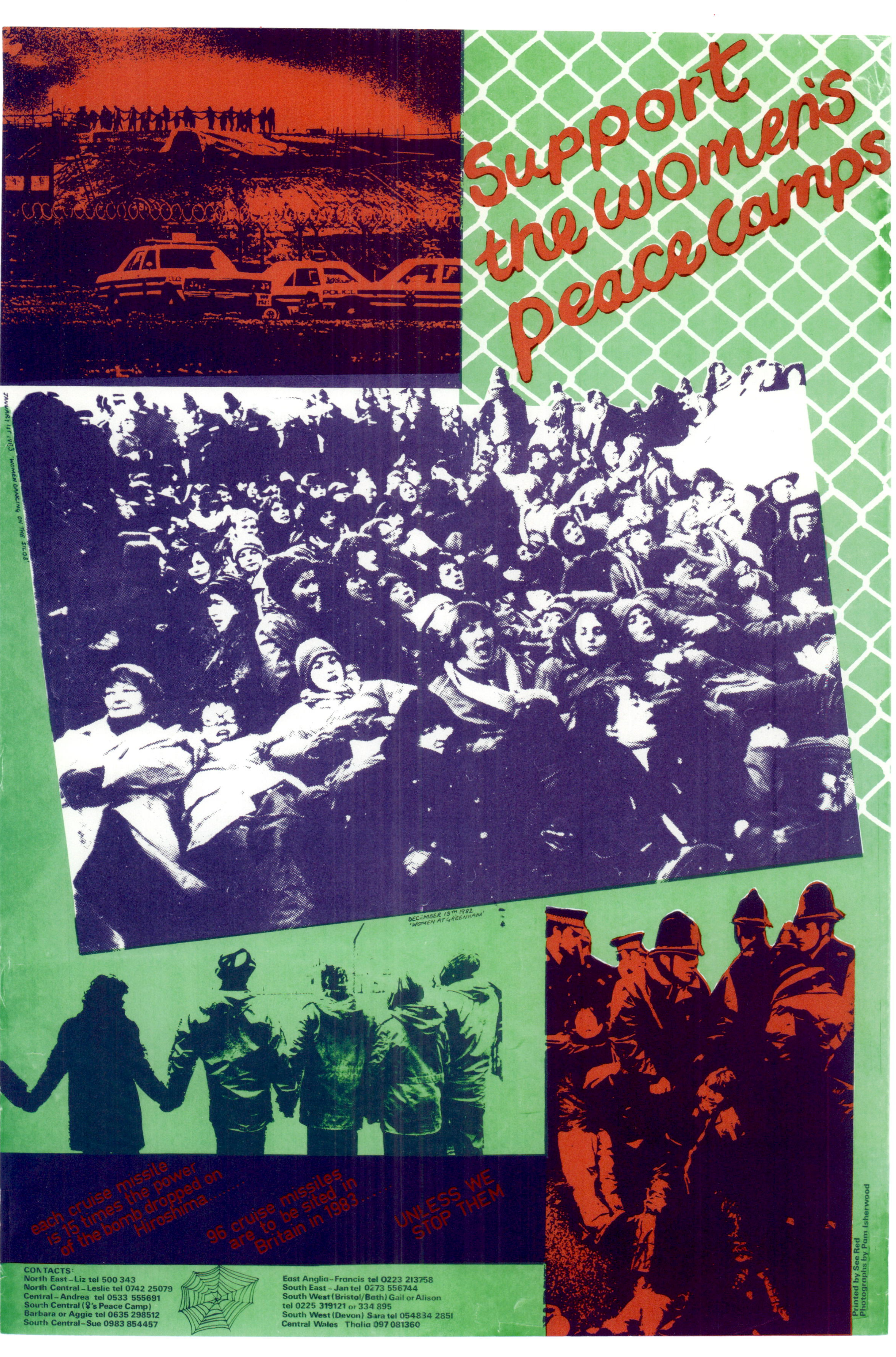

Support the women's Peace Camps
DECEMBER 13th 1982
'WOMEN AT GREENHAM'
each cruise missile is 15 times the power of the bomb dropped on Hiroshima......
96 cruise missiles are to be sited in Britain in 1983......
UNLESS WE STOP THEM
CONTACTS:
North East – Liz tel 500 343
North Central – Leslie tel 0742 25079
Central – Andrea tel 0533 555691
South Central (♀'s Peace Camp)
Barbara or Aggie tel 0635 298512
South Central – Sue 0983 854457
East Anglia – Francis tel 0223 213758
South East – Jan tel 0273 556744
South West (Bristol/Bath) Gail or Alison tel 0225 319121 or 334 895
South West (Devon) Sara tel 054834 2851
Central Wales   Thalia 097 081360
Printed by See Red
Photographs by Pam Isherwood

**The South London Hospital For
Women Will Not Close**

Women's hospitals had come to be seen as
old fashioned before the Women's Liberation
Movement and its critique of how women
were treated by the male medical profession.
Now such valuable resources needed to be
defended. In 1983, the Wandsworth Health
Authority announced the impending closure
of South London Women's Hospital. A campaign
developed with public protests and a 'work in'
by hospital staff in 1984. After the last
inpatients departed in the summer of 1984,
hundreds of women protesters began a lively
nine-month occupation of the hospital to
prevent equipment and furniture being moved
out and to campaign for re-opening. During this
time the occupied building also became an
activist and social space for various other
women's groups and campaigns. An important
precursor was the campaign begun in 1976
to prevent the closure of Elizabeth Garrett
Anderson Hospital in central London.

See Red Calendar 1984

(*over the page*) We made this calendar with
input from *Outwrite*, who supplied many of the
images, with the aim of promoting them as well.
The rifle in the women's symbol logo was
inspired by the women's solidarity mural in west
Belfast (shown in the photograph for March) and
the source of some collective debate. We also
found that some feminist outlets did not want
to stock it because of this aspect.

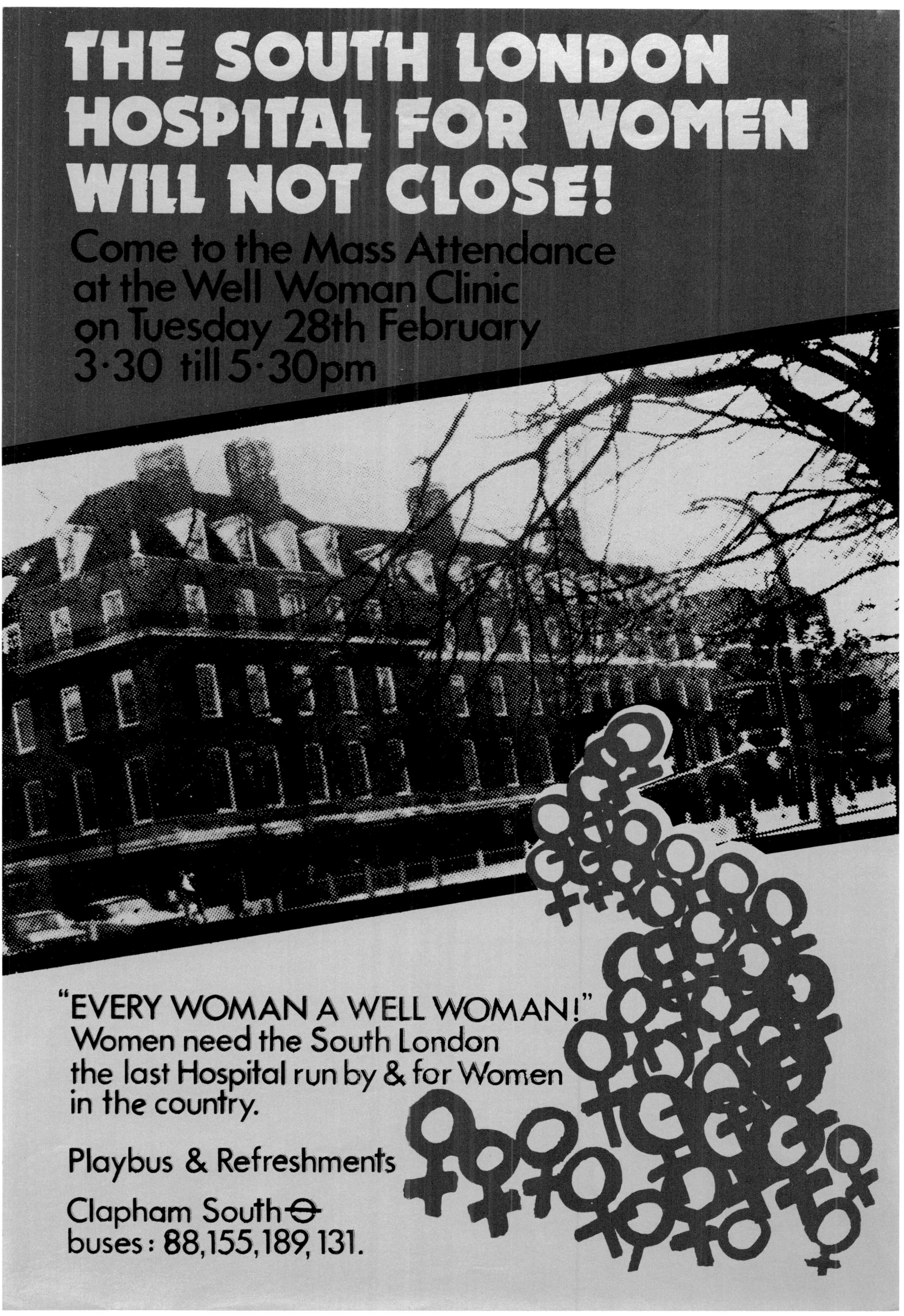

THE SOUTH LONDON HOSPITAL FOR WOMEN WILL NOT CLOSE, 1984 43 × 29.5 cm

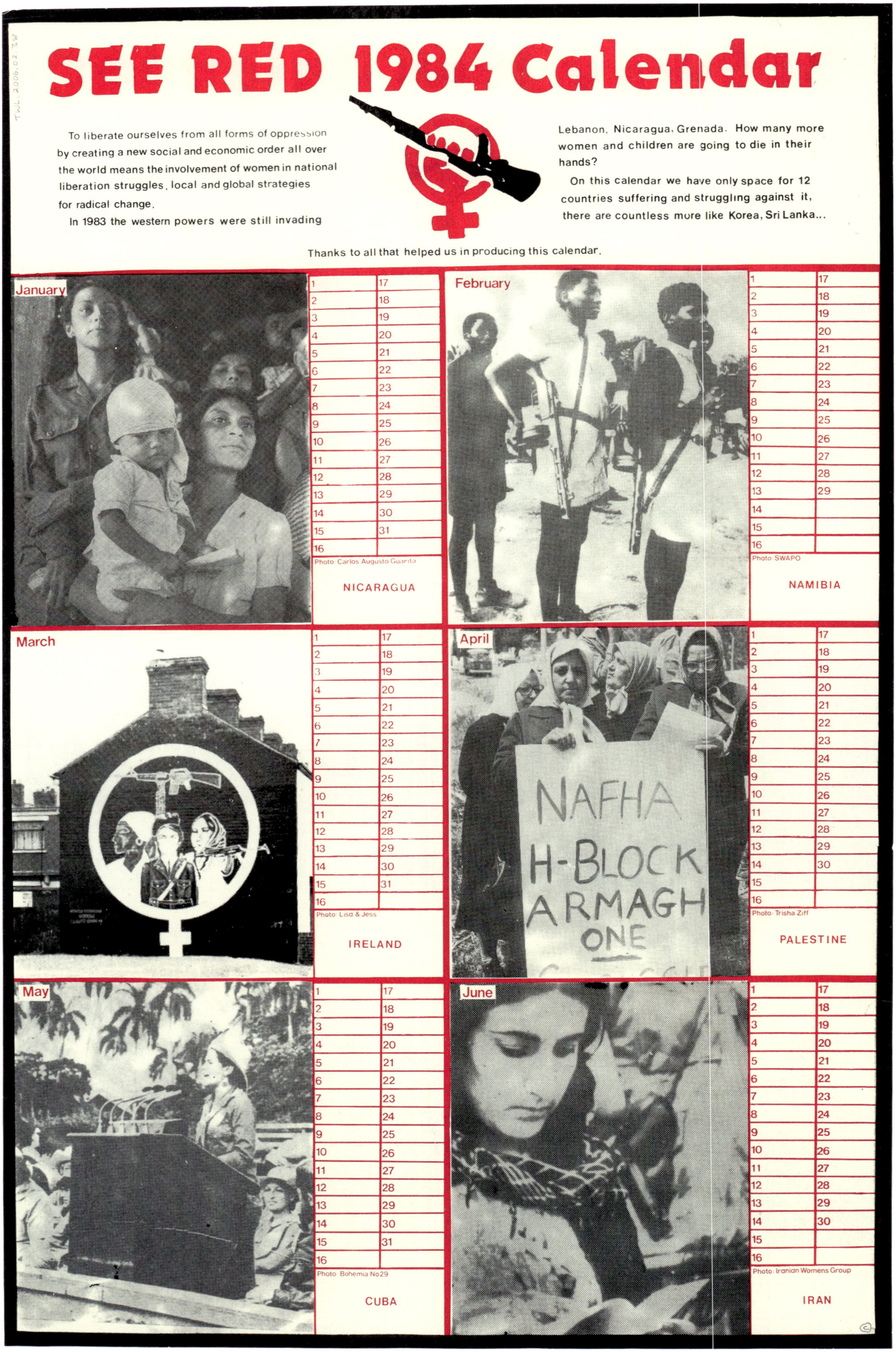

SEE RED 1984 Calendar

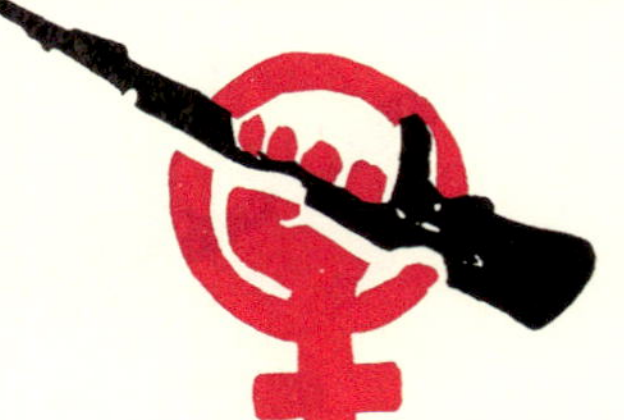

To liberate ourselves from all forms of oppression by creating a new social and economic order all over the world means the involvement of women in national liberation struggles, local and global strategies for radical change.

In 1983 the western powers were still invading Lebanon, Nicaragua, Grenada. How many more women and children are going to die in their hands?

On this calendar we have only space for 12 countries suffering and struggling against it, there are countless more like Korea, Sri Lanka...

Thanks to all that helped us in producing this calendar.

January

Photo: Carlos Augusto Guarita

NICARAGUA

February

Photo: SWAPO

NAMIBIA

March

Photo: Lisa & Jess

IRELAND

April

Photo: Trisha Ziff

PALESTINE

May

Photo: Bohemia No 29

CUBA

June

Photo: Iranian Womens Group

IRAN

SEE RED CALENDAR, 1984   75.5 × 50 cm

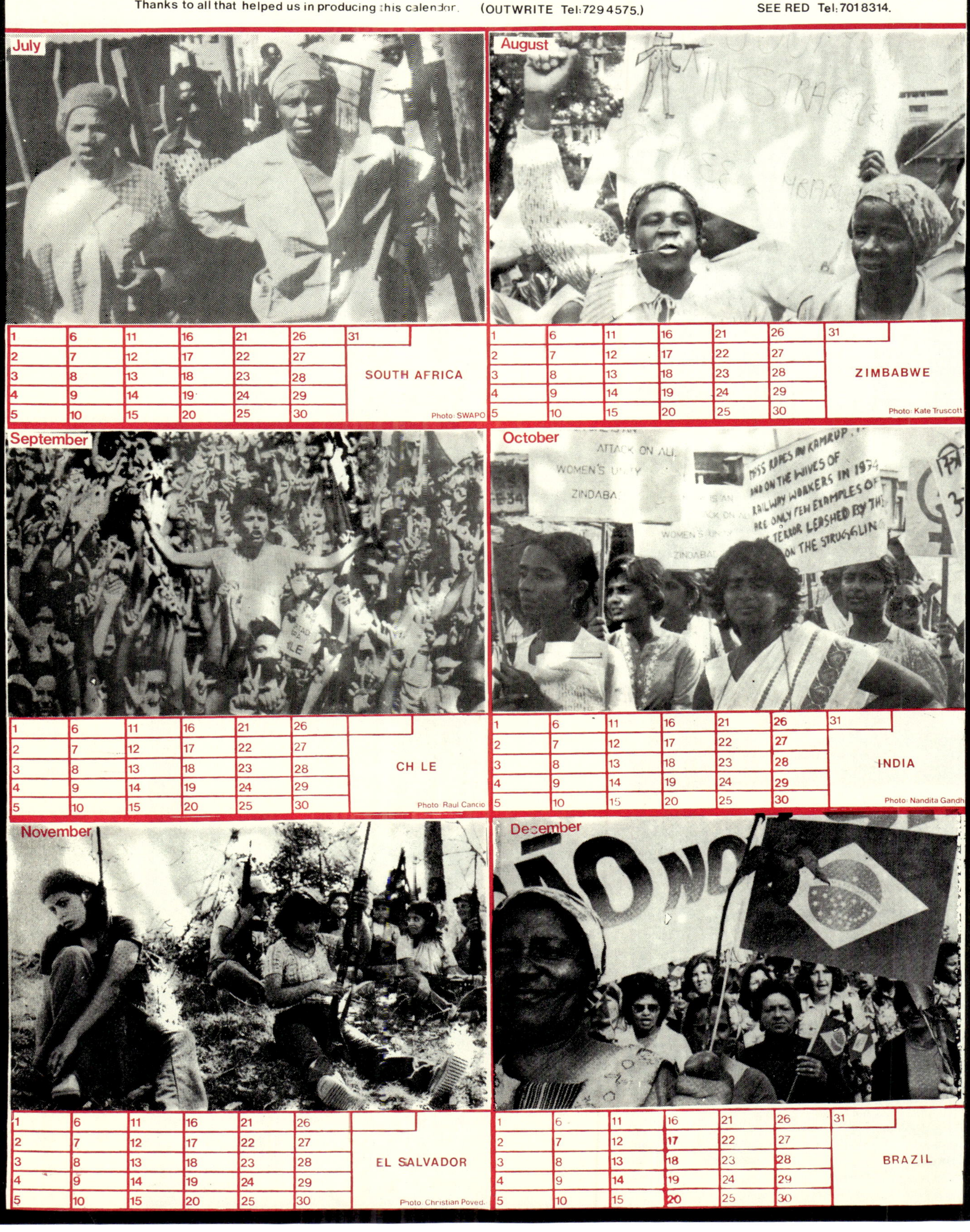

SEE RED CALENDAR, 1934   75.5 × 50 cm

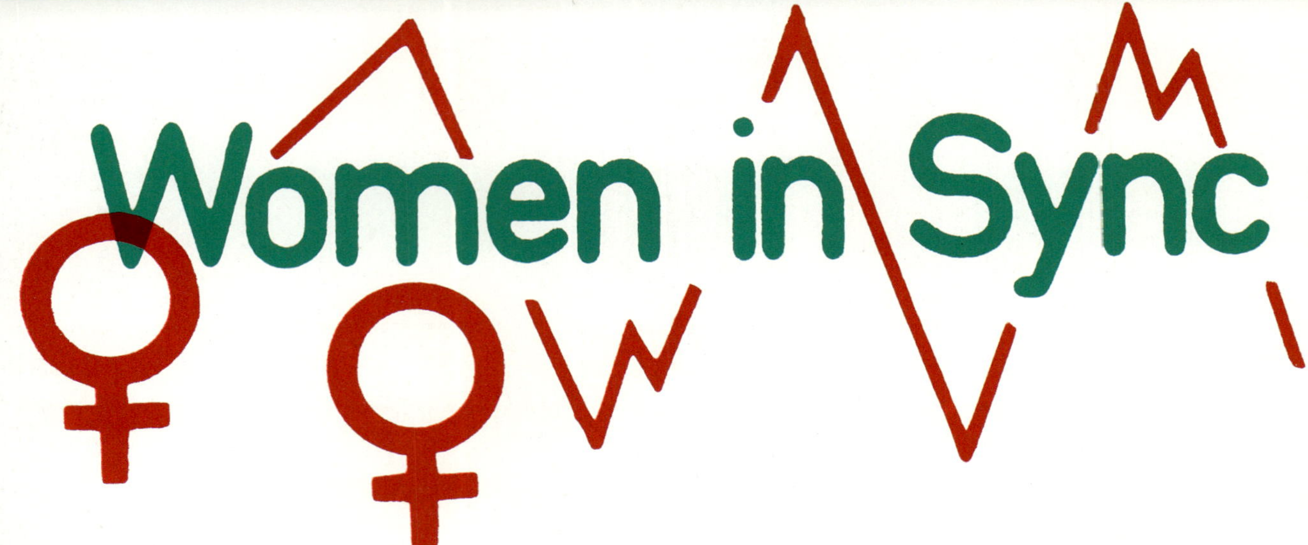

A WOMEN'S VIDEO RESOURCE

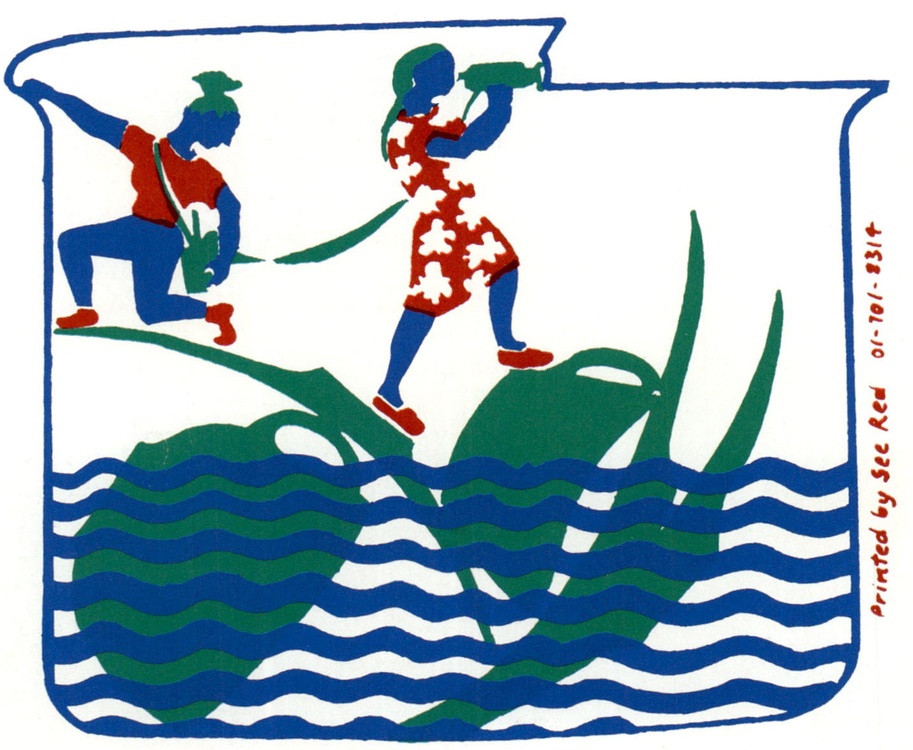

WRITE TO — Room 1/2
38, Mount Pleasant
London WC1

PHONE — 278~2215

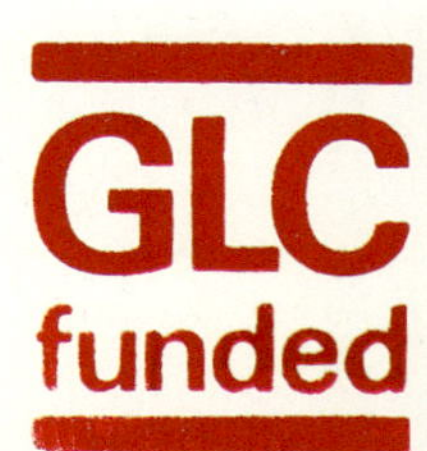

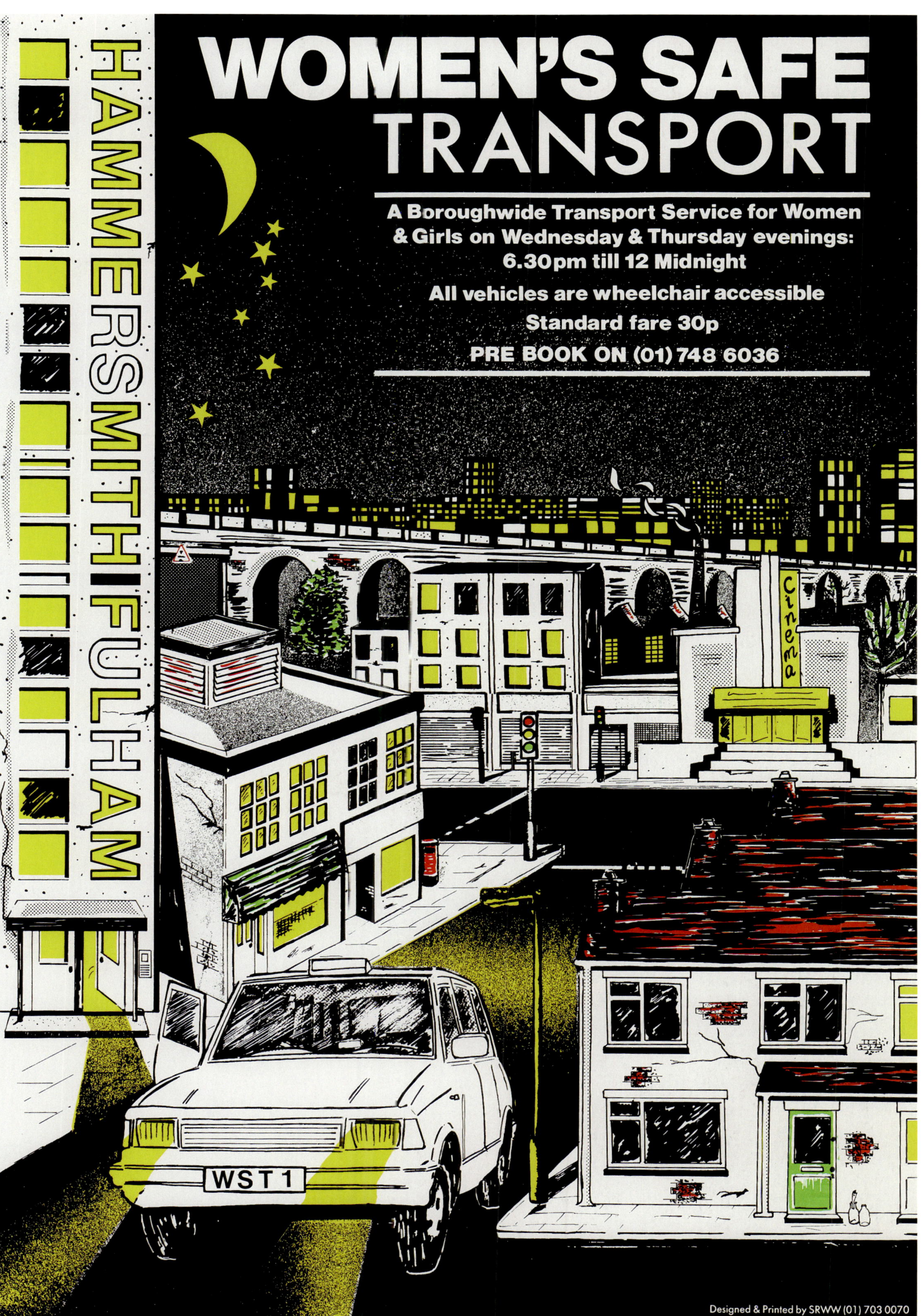

   WOMEN'S SAFE TRANSPORT, 1987/88 *42 × 29.5 cm*

BLACK LESBIAN & GAY CONFERENCE, 1987 42.5 × 59 cm

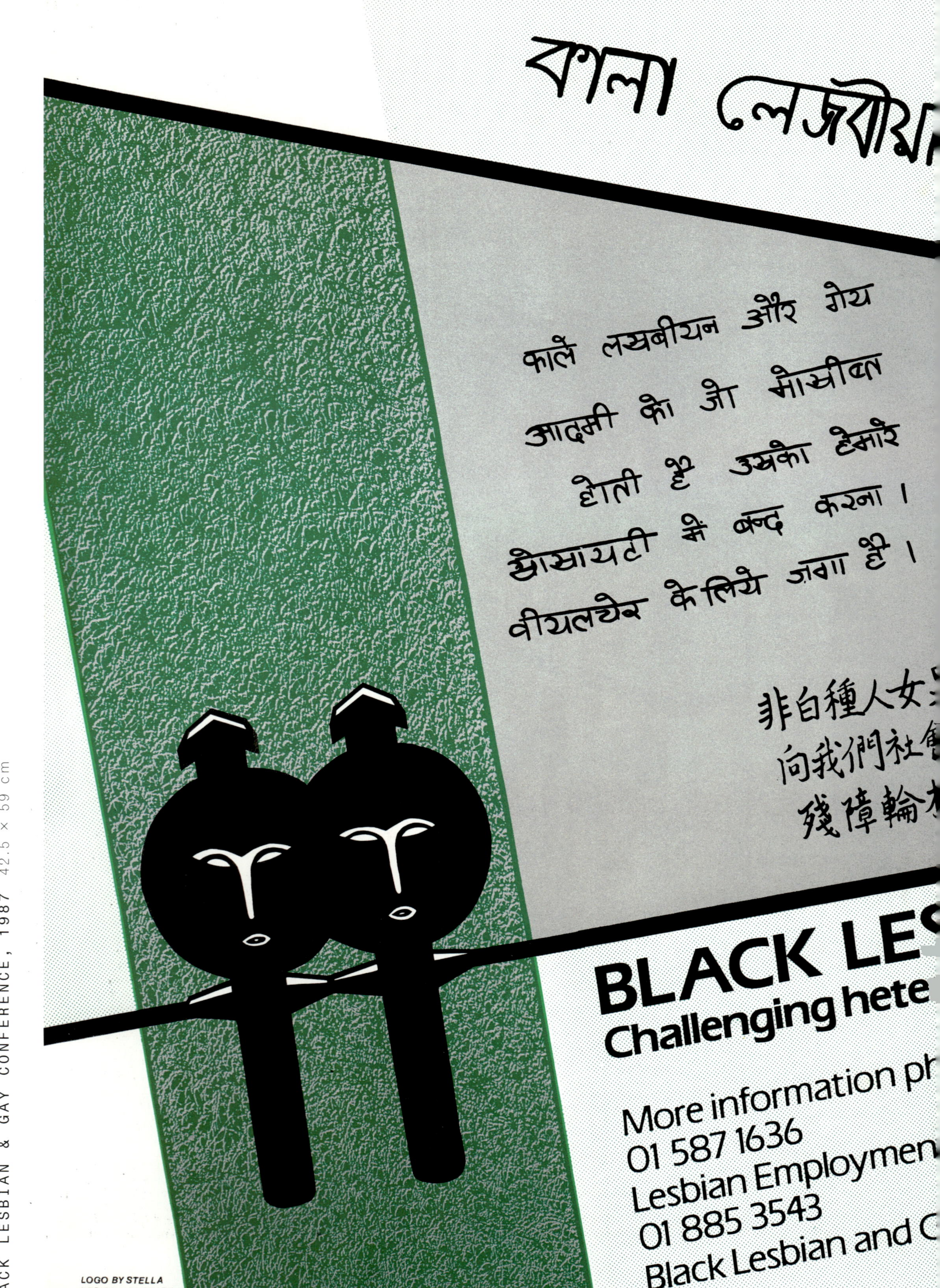

LOGO BY STELLA
DESIGN & PRINT BY
SRWW 01 703 0070

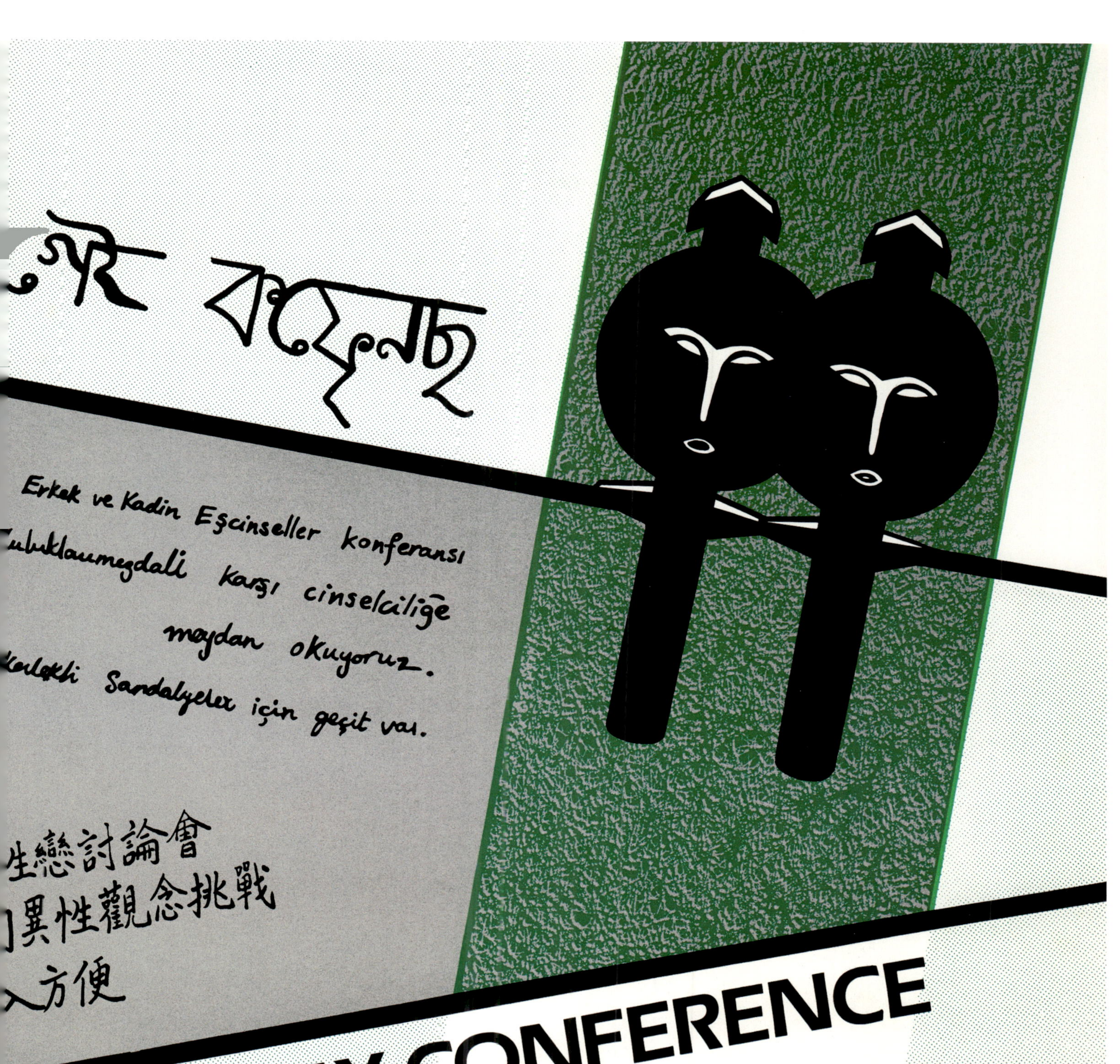
Erkek ve Kadin Eşcinseller konferansı
Tutuklaumegdali karşı cinselciliğe
maydan okuyoruz.
Keilokli Sandalyeler için geçit var.

生戀討論會
異性觀念挑戰
入方便

AN & GAY CONFERENCE
xism in our communities

Turnpike Lane
221, 121, 123, 144,
41, 29, W/2, 67,
Good access
Signers
Creche

hts

entre

MARCH 21st
Saturday 10am–6pm
Disco 8pm–11pm
West Indian Cultural Centre
Clarendon Road
London N8

See Red
Women's Workshop
1974–1990

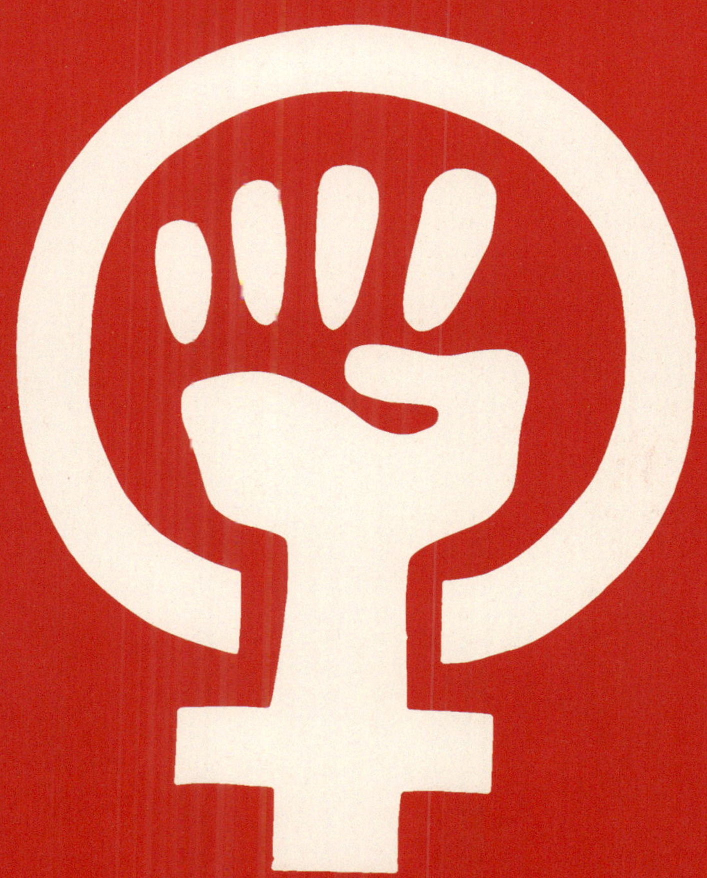

More than 40 women joined See Red Women's Workshop over 16 years: we would not have survived without everyone's commitment and participation. The following list is compiled from our very incomplete meeting minutes and notes — at the time we had no eye for posterity. We are aware that more women who worked with us during this time may be missing from this list and we can only apologise for this.

Pru Stevenson 1974–83 · **Suzy Mackie** 1974–82

Julia Franco 1974–80 · **Sarah Jones** 1975–83

Christine Roche 1974 · **Jo Spence** 1974

Michael-Anne Mullen 1974 · **Margaret Edney** 1974

Pauline · **Hazel** · **Dana** · **Sharon** 1975–76

Nina 1975 · **Bertha Husband** 1975–77

Leslie Ford · **Bejhat** · **Sharon** · **Denise** · **Charmian**

Caroline · **Dawn** · **Mel** · **Kehinde James** 1979–82

Bev Zalcock 1980 · **Maralyn** · **Laura**

Sue Winter 1980–83 · **Sue Field Reid** 1980

Lesley Mitchell 1981 · **Magdalena Arias** 1981–82

Ginette 1981 · **Anne Robinson** 1981–83

Kathleen Brady · **Sandra Hopley**

Jess Baines 1982–84 · **Yael Hodder** 1982–90

Jacquee Bruce 1983–90

Carmen Gloria Diaz 1983–86

Norma Rodriguez · **Cath Coleman** 1984–90

Sarah Jones See Red 1975–83

Well versed on the issues around gender and a strong campaigner, Sarah wanted to improve the lives of women and make a difference. Sarah joined See Red soon after leaving university in 1974 and brought huge amounts of energy, inspiration and determination into See Red where she shared her numerous skills and knowledge freely. Sarah was the most organised and hers was the calming voice in heated debates and discussions: she was the linchpin that held See Red together — a great teacher and mentor who was universally liked. During her time at See Red, Sarah worked part time for TIN (Tin age Information Network) where she taught arts and craft: on leaving See Red she worked there full time, eventually going on to run the organisation. Sarah was part of the collective that founded and produced *Lower Down*, a radical south London newspaper. Sarah went on to be a student advisor and counsellor at Southwark College and Westminster College. She then qualified as a psychotherapist and worked for the Ashbourne centre — a Gestalt community offering counselling, support, and life skills, prioritising, people on low incomes. Diagnosed with advanced ovarian cancer in 1995, strong and determined Sarah confounded health professionals by living another 12 years. Sarah Jones died in 2007.

Julia Franco See Red 1974–80

1980 was a very sad year for us as one of our founders, Julia Franco, died. Julia was a key part of our early poster ideas and direction. Having been born in the USA, Julia's style brought an ironic attitude towards debunking and challenging the American dream. *My Wife Doesn't Work* came from her own experiences as a wife and new mother. *Bite The Hand* is still as angry and relevant nowadays as it was back then. She also had the original idea for *Right On, Jane*, developing an alternative version of the Ladybird pages and creating one of our most popular posters. She challenged the roles society had laid out for women and mothers: she was a rebel, and her designs resonated strongly with many women in similar situations. Julia was a formative part of our communal household in Stockwell and we are very happy that her daughter Bronnie, now a mother herself, is working with us.

Memories of See Red

Sue Field Reid

I remember being very pleased to be invited to join See Red; I knew I believed in the ideas they wanted to put out in the world.

I enjoyed the atmosphere and was glad to be part of the ups and downs.

In my memory there were quite a few downs, mistakes and mis-printings, high emotions and disagreements but then I suppose this happens whenever there is a group of people working very hard, with little financial support, with the serious aim of spreading important ideas in an uncaring selfish world. We needed to express these messages clearly and visually and that took much thought and discussion until everyone was in agreement.

The up times came when we finished the annual calendar or a series of posters and could go off to a conference with them where they were snapped up by enthusiastic conference-goers; it then felt hugely positive and satisfying.

Magdalena Arias

I came to London from Colombia as a political refugee. I was trying hard to settle and had few friends when a community worker brought me an advert about See Red, inviting women to join them. I went to their workshop the following day and began going regularly as an apprentice once or twice a week. We discussed ideas for new posters and I learned to print by printing them.

Ginette, who was from Chile, and I designed a poster about the South American struggle for economic and political freedom. Even in the designing and discussions for posters like this one, we were raising awareness of what was going on in that part of the world. To work and share ideas with the See Red women was inspiring. Their solidarity, their determination to get their message across through posters, was not only a great idea, it was encouraging and liberating for me and for other women.

Bev Zalcock

I was invited to become a See Red apprentice by Suzy around Spring 1980. I was flattered and thrilled as I was a great admirer of the posters: I remember pinning some on the wall at my place of work — Tower Hamlets Adult Education Centre — and being informed that I had to take them down as they were 'political'. I felt this was a bit rich, given that there was bunting celebrating the Silver Jubilee, all over the building!

Sarah, was my trainer, and I remember it being fun but also very hard work, which is probably why I only lasted a year! In fact, I had a teaching job at the time, and was also quite heavily involved in local activism. But I did learn to screen print, or at least understand the process, which I found fascinating and so different from my own artistic practice, filmmaking.

I distinctly remember helping to print Julia's Ladybird pastiche, and the first time being slightly terrified at the amount of paint we were pouring on to the screen. This was an experience that is still vivid in my mind; pools of colour — the smell, the texture and the precision required, all stay with me.

Sue Winter

I was trying to understand what the social function of art could be and See Red was doing something that seemed clear to me, using imagery to combat sexism, to raise awareness and counterbalance media images of women. I only had rudimentary printing skills and learnt everything on the job. The others were really inclusive, they encouraged me and I felt my input was valued.

The posters covered a lot of issues relevant to the women's movement. They went into youth clubs, onto the walls of women's centres and advice centres and they offered the women and girls that went through these places a different view of being a woman or girl. I really enjoyed printing a good run of posters, especially when it went well, the physical activity of it: there'd be 50 in the rack and you had a sense of achievement, especially if it was a poster that you really liked.

About the Authors

Prudence Stevenson
See Red 1974–83

After See Red, Pru taught art in HMP Holloway 1983–85. She publicly resigned on BBC Newsnight to draw attention to the inhumane conditions on the psychiatric wing. Pru was then banned from entering the prison and went on to work for the campaign group Women in Prison 1985–87. She co-wrote *Breaking the Silence*, a report on women's prisons in England and Wales 1986 (GLC Women's Committee) and *Insiders: Women's Experience of Prison* (Virago 1988).

Pru founded the advocacy and campaigning group WISH (Women in Secure Psychiatric Hospitals) in 1987 and was Director 1987–96. Pru was awarded the Freedom of Information award in 1987 and the Guardian Jerwood Award 1992 for Individual excellence in the charity field.

She co-ran a campaign of education and deterrence for FPWP/Hibiscus 1997–2012 in Jamaica, Nigeria and Ghana aimed at women vulnerable to smuggling drugs. In 2012 she founded the Paddington Children's Holiday Scheme, enabling inner city children in social or economic need to have a holiday in the countryside. Pru continued drawing, painting and producing prints throughout.

Susan Mackie
See Red 1974–82

A part-time arts and crafts youth worker whilst at See Red, Suzy left in 1982 to study community-based social work, after which she was at Lambeth Women and Children's Health Project, a self-help health & community development project, for eight years. Then to the NHS, working on sexual health promotion and HIV prevention projects, and training those who worked with vulnerable young women. Suzy was (FPA) Family Planning Association England Training Manager (1998–2005), designing sexual health courses, participating in national guidance and policy development, contributing to publications for young people, and writing training manuals on sex and relationships for carers and youth workers that were recognised as best practice by the Teenage Pregnancy Unit. Training Manager at Fostering Network England (2006–2008), Suzy managed courses, developed training publications, and worked with carers and the government on the development of professional standards for foster care. Her work involving carers and young people in delivering training and promoting celebration of their achievements was recognised by the Children's Workforce Development Council in 2010. Freelance from 2008, Suzy continued to work with foster carers, youth workers and young people's peer mentoring projects.

Anne Robinson
See Red 1981–83

Following her particpation in See Red, Anne got involved in artists' films, community video and feminist/queer collaborations with the Poison Girls, Wildtrax collective and Square Peg. She then studied film at St Martins and began teaching. She continues to work with film as an artist educator, currently at London Metropolitan University and Camberwell and completed a practice-led PhD on temporality, painting and film in 2012. Based in east London, her art practice is concerned with the perception and politics of time passing, working experimental y with painting, film, sound and performance. Works include:*Thrashing in the Static* (2014), *Que Sera* (2010) and *Inside Out Blues* (2013), shows including Deptford X, Cass and Stamford University and collaborations with the Comm(o)nist Gallery and Rachael House's Feminist Disco. She remains politically engaged with collective practice. Curatorial projects include: *Over Time* (2014) on the Thames foreshore and Supernormal experimental arts festival (2010–15).

Jess Baines
See Red 1982–84

After 1984, Jess spent another decade working in various London radical printshops before enrolling at Camberwell School of Art in the mid 1990s. At Camberwell she continued with concerns that had been part of the discussions at See Red: a feminist representation of women, although now in a 'post-feminist' era... Ongoing interest in issues of gender and representation led to involvement in the Transgender Film & Video Festival while it was based in London. A lengthy art project relating to the demolition of social housing led to further study at Goldsmiths College. In the early 2000s, she began teaching cultural and historical studies at London College of Communication (UAL), where she still works. In the late 2000s, she embarked on a research project about the history of late twentieth century radical printshops in Britain, which she continues to write and give talks about.

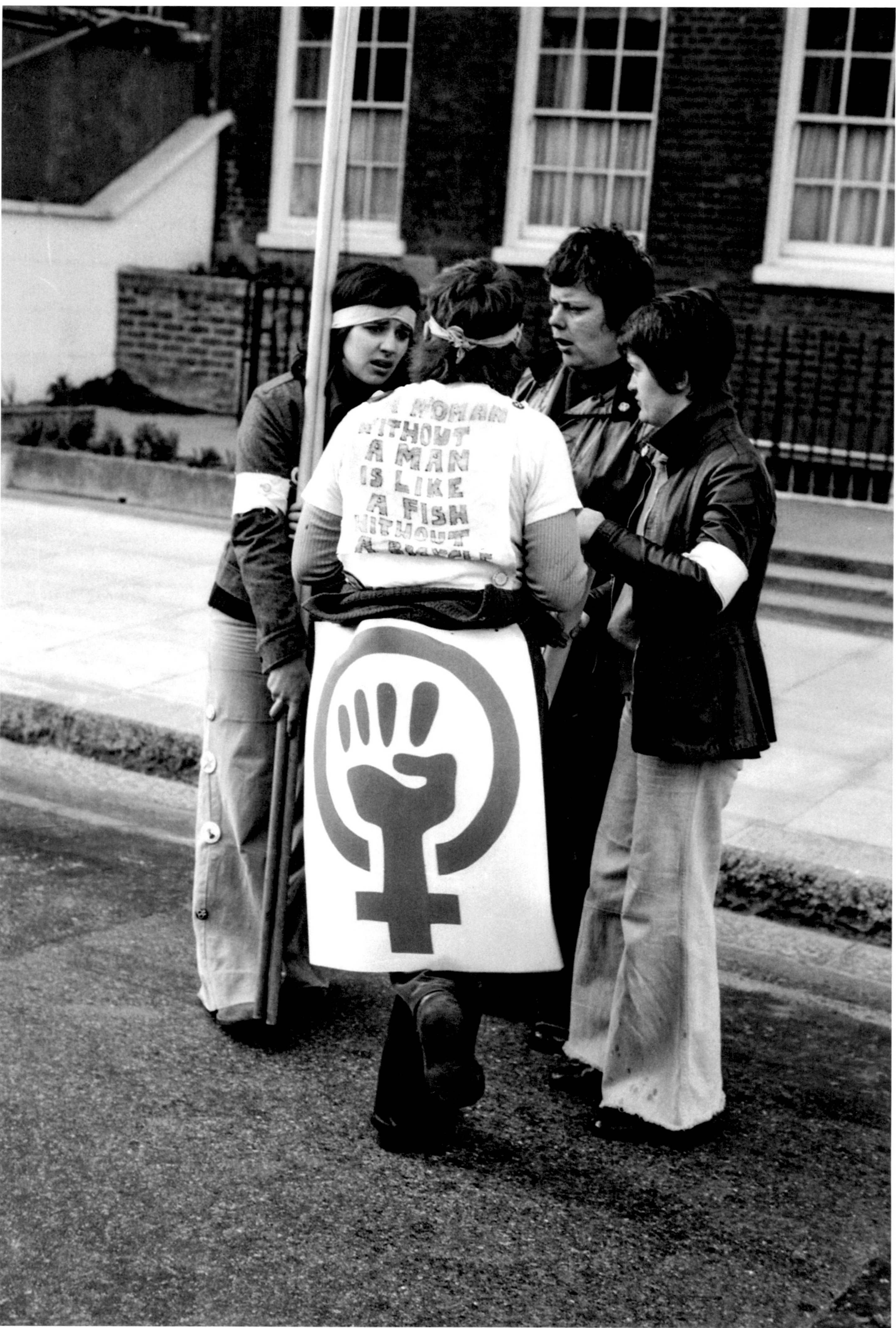
A WOMAN
WITHOUT
A MAN
IS LIKE
A FISH
WITHOUT
A BICYCLE

Index

The page numbers of images are indicated with italics

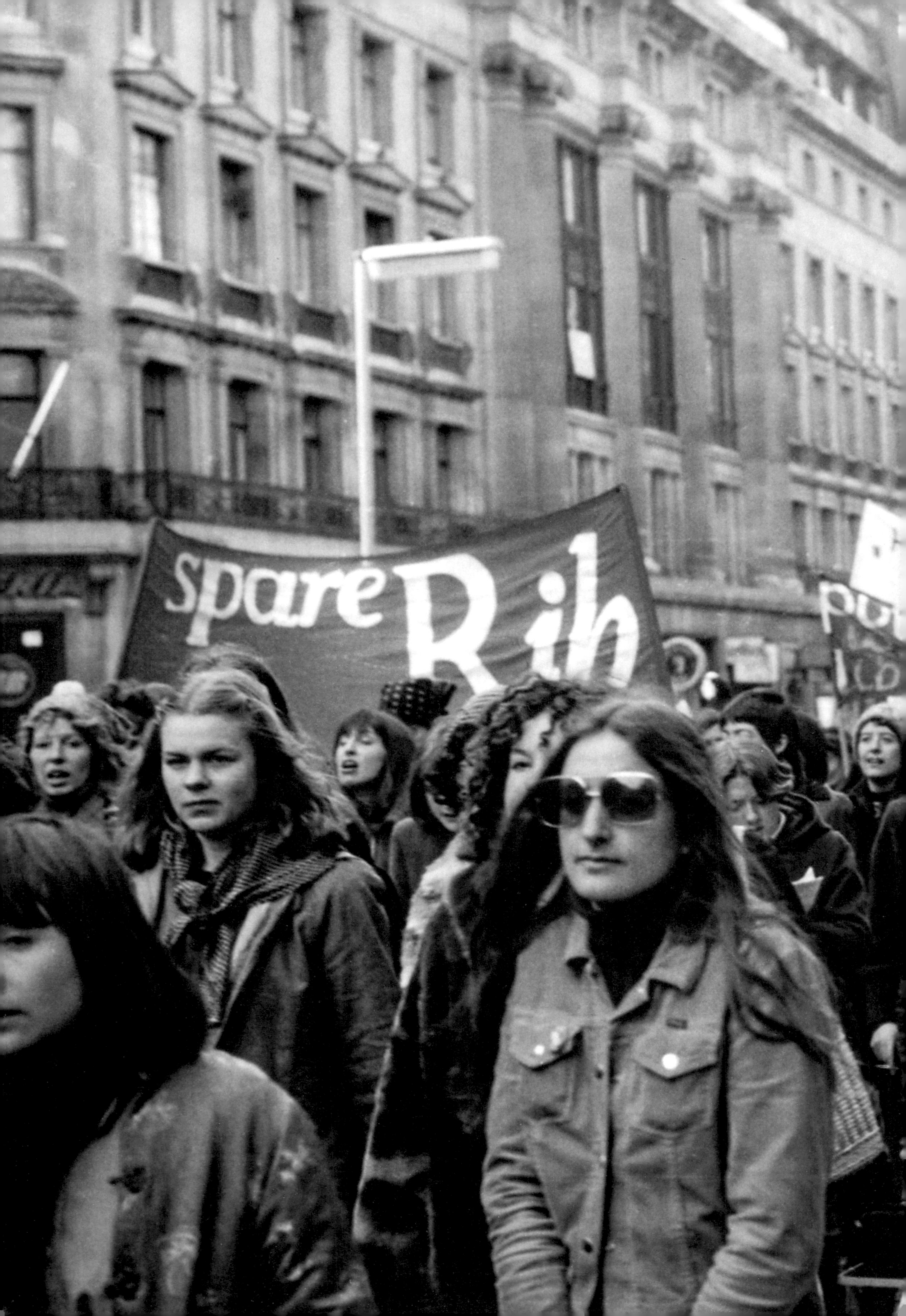

spare Rib

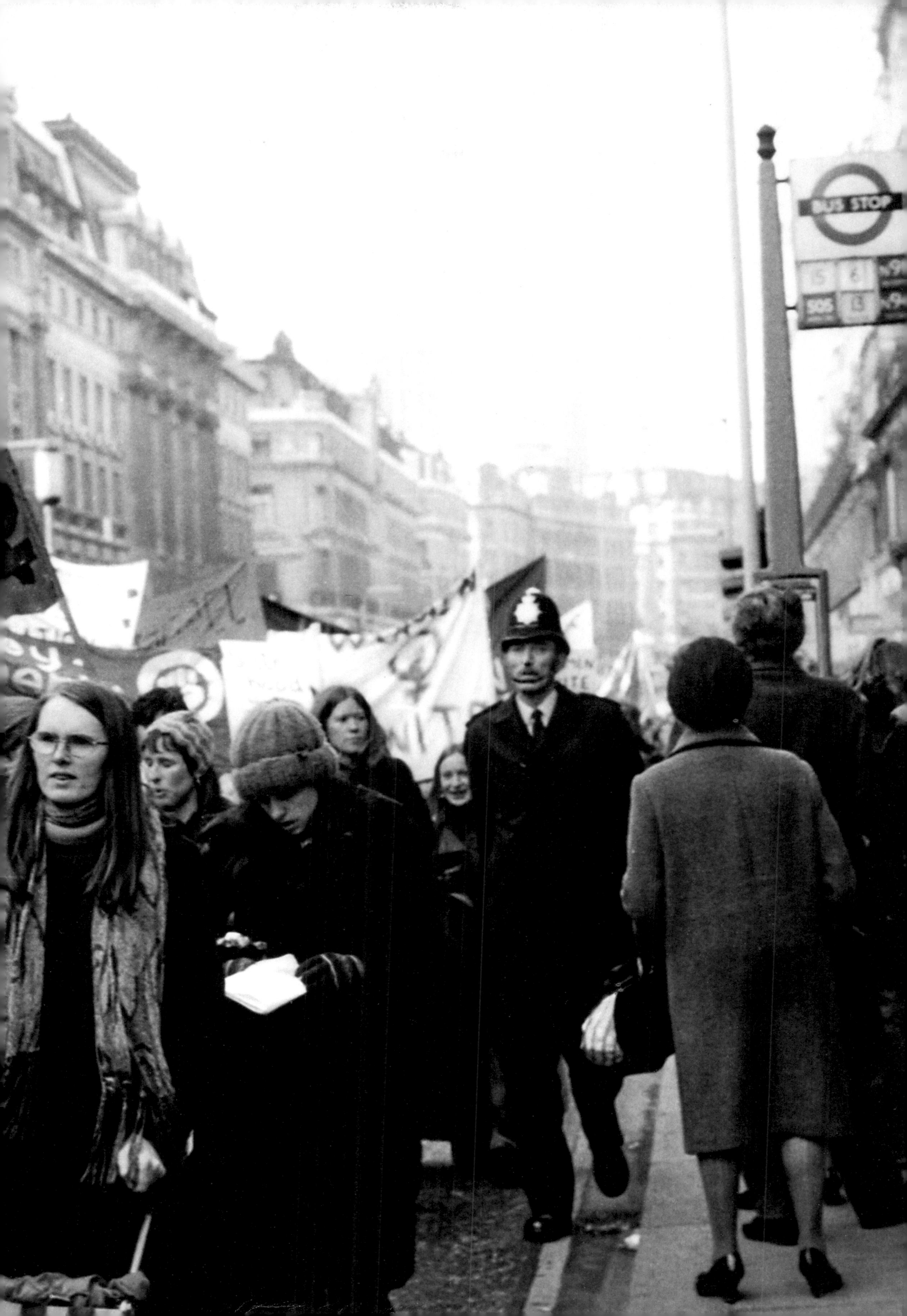
BUS STOP

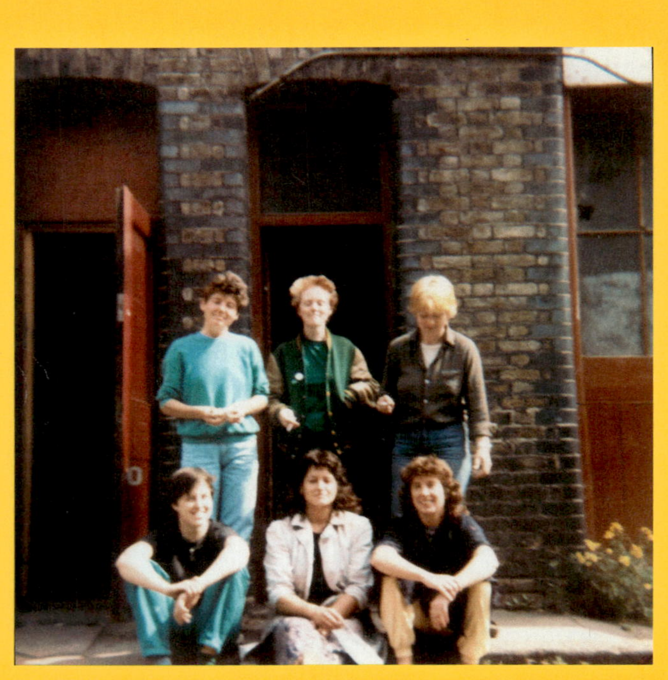